THE INDIVIDUAL, WORK
AND ORGANIZATION

THE INDIVIDUAL, WORK AND ORGANIZATION

Behavioural Studies for Business and Management Students

Robin Fincham and Peter S. Rhodes

WEIDENFELD AND NICOLSON · LONDON

First published in Great Britain by
George Weidenfeld & Nicolson Limited
91 Clapham High Street
London SW4 7TA

ISBN 0 297 791389 cased
ISBN 0 297 791397 paperback

Filmset by Deltatype, Ellesmere Port
Printed in Great Britain by
Butler & Tanner Ltd.,
Frome and London

Contents

CONTENTS

Tables

Figures

Introduction

THE NATURE OF BEHAVIOURAL STUDIES

Our reasons for wanting to write this book arose initially from a quite common experience of academics, that of teaching in an area for which there seemed to be no adequate textbook. Indeed, in our case, there appeared to be no text at all. This impression has to be put into context immediately, for there is certainly a well-developed literature covering a variety of 'behavioural' disciplines. However, we would argue that very little of this really covers the scope of the subject we take to be behavioural studies. The most significant of these related subjects, organizational behaviour, is squarely based on occupational psychology, with the addition of an account of organization theory usually from a psychological perspective. There are also other versions of behavioural studies (e.g. Boot, Cowling and Stanworth, 1977) drawing in the main from sociological studies of work and organizations.

In contrast, our approach has been to develop behavioural studies by drawing equally on the two major disciplines of psychology and sociology – or, to be more precise, on a number of specific areas of these disciplines. The way in which these are selected and integrated will, we hope, become clearer as we go along.

The development of behavioural studies has been very much a part of the development of vocational education as a whole, and particularly that of business and management studies. On the vocationally oriented degrees taught in many polytechnics and colleges, a discipline-based approach is usually thought of as being too narrow to encompass the many-faceted nature of the problems that occur in business and professional contexts. Instead, the trend favours an interdisciplinary emphasis, where the problems of vocational education are tackled by bringing together the relevant parts of various disciplines. Early formulations of business studies degree courses placed economics and accounting as major building blocks, with emphasis on the central business topics of corporate policy and decision-making gradually taking precedence in later years. Nowadays information science plays a key

1

role, and can permeate all subject areas as well as being a subject in its own right. The psychological and sociological sciences, integrated with equal weight to form behavioural studies, were seen as a third major part of the foundation. Broadly intended to give an understanding of the 'human' problems of work, they were also meant to form the basis of more advanced study in the main areas of human resource management, such as manpower studies and industrial relations.

Integration

It is important at the outset to have a clear idea of the basis on which the subjects of psychology and sociology are being brought together. Attempts to integrate different academic disciplines have sometimes been confused because of the term itself being defined rather loosely. Part of the problem is that a fully integrated, or interdisciplinary, approach involves a true synthesis between disciplines. And this would mean, in effect, a new discipline being created with its own distinctive methodology and theory. The great demands that such an approach would make on the teacher mean that in practice something more modest is usually attempted, and different disciplines are brought together in a coordinated fashion whilst retaining their distinctive identities. In this way, the developed theories and subject matter of the separate disciplines can still be drawn upon.

The model of integration that we have employed to some extent reflects both the above options. On the one hand, the individualist perspective of psychology and the structural perspective of sociology are quite distinctive, so it is appropriate that they should be developed as complementary but separate frameworks. In addition, though, something much closer to a true integration of the two subjects occurs in the subdiscipline of social psychology. The study of groups, with which social psychology is concerned, is an area of common ground on which the individual and social perspectives overlap.

The applied context

This kind of subject integration follows directly from a commitment to an educational philosophy which is very clear about its applied emphasis. The belief in the promotion of managerial effectiveness, and the study of business as an entity in its own right, have meant a shift from a strictly 'academic' approach.

In this context, the topics covered in this book reflect an abiding concern with the practical problems of the workplace. Topics of central relevance to managerial efficiency and effectiveness – such as the development of occupational skills, the control of effort and motivation, and organizational goals – are all treated prominently. At the same time, there are other issues not reflecting quite so directly on human performance which are still of great practical interest. The basic processes of human behaviour, such as learning and group interaction, fall into this category, as do the more critical sociological topics, like the impact of technology on work and the role of women in employment.

Of course, these issues also constitute intellectual problems, the study of which supports broader educational aims. In this book we have tried to do justice to the theoretical developments of behavioural science. For we believe strongly that there is a place for a critical behavioural science within a business and management context, and that vocationally oriented students are not averse to such an approach so long as its relevance to real-world problems is clearly established. Nor are they averse to an analytical framework being developed if this can broadly be seen to support the understanding of practical issues.

These practical and educational concerns affect each other in several ways. At one level, we have attempted to provide a rigorous and thorough introduction to a range of central topics in behavioural science. However, for the students for whom the book is intended, a fully developed introduction to psychology and sociology would hardly be appropriate. These subjects are not being studied primarily for their own sake, but for their wider relevance. This does not mean that we have abandoned all concern with theory and method. Rather, the emphasis will be on treating them in the context of discussions about concrete issues and problems.

Selection of topics

The original idea of behavioural studies as a combination of two established disciplines does give rise to constraints of space, and the upshot of this has been the adoption of a *selective* approach in formulating its contents. Not everything within the disciplines concerned can be covered, even in an introductory fashion; and there are good reasons for taking fewer topics in order to treat the ones selected in some depth. It is important to show how debates have taken shape, and how empirical evidence has been used to support or refute particular arguments, especially if knowledge is ever to be put to practical use.

Our own selection of materials inevitably contains some personal bias, and others no doubt would have chosen differently to some extent. The reasoning behind our choice of topics reflects a range of concerns. The desire to provide a foundation in the behavioural disciplines, and to pick out areas which have an applied emphasis, obviously were prime criteria. But the problem of translating a 'vocational' criterion into actual teaching materials is not always straightforward. We have tended to stick closely to the work setting, and to emphasize 'objective' areas of study – so that, for example, topics relating more broadly to industrial society or to subjective processes of interaction have been played down, although certainly not omitted entirely. We have also tried to give a flavour of some of the modern debates and key contemporary issues in occupational psychology and the sociology of work and organizations.

Level of topics

The selective emphasis and limitations of space can also give rise to problems to do with the *level* of materials in what is after all an introductory subject. Of course, a core of introductory materials remains the basis of the book. But there is certainly much less of an emphasis on building this up than there would be on a standard, discipline-based course. Because students frequently have a limited exposure to behavioural studies, the staff teaching the subject will want to progress as far as possible in the time available. This tendency is reinforced from within the areas of business and management studies, where naturally there is a demand for the most up-to-date arguments that behavioural science has to offer. Certainly the trend of continually bringing forward topics from later years seems widespread in business and management degree courses. These courses often develop over time by way of the gradual elimination of introductory materials and 'standard' topics in favour of more relevant advanced-level topics (which have themselves probably been displaced from later years of degree courses by the expansion of more central business topics).

All this can mean that quite early on students, who are not studying a single discipline, may be required to assimilate materials that many of their counterparts on single-discipline degrees would not come to until the later years of their courses, after a solid foundation in the subject.

These difficulties, which are very common in vocational education, can be tackled in several ways. In some cases the topics being considered are not necessarily complex in themselves; rather, they relate to a particular context in some vocational area, and once their relevance has been established then no further problems arise. But for other topics which are perhaps rather difficult to grasp – the managerial uses of power, for example, can present these sorts of problems – then *presentation* becomes vitally important. The emphasis on making issues as clear and understandable as possible, avoiding the use of unnecessary jargon, is a prime responsibility, and one which relates directly to the broader relevance of behavioural science. The critical test of relevance is whether the most important findings and arguments of behavioural science can be made intelligible to the non-specialist, and their connection with real-world problems spelled out.

THE BEHAVIOURAL SCIENCE DISCIPLINES

Like all systems of rational enquiry, the behavioural sciences provide a set of conceptual tools which help in classifying and explaining the phenomena in their area of study. Unlike most other disciplines, however, the subject matter of behavioural science – the structures and processes shaping the social world and human behaviour within it – makes up the everyday experience of the general population. This means there is a pre-existing 'baseline' of common-sense understanding of the social world with which the explanations of behavioural science have to compete.

The claim of being able to advance from common-sense understandings of human behaviour and society rests on the use of developed theoretical frameworks and research methods. Firstly, it can be argued that much common-sense knowledge is flawed by the limitations of everyday experience. People's knowledge of the social world necessarily reflects the set of experiences that have occurred during their lives. Thus, for example, it would be difficult for an individual to form abstract propositions about the functioning of the labour market – such as the level of job choice available – when his or her experience has been restricted to one occupational group, and knowledge of other parts of the market is based only on anecdotal evidence. There are also biases present in people's thinking which produce a great deal of selectivity in what is noticed, understood and remembered. People tend to think in the form of attitudes and stereotypes which oversimplify complex patterns of social interaction. In contrast to this, the analytical frameworks and theories that behavioural scientists develop provide a much sounder basis for understanding human social behaviour.

Secondly, behavioural scientists claim that they can improve on the baseline of common-sense understandings by using research techniques to collect data more systematically than the layperson could. Research methods include laboratory experimentation, questionnaire and interview surveys, and participant observation. The value of the first of these three can be greatly enhanced by using statistical techniques that enable propositions about the social world to be tested. For example, if we are interested in the effects of certain *variables*, such as social class, intelligence and the type of school attended, on the qualifications that individuals leave school with, we can, by using statistics, isolate both the specific effect of each of these variables and their interaction – thus, being intelligent in one kind of school might have more effect on the level of examinations passed than it does in another institution.

Laboratory experimentation involves careful manipulation of aspects of the experimental setting, known as the *independent variables*, and seeing what effect these have on the *dependent variable*. Occupational psychologists have for some time been interested in the effect of the environment on people's work rate. Thus, independent variables have included levels of heat, lighting, noise and humidity; and these have been related to dependent variables like workers' output per hour, their level of fatigue and their job satisfaction. Laboratories have also been used to study complex social phenomena. For example, the emergence of a leader in a small group can be observed and perhaps related to the amount that that individual contributes to the group's discussion. Although critics claim that laboratories are an artificial situation which necessarily generates artificial knowledge, a lot of evidence suggests that individuals can quickly forget the setting and participate in the activity, virtually unaware of being observed. In fact, in one notable study in which subjects were given the tasks of playing the parts of prisoners and prison warders, the researchers had to stop the experiment because subjects were playing their parts too realistically – prison warders had become aggressive and prisoners had become withdrawn (Zimbardo *et al.*, 1973).

Questionnaire and interview surveys are also powerful techniques for the collection of data on a range of biographical and attitudinal variables. Questionnaire design and interviewing both require a high degree of skill and experience. A well-constructed questionnaire uses no ambiguous words and phrases, and is lengthy enough to obtain the information needed but not so long that it taxes the stamina and goodwill of the respondent. Surveys of this kind can be used extensively, covering hundreds or even thousands of respondents, and where the data collected is necessarily standardized and fairly superficial; or they can be used intensively to obtain much more detailed information, though usually from fewer respondents.

While laboratory experimentation and survey techniques mainly collect *quantitative* data, participant observation is especially useful for collecting *qualitative* data. Here, the experimenter actually becomes involved with the individuals who are being studied, often engaging in the same activities. The assumption is that whatever is lost in terms of not being able to control the experimental environment is made up by gains in the realism of the observations. The insights gained by attempting to experience the world in the same way as the people being studied, and to establish the 'rules' which structure their behaviour, can be particularly valuable. Some of the most notable studies of real-life organizations, such as factories, schools and mental hospitals, have been carried out using this method.

All this is not to say, however, that behavioural scientists are necessarily dispassionate or detached observers of the social world. They possess, as much as anyone else, values, beliefs and principles; and they often pursue particular social or political ends. But the important point is that such values should not be allowed to compromise the objectivity of research. Research groups within the behavioural sciences manage, on the one hand, to make their values explicit, whilst on the other demonstrate integrity in their research. To do otherwise would be counter-productive. If researchers were to cut short proper research procedures they would reduce the chances of their conclusions standing up to critical scrutiny, and therefore ultimately damage their cause.

If behavioural scientists' claims about being able to improve on the everyday understanding of the social world are correct, then their skills will be especially useful in the workplace – an area where competing interests and perceptions often generate misunderstanding and prejudice. This means, however, that the behavioural sciences can be challenging for business and management students, because research often opposes existing interpretations, or theories may make totally different assumptions about events from those the students are used to. But while the behavioural sciences can and do produce critiques of existing workplace practices, this relationship between academics and practitioners is not the only one available. Very often the insights provided by behavioural scientists can join with managerial thinking and practice. And behavioural scientists themselves may become involved in the workplace as *change agents* – using diagnostic skills to enhance organizational effectiveness and employee well-being. A strong claim can therefore be advanced for the practical contributions that each of the behavioural science disciplines has made to positive change in the workplace. Occupational psychology has had a significant impact on selection, training and job design. Social psychology, with its group dynamics emphasis, has formed the basis of management development. And industrial and organizational sociology have helped in the wider policy study of issues such as the impact of technology on work and the role of women in employment. It is to brief accounts of the separate disciplines that we now turn.

The psychological perspective

Psychology is a highly diversified field of study which bridges the gap between biology and sociology, and has as its chief focus the individual and the individual's interaction with the environment. All psychologists try to respond to one key question: why did this person behave in this way? An adequate answer involves not only explaining why the particular behaviour occurred in the particular situation, but also, more importantly, producing a theory of the psychological processes which caused the behaviour, and cause it in similar situations. By developing such theories future behaviour can be predicted. This means that psychological theory can be of great value in the workplace, where effective decision-making requires accurate information about human psychological functioning.

The list of the basic processes investigated by psychologists includes perception (the functioning of the senses), human information-processing, memory, and learning. All of these have considerable practical implications. Human information-processing, for example, is concerned with the way people detect and respond to signals in the environment. The simplest question here is, how long does it take to perceive a signal, say a light or tone, and respond to it? More complex questions might ask, what are the boundaries to human information-processing capacity for a given unit of time, and how do we cope with these limits? Psychologists have demonstrated that there are indeed limits to the amount of information that can be processed (about one bit of information per second) and that we are unable to perform other actions while the nervous system is occupied with this task. To compensate we develop various 'search strategies', so that what information-processing capacity we have is used economically. It has also been shown that our attention is highly selective – in general we cope by processing only a small fraction of the incoming signals.

Much of the research into information-processing has been funded by military sponsors who needed guidelines for the design of man-machine environments, such as aircraft cockpits and air-traffic control systems. However, information-processing is an example of a universal psychological process, and increasingly industrial jobs make considerable demands on human information-processing capacity. The limits of that capacity, and the search strategies we develop to cope, are psychological properties that all individuals bring to the workplace, and some of their implications for an understanding of workplace behaviour are described below, in Section One, when we consider skill acquisition and stress.

Some psychologists, however, are more concerned with the ways in which people differ, and the study of these differences represents a key area in the modern discipline of psychology. Much research effort has gone into discovering the fundamental dimensions along which people's personalities and intellects vary. Closely associated with this research is a branch of psychology known as psychometrics, the measurement of the various attributes that have been identified within the broader field of psychology.

Like the study of processes within individuals, research into individual differences also has important applications in the workplace. If psychologists have discovered the fundamental ways in which people's personalities and intellects differ from one another, to what extent do these differences predict variations in job performance between individuals? In Chapter 3 we will look at psychologists' success in answering this question.

In sum, then, psychology clearly has an important role to play in understanding workplace behaviour, and as we will see it has made a major contribution to the design of, for example, training programmes, employee selection procedures and physical working environments – and thus ultimately to the whole of the quality of working life.

The social-psychological perspective

Social psychology has as its basic unit of analysis the social group. Social psychologists assume that an individual's behaviour can be better understood if reference is made to the groups which he or she identifies with or is a member of. In this sense, social psychology represents the interface between psychology and sociology, since it describes and explains how social structures can become *internalized* by individuals and thus affect their psychological make-up – their attitudes, perceptions and beliefs – which in turn affect behaviour. These structural forces, generated on the wider social stage or in specific groups, form the chief part of the subject matter of social psychology.

Within groups there emerge customary ways of behaving among members, the observance of special rituals, or even a shared style of dress. Similarly, specific patterns of behaviour will be enacted by individual members – the roles of leader and follower are two very common ones – and each member will enjoy a particular standing or status within the group. The point to bear in mind is that although we usually think of concepts like role and status as qualities which inhere in individuals – we frequently think of roles in terms of the behaviour of the people filling them, whilst the possession of status also seems to be an individual characteristic – in reality these are social factors generated in the process of interaction. The truth of this can readily be demonstrated if roles are regarded as rather like 'scripts' written for us by society; we may interpret them in individual and personal ways, but we are still expected to 'act out' the basic role according to the images that other people hold. Similarly, the example of changes in status – of enjoying high status in one social group but low status in another – is a common experience, and again it shows the social character of this process. In both cases the distinctive feature of group structure is evident, namely the existence of forces outside the individual and present in the social group as a whole.

What is also evident is that the behaviour and attitudes of individuals are being modified by their membership of groups – they are having to conform with ways of behaving already established. Much of this doesn't take an oppressive or coercive form at all. It will seem natural to individuals, on entering new situations, to learn the accepted manner of interaction with other people. What social psychologists have observed, however, is the massive potential that groups seem to have for enforcing conformity, whether unconsciously or through more coercive means.

Over and over again it has been shown that groups have quite astonishing powers to induce members who might otherwise want to express some non-conformist behaviour – an independent opinion, or resistance to some group norm – to fall into line. Even where group members do manage to resist having to conform, the very pressures they have to withstand in order to retain their independence demonstrate the forces of control that groups are bringing to bear. For instance, in a famous series of experiments conducted by the American social psychologist Asch, subjects were persuaded to change their identification of various images and pictures presented to them – literally to deny the evidence of their own eyes – merely because the other group members had already given their answers and established a group consensus.

This is all the more remarkable when one is reminded that the controls in question may be purely social in nature. In real-life situations people's careers or other major rewards may depend upon their conforming, but these pressures can also be reproduced without any 'material' controls acting on the individual. Group conformity can be obtained simply via social rewards, like acceptance in the group, or through the threat of negative sanctions, such as ostracism or ridicule. These effects can readily be reproduced in the laboratory, and newly set-up experimental groups quickly generate such normative patterns of behaviour. Yet the dynamics of group interaction are often so subtle that it can be difficult for the outsider to detect what is taking place.

The practical uses of such research findings – which form the main topic of the chapters in Section Two – become apparent when we recognize that virtually all interaction in organizations can be tied down to groups of one form or another. In the work setting, for example, it is common nowadays to find group techniques being used to improve the environment for workers (see Chapter 8). Also, the recognition of the power of informal groups and friendship cliques to influence workers' behaviour has served, and still serves, as the impetus for an enormous research effort.

In addition, there is now increasing interest in decision-making situations. It can readily be seen that many, perhaps most, important decisions are taken not by individuals acting alone but by small groups of influential or technically qualified people. On the flight deck of modern aircraft, for example, the decisions are taken by a triad of pilot, co-pilot and flight engineer. And more generally within large organizations the 'corporate group' which holds real power will often number, say, five or six senior managers. In these sorts of situations, it has been shown that processes of conformity and integration within groups may compete with technical expertise, and that group pressures may even have the power to override the habits of training. All the more important, then, that the dynamics of groups are understood so that optimal use may be made of the skills possessed by decision-makers.

The sociological perspective

The role of sociology on business and managerial degree courses, as McKenna (1983, p.6) notes, has always been more problematic than that of psychology, the reason being the prominence of radical theory within the discipline and the decline of consensus-based theories that were once popular. McKenna's own definition of behavioural studies, as a 'hybrid sub-discipline with an analytical dimension which fits comfortably into a Business Studies programme', is clearly meant to suggest that only 'conventional' sociological explanations should be included. He argued that radical or Marxist accounts should be restricted to explanations of social conflict. Problems of this sort have led to the concern that sociologists would either have to compromise their discipline or risk antagonizing students (Brown and Harrison, 1980; Deem, 1981). As a result, views of sociology's role have in the past had an unfortunate tendency to polarize – one camp in effect saying that the discipline should remain separated from business and management studies, and the other stressing that sociology should deploy only theories from the body of the discipline which are sympathetic with a business ethic.

The approach we have taken here is neither of these. We would argue instead that an approach which draws on the full range of the discipline, including radical ideas, can usefully engage with business and management interests – and indeed that today this is the only approach that is really tenable. Advances, both in teaching in the areas of business, management and professional studies, as well as in behavioural science itself, have outflanked these other views. The degree courses involved have 'come of age' and are fully able to benefit from a range of alternative perspectives (Alan Smith, 1981). And radical theories, for their part, are now inseparable from broader sociological concerns. As

Thompson (1983, p.36) has asserted, we now have a 'new sociology of work' in which radical theories and an existing tradition are joined in an exciting and fruitful debate.

Explanations that sociology provides are based on the idea of social action as a *duality* comprising the structures of behaviour to which people conform, and the more creative and active role played by the human agent. As before, structure refers to the patterns of expectations and forms of behaviour which have become ordered and which persist over time. It suggests that society consists of a 'world out there' existing independently of any one of us. This is only part of the picture, though. Even at the social level behaviour obviously originates in the interaction between people – and the intervention of these interests and motives introduces the possibility of changes and developments. Together, structure and agency account for the opposing forces of stability and change present in all human affairs.

Social structure   As noted above, structural forces overlap at the group level. However, an aspect of structure which is wholly a product of the societal level is *social class*. Although the class structure has long been one of the chief interests of social scientists, our focus on the work context means that we shall not be concerned with these broad patterns of inequality. In keeping with the aims of the book, we have attempted to treat class not as an issue in its own right but as something which can throw light on the nature of work and occupations. But as an issue class does arise in at least two ways in Section Three.

Class may firstly be thought of as a *relationship*. In the work context this translates into the relation between the employer and employees. Analysis of the employment relationship in class terms has been vital in understanding one of the major issues of industrial sociology, namely the problems of conflict in the workplace. Secondly, class may be thought of in *occupational* terms. Nowadays an individual's class position is based on his or her occupation, and changes that affect occupations also affect the class structure. The power of occupations to attract material rewards and status represents a dynamic and changing aspect of social class.

Human agency and meaning   Aside from structure, sociology's emphasis on the creative aspects of social action shares with psychology a concern with the individual. But unlike psychology this is not here a question of individual processes or differences. Rather, the concern is with the subjective responses shared within particular groups of people – how a workforce experiences its employment, for example, or the manner in which a community perceives some event that impinges upon it. In other words, the concern is not simply with opinions or attitudes, but with the social character of the *meanings* that people assign to situations they find themselves in. Social situations turn out to be complex, many-sided events, giving ample scope for different groups affected to perceive them in quite different ways.

The meanings that people assign – how *they* understand and define situations

11

– take on a concrete reality. Meanings become self-fulfilling 'social facts' because they form the basis on which people act. This viewpoint provides an answer to another criticism often levelled at sociology, that it is only concerned with subjective factors and not with objective events in the real world. The answer we can give is to point out that subjective meanings have an objective reality, because people's understanding is the basis of the response they make. In the discussion in Sections Three and Four we will encounter several cases where a knowledge of how particular groups define their work situation is the key to understanding behaviour.

Social conflict   Another difference of emphasis between the psychological and sociological perspectives hinges on the question of conflict. On the whole the individualist approach is not concerned with issues of conflict – unless the resolution of personality conflicts is considered, or perhaps the conflict between external demands and human needs that causes stress. But as we move to the social level, structural conflict comes much more clearly into focus.

Concern with the conflictual aspects of social relationships lies behind another criticism of sociology, namely the complaint that the discipline is not 'scientific' nor can it provide 'solutions' to real-world problems. The response we might give is that social life itself involves conflicting interests, and that solutions to complex problems are rarely unambiguous technical answers, but options and choices which emerge from the interplay of more than one set of interests. The mobilization of power in pursuit of interests is part of day-to-day reality – and nowhere is this more evident than in the work context and in organizations. Sociological analysis recognizes this, stressing that conflict is not irrational, nor always the result of misunderstandings; it must be explained and explored in its own right.

This readiness to take issues of conflict seriously reveals the critical nature of sociological analysis, for academic disciplines cannot divorce themselves from their own subject matter. Virtually all of the topics we cover in Section Three, and many in Section Four, attract some very different views and opinions, and part of our aim will be to explore these alternative perspectives and debates.

THE STRUCTURE OF THE BOOK

Levels of Analysis

The psychological, social psychological and sociological approaches discussed above broadly correspond with the structure of this book, which divides into three distinct levels of analysis: individual, group, and work/organizational.

In Section One, we look at the ways in which various *individual differences* affect behaviour. As we have suggested, the psychologist wishes to know how processes *within* individuals, such as learning and motivation, are manifest in behaviour – and also how differences *between* individuals, in terms of their aptitudes, abilities and personalities, can be studied. Further, the occupational psychologist is concerned with applying these explanations to the work setting.

In Section Two the processes that occur in the context of the work group are explored. The emphasis here is on *social interaction* and the ways in which behaviour in organizations is generated and adapted in face-to-face situations. The main forms of group dynamics, including the emergence of basic rules of human interaction, the processes of group formation, and the leader-follower relationship, are all of special interest here.

Sections Three and Four adopt a wider *social* level of analysis applied to the work and organizational contexts respectively. As we have noted, the sociologist is concerned not so much with the properties of individuals, or with the nature of group-based interaction, but with relatively enduring social structures. Industrial sociologists apply these broader categories, looking at the relationship between employers and workers considered as classes, for example, or the role of gender in employment, while organization theorists have developed accounts of the functioning of modern, large-scale organizations. There is also concern with wider social and economic structures, such as the labour market, within which organizations operate.

Using these distinctive levels of analysis should help provide a holistic view of the human problems of work. Complex, multi-dimensional problems depend for their resolution on a variety of different approaches and perspectives being applied – one approach rarely has all the answers. Indeed, as Gowler and Legge (1982) have observed, 'problems although surfacing at one level in the organization are likely to have antecedents and effects at different levels'.

The central task of behavioural science, according to Landy (1982), is to describe the functional relationship that exists between these levels and estimate their relative importance in understanding behaviour. Behavioural scientists have shown an increasing willingness to consider the interaction between different levels of analysis, their underlying assumption being that one level provides the context or environment for the next. This is the real basis of an integrated approach to understanding the human problems of the workplace.

THE INDIVIDUAL AND WORK

By the beginning of the First World War many psychologists in Europe and the United States had recognized that there were problems within the workplace which could be both analysed and remedied using the concepts and methods developed more broadly within their own discipline. As with many other areas of research with military or industrial applications, wartime conditions provided the impetus for a rapid development of industrial psychology. Firstly, the armed forces began to realize the value of a systematic psychological assessment of recruits as an aid to decisions about a soldier's rank and suitability for technical training. Secondly, the increased demand for output and the reduction in available manpower produced by wartime conditions prompted many managers to seek the assistance of psychologists to improve the productivity of the residual workforce.

After the First World War, interest in industrial psychology was consolidated by groups of psychologists who wanted to offer their skills to employers forming research and consultancy companies such as the National Institute of Industrial Psychology in Britain and the Psychological Corporation in the United States.

Industrial psychology in these formative years, therefore, was attempting to answer two broadly inter-related questions. Firstly, what factors increase a worker's productivity? And secondly, how can the match between the employee and the job be improved?

Early attempts to answer the first question involved the careful measurement and manipulation of environmental factors such as temperature, lighting, noise levels, humidity and aspects of work like the length and number of rest breaks, and establishing their effect on a worker's productivity. This approach produced some remarkable early successes. For example, a wartime study demonstrated that a drop in daily hours from twelve to ten actually increased productivity and brought about a large decrease (50 per cent) in the accident rate. At the time, industrialists had believed that output could be improved by increasing working hours.

It was gradually realized, however, that the relationships between objective work conditions and productivity were moderated by subjective phenomena, such as the employee's attitude to work and job satisfaction. Thus, seemingly straightforward concepts like fatigue were found to involve physiological processes such as the build-up of lactic acid in muscle tissue, as well as the psychological willingness of the individual to work.

The second question – how to improve the employee-job match – produced a variety of answers. Some psychologists believed the answer lay in more careful *selection* of employees. This involved preparing an inventory of the relevant skills, aptitudes and temperaments required for high job performance, and constructing psychological tests which identified individuals who possessed these qualities. Other psychologists developed the 'training solution', allowing individual deficiencies to be compensated for by training employees up to the required standard. Finally, a solution which emerged during the Second World War – the 'equipment solution' – proposed a radically different approach to the problem. It suggested that a better match could be achieved by applying psychological knowledge of human capabilities and particularly their limits to the design of man-machine systems. The body of knowledge these psychologists produced became known as ergonomics.

What answers to both questions – improving productivity and the employee-job match – had in common was the assumption that solutions could be sought based on the individual employee as the fundamental unit of analysis. In this first section, we will examine the main research findings based on this assumption and which underpinned the solutions to the initial questions psychologists were asked to provide answers for.

In Chapter 1 we look at the research on the training solution which seeks to explain how people acquire complex occupational skills. Humans, as we will see, have a remarkable capacity to learn; in fact virtually all of our behaviour is acquired through learning. The practical implications of this in the workplace are considerable, and an understanding of how learning occurs obviously enables better training programmes to be designed.

While Chapter 1 describes the remarkable adaptive capacities of humans, Chapter 2 explores one consequence of the limits of this capacity, stress. Trying to adapt to certain types of environment involves severe mental and physical health risks, but the problem of stress at work has been recognized only recently by psychologists and employers. We will examine some of the types of stress that have been identified in the workplace and discuss methods of reducing their damaging effects.

In Chapter 3 we look at the research on which the selection solution was based. We focus on personality and intelligence, perhaps the most important ways in which individuals differ from one another. We explore what implications differences in personality and intelligence have in the workplace and discuss two methods of assessing them: the interview and the psychological test.

Finally, in Chapter 4 we examine the two most significant contributions psychologists have made to the understanding of employees' productivity: the concepts of motivation and job satisfaction. As we suggested above, although early successes were achieved by manipulating objective aspects of the workplace, it was soon realized that subjective factors, particularly the *needs* workers brought with them to the workplace and the way employees felt about their jobs, also affected their productivity. This realization, combined with the rising expectations of employees after the Second World War and relatively full employment, prompted an enormous amount of research and discussion on how employees' needs could be met and thus how a motivated and reasonably satisfied workforce could be created.

1

Learning

Perhaps most fundamental of the questions psychologists ask – a question that applies in the work context as well as in the wider social one – concerns how people acquire the various abilities needed to survive in a social world and to interact with others. It is in this context that *theories of learning* form the basis of our understanding of human behaviour. The development, via evolution, of a relatively large brain has provided us with an enormous mental capacity which has meant that learning has displaced instinct. Instinctual behaviours seen in other animals appear only briefly in the first year of human life and then recede.

Learning is also central to the explanation of behaviour in the workplace, where individuals need to acquire very specific responses and skills to carry out the tasks that make up their jobs. In fact, much of the interest in the psychological processes of learning stems from the practical implications of research findings. The design of effective training programmes is increasingly linked with models of the learning process, particularly where workforces are needed that can adapt quickly to technological change. Training designed with an awareness of the learning process is more likely both to help learners acquire new skills and, perhaps more crucially, increase confidence in their own learning abilities. As Baroness Sear (1985) pointed out:

> What people need above all else is the ability and the will to learn and the conviction that it can be done. No one can say precisely what demands will dominate the labour market over the next twenty years. But if people can be given the confidence that they can learn what is needed, then the uncertainty of future demands loses much of its menace. The ability to learn and the flexibility it makes possible must be the key to future success.

It is in the context of training for the future that learning theories which identify key features of the learning process are increasingly valuable.

Learning theories have other practical applications. If they can explain how people acquire competence they may also be able to tell us what differentiates excellent from merely competent individuals. In many jobs this difference can be accounted for by motivation, personality, intelligence or aptitudes.

However, there are often key differences between the way excellent and competent individuals perceive and comprehend their environments. If identified, these can become the basis of training programmes aimed at bringing about the changes in perception and comprehension necessary for improved performance.

Learning theories can also help when considering how occupational activity is best described. Trainers need valid methods of describing what people at work do in order to identify what skills individuals need to do a job and what opportunities a job provides for the development of skills in individuals. Traditionally the main concern has been to develop ways of describing the tasks that people actually perform. Learning theories also suggest that it is often as important to describe skills, how people accomplish the tasks involved in their jobs and the learning processes involved in acquiring these skills (Downs and Perry, 1986).

In this chapter we will examine the two main types of learning theory: stimulus–response and skill theories. The former focuses on conditions *external* to individuals. A stimulus is something perceived by an organism in the environment. A doorbell, a supervisor's request, and the smell of food are all examples of stimuli. A response is a unit of behaviour (usually observable) emitted by an organism. Answering the door, anxiety, and salivating are all responses which might be found to be associated with the respective stimuli. Stimulus-response theorists explain how responses are acquired by examining what precedes the response and what happens in the environment after the response has occurred. Many researchers, however, have preferred to stress the part *internal* cognitive processes play in learning, and use larger units of learning such as skill; they relate changes in the way people make sense of their environments to improvements in the performance. As we will see, both approaches have contributed a great deal to our understanding of how learning, perhaps the most important of human capacities, occurs.

LEARNING THEORIES

Stimulus–response theories I: classical conditioning

The initial concern of the Russian physiologist Pavlov (1849–1936) was the innate reflex responses of animals. While studying one of these reflex responses, salivation, he noticed some dogs would sometimes salivate when the lights in the laboratory were switched on in the morning or when they were removed from their pens. At first he found these 'psychic secretions' a nuisance since they disrupted his experiments. He soon realized, however, that these responses were far more important than the simple physiological reflexes he had intended to study. He began a series of experiments to investigate them in more detail. In a typical experiment Pavlov would present a dog with a neutral stimulus such as a tone or a bell. This would be quickly followed by meat powder to which the dog would automatically salivate. If the pairing of a neutral stimulus with the meat powder occurred enough times, Pavlov found the salivation response could be elicited by the tone or bell alone. The dog had been *conditioned* to respond to the neutral stimulus.

Pavlov's contribution to the explanation of learning has proved to be of immense significance. It explains how a wide range of human responses are acquired. It has also helped in the treatment of a number of behavioural problems, from phobias to sexual difficulties such as impotence.

In order to generalize Pavlov's research methods to other situations, a specific vocabulary describing the components of conditioning has been devised. The original reflex is composed of an unconditioned stimulus (UCS) and an unconditioned response (UCR). In Pavlov's experiment the meat powder was the UCS and the dog's salivation the UCR. The neutral stimulus, the bell, buzzer or tone is known as the conditioned stimulus (CS). When salivation occurs after the presentation of the CS on its own it is termed the conditioned response (CR) (Figure 1.1). The CR is never quite as strong as the original UCR. In Pavlov's experiments the dogs salivated less for the CS than the UCS. If the CS is presented on a number of occasions without the UCS the CR will decline further in strength. This decline in the CR is known as *extinction*. Zero extinction is said to occur when the CS does not elicit a CR at all. However, even at zero extinction the association between CS and CR does not disappear altogether as relearning the CR requires fewer pairings than were necessary for the original conditioning.

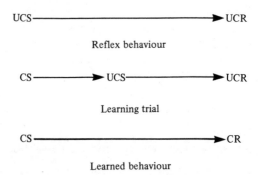

Figure 1.1 *The classical conditioning sequence.*

Two important features of the conditioning process have been identified: *generalization* and *discrimination*. Generalization refers to the organism's capacity to respond in a similar way to stimuli that are similar in certain respects to the original CS. For example, young children sometimes refer to all adult males as 'daddy'. Generalization in evolutionary terms is highly useful; it reduces the complexity of the stimulus environment since the organism can apply the same response to a range of stimuli. However, as we shall see later, generalization can also be maladaptive if the learned response is generalized to situations in which it is inappropriate. Discrimination is the opposite tendency, allowing organisms to respond differently to similar stimuli. The young child eventually learns to apply the word 'daddy' to one adult male only.

Classical conditioning has been observed in a number of human and animal subjects and there seems little doubt that it is a basic learning process. However, when it came to more complex behaviours Pavlov believed that these could be acquired through *secondary conditioning*. This occurs when the CS–CR connection is so well established that a CS acts as a UCS in subsequent conditioning. For example, if a child automatically responds to an unpleasant stimulus (UCS) such as a smack from a parent by experiencing anxiety (UCR), words which precede the blow, such as 'no' or 'stop that', can become conditioned stimuli. Through conditioning, then, these words may be enough to control a child's behaviour without resorting to physical punishment. Through secondary conditioning the child may even learn that particular facial expressions precede these words so that they, in turn, become the conditioned stimuli which elicit the anxiety response. In this way the child learns to recognize increasingly subtle indications of parental disapproval.

Classical conditioning is particularly useful in explaining behaviour mediated by the autonomic nervous system. This is the part of the nervous system which controls reflex action and emotional states such as pleasure and anxiety. Extreme emotional reactions, phobias, like the fear of heights, crowds or small spaces, can be acquired through classical conditioning. If phobias are acquired through classical conditioning they can also be cured by helping individuals to 'unlearn' the phobia by replacing the conditioned anxiety with a more neutral emotional response. In fact, treatment based on conditioning principles is now commonplace and has very high success rates. Weaker emotional responses such as the emotions that inanimate objects like buildings, rooms and food can elicit are also often the result of classical conditioning. An aversion to a particular food, for example, can be the result of a single pairing of the food (CS) with a powerful aversive stimulus (UCS) such as food poisoning. The single pairing may be sufficient for the food to elicit anxiety or nausea (CR) on subsequent occasions and the food is therefore avoided.

Conditioning can provide us with what are termed *patterns*, that is 'conditioned feelings, thoughts or behaviours which are unresponsive to what is new and changing in situations' (Evison and Horobin, 1983). These patterns are formed during experiences which have caused an individual distress. In childhood, distress is particularly significant because it tends to be associated with situations which occur frequently. Being simpler than adults, children are also less likely to understand what the causes of distress are. Distress is then generalized so that it can be elicited by a range of situations.

Once patterned, we can only pay attention to the characteristics of the situation which elicit distress. This means we are unlikely to acquire improved methods of dealing with these situations, so that, for example, it can be difficult to shed the patterns we acquire in childhood to cope with authority figures. Hence we will continue to experience distress in the presence of authority figures and perceive them as threatening even though in reality they no longer are. Our conditioned distress will prompt the same rapid and unthinking response that it did in childhood. For example, we may find we automatically acquiesce to requests from our supervisors since this quickly reduces the unpleasant feelings restimulated by these situations.

Management training programmes often attempt to make trainees aware of their own patterned feelings, thoughts and behaviours. Trainees can then begin to explore more effective methods of dealing with the situations which elicit their maladaptive patterned responses.

Classical conditioning also has implications for task performance and training in organizations. We have a fixed capacity to attend to a given task. The capacity available for any task depends on the number of other demands on our attention. Thus, pleasant or unpleasant feelings evoked at work demand part of an individual's attention and will interfere with his or her ability to attend to a task. This impairs an individual's performance and can increase the likelihood of accidents. Coercive or punitive supervisors can become the conditioned stimuli which elicit negative feelings. The conditioning may be generalized so that these feelings are evoked by all managers.

In training programmes some trainees may already have conditioned negative feelings about instructional situations and instructors. Trainers on government training schemes for young people who have recently left school are especially faced with the problem of often having to deal with individuals who have conditioned negative feelings elicited by learning environments. Individuals who experience these feelings are both unlikely to learn much and likely to prove disruptive to other trainees. A good deal of research has been undertaken recently to devise training programmes in which the anxiety that learning situations have normally evoked is 'unlearned' and replaced with more positive feelings (e.g. Downs and Perry, 1984).

Stimulus–response theories II: operant conditioning

Learning of stimulus–response associations also occurs through operant conditioning. An operant is a unit of behaviour emitted by an organism; eating a meal, placing a bet and smoking a cigarette are all examples of operants. The most noted operant theorist, B.F. Skinner, believed that the environment *shapes* an individual's behaviour by maintaining certain responses and suppressing others.

Skinner's major contribution has been to outline how the shaping of an individual's responses by the environment occurs. He believes the most powerful shaping mechanism is *reinforcement*. If we return to the hypothetical example of the patterned behaviour elicited by authority figures, classical conditioning, as we saw, explained why anxiety was experienced. Situations in which authority figures make demands are perceived as threatening. This perception elicits the classically conditioned anxiety response, which in turn is followed by an operant: acquiescence. In operant conditioning the key question is, what occurs after a response? In this example the response caused an immediate reduction in anxiety. In operant terms the response was *reinforced*. This reinforcement has been powerful enough to stamp the response into an individual's behaviour pattern.

Reinforcement operates either negatively or positively. *Positive reinforcement* occurs when a pleasant stimulus follows a response. Money, status, recognition and praise can all act as positive reinforcers since they all increase the likelihood of the preceding response being emitted again.

Any response which reduces the intensity or removes an unpleasant stimulus is said to *negatively reinforced*. Like positive reinforcement, negative reinforcement increases the probability that the response will reoccur. Negative reinforcement produces two types of learning: *escape* and *avoidance*. Acquiescing to the demands of authority figures in the example above falls into the first category since it allows individuals to escape from their conditioned distress. An individual could also learn to avoid supervisors and thereby reduce the threat of anxiety-loaded encounters.

Skinner believed escape and avoidance behaviours were very common in human society. Aversive conditions are, wittingly or unwittingly, frequently created by other people. Unwittingly, other people can be boring, annoying or unpleasant, and we quickly develop avoidance relationships with them. Aversive conditions are created intentionally as a method of social control. A supervisor, for example, may become more autocratic, coercive and punitive to increase output. To escape these aversive conditions, workers may increase their work rate which, in turn, reinforces the supervisor's belief in the effectiveness of an autocratic style of supervision. However, other escape behaviours can be learned: striking, sabotage or displacing the aggression their aversive environment has caused on to people outside the workplace are all possible consequences. Alternatively, workers may acquire avoidance behaviours which put them out of the aversive stimuli's range, for example, by staying at home or changing job. Proponents of operant conditioning believe a number of social phenomena are explained by avoidance or escape learning. Conformity, for example, may be not so much the result of the positive reinforcement of behaviour by others but learning to perform in a way that avoids their contempt.

While positive and negative reinforcement serve to increase the strength of responses, *punishment* and *omission* have the opposite effect. Punishment involves an aversive stimulus following a response. Contact with aversive stimuli very quickly reduces the probability of a response reoccurring. A child who puts his or her hand on a hot oven ring is unlikely to do it again. In adult life we learn to withhold the responses that have attracted contempt, ridicule or criticism. The term omission is used to describe the removal of pleasant stimuli after a response. Parents make use of this contingency when sending a child who misbehaves to bed. This removes pleasant stimuli such as television or the company of siblings. Table 1.1 below provides a summary of these four response categories.

Table 1.1 *The four types of reinforcement proposed by Skinner.*

	PRESENT	REMOVE
PLEASANT STIMULI	Positive reinforcement	Omission
UNPLEASANT STIMULI	Punishment	Negative reinforcement

Operant theorists believe that reward is a more powerful method of shaping behaviour than punishment. Reward has the virtue of indicating what behaviour is required, while punishment only indicates what response an individual should withhold. Punishment can also cause anxiety, hostility and resentment in an individual. Aversive stimuli, as we have already seen, can also lead to avoidance learning. The individual can learn to avoid the parent, teacher or supervisor or to perform the undesired response out of their range. Skinner (1971) believed that society in general has gradually shifted from systems of control based on the use of aversive stimuli to ones which use reward. Teachers now try and make children want to learn through reward rather than through punishment. Parents increasingly offer rewards to their children in the form of approval rather than using punishment to shape their children's behaviour. And some organizations have replaced aversive auto-cratic managerial practices with the potentially more rewarding democratic supervisory styles.

Skinner was also interested in the effect of what he termed *schedules of reinforcement* on behaviour. The simplest schedule is one in which every response is followed by a reward. However, in everyday life, this schedule, known as *continuous reinforcement*, is highly unlikely: teachers, parents, colleagues or supervisors cannot reinforce every desired response. You are more likely to experience *intermittent reinforcement schedules* in which your behaviour is not always reinforced. For example, you were not rewarded as a child each time you performed a desired response such as sharing a toy but you may have been rewarded intermittently. Experiments have found that intermittent schedules of reinforcement exert a more powerful influence on behaviour than a continuous schedule since we seem to learn not to expect reinforcement each time we make a particular response. This means behaviour persists in the absence of reinforcement whereas responses learned with a continuous schedule, where an organism expects reinforcement after every correct response, rapidly disappear when not reinforced. In fact, intermittent schedules can often have a major influence on behaviour in return for very little reward. For instance, a gambler does not need to win very often to sustain the habit.

Reinforcement schedules have been used to explain a number of workplace phenomena: motivation, absenteeism, and the effects of different payment systems. Ferster and Skinner (1957) argued that there are two basic types of intermittent schedule. Firstly, there are those schedules in which reinforcement occurs after a fixed number of the desired responses has been made or after a fixed period of time has elapsed. Secondly, there are those in which reinforcement occurs regularly or irregularly. By combining these two criteria four intermittent schedules are created, which they believed had different effects on behaviour.

(1) A *fixed-ratio schedule* is one in which reinforcement occurs after a given number of responses. This schedule can produce a great deal of the desired behaviour for very little in return. Piecework, where an employee is paid for producing a fixed number of units, is an example of a fixed-ratio schedule. In theory, piece-rate working ought to produce the response pattern normally associated with the fixed-ratio schedule: a high and constant response rate. In practice, however, many employers have found a pay structure which attempts to link specific response rates with pay too cumbersome and have opted for a 'flat' weekly wage. In a car plant, for example, the rate of pay for each of the thousands of assembly tasks has to be negotiated and renegotiated every year. Employees also tend to learn a work rate which is not high enough to cause management to increase the response–earnings ratio and not so low as to reduce earnings below a desired level.

(2) A *variable-ratio schedule* can be even more effective in terms of the effort–reward ratio in producing the desired behaviour than a fixed-ratio schedule. A gambling machine, for example, pays out on average once in fifteen bets. Since a variable ratio makes it difficult to know when a payout is likely, gamblers are prepared to place bets at a constant (often high) rate. Some payment systems are variable-ratio schedules. One of the present authors has carried out research in a firm which sold pension plans. Sales staff were paid according to the number of plans they sold. To sell a plan it was necessary on average to make about thirty calls. Some weeks the ratio for a member of staff would stretch to well above this level. Like the gambling machine, it was impossible to know whether a response would be rewarded and work rates were therefore high and constant.

(3) In *fixed-interval schedules*, reinforcement occurs at regular intervals, regardless of what response precedes it. Monthly or weekly payment systems are examples of this schedule. Fixed-interval reinforcement produces a distinctive pattern of responding. As the reward time approaches the response rate increases, dropping immediately after reinforcement. This drop in

response rate indicates the organism has learned there is no relationship between response and reward in the period closely following reinforcement. The absence of any relationship between response and reward immediately following reinforcement in this schedule may help to explain higher rates of absenteeism found in organizations after a pay day.

(4) The length of time between reinforcement in a *variable-interval schedule* varies around some average value. This schedule elicits moderate and constant response rates. For example, if the time between assessments of suitability for promotion varies in an organization, employees learn their performance needs to be consistently good to ensure a favourable rating.

Stimulus–response theories: a technology of behaviour?

Skinner has argued that operant theory provides the framework for a 'technology of behaviour' – enabling environments to be designed so that desired responses are systematically strengthened while less desirable responses are weakened.

An important instance of the application of operant principles is known as *behaviour modification*. This is often found in clinical settings, although behaviour modification can be applied equally well in an organizational context. For example, Nord (1969) argued that organizations tend to be designed in ways which largely ignore the recommendations of operant theory. Firstly, staff may be unaware of what they have to do to gain rewards such as a rise in pay or status. Secondly, hard work is sometimes punished, rather than reinforced, by loading more work on to conscientious staff. Thirdly, group or departmental productivity bonuses weaken the link between individual performance and reward. Finally, managers tend to think reinforcement can best be achieved via monetary reward. But while this may well be the case generally, for some staff recognition and praise can be more potent reinforcers.

Luthans and Kreitner (1975) were the first to outline clearly how operant principles could be applied to organizational behaviour. Their programme begins with the identification of *critical behaviours*. These are the responses thought to be necessary for effective performance in a job. For example, the initial approach to a customer may be a critical behaviour for effective selling. The second phase establishes the *base rates* for target behaviours. These are the rates at which these critical behaviours normally occur. Identifying base rates enables the impact of the programme to be assessed at a later stage. The third stage, termed *functional analysis*, involves careful observation of what normally precedes and follows various types of work behaviour. For example, a functional analysis may reveal that customers are normally only greeted if they approach a member of the sales staff. After the functional analysis has been completed an *intervention strategy* is devised. This makes rewards contingent on critical behaviours. Finally, there is a *systematic evaluation* of the intervention strategy. The rate at which target behaviours are now displayed is compared with the base rate.

Luthans and Kreitner argued that this procedure offered significant benefits in training programmes, and collected a good deal of evidence to support their claim. One study of sales staff in a large department store attempted to change staff performance on a number of critical behaviours (Luthans, Paul and Baker, 1981). The base rates for attendance, stock-keeping and various aspects of interaction with customers were identified. The functional analysis revealed what responses were linked to successful selling. They found, for instance, that sales staff needed to stay close to their goods, greet customers as soon as they appeared, and keep display shelves at least 70 per cent full. The researchers divided sales staff into two groups. For one group they devised an intervention strategy which for a period of time made such rewards as time off with pay and free package holidays contingent on critical behaviours. These rewards were not made available to the second group. The behaviour of both groups was observed for the twenty days incentives were available and for a further twenty days. The performance of the intervention strategy group was significantly better relative to the second group in both observation periods. On the basis of this and other studies, Luthans believes operant principles can be applied in the workplace in such a way that significant benefits occur for both staff and management.

As yet, organizational behaviour modification has not been widely employed by British managements. Nonetheless, some insights provided by operant conditioning are clearly pertinent: motivation and performance can be low because contingencies are unclear, rewards insufficient or inappropriate, and desirable performance punished rather than rewarded.

A second example of Skinner's 'technology of behaviour' is *programmed instruction*. For example, if you were to enrol on a mathematics course which used this method, you would interact not with a tutor but with a teaching machine. The machine would take you through the course by presenting you with a series of *frames*. These would contain a small amount of information, for instance, a worked example of multiplying fractions, followed by a question. If your response to a question is correct the machine moves you on to the next frame. Two views have developed about the place of *incorrect responses* in programmed instruction. Skinner (1954) believed programmes should be designed to make the chances of a learner making a mistake as close to zero as possible. This means material has to be broken up into a large number of frames, each containing a small amount of information. With a mathematics programme a number of examples of the same procedure would be used, each frame presenting a question only slightly more difficult than the previous frame. The increase in complexity in the material between each frame is therefore kept to a minimum. The disadvantage of these *linear programmes* is that learners are all presented with the same order of frames whatever their previous knowledge may be. *Branching programmes* (Crowder, 1960) attempted to create more flexible instruction by using errors diagnostically. If your response is incorrect you are 'shunted' into a series of remedial frames until a response indicates you are able to rejoin the main programme. Since larger increases in the complexity of material between frames are possible with branching programmes, learners familiar with some of the programme's content can progress rapidly through mainstream frames until they reach a point where their responses indicate remedial frames are necessary.

The availability of relatively cheap and increasingly powerful small computers has meant that very sophisticated branching programmes can now be written and made widely available. Similarly, linear programmes need not involve expensive equipment. For example, a series of cards each of which is a frame and a piece of cardboard to mask answers can constitute a linear programme.

Programmed instruction has been utilized in commercial, industrial, military and educational settings and a number of advantages have been claimed for it.

Firstly, it enables organizations to specify what is termed *terminal performance*, what trainees will need to do to pass the *criterion test* at the end of the programme, and *pre-entry behaviour*, the level of competence required before training commences.

Secondly, it enables employees to use free time available for training as and when it occurs. In many occupational settings training may only be possible at irregular times of the day.

Thirdly, it allows the slow learner to learn at his or her own pace, thus experiencing less anxiety and embarrassment than when learning with a teacher and peers.

Finally, it is thought to be highly cost-effective, with savings in training time more than offsetting the capital cost of any equipment involved.

However, programmed instruction does have some disadvantages. Firstly, producing a good course based on programmed instruction is very difficult. Programme writing is a highly skilled task requiring a knowledge of both the subject and operant principles. In addition, there may not be a simple correspondence between a learner's responses and his or her comprehension of material. Learners do not always fully understand why their responses are correct or incorrect. There are also some studies indicating that learning achieved with programmed instruction is not necessarily superior, in terms of retention of material over time, to what is possible with conventional methods (Nash, Muczyk and Vettori, 1971). However, programmed instruction, particularly when combined with computers, is still in its infancy compared to traditional methods. The potential of the technique is only just beginning to be realized.

Both these applications of operant theory produce changes in behaviour by establishing a link between certain responses and the environmental outcomes an individual experiences. In organizations the principles of operant conditioning suggest that work settings should encourage employees to perceive some relationship between their effort and some valued reward. And, in contrast, the condition that should be avoided in organizations is *learned helplessness*, where employees believe there is no link between the events they experience and their behaviour (Seligman, 1975). Organizations that create environments which foster a sense of helplessness in employees face the immense problem of managing staff whose motivation has been drastically lowered. Organizations, therefore, should always create conditions in which it is difficult for employees to learn helplessness.

Many researchers have argued that stimulus–response theories are overly mechanistic and reductive. Mechanistic because by using only observable phenomena such as stimuli and reinforcement schedules and treating humans as passive recipients of them, they take no account of the mental activity which may occur in individuals during learning. Reductive because the theories have to break down complex behaviour into small stimulus–response units in order to explain how they are acquired. Critics of stimulus–response theories have claimed we need to develop more holistic units of analysis and accept that internal mental processes, though difficult to monitor, do play an important part in the learning process.

There is some empirical support for the claim that these mental or *cognitive* processes do need to be included in explanations of learning. For example, studies during the Second World War of air-gunners tracking simulated enemy aircraft found they often displayed negative response times. They were able to respond before the stimuli appeared. This indicated that gunners had developed mental models of the flight paths of enemy aircraft which enabled them to predict positions of aircraft and respond before they appeared. Similarly, in a classic experimental study of behaviour analogous to that of refinery process workers, Crossman and Cooke (1962) found the behaviour of their subjects could not be explained adequately within a stimulus–response framework. Their subjects were simply asked to control the temperature of boiling water by using a thermometer and adjusting a thermostat dial. If a subject's performance was shaped simply by feedback of response outcomes, the size of the adjustments should have correlated with the size of temperature error and its rate of change. These correlations appeared in inexperienced subjects only. Experienced subjects were able to predict the effect of adjustments on temperature, and this indicated that they had developed a mental *model* of the process. Experienced subjects' actions were therefore not simply controlled by information provided by the thermometer.

THE ACQUISITION OF SKILL

There is some evidence, then, that complex human activity does not fit easily into a stimulus–response framework. What seems to happen is that people actively develop models of the systems they are interacting with. In other

29

words, individuals do not respond directly to the environment, as stimulus–response theories assume, but to the models they construct of it. A number of researchers have claimed that a concept which can accommodate these less observable aspects of learning is *skill*. The definition of skill is complicated by its wide use in ordinary language. In industry it is used to mean 'time served', or qualified to carry out a craft or trade. Work is often classified into skilled, semi-skilled and unskilled. But in behavioural science the term is used in a much wider sense to refer to all the factors which go to make up a competent, expert, rapid and accurate performance. Skills in this sense are seen as natural units of activity which cut across task boundaries. This means that though two jobs involve different tasks they can require similar skills for effective performance.

Skill theorists believe that improvements in performance can be related to changes in the models people possess of the systems they are interacting with. Gibson (1968) has provided an influential description of the changes that human perceptual systems progress through. He proposed a sequence of developmental stages, each representing an increase in the ability to process, store and cross-reference information from different perceptual systems. Gibson suggested that at first we learn the range of stimulus inputs. We can understand a specific input better if we are able to relate it to the entire range of inputs. A learner driver, for example, will learn to discriminate between engine noises by learning the range of possible engine noises. This is the basis of what Gibson termed *learning affordances*, understanding what meaning or value an input has and what its implications for action are. This involves individuals developing *categories* for processing information. A learner driver, for example, develops categories for processing ranges of engine noise which indicate whether he or she should accelerate, decelerate, change gear or take no action.

The concept of categorization has important practical implications. Techniques have been developed which enable differences in the categories used by skilled individuals and beginners to be identified, thus providing important insights into the nature of the skill and a firm basis for the design of training programmes.

Gibson suggested individuals will then establish the covariation between inputs from different perceptual systems. We can make more sense of an input if we can associate it with inputs or cues from other senses. In many skilled activities it is essential to learn the auditory, tactile and balance inputs associated with a visual input. This also enables the skilled individual to make more use of sensory information derived from receptors in muscles and joints. These *kinaesthetic* cues are more immediate than visual cues and so make possible increases in the rapidity and accuracy of movement. Knowing what efficient performance 'feels like', gear-changing for example, is an important guide to skilled activity.

We also acquire what are termed *constancies*. These allow us to perceive certain characteristics of the visual world, shape, size, colour and brightness, as constant. Without constancies the visual world would be extremely confusing; objects would appear to change shape if viewed from different angles, they would very rapidly diminish in size as they move away from us, and would vary in colour and brightness according to the specific lighting conditions in which they are viewed. A dinner plate, for example, appears circular if viewed directly from above; if seen at an angle the shape formed by the parcel of light rays reflected from it on to the retina is an ellipse. The plate does not, however, change its shape as we change our angle of view. Constancies appear to be learned early on in life but can break down and need to be reacquired. Colour constancy, for example, disappears with unfamiliar objects, and size constancy can fail in specific visual environments such as when travelling at very high speeds.

Next our perceptual system incorporates what Gibson termed the *invariants in events*; these are the unchanging characteristics of the systems we interact with. We first learn the laws which determine how objects fall, roll, collide, break and pour. We then move on to learn more abstract invariants such as inertia.

These developments in the perceptual systems of individuals increase the *selectivity* of attention, enabling more efficient monitoring of both performance and the environment: 'only the information required to identify a thing economically tends to be picked up from a complex of stimulus information' (Gibson, 1968, p.286). This means skilled individuals need less information to select a response. The skilled driver, for example, requires less visual information than the learner driver to be able to perceive a shape in the distance as a child emerging from behind a parked car. Similarly, skilled process workers in refineries can assess the state of the system with quick and infrequent inspections of display panels (Bainbridge, 1978).

Constructing models of the environment which categorize and store inputs also reduces the demand on memory. Descriptions of human memory usually assume two stores, termed primary or short-term memory and secondary or long-term memory. This division implies that two processes are involved in the storage of information. Primary memory appears to be the conscious or working store in which information can be stored for a few seconds. If important, information is transferred to a secondary, long-term store. Primary memory is thought to be located in circuits in the frontal lobes of the brain, whereas secondary memory appears to involve irreversible changes in the molecular structure of brain cells. Primary memory is a fragile store and is easily disrupted. For example, if you have to attend to another input while trying to memorize a telephone number you are unlikely to be able to remember what the number was. Fatigue and stress also disrupt the primary memory.

As well as being a fragile store, primary memory also appears to have a limited capacity. Whereas secondary memory has an almost infinite storage capacity, primary memory seems able to hold only a small amount of information. In fact its capacity seems to be between five and nine 'chunks' of information (Miller, 1956). These chunks need not represent individual items such as numbers. By subjectively grouping items more information can be contained in the primary store. A nine-figure phone number, for example, can be remembered as three chunks each containing three digits. Skilled workers seem to be able to deal with many more items of information by chunking them according to the action-relevant categories they have developed. By reducing the load on short-term memory, skilled individuals considerably increase their resistance to the effects of stress and fatigue.

Skill theorists believe that it is useful to think of skill in terms of two dimensions: horizontal and vertical.

The horizontal dimension refers to the organization of activity over time. Unskilled performances are marked by a confused response order and imprecise timing. Learner drivers, for example, usually stall at the points where they are required to make a number of responses in a particular order with reasonably precise timing.

In the training context this implies that 'micro'-behavioural training, in which trainees acquire a specific response routine, for example, sales trainees who are drilled with 'scripts', may be inadequate. The correct sequencing and timing of responses may vary in specific contexts and a trainee's ability to vary the order and timing of responses will depend on more macro-cognitive learning, for example, understanding how to provide information at a rate which corresponds to the client's ability to understand it.

The vertical dimension reflects the hierarchical organization of skills. It is believed that skilled activity differs in the extent to which it involves conscious awareness. Some behaviours, termed *subroutines*, are so well learned that they can be retrieved from secondary memory and employed without passing through our conscious or primary memory. For highly skilled individuals so much of their activity consists of automatized subroutines that their conscious memory has little to do. This can give rise to the strange feeling they often report, of being able to 'step outside of themselves' during an activity which appears to observers to involve a great deal of conscious effort. Further up the hierarchy are *operating programmes* (Randall, 1981). These convert the contents of our models into behavioural outputs by triggering patterns of subroutines. The model is then updated to include outcomes of the action. Operating programmes can themselves be relegated to subroutine status if they are so well learned that they can be elicited without conscious awareness. At the apex of the hierarchy is the *executive programme* which selects the skill most appropriate to a situation.

Improvements in performance occur when either the model or the operating programme develop. The model contains more powerful representations of the situation, the operating programme acquires new sequences of subroutines. These improvements need not happen in parallel; the operating programme and model can move out of phase with each other, one leapfrogging over the other. For example, when an individual's modelling of a system, whether mechanical, human or administrative, improves, the model is able to include enhanced states of that system. However, for this new state to be achieved, the operating programme must acquire new responses. This process continues until the operating programme is unable to produce a sequence of subroutines which would result in outcomes not already contained in the model. Similarly, the model reaches a point where it both deals economically with all relevant inputs and cannot produce improvements in the state of the system that are not already included in it. What sets the upper limit on the refinement of model and operating programmes is the individual's level of *motivation*. Highly motivated individuals will always struggle to improve their modelling of a situation and the ways they are able to respond to their models. A racing car driver, for example, requires a more highly developed model and operating programme for driving than an ordinary driver. A highly motivated student will try to comprehend how academic performance can be improved upon and attempt to acquire the information-gathering, analytical and writing skills that enable the improvements to be realized. In general, the development of models and operating programmes slows down once we feel we have mastered the system we are interacting with.

Skills at work

Skill theory has considerably improved our understanding of the way in which people acquire complex behaviours. It is now possible to appreciate the crucial role that people's construction of their environment plays in their level of skills. We can see that skilled activity is in a sense an extension of their understanding of the systems they are interacting with into the external environment. These insights are important since they provide clues about the practical analysis and development of skills in training programmes.

Developing a satisfactory *skills appraisal* is the starting point for satisfactory selection or training procedures. With complex jobs it is often necessary to construct both a task description to indicate what the skilled individual does and a skills appraisal to explain how the tasks are accomplished. Singleton (1978) suggested the transition from the task to the skills domain could be accomplished by:

(1) discussing the skill at length with the skilled individual; supplementing this information by talking to his or her supervisors and subordinates;
(2) making the verbal communication from the skilled person more explicit by focusing on the categories he or she uses to distinguish inputs and the way he or she copes with specific events or problems which occur in his or her work;
(3) observing the development of skill in trainees;
(4) structuring the activity by identifying the dimensions skilled individuals use to perceive their environments and make decisions, and where possible developing measures for each dimension;

(5) checking the conclusions of this analysis by direct observation, performance measurement and experiment.

This form of skills analysis has provided useful insights into the nature of a number of complex occupational skills. Bainbridge (1978), for example, found that process controllers developed two internal representations of the environment, a working memory which contained information about the current state of the process and a more abstract model which housed their knowledge of the dynamics of the refining process. From time to time controllers updated their working memories on the basis of what was in their primary memories. This revealed what categories skilled controllers used to reduce raw display panel data to quantities that could be managed by their primary memories.

This approach to skills appraisal has also been helpful in the analysis of managerial skills. Moorhouse (1981), for example, clearly identified differences between the key skills necessary for departmental managers within a factory and the overall production manager.

Skills appraisals of various complex occupations have found the ability to refer between different domains of information is a crucial component of skilled performance. Managers, particularly, are often required to weight and synthesize limited information from different sources when making decisions.

The concern with skills has prompted the development of packaged skills appraisal systems to describe the skills needed for less complex jobs. Most of the research that has underpinned these systems has been sponsored by the government's Manpower Services Commission. Their ultimate goal was to provide a common language to describe the world of work in order to relate what people are capable of to what jobs require. This objective has not however been realized. People involved in activities like training, careers guidance and wage-setting all seem to require different forms of description, and within each of these specialisms different levels of analysis are possible. So research is now geared to developing appraisal systems that meet specific training or labour market needs. Basic skills analysis (Freshwater, 1982), for instance, was designed to analyse the skills required by young people entering the labour market. It consists of nearly 400 descriptive statements grouped under six skill headings: basic calculations; measurement and drawing; listening and talking; reading and writing; planning and problem-solving; and practical skills. The item-checklist enables the trainers to identify quickly the training needs of individuals and the opportunities for skill development provided by jobs. The trainers do this by indicating whether a basic skill item is a prerequisite for a particular job, that is, trainees should possess it before training begins, or whether the skill can be taught.

The skills involved in a broader range of occupations can be identified using an appraisal system known as the job components inventory or JCI (Banks *et al.*, 1982). Items in this system are grouped into five skill areas:

(1) use of tools and equipment;

COMMUNICATION AND INTERPERSONAL SKILLS	Professional Technical	Professional Managerial	Clerical with figures	Secretarial/Typing	Active Clerical	Clerical without figures	Receptionist	Clerical public contact	General Clerical	Selling
Receive written information	●	●	●	●	●	●	●	●	●	●
Advise or help colleagues or workmates	•	●	○	○	•	○		○		○
Complete standard forms or letters	●	●	●	•	●	●	●	●	•	•
Use codes	•	●	●	●	●	●	●	●	●	●
Write notes, letters, memos, short reports	●	●	●	●	•	●	●	●	●	•
File or sort things	●	•	●	●	•	●	●	•	●	•
Fill in a record book or manual	●	•	○	•	•	●	●	•	●	
Look up written information	○	●	●	●	○	●	●	●	●	•
Advise or help customers or clients	•	●	○	○	○	○	○	●	•	●
Receive complaints	○	•	•			○	○	●		•
Negotiate with colleagues or workmates		•		○	○			•		○
Use a manual or follow written instructions	•	○	○	○					○	
Instruct or train other people							○			○
Use or react to signals		○								
Persuade colleagues or workmates		○								
Negotiate with customers or clients		•					○	○	○	○
Persuade customers or clients		•								•
Interview people – simple information										
Interview people – queries								○		
Interview people – formal										
Give talks										

Figure 1.2 *Extract from a skills matrix using the job components inventory. Large black dots indicate very frequent usage of the skill, small black dots frequent usage of the skill, large white dots occasional usage of the skill and a blank cell indicates that use of the skill is extremely rare or never occurs.* From M. Banks, P. Jackson and E. Stafford (1982) *A Skills Compendium.* Sheffield: Manpower Services Commission.

(2) perceptual and physical skills;
(3) mathematical skills;
(4) communication skills;
(5) decision-making and responsibility in the job.

Three kinds of question are asked when completing this inventory; whether the skill is used or not, if it is used then how often, and what the skill is used for. The frequency with which a skill is used in a job can therefore be indicated in the inventory (Figure 1.2).

The potential of data gathered using these appraisal systems is increasingly being realized. Data can be used to produce:

(1) skills matrices which compare skill requirements of different job categories (e.g. between clerical and selling jobs);
(2) skill wheels, which assess the relative skill requirements of closely related jobs (e.g. different clerical jobs). This information is important in deciding on regrading or wage setting;
(3) job profiles which convert checklist data into narrative form. Job profiles are more easily understood by the general public and so can be used when preparing job specifications in management–union negotiations on wage-setting and regrading issues.

Skill matrices and wheels enable trainers to create more broadly based training programmes by identifying what are termed *portable* or *transferrable* skills, that is, skills which can be used in a variety of occupations. Identifying these skills and designing training programmes around them is a central theme of current government training policy. This is because it is thought that nowadays young people starting work will have to be able to adapt to rapid technological and job changes, so training ought to concentrate on the skills that can be used in different work settings.

Skills that are perhaps most transferrable are the *learning skills* identified by Downs and Perry (1984), which include: observing; questioning; memorizing; recording; assessing own performance; following instructions and diagrams; error identification; listening; comparing and contrasting. These learning skills are involved in acquiring skills as different as balancing a cash till and deciding how a company should respond to changes in exchange rates (Downs and Perry, 1986). The practical implication of learning skills research is that people can become more skilful in learning. Thus, training can be designed in such a way as to encourage the acquisition of learning strategies in general and the ability to choose the correct strategy for a particular task. Learning difficulties from this perspective occur when people choose an inappropriate strategy, for example, memorizing rather than trying to understand concepts. In one study three groups of students sat an 'O'-level paper: 45 per cent of the experimental group who had attended a 'learning to learn' course gained an 'A'-grade pass compared with 8 and 26 per cent in the comparison groups (Downs and Perry, 1982).

The learning skills research has been extended by the development of the job learning analysis (JLA) inventory (Downs and Perry, 1986). This can be used to identify what learning skills are involved in a job and their relative weight. Training can then be assessed according to whether it involves these learning skills. In one instance, by using the JLA they were able to demonstrate that a training programme involved only memorizing and understanding, whereas trainees needed to learn how to make judgements and predictions and to interpret manuals. On the basis of the JLA data they were able to produce a syllabus which matched the learning needs of the job.

Downs and Perry believe that training must now be designed to improve the fundamental skills of learning if the objectives of current training policy, the creation of active, confident and versatile young people, capable of dealing with changes in their jobs by being able to learn quickly and effectively, are to be achieved. Designing training programmes that concentrate on how people learn requires a radical revision of approach on the part of trainers and teachers more used to thinking about *what* people learn. However, those seeking to bring about these changes now have a sound basis of theory and research to guide their attempts to produce more effective training programmes and policies.

FURTHER READING

Bandura, A. (1969) *Principles of Behaviour Modification*. London: Holt, Rinehart and Winston.

Hill, W.F. (1982) *Principles of Learning: A Handbook of Applications*. Palo Alto, Calif: Mayfield.

Hill, W.F. (1985) *Learning: A Survey of Psychological Interpretations* (4th ed.). New York: Harper and Row.

Holding, D.H. (1981) *Human Skills*. Chichester: Wiley.

Kolb, D.A. (1984) *Experiential Learning: Experience as the Source of Learning and Development*. London: Prentice-Hall.

Machan, T.R. (1974) *The Pseudo-Science of B.F. Skinner*. New Rochelle, New York: Arlington House.

McGinnies, E. and Ferster, C.B. (eds.) (1971) *The Reinforcement of Social Behaviour*. Boston: Houghton Mifflin.

Singleton, W.T. (1978) (ed.) *The Analysis of Practical Skills*. Lancaster: MTP Press.

Skinner, B.F. (1971) *Beyond Freedom and Dignity*. Harmondsworth: Penguin.

Skinner, B.F. (1976) *Walden Two*. New York: Macmillan.

Welford, A.T. (1976) *Skilled Performance*. Brighton: Scott, Foresman.

2

Stress

In the previous chapter, the processes were examined which enable people to adapt to and integrate with their environments. These adaptive capacities, however, have limits and risks attached to them. For example, the person who constantly struggles to master a turbulent environment or a demanding task faces an increased risk of peptic ulcers, mental illness, hypertension and coronary heart disease. Less dangerous but still serious symptoms, like headache, eyestrain, dizziness, loss of appetite, depression and nervousness may also occur. And these can result in responses, like the increased consumption of tranquillizers or alcohol, which only compound the problem.

These are all stress-related symptoms, and their prevalence in occupational and wider contexts has given rise to much interest in the causes and alleviation of stress. There is probably no doubt that this has sometimes had rather 'elitist' overtones, as stress has traditionally been associated with executive and managerial occupations. But, in point of fact, stress never has been a 'middle-class disease'; incidents of stress-related symptoms are just as frequently caused by factors like shift-working or excessive fatigue, which are typical of manual jobs. Also, nowadays the new technologies are making stress increasingly a problem in manual and low-grade white-collar work. There is growing concern, for instance, over the impact of word-processing on secretarial work, and the incidence of stress-related symptoms among typists.

In this chapter we will examine some of the major theories of stress and some of the recent attempts to reduce the impact of stress on individuals.

WHAT IS STRESS?

The earliest and most influential conceptualization of stress came from Selye (1936). He observed an identical series of biochemical changes in a number of organisms adapting to a variety of environmental conditions. He termed this series of changes the *general adaptation syndrome*. During the initial phase, termed the *stage of alarm*, the organism orients to the demand the environment is making on it and begins to experience it as threatening. This state cannot be maintained for very long. If the stimulus which has elicited the alarm response is too powerful (for example, a poison) the organism dies; if survival is possible the organism enters the *stage of resistance* in which the organism musters the resources to cope with the demand. If the demand continues for too long these adaptive resources are worn out and the organism reaches the *stage of exhaustion* in which serious damage can occur. Selye was not sure what it was that an organism lost in the stage of resistance that caused it to pass into the stage of exhaustion, although he was convinced it was more than simple calorific energy (Selye, 1983). The general adaptation syndrome can operate at different levels, from a subsystem to an entire organism. Certain kinds of athletes (footballers, for example) make severe demands on specific ligaments and joints in their training and performance. The general adaptation syndrome and the consequences of the stage of exhaustion will therefore tend to be localized.

Selye's discovery of the biochemical and physiological pathways of the stress response has been of immense significance. A number of researchers, however, have not followed Seyle in seeing stress as simply a response. One major group of writers has argued that stress has to be seen as a function of an individual's *appraisal* of a situation. As we saw in our earlier discussion of skills, people do not respond directly to a stimulus but to the meaning a stimulus may have in relation to their model of the environment. This implies that events in the environment are not of themselves stressful; they must be perceived by the individual as a threat before the stress concept can be applied (Lazarus *et al.*, 1980). The stress experience, according to this view, is therefore determined by the *appraisal of what is at stake* and the analysis of the resources available to meet the demand.

The notion of appraisal broadens the concept of stress to include psychological factors, particularly personality variables such as 'the need for power' and 'locus of control' (see Chapter 3). In other words, what one person sees as a threat, another may see as a challenge. These different appraisals seem to produce specific physiological changes which, in turn, have different implications for the health of the individual. Some evidence has supported the view that appraisal plays a crucial role in determining the impact of a stressor on an individual's health. Jemmot *et al.*, (1983), for example, found the secretion rate of the immune systems of a group of students under academic pressure was not uniform. The relationship between exam pressure and the activity of the immune system was moderated by certain personality variables. Similarly, Arsenault and Dolan (1983) found the relationship between job stress and work outcomes, such as absenteeism and performance, varied according to the subject's personality type.

The concept of stress which dominates current research is an extension of the appraisal hypothesis that stress represents a relationship between a stressor and an individual's reaction to it. Current research is based on the assumption that stress, inferred from physiological, behavioural, psychological and somatic signs and symptoms, is the result of *a lack of fit between a person (in terms of their personality, aptitudes and abilities) and the environment*, and a consequent inability to cope effectively with the various demands it makes of him or her. One study which tested this view found that while neither a worker's report of the actual complexity of a job nor the level of complexity a worker wanted was related to a measure of depression, there was a strong relationship between measures of the person–environment fit and depression. The relationship the researcher found was curvilinear; when the person–environment fit was exact, depression was minimal but when there was either too much or too little complexity present in the work, the depression score was increased (Harrison, 1976).

TYPES OF STRESS AT WORK

Role interaction

Though individuals' perceptions of the environment play an important part in determining the experience and consequences of stress, it is nonetheless possible to identify objective features of work which are likely to be perceived as threatening. An individual's activities within an organization are a function of what *role(s)* he or she occupies in it. A role can be defined as the set of expectations that others have of a role incumbent's behaviour. Research has identified the ways in which roles become stressful. Firstly, in what is termed *single role conflict*, the various components of a given role become difficult to reconcile. For example, the expectations of a supervisor's staff may include defending their interests, taking an interest in them and affording them a significant degree of freedom in their work. The supervisor's managers, however, might have very different expectations. They may expect the supervisor to represent the interests of senior and middle management and to employ a much tougher style of supervision. Secondly, *multiple role conflict* stems from the fact that people invariably fill many different roles; and here the demands of one role clash with those of another an individual occupies. For example, a manager who is also the factory's safety officer might find the demands of each role difficult to reconcile, which may mean taking certain short cuts such as removing safety guards. In a wider context, women, particularly when married with children, can experience conflict and stress when attempting to combine familial and work roles (Lewis and Cooper, 1983).

Some roles, such as negotiator or salesperson, because they involve relating the activities of the organization to the outside world, seem to carry a higher than average level of stress. Miles (1980) developed a typology of these *boundary-spanning roles* which he claimed discriminated between high- and low-stress jobs of this type. The most stressful boundary-spanning job, according to his typology, would be one which involved performing complex tasks in a changing environment with a variety of outside parties to whom there is a long-term commitment, and where there are clear performance criteria and independent sources of information on achievement available to the parent organization. Thus the role incumbent is exposed to numerous novel and unanticipated problems, as he or she attempts to develop relationships with different types of client, while the availability of hard performance data means that employers can press the individual for results and ignore the delicate processes involved in a boundary-spanning role.

Another common source of role stress, termed *role ambiguity*, occurs when an individual is uncertain what tasks, responsibility and authority have been assigned to the role he or she occupies. Complex, flexible, non-bureaucratic organizational structures can cause role ambiguity since roles include responsibilities within a project team in addition to the individual's regular functional (personnel, marketing, finance or production) duties.

An increasingly common source of stress occurs when individuals feel *locked into* roles. Such stress is particularly common in large bureaucratic organizations where employees may believe they are unable to change their job, because very few job opportunities are available or they are not sufficiently able or qualified to move into another post. This can be caused by distortion in the promotion patterns in organizations. If an organization has recently been reorganized or created, new senior posts may be filled by relatively young people. Once these posts are filled there is little opportunity for promotion within the organization. The stagnation experienced when career paths are blocked leads to frustration, apathy and eventually to what Daley (1979) termed *burnout*, when the initial enthusiasm for a job is replaced with negative attitudes. Personnel departments and senior management in large organizations are increasingly recognizing the problems in terms of reduced physical and mental well-being of staff feeling locked into roles. Strategies for reducing burnout attempt to reduce the concern an individual has with the limitations of his or her current position within a hierarchy by negotiating career plans which may involve sideways as well as upward moves or by setting up project teams which create new networks of responsibility and authority in addition to the existing ones. It may also be possible to provide realistic career changes for people by a general restructuring of career scales within an organization.

Decision-making stress

One of the most potent types of stress in organizations occurs as a result of having to make difficult decisions. Janis (1982) suggested two reasons why this may be so: people's awareness of their limited knowledge and problem-solving capacities, and their awareness of the various losses which may result from choosing any of the options available. Janis argued that *decisional stress* significantly reduces the quality of an individual's decision. At its most extreme, this can cause people simply to withdraw from a situation and make a decision without seeking out or considering relevant information. More usually, however, individuals' attempts to deal with decisional stress fall into one of five categories:

(1) unconflicted adherence where behaviour is unchanged and information about the risks of continuing in the same way is ignored;

(2) unconflicted change which involves uncritically adopting whichever course of action is most salient or most strongly recommended without making contingency plans and without psychologically preparing for setbacks;

(3) defensive avoidance where the individual procrastinates but eventually chooses the least difficult alternative, ignoring any information that suggests this decision may be wrong;

(4) hypervigilance which involves searching frantically for a way out of the conflict and seizing upon any plan which seems to offer an immediate solution;

(5) vigilance which consists of a careful search for relevant information followed by a thorough appraisal of the alternatives.

Of these five strategies, Janis suggested vigilance was the only one which involves enough cognitive work to meet the criteria of true decision-making. Hypervigilance, where attention shifts on to a variety of sometimes quite trivial cues, introduces the most error into a decision. The individual's thinking in this condition tends to be based on simple stereotypes and can involve obsessional dwelling on the worst possible outcomes. Janis saw 'time pressure' as the main cause of hypervigilance. When individuals are constantly overloaded with urgent business, they are more likely to commit themselves impulsively to courses of action which soon after appear to have been inappropriate.

One approach to reducing the stress experienced by individuals when making important decisions, known as *stress inoculation*, seeks to provide individuals with resistance to decisional stress by improving both their understanding of what causes it and their ability to cope with it. Cameron and Meichenbaum (1982), for example, developed a programme based on the appraisal concept of stress, that stress is a function of an individual's perception of a situation and his or her resources to cope with it. The programme consists of three stages:

(1) conceptualization, in which the individuals' understanding of decision-making situations and their own experiences in them are improved by explaining the appraisal model of stress. Meichenbaum suggested that this model provided individuals with a highly effective conceptual framework within which they could organize their own experience of stress. To achieve accurate appraisal, they are encouraged to recognize that appraisals of situations are often inaccurate or incomplete and that allowances have to be made for the biases which creep into their perceptions. Individuals then consider the skills which enable pertinent evidence to be examined and reasonable propositions to be formulated;

(2) skill acquisition and activation. This part of the programme examines whether an

individual lacks a particular skill for accurate diagnosis of a situation, or possesses it but does not apply it. A relevant skill might be efficient gathering of information about the likely outcomes of a decision;

(3) rehearsal and application. In this final phase of the course, the individual practises and applies the newly acquired coping skills using role-play techniques. It is hoped that these skills can then be transferred to help deal with real problems.

Moos and Billings (1982) have argued that the attitudinal, personality and cognitive factors that provide the psychological context for coping with decisional stress are relatively stable characteristics of individuals. They believe that complex changes, particularly in an individual's sense of *self-efficacy* (how competent individuals feel), are necessary before improvements in coping with decisional stress can occur. At present it is unclear therefore to what extent short interventions like Meichenbaum's, aimed at providing coping skills, can bring about changes in the underlying psychological dimensions of coping.

Over- and understimulation

Welford (1973) suggested that humans and many other organisms appear to have evolved to function under conditions of moderate stimulation. Such aspects of the environment as noise, temperature, light, humidity and barometric pressure are tolerable at moderate levels but cause stress if they are too high or too low.

In the work context, the level of stimulation a job provides is likewise associated with the amount of stress it can cause employees to experience. Understimulation can occur in jobs which involve repetitive work and underutilization of skills. The emotional responses to these jobs are apathy, boredom and reduced levels of motivation (Caplan *et al.*, 1975). Behavioural responses are likely to be less well organized than they would have been at higher levels of stimulation. Many studies have shown that people who do repetitive work also face increased risks of stress-related illnesses (e.g. Ferguson, 1973). Cox (1980) has suggested that the effect of repetitive understimulating work on health occurs through what he termed an emergency stress response. This occurs when someone performing a repetitive task has to suddenly readjust his or her attention because it had drifted away from the task. He argued that because of the increased physiological 'wear and tear' these adjustments involve, the higher frequency of attentional shifts inherent in repetitive work was detrimental to health. His explanation however is tentative at present and it remains unclear why repetitive work carries health risks.

Many people at work, however, face the opposite problem of having to cope with too much stimulation. Overstimulation can be as stressful, if not more so, than understimulation. Perhaps the classic example of a job in which large amounts of variable information have to be coped with is air traffic control. The health costs in terms of ulcers, skin disorders, hypertension and respiratory complaints have been well documented (Martindale, 1977; Rose, Jenkins and Hurst, 1978). In fact it was noteworthy that American air traffic controllers were involved in a particularly bitterly fought strike in 1981 largely in an attempt to improve their working conditions. And several of the issues at stake involved reducing the variety and quantity of stimulation they were having to cope with.

Type As and type Bs

Even though occupations vary in the stress-related health risks they carry, it is now accepted that individuals similarly differ in their proneness to stress-related health risks. As early as 1868 a German doctor, Von Dusch, noted that people who developed coronary heart disease (CHD) were often excessively involved in their work. In 1943 another doctor, Dunbar, noted that his CHD patients could frequently be characterized by compulsive striving, self-discipline and an urge to get to the top through hard work. In the late 1950's, Friedman and Rosenman began a series of studies on managers in a range of companies. In an early study, fifty accountants were monitored for six months. Blood samples were taken every fortnight to gauge their cholestorol levels which were then compared with their diaries where they reported the amount of stress present in their work and homes. With other factors such as diet and exercise held constant, they found cholesterol levels went up and blood coagulation times went down during periods of stress. In 1959 Friedman and Rosenman made their most controversial contribution to the understanding of the relationship between stress and heart disease. They operationalized a behaviour pattern, termed type A, which they believed encapsulated what Von Dusch, Dunbar and others had observed in their CHD patients. This behaviour pattern, they argued, carried a risk of CHD independent of all other known risks. Individuals who fall into the type A category display:

(1) a strong and sustained drive to achieve poorly defined goals they have set for themselves;
(2) an intense desire to compete;
(3) a desire for recognition and promotion;
(4) involvement in numerous and varied activities which have deadlines;
(5) habitually fast completion of physical and mental functions;
(6) high levels of mental and physical alertness.

In extreme instances type A behaviour involves tense facial and body muscle tone, rapid body movements, hand- or teeth-clenching, excessive gesturing and explosive speech characteristics. Conversely, the type B individual displays less striving, aggression, hostility and competitiveness, and is in general more relaxed. While these are extremes, most people do in fact fall into only one of the categories, 40 per cent being type A and 60 per cent type B (Glass, 1977).

A large body of evidence has been accumulated which has confirmed the association between type A behaviour and CHD. One series of studies observed a sample of over 3,500 men over a fifteen-year period. Of the twenty-five deaths caused by CHD, twenty-two had been classified as type As. This yielded a risk factor in the type A group for CHD some six times larger than that for type Bs (Rosenman *et al.*, 1975). Why does type A behaviour carry such an increased risk of CHD? Chesney and Rosenman (1980) argued that some behaviours in the type A constellation are more predictive of CHD than others. They saw four facets of type A behaviour as particularly predictive of CHD:

(1) *time urgency*; type As feel time passes too quickly;
(2) *their competitive and hard-driving style* makes type As work harder and faster than type Bs, even when no deadline is present. Type As seem to impose deadlines on themselves. This enables type As to maintain and even enhance their performance on multiple tasks compared to a fall in performance by type Bs (Fazio *et al.*, 1981);
(3) *suppression of symptoms*; though type As work harder and faster than type Bs, they report less fatigue and complain less. In fact, hard work and self-imposed deadlines seem to reinforce their suppression of symptoms since it is only at times when the pressure has eased that symptoms are experienced;
(4) *hostility and aggressiveness* are thought to be the facets of type A behaviour which best predict CHD. Type As are more impatient, aggressive and irritable with others. When provoked, type As are much more hostile than type Bs in similar circumstances (Carver and Glass, 1978).

The motivational basis for type A behaviour is thought to be their 'need for control'. Type A behaviours are elicited by situations in which type As feel challenged, under pressure or threatened. It is at these times that differences in blood pressure, heart rate, and adrenalin level are observed between type As and Bs. Carruthers (1980) tentatively suggested that adrenalin accelerates the ageing of the cardiovascular system and so increases the CHD risk.

In a work-oriented society, type A behaviour is not seen as a clinical problem. If anything it tends to be rewarded. Measures of type A behaviour are positively correlated with occupational status (Mettlin, 1976), though, interestingly, type Bs are most prevalent at the top of organizations (Friedman and Rosenman, 1974). Healthy type As are obviously a great asset to organizations, given their hard-driving style may be necessary to cope with the work environment. For example, Rose, Jenkins and Hurst (1978) found type A air traffic controllers had higher rates of stress but the largest single chronic illness in the sample, hypertension, was suffered by type Bs. This finding is consistent with the view that stress results from a mismatch between an individual and the work environment. Air traffic control, a type A job, produced more stress-related illness in type B controllers.

Type As' increased risk of CHD, however, often confronts them with the choice of either curtailing their ambitions and accepting positions of lower status with less responsibility, or learning to face challenges without eliciting the health-damaging physiological responses. We will now examine some of the recent developments in occupational stress-management which provide type As with the second option.

OCCUPATIONAL STRESS MANAGEMENT

There is a good deal of research on the coping strategies found either among individuals dealing with general family and work stresses, or in specific situations such as retirement (Kasl, 1980), or job transfer (Brett, 1980) which can be used to support counselling and guidance of staff. In addition, there are packaged stress management programmes which advocate specific remedies for occupational stress.

Moos and Billings (1982) have provided the most comprehensive classification of general coping strategies, which proposes three broad categories.

(1) Appraisal-focused coping. This includes *logical analysis*, where individuals try to identify the causes of their current difficulties, considering one aspect of their work-situation at a time and using their past experience to predict the possible outcomes of their actions. Individuals may attempt some *cognitive redefinition* of their work problems – accepting their situation but trying to find something favourable in it which makes it possible to perceive it as less stressful. Some individuals use *cognitive avoidance* – attempting to cope with the situation by denying the fear or anxiety they are experiencing, or by trying to forget that the problem exists.

(2) Problem-focused coping. In these strategies individuals actively tackle the problems that are causing their stress. Firstly, by utilizing the social support system available at work individuals can *obtain guidance* on how best to deal with a situation. Secondly, by *taking direct action* an attempt can be made to modify or eliminate the source of stress. For example, an individual could, by renegotiating a work role, remove ambiguities in his or her present position. Finally, some individuals *develop alternative rewards* by substituting rewards which had been difficult to obtain with rewards that are more easily obtainable.

(3) Emotion-focused coping. These strategies provide ways of dealing with the emotional consequences of stress. Firstly, by *affective regulation* individuals try to avoid paying attention to their feelings – perhaps best summed up as showing a 'stiff upper lip'. Secondly, by *resigned acceptance* individuals can passively accept the situation and expect that the worst is likely to occur. Finally, individuals can attempt to cope with their emotions by *emotional discharge* – 'letting off steam'. This form of coping, however, can involve behaviours such as spreading rumours, stealing, damaging property and violence, which will actually increase the problems an individual faces.

This classification provides people involved in stress counselling with the means to explore an individual's method of coping with stress and to facilitate effective coping. Clearly an individual's coping strategies moderate the relationship between stressful events and their psychological and physical consequences. Specifically, Billings and Moos (1981) found that people using the active and cognitive strategies experienced fewer harmful physical and psychological outcomes than those using the avoidance methods.

Alternatively, in the work situation, where there is often less time for individual counselling, 'off the peg' programmes can be usefully introduced. The stress management methods employed in worksite programmes have included physical exercise, muscle relaxation, biofeedback (teaching individuals how to control their blood pressure, heartbeat and other involuntary physiological responses), meditation, and behavioural skills training (Murphy, 1984).

Physical exercise and fitness facilities are usually offered by organizations in the context of general health promotion programmes, but have also been found to be useful for individuals coping with stress (e.g. Durbeck et al., 1972; Heinzelmann, 1975). For example, Durbeck's study of NASA employees found that after a year of regularly using exercise facilities provided on the site, the subjects reported less stress and indicated they felt able to handle stress more effectively. Selye (1975) suggested the reduction in stress produced by exercise stems from what he termed the cross resistance effect, whereby the increased strength of one bodily system or process has an impact on another bodily system or process and thus affords physically fit organisms some protection from environmental stressors.

The systematic evaluation of programmes designed specifically for reducing occupational stress has really only just begun. One key question is the extent to which methods which have proved useful in laboratory and clinical settings can transfer to the work environment. For example, biofeedback training can provide individuals with a degree of control over their level of physiological arousal in laboratory settings, but this control is easily disrupted by stressors present at work and thus does not transfer easily (Holroyd and Lazarus, 1983). Even when worksite programmes appear to be able to produce reductions in reported and measured levels of stress, it is often difficult to establish why the improvements have occurred. The fact that many programmes use more than one method makes it difficult to disentangle the effects of any one of them. The research on worksite programmes also indicates that control groups often show as many changes on physiological and self-report psychological measures of stress as the experimental groups (Drazen et al., 1982; Murphy 1984). This implies that a number of effects, over and above the specific factors being tested for, are operating to reduce stress levels. As Murphy (1984) pointed out, 'nonspecific factors inherent in all training strategies like sitting in a comfortable position, the intention to relax, a credible training strategy, and motivation due to self-selection into the study, are responsible for some of the observed self-report changes and physiological changes'. At present, however, we know that many of the multi-method programmes currently being used on worksites do help to bring about improvement on both objective and subjective indices of stress. There is also some evidence to suggest that reduced absenteeism, and other benefits quite unrelated to stress, more than repay the costs of such programmes to organizations (Murphy, 1984).

The major criticism these programmes face comes from writers who argue that organizations can use these methods to adapt employees to poorly designed work environments and so avoid the need for reorganization (Newman and Boehr, 1979). Instead, they suggest, attention ought to be given to reducing the prevalence of objective stressors in organizations by increasing communication, participation, autonomy and training.

Although this represents a valid criticism there are at least two reasons why the need for occupational stress management programmes remains. Firstly, as Ganster *et al.* (1982) point out, many stressors cannot be designed out of organizations, for example, deadlines like the end of a financial year. And secondly, as Murphy (1984) argues, many organizations are unwilling to change their structure and practices, which means the programmes are the only way of reducing occupational stress and thus improving employee well-being.

FURTHER READING

Beech, H.R., L.E. Burns and B.F. Sheffield (1982) *A Behavioural Approach to the Management of Stress – A Practical Guide to Techniques.* Chichester: Wiley.

Bronner, R. (1982) *Decision Making under Time Pressure: An Experimental Study of Stress Behaviour in Business Management.* Lexington, Mass.: Lexington Books.

Charlesworth, E.A. and R.G. Nathan (1986) *Stress Management: A Comprehensive Guide to Wellness.* London: Souvenir Press.

Cherniss, C. (1980) *Staff Burnout: Job Stress in the Human Services.* London: Sage.

Cooper, C.L. (ed.) (1983) *Stress Research: Issues for the Eighties.* Chichester: Wiley.

Corlett, E.M. and J. Richardson (eds.) (1981) *Stress, Work Design and Productivity.* Chichester: Wiley.

Goodworth, C. (1986) *Taking the Strain: Managing Stress at Work.* London: Hutchinson.

Meichenbaum, D. (1985) *Stress Innoculation Training.* Oxford: Pergamon.

Norfolk, D. (1986) *Executive Stress.* London: Arrow.

Paine, W.S. (ed.) (1982) *Job Stress Burnout: Research, Theory and Intervention Perspectives.* Beverley Hills, C.A.: Sage.

3

Individual Differences

While many psychologists attempt to identify processes which are common to all individuals – the way information is processed and stored, for example – others are preoccupied by the differences they observe between people. In general, because of their practical applications in clinical, educational and work settings, the study of individual differences has concentrated on two areas: personality and intelligence.

Common to the study of both are a number of key assumptions. The first is that although individuals are *unique* they are also *consistent*; character and intelligence are developed early and remain much the same throughout adult life. Thus, a bright, sociable child becomes a bright, sociable adult. Secondly, although differences between individuals' intellectual abilities and personalities seem bewilderingly complex there are, in fact, just a few *underlying dimensions* along which these attributes vary. And finally, reducing the complexity of observed differences between individuals is usually achieved by making the assumption that individual differences are *normally distributed* (Figure 3.1).

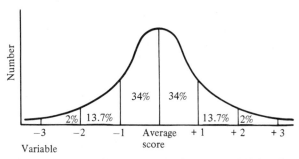

Figure 3.1 *Normally distributed variables produce this characteristic bell-shaped curve. With a measure of dispersion – the standard deviation – it is possible to calculate the proportion of a population falling above or below a particular point on the scale. It can be seen that 68 per cent of the population fall within +1 and –1 standard deviation of the average score for the population.*

The idea that the normal distribution – which had been shown to apply to physical characteristics such as height and weight – could also be applied to psychological attributes was first suggested by Francis Galton (1822–1911). By assuming a normal distribution psychologists can use sophisticated statistical techniques which both identify connections between aspects of personality or intelligence and describe an underlying set of personality or intelligence factors which explain the observed associations.

In the workplace the study of individual differences is useful in at least two ways. Firstly, a sounder basis for the prediction and understanding of behaviour can help those whose jobs involve dealing with other people. Secondly, it is important to have the best possible match between people's personalities and intellectual abilities and their jobs since a bad match leads to poor performance and stress. Thus the ability to identify and measure the individual differences associated with high job performance enables organizations to select and recruit individuals with these attributes.

In this chapter we will examine the extent to which psychologists have managed to identify the key dimensions of personality and intelligence and what relationships these dimensions have with job performance. Finally, we will discuss the relative merits of two common methods of assessing individual differences in the workplace: interviews and psychometric tests.

PERSONALITY

We all at times need to develop accounts of other human beings in order to make sense of their current behaviour or to be able to predict future behaviour. To do this, often without realizing it, we develop and use concepts that describe their personality. Normally our judgments about other people's personalities are based on their behaviour. For instance we might say, 'she behaved *conscientiously*'. If she often behaves like this we might be prepared not only to use the adverb to describe her behaviour but also to employ the adjective *conscientious* to describe her as a person. Eventually, we may find ourselves – by using the noun *conscientiousness* – inferring the existence in her of something called a *trait*. The important point to bear in mind is that, though traits are nouns, seemingly representing mental structures, they are, in fact, *dispositional concepts* which reflect a person's characteristic behaviour.

Behavioural scientists define personality as the relatively enduring combination of traits which makes an individual unique and at the same time produces consistencies in his or her thought and behaviour.

Normally, if asked to produce character descriptions we would be unlikely to apply the same traits to each person, since some would appear highly relevant to some people but not to others. Each individual would probably elicit a unique set of traits. This is termed an *idiographic* description. This type of description also occurs in certain professional contexts, psychiatry for example, where each patient's character is explored in considerable depth. Many behavioural scientists however use what are termed *nomothetic* descriptions where a trait is applied universally. The advantage of this approach is that it enables standardized assessments of groups of individuals, such as job applicants, to be made.

In this section we will examine three perspectives that have made significant contributions to our understanding of personality.

Firstly, from the nomothetic perspective, we will describe some dimensions of personality produced by a statistical technique known as factor analysis. Secondly, we will outline the model of personality developed within the idiographic tradition by Sigmund Freud. His view of the developmental processes which shape people's personalities from childhood has been both controversial and influential since its appearance eighty years ago. And finally, returning to the nomothetic perspective, we will examine some personality dimensions proposed by psychologists who believe *social learning* – the learning that occurs through interaction with others – has effects that are permanent enough to be considered part of a person's personality.

Personality factors

A factor analysis of personality begins by collecting data from a large sample of individuals using a variety of rating scales and behavioural measures. On the former, subjects would rate themselves along scales measuring very specific traits such as patient–impatient or conscientious–expedient. On the latter, subjects would provide information about fairly specific behaviour patterns, for example how many hobbies they had or how often they went to parties.

The next step is to identify what associations exist between the various measures. This is achieved by calculating the correlation between two sets of scores. A correlation coefficient indicates the strength of any linear relationship between two measures. It varies from +1.00, a perfect positive relationship in which the subject's position on one scale corresponds exactly with his or her position on the other, through 0.00 where there is no relationship between subjects' scores on the two measures, to -1.00, a perfect negative relationship in which the subject's position on one scale is the opposite of his or her position on the other (Figure 3.2). Thus, for example, there may well be a positive correlation between the behavioural measure of party-going and the trait scale patient–impatient, subjects who attended numerous parties also tending to rate themselves as impatient.

The third stage of a factor analysis is the construction of a *correlation matrix* in which the correlation between each of the behavioural measures or rating scales is plotted against all the others used in the survey (Figure 3.3).

A factor analysis then attempts, by using some sophisticated mathematics, to identify the smallest number of *factors* that need to be postulated to explain the

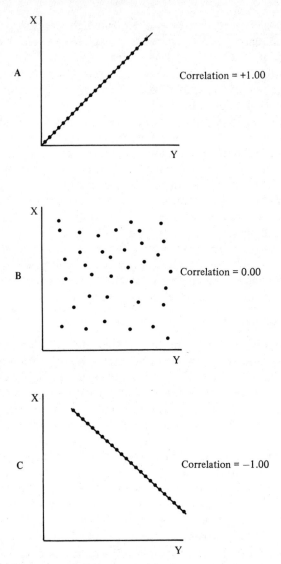

Figure 3.2 *Correlation representing the association between two variables. In A and C subjects' scores on variables x and y are perfectly correlated (directly in the former and inversely in the latter). In B, however, there is no relationship between individuals' scores on the two scales.*

pattern of associations found in the correlation matrix. Factors are given names by examining which of the original behavioural measures or rating scales correlate best with the factor – although some researchers prefer to invent names for their factors to remind us that we are dealing with statistical abstractions that may not necessarily correspond exactly to the psychological make-up of individuals.

TESTS	2	3	4	5	6	7	8	9
1	.4	.6	.0	.1	.1	.1	.1	.1
2		.4	.4	.3	.4	.1	.2	.1
3			.1	.0	.2	.1	.1	.1
4				.3	.6	.0	.1	.1
5					.4	.1	.1	.2
6						.0	.0	.0
7							.5	.4
8								.4

Figure 3.3 *An example of a correlation matrix (based on Guilford, 1967). The outlined figures represent significant correlations between scores on tests. The three groups of correlations indicate the presence of three underlying factors.*

The best known advocate of factor analytic techniques in Britain is Hans Eysenck. Since the late 1950s, Eysenck has used the technique to derive, test and modify his personality theory. He has proposed that most of the differences we observe between people's personalities can be accounted for by just three factors, expressed as bipolar dimensions.

(1) Introversion–extraversion. Individuals at the extravert end of the dimension are characterized as 'stimulus hungry', requiring a variety of stimulus inputs. Extraverts meet their need for stimulation by engaging in a variety of social and physical activities. Extraverts also tend to be aggressive and unable to keep their feelings under control. At the other end of the dimension, introverts are quieter, have fewer friends, are less active, have fewer interests, are serious-minded, conscientious, and manage to keep their feelings under control.

(2) Neuroticism–stability. High-scoring individuals report anxiety, moodiness, worry, depression, and sleep loss, are easily upset and if upset take a considerable time to return to an even keel. Conversely, stable individuals experience less emotional upset, embarrassment and worry. When upset, stable individuals quickly return to their emotional baseline.

(3) Psychoticism. Introduced some time after the first two factors, psychoticism is unlike them in that most individuals have low scores. Moderate scores are obtained by displaying lack of empathy, sensitivity and regard for others. The high scorer is hostile even to relatives and friends, enjoys making fools of others and enjoys indulging in dangerous or bizarre activities.

By combining the first two dimensions, four broad characterizations of personality are created: stable–introvert, stable–extravert, neurotic–introvert, neurotic–extravert. Interestingly, this modern statistically derived typology corresponds to that developed by Hippocrates in ancient Greece: phlegmatic, sanguine, melancholic and choleric. Hippocrates attributed these four temperaments to the relative level of four essential body fluids or 'humours': blood, yellow bile, black bile and phlegm.

Eysenck also gave his typology a biological basis linking it not with body fluids but with the central nervous system (introversion–extraversion) and the autonomic nervous system (neuroticism–stability). He proposed that individual differences on the first dimension – introversion–extraversion – are explained by inherited differences in the *excitatory potential* of central nervous systems (CNS). Individuals whose excitatory potential is low are predisposed towards extraversion since the bias in their CNS is towards cells being inactive (inhibition) rather than active (excitation). This means extraverts require more going on around them for their brains to function adequately, and thus maintain a reasonable level of alertness, than introverts do. Extraverts not only have a CNS which switches off more readily, they also take longer to dissipate the inhibition that has built up in their CNS while attending to a stimulus. Conversely, introverts, through their higher excitatory potential, are already reasonably alert and thus less prone to switching their attention to other sources of stimuli, in other words, are less easily distracted. They will also be less likely to have what are termed 'micro-sleeps' (switching off for a few seconds) since they dissipate any inhibition much more rapidly than extraverts.

Even before Eysenck's theory was available, large individual differences had been observed in the ease with which individuals in some occupational settings doing jobs like radar and sonar operating could cope with the low levels of stimulation the jobs involved. In such jobs, some operators missed critical signals on their screens or reported signals when none were present, while the performance of others seemed relatively unaffected by the low level of stimulation. Eysenck's theory seemed to offer an explanation of this and other similar differences in behaviour. Extraverts, because of the low level of activation in their central nervous systems, find it difficult to cope with environments which provide low levels of unvarying stimulation. Introverts, on the other hand, with central nervous systems already reasonably activated, find these environments ideal. Conversely, they would be 'swamped' by high levels of stimulation, which would cause a considerable reduction in their task performance.

Much of the impact of this *physiological* difference on *psychological* differences between individuals was presumed to arise from its effect on an individual's 'conditionability'. Introverts, since they build up inhibition slowly, are easier to condition than extraverts. This implies that introverts are constitutionally more likely to assimilate, through conditioning, the rules, obligations and attitudes of their social environment. Conversely, the impact of socialization on extraverts is attenuated by their weaker conditionability. Extraverts are therefore less likely to acquire conforming and conscientious behaviour patterns than introverts.

Though Eysenck for the most part has concentrated on exploring the biological substrate of the introversion–extraversion dimension, he has suggested that an individual's position on the second dimension – neuroticism–stability – reflects the stability of his or her autonomic nervous system (ANS). The ANS is the part of the nervous system not directly under conscious control that carries a number of reflex activities; it is also involved in certain emotional responses. Some individuals inherit a *labile* ANS which responds vigorously to stress and also takes some time to return to baseline. In addition, they will experience more spontaneous activity, that is, shifts in activation which are not clearly attributable to external events. Conversely, some individuals are born with a *stabile* ANS characterized by weaker responses to stress, a more rapid return to baseline and less spontaneous activity. This means individuals with a labile ANS are constitutionally more prone to worry, anxiety, embarrassment and stress than those with a stabile ANS. Thus individuals towards the neuroticism end of the dimension have a greater amount of 'free-floating' anxiety which, through conditioning, can become attached to events or people. This may mean, for example, that social interaction can for some individuals become 'loaded' with a considerable amount of anxiety. However, an important implication of Eysenck's theory is that neuroticism is normally distributed along a continuum. In other words, there is not a discontinuity between 'normal' people and neurotics. Thus, the difficulties experienced by people with conditions such as agoraphobia (fear of open spaces) are simply the result of somewhat higher levels of anxiety being paired with certain stimuli. It follows that such symptoms can be easily treated with behaviour modification programmes in which the individual 'unlearns' the existing anxiety response and learns a more neutral response, so enabling him or her to resume a normal life.

The third factor, psychoticism, is again presumed to reflect physiological differences between individuals. The relationship here has only been tentatively sketched by Eysenck and Eysenck (1976). They pointed out that since the behaviours that load on to the psychoticism factor are essentially 'male', variation in the levels of androgen, a male hormone, in a population could be responsible for this factor. This claim, as yet, awaits empirical support.

Eysenck's theory attempts, then, to provide both a fundamental *description* of personality and an *explanation* of personality. Not surprisingly, a theory which suggested firstly that personality can be described using only three dimensions and secondly that it is ultimately reducible to physiological differences has attracted a great deal of attention. Much of the research using the factors has demonstrated differences between introverts and extraverts on other measures. For example, from about age 14 onwards, introverts tend to do better at school and college (Entwistle and Wilson, 1977; Rhodes, 1983). But the connections between physiology and personality suggested by the theory have not all been confirmed. Claridge (1970) for example, found that tolerance to sedatives which, because introverts are presumed to have a higher level of central nervous system activation and hence greater tolerance to sedatives, should be predicted by the introversion–extraversion factor alone, was best predicted by a combination of introversion–extraversion and neuroticism–stability scores. The assumption of a general conditionability trait by Eysenck has also not been clearly supported. Conditioning appears to occur at different rates for particular types of response within the same individual. For example, conditioning an individual's eye blink to occur after a click might be achieved relatively rapidly but conditioning another autonomic response in the same individual may occur relatively slowly. While the precise nature of the links between Eysenck's dimensions and physiology are unclear, most factorists would agree that the three factors account for a considerable proportion of the differences we observe between personalities.

Eysenck's dimensions were produced by a type of factor analysis which extracts what are termed *orthogonal* factors. These are large factors, each accounting for a considerable proportion of the observed differences in personality. They are also independent of one another, which means that an individual's score on one of the dimensions is unrelated to his or her score on any of the others. Extracting orthogonal factors from personality data produces what is termed a *type* description.

Some factorists feel that Eysenck's approach to factor analysis loses a good deal of more specific information about human personality. In some contexts like personnel selection and clinical assessment, the use of only three broad personality factors means that a number of important aspects of a candidate's or patient's personality may be concealed. For example, introversion–extraversion can be divided into a number of factors such as assertiveness, self-control, sociability, conscientiousness and conformity which may be of great value in personnel selection or patient assessment. Deriving a number of somewhat intercorrelated *oblique* factors produces what is termed a *trait description*. The most widely used trait profile was produced by Cattell (1967). He found sixteen trait factors in his data. His traits have been used to show the average profiles of individuals, from successful students and salespersons to sufferers from anxiety, neurosis and psychopathy (Figure 3.4). We should stress that Cattell and others who use trait profiles do not deny the existence of Eysenck's factors – indeed data from Cattell's profile, if factor-analysed, produces Eysenck's factors – they simply prefer to use a more detailed description of an individual's personality.

One disadvantage of oblique factors, however, is that they are not as robust mathematically as the larger orthogonal ones. This means that they do not always appear with the same clarity as the larger dimensions when factor-analysing data (Kline, 1983). Ultimately, the choice between oblique and orthogonal descriptions depends on subjective judgments about the nature of personality and the context in which the personality description is used. Factor-analytic techniques currently provide the most systematic method of investigating the basis of differences between individuals' personalities. The fact that many of the dimensions produced by this method are able to improve predictions about various aspects of behaviour lends weight to the view that

FACTOR	LOW SCORE DESCRIPTION	TRAIT 1 2 3 4 5 6 7 8 9 10	HIGH SCORE DESCRIPTION
A	Reserved		Outgoing
B	Less intelligent		More intelligent
C	Affected by feelings		Emotionally stable
E	Humble		Assertive
F	Sober		Happy go lucky
G	Expedient		Conscientious
H	Shy		Venturesome
I	Tough minded		Tender minded
L	Trusting		Suspicious
M	Practical		Imaginative
N	Forthright		Shrewd
O	Self assured		Apprehensive
Q1	Conservative		Experimenting
Q2	Group-dependent		Self-sufficient
Q3	Undisciplined self-conflict		Controlled
Q4	Relaxed		Tense

Percent of population obtaining score

1	2	3	4	5	6	7	8	9	10
2.3	4.4	9.2	15.0	19.1	19.1	15.0	9.2	4.4	2.3

Figure 3.4 *Cattell's sixteen personality factors. Each individual is profiled on the basis of his or her answers to a questionnaire which takes about thirty-five minutes to complete. Scores for each factor are assumed to be normally distributed, here divided into ten, thus 38.2 per cent of the population fall within the middle band. Since a large amount of data on various occupational groups is available, Cattell's personality factors are used widely in selection and vocational guidance. As well as being predictive of job performance the profile has also been used to build effective staff and managerial teams. The profile shown here belongs to one of the authors.*

they represent fundamental attributes of human personality and are not merely statistical artefacts.

Freud and the dynamics of personality

Many researchers believe personality is the outcome of processes too dynamic to be captured by any statistical technique. The best known of these dynamic theorists is Freud. His theory of personality represents one of the major intellectual achievements of this century, and we can only hope to provide a glimpse of its complexity, scope and applications.

One of Freud's basic propositions was that most of the material in our minds was housed in what he termed the *subconscious*, a vast repository which for most of the time was inaccessible to us. What was available to individuals in the conscious mind represented just the tip of the iceberg (Figure 3.5). Between the conscious and subconscious mind lies the *preconscious*, similar to what we would usually term the 'back of our minds'. Here information is more readily available than if it were in the subconscious. Appointment times or the chores for a day are examples of the sort of items which might be stored in the preconscious.

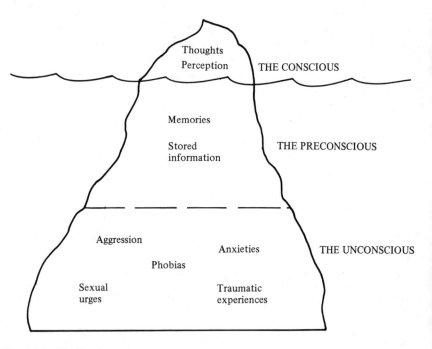

Figure 3.5 *The Freudian iceberg.*

Freud also proposed a tripartite structure for personality, consisting of *id*, *ego* and *superego*. The id is driven by a fixed source of instinctual 'psychic energy' which fuels two innate *drives*: sex and aggression. (It should be noted that what Freud meant when he employed the term sex was very different from its current meaning. Freud meant the term to include all forms of sensual experience and certain 'sublimated' substitutes such as friendship.) The id operates on what Freud termed the *pleasure principle*; it seeks immediate gratification of impulses produced by its two drives. The social world, however, is not organized in a way that makes this possible; its demands are housed in the ego. Using the *reality principle*, the ego strives to relocate the id's impulses to times or activities in which their gratification is possible. Freud saw the ego as existing only partly in the conscious mind, much of it, like the id, being housed in the unconscious and preconscious. The superego is also concerned with control of the id and further restricts the range of situations in which the id can be gratified. It differs from the ego in that it incorporates values and morals. Whereas the ego may restrict gratification of the id to a range of feasible situations, for example, the release of aggression in contact sports only, the superego further restricts the range to situations which are morally acceptable as well. This, for example, may mean that boxing is dropped from the set of contact sports in which aggressive impulses are gratified because it is found morally unacceptable, whereas fencing is continued. The superego, also, is not wholly conscious since it is acquired through a long process of internalizing parental and societal values.

Freud's theory of personality set the scene for a struggle between the id and the superego for control of the ego. The superego will contain various negative prescriptions forbidding behaviour of certain sorts, often leaving little room for the gratification of basic desires sought by the id. This conflict, besides absorbing a large proportion of the fixed amount of 'psychic energy' available to the individual, was assumed, if severe, to result in abnormal behaviours such as are found in obsessional and neurotic disorders.

Freud proposed a number of ways in which the unconscious mind develops mechanisms which enable individuals to live with these conflicts. They have the general label of *defence mechanisms*. The principal defence mechanism is *repression* or motivated forgetting. Extreme instances involving total loss of memory (amnesia) are often traceable to a single traumatic event. Freud believed the memory of the event was not lost but buried with other details of the individual's identity in the subconscious. The material can become available again through associations, dreams and psychotherapy. In less extreme cases of repression, memories of painful past experiences are kept out of consciousness or can lead to forgetting to do things loaded with anxiety, like visiting the dentist.

Another way in which individuals can be protected from their anxieties and conflicts is through *projection*. This defence mechanism achieves its defensive function by projecting the problem on to other people. For example, feelings of inferiority can be projected on to other people assumed to be of lower status. Other defence mechanisms include *reaction formation*, in which the individual develops a trait which is the opposite of the original predisposition – for example, sexual preoccupations are transformed into exaggerated prudishness; *denial*, where an individual struggles not to notice potentially ego-threatening events; *regression*, during which an individual retreats into the behaviour patterns of an earlier stage of development; and *displacement*, where an individual redirects unacceptable impulses.

One of the major determinants of people's personalities, in Freud's view, is what happens in early childhood when the conflicts between the id and the outside world first occur and when methods for dealing with them are first acquired. Freud believed childhood could be divided into *stages* corresponding to the principal sources of physical pleasure for children. The adult personality, he believed, contains residues of the conflicts experienced at each one. If, however, conflicts were experienced which were not satisfactorily resolved at the time, the individual becomes *fixated*, progresses no further and displays the cluster of traits associated with that stage.

Since the mouth is the primary source of satisfaction of the very young infant's bodily needs, the infant begins life in the *oral* stage. The infant is also assumed to derive pleasant physical stimulation from sucking. Freud suggested that oral fixation stems from too much or too little oral gratification. Too much gratification produces the oral-optimistic character, characterized by dependent and trusting attitudes. Too little gratification creates the oral-pessimistic personality in which the individual is sarcastic, caustic, or even sadistic.

Freud suggested that at about 2 years old, as control of the muscles employed in elimination is acquired, the focus of pleasure shifts to the anus, since pleasant sensations can now be derived from the expulsion or retention of faeces. He therefore termed this the *anal* stage. It is at this point that the outside world begins to oppose the id. The conflict for the child is between parental authority, in the form of toilet training, and gratification of the desire to retain or eliminate faeces. Fixation here occurs through too strict or too weak toilet training. Toilet training that is too severe produces the anal or obsessional personality in which the individual is excessively neat, pedantic, orderly and controlled. There is some statistical research supporting the notion of the obsessional personality (Kline, 1983), though these researchers would not necessarily agree with Freudians about the way it develops. Conversely, where toilet training has been too weak the child may become untidy and sloppy in adult life.

At about the age of 4, children enter what Freud termed the *phallic stage*, as he believed the child's sensual experiences were essentially penetrative and thus masculine in character. Freud suggested that in this stage, to avoid the guilt associated with the experience of attraction towards the parent of the opposite sex, the child begins to identify with the parent of the same sex. During the *latency* period, which begins at about the age of 5 and ends at puberty, the id appears to be relatively quiescent. Finally at puberty we enter the *genital stage* where we leave behind the self-centredness of childhood and begin to seek pleasure through satisfactory sexual relationships.

Freud's analysis of personality and behaviour has attracted a great deal of criticism. People in Freud's time, during the culturally restrictive Victorian era, found the explanation of behaviour in terms of sexuality, particularly infant sexuality, very difficult to accept. More recently, the theory has been dismissed as unscientific. One view is that for a theory to be considered scientific it must generate testable propositions so that it can in principle be disproved. The number of non-observable concepts in Freudian theory and the difficulty of generating specific testable predictions from it has meant that many psychologists, especially those who advocate factor-analytic methods, consider the theory worthless (e.g. Eysenck, 1985). Despite these problems, many people have continued to use and develop the Freudian theoretical framework, believing it to be a powerful tool for the exploration of human personality.

Personality dimensions and social learning

(1) Locus of control

One problem with Freud's analysis of personality development which many of those who are currently developing the theory have sought to rectify is his neglect of the effects of interacting with the social world. Many personality theorists believe that the social learning that occurs when interacting with siblings, peers, parents and teachers produces cognitive changes in individuals which are sufficiently enduring to be considered as stable personality traits. Two traits identified by social learning theorists have been found to be particularly useful in predicting behaviour in a variety of contexts.

Firstly, *internal vs external locus of control* represents the extent to which people have built up the generalized expectation that they can exercise control over their environments. If our experience of the world teaches us that we can influence events, we tend to acquire an internal locus of control. If, however, the environment seems to be largely beyond our control we develop an external locus of control (Rotter, 1966). An extreme example of this type of learning would be if a child experiences the death of a parent at an age when he or she cannot understand why this should happen. The child may therefore come to believe that he or she has very little control over events. A great deal of research suggests that the locus of control we develop has important implications for behaviour in later life. For example, Brown and Harris (1978) found that depressives were far more likely to have lost a parent before the age of 5 than non-depressives. In occupational settings, research has found that internals tend to achieve higher status and incomes than externals, who in turn are more likely to feel that their workload is high and their working conditions are poor. Because internals tend to believe that they have control over the outcomes they experience, they believe that there is a connection between their performance at work and their reward level and thus are more easily motivated than internals, who feel there is less connection between effort and outcome.

Because locus of control is produced by people's experience of the world, it is not a completely unchanging aspect of personality. Significant changes in the control people can exercise over their environment may produce changes in their locus of control. At work, for example, experiencing participative decision-making procedures may cause a shift towards an internal locus of control in employees (Frese, 1982).

(2) McClelland and need for achievement

Secondly, differences in social learning were also seen as the explanation of variation in David McClelland's dimension the *need for achievement* (N-ach). A considerable amount of research carried out by McClelland suggests that the learning that fixes an individual's position on this dimension occurs early on in life and so can be considered as a relatively stable feature of personality. Child-rearing practices and the father's occupation were seen as combining to influence the child's level of achievement motivation. Families producing high N-ach children tended to stress self-control, high standards, and individual initiative and independence, whereas low N-ach children came from families which emphasized compliance, dependence, a collective orientation, and getting on with others.

One of the most interesting aspects of McClelland's work was his attempt to show that the general level of achievement in individuals was linked with economic and technological growth in society as a whole. Children who have grown up in cultures and families that stressed achievement are more likely to engage in entrepreneurial activity in adult life. In *The Achieving Society* (1961), McClelland put forward his well-known hypothesis that increases in achieve- ment motivation spread throughout a society precede periods of economic and technological innovation. One notable form of evidence for this was to derive measures of achievement imagery in children's books in different cultures at different times. He found that the amount of achievement imagery predicted economic activity in the society a generation later.

Many researchers have found McClelland's concepts useful in exploring other achievement-related issues such as women's achievement. This research typically uses a projective test known as the Thematic Apperception Test, which requires subjects to write a story about an ambiguous figure thus prompting them to project their own personalities on to the image in order to provide it with meaning. The story is then analysed and scored for the degree to which achievement imagery is present. For men, early research found that this measure of achievement motivation predicted achievement behaviour reason- ably well. For women, however, the results were more complex, inconsistent and puzzling. There was often no correlation between the achievement imagery a woman used on the test and her achievement behaviour. One intriguing explanation was that women who do want to achieve also acquire through social learning a fear of success (Horner, 1972). This conflict between need for achievement and fear of success creates tension, anxiety and stress in women whose need for achievement is high. This stress will only be reduced by radical changes in the social learning that occurs in females during childhood and adolescence.

INTELLIGENCE

Conceptions of intelligence

The concept of intelligence probably has attracted more public attention and aroused more controversy than any other in the field of individual differences. This is partly because it has affected more people's lives than any other psychological construct. The old tripartite educational system of grammar, secondary and technical schools formed the basis of public education in the period between 1944 and 1971; and this was founded on the assumption that the ability of a child to benefit from a grammar school education could be predicted at the age of 11 from his or her score in an intelligence test. Similarly, many large organizations believe an individual's ability to perform in professional or administrative roles can to an extent be predicted from an intelligence test score. Controversy has particularly surrounded the use of test scores to support arguments about the heritability of intelligence and its distribution in different racial groups.

While the use and abuse of intelligence tests and test data aroused a level of concern that spread to the general public, another important debate was taking place between academics about what the term itself actually meant. Sternberg (1985) has provided a useful classification of conceptions of intelligence. He suggested the major distinction is between *explicit* and *implicit* theories. The former are 'based on data collected from people performing tasks presumed to measure intelligent functioning'; whereas implicit theories are based on intuitive assumptions about the nature of intelligence.

Explicit theories can be based either on dimensions of intellectual abilities that have emerged from factor analysis, such as verbal comprehension or spatial reasoning, or on assumptions about the cognitive processes that contribute to intelligent functioning. The former differ in the number of factors they propose, ranging from one (Spearman, 1927) to one hundred and fifty (Guilford, 1982). The latter differ in the level of cognitive processing that they use to explain intelligence. Cognitive processes assumed to represent the basis of intelligent functioning have included: (1) the *pure speed* of an individual's information-processing measured by simple reaction time experiments; (2) *choice speed*, an individual's ability to make a quick choice between two simple stimuli measured by choice reaction time experiments; (3) *speed of lexical access*, the time taken by an individual to retrieve information from long-term memory; and (4) *speed of reasoning* processes, an individual's speed at higher order information-processing such as completing a series of numbers. Thus, both types of explicit theory develop tests which are assumed to isolate and provide measures of the important aspects of intelligence.

Implicit theories have included: (1) the power to generate accurate responses; (2) the ability to use abstract thinking; (3) the ability to adjust to the environment; (4) the ability to adapt to new situations; (5) the capacity for knowledge and knowledge possessed; and (6) the capacity to learn or to profit by experience.

Because psychologists are mainly interested in measuring intelligence, they have preferred to use the more quantifiable explicit theories. Thus, although in this section we will describe only explicit theories, we should stress that implicit theories dominate the assessment of intelligence in everyday life – during the conversations and interviews we have at work, college or in informal social situations it is implicit theories that we use to make inferences about other people's intelligence.

Measurement of explicit intelligence factors

Of the explicit theories, those based on factor analytic techniques have been highly influential in the field of intelligence research. Unlike personality which, as we have seen, can be broken down into a number of factors, there is a considerable amount of agreement that a large proportion of the variance in intelligence scores can be accounted for by a single, large factor: G. This general factor permeates all our intellectual activity, determining to a large extent how well we do on spatial, verbal, numerical, memory and other types of test. G seems to account for just over half the observed differences in test scores in a group (Vernon, 1971).

The belief in a general intelligence factor can be traced back to the work of Spearman (1904). He used a technique of factor analysis similar to that used by Eysenck in personality research which extracts factors independent of each other. G was produced by the correlations of scores on all ability tests. Individuals who did well on one type of test tended to do well on all the others. There was, however, a certain amount of variance specific to each test. So, for example, an individual's score on a vocabulary test was determined firstly by his or her level of G and secondly by his or her standing on a factor specific to that test.

As we have already seen, it is possible to use factor analysis to provide a larger number of less independent factors. Some researchers have therefore preferred to break G up into a number of more specific abilities. Thurstone (1938), for example, described what he termed seven *primary abilities*:

(1) spatial ability;
(2) verbal reasoning;
(3) perceptual speed;
(4) numerical ability;
(5) memory;

(6) verbal fluency;
(7) inductive reasoning.

Though tests devised to measure individuals on each of these factors will provide more specific information about their abilities, test scores on each will tend to be inter-correlated. Vernon (1971) proposed that by deriving different types of factorial solution from test data a hierarchical model of intellect can be constructed which identifies four levels of ability: G; major group factors (verbal–educational ability and practical–mechanical ability); minor group factors; and specific factors (Figure 3.6).

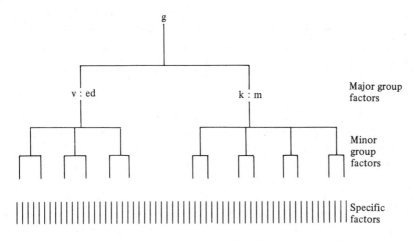

Figure 3.6 *Vernon's model of the structure of human abilities.* From Vernon (1971).

In a sense, then, as far as explicit theories are concerned, the question of how best to describe the structure of intellect is a technical question: what is the most compelling factorial solution to a set of data? With the availability of cheap computational facilities it has become easier to explore the various methods of factor analysis and so some agreement has recently developed about what requirements a factorial solution to test data should meet (Barret and Kline, 1980). Applying these criteria has produced a refinement in the notion of G: fluid ability, Gf, and crystallized ability, Gc. Essentially, the distinction represents the difference between an individual's reasoning *processes* (Gf) and the outcomes or *products* of these processes (Gc). Thus, tests which measure an individual's ability to solve problems or respond to novelty, tests of spatial reasoning for example, provide measures of Gf, whereas tests which measure knowledge acquisition, tests of vocabulary for example, provide measures of Gc. Logically, then, Gf is the precursor to Gc, and since performance on tests of Gc will also have some reasoning component, measures of Gc and Gf tend to be somewhat inter-correlated.

The Gf and Gc constructs have become the factors which many contemporary psychometricians believe account for a large proportion of the variance in scores on any aptitude or attainment test (Kline, 1986).

PERSONALITY AND INTELLIGENCE IN THE WORKPLACE

If we turn now to look at the application of the above concepts of intelligence and personality in the work setting, an understanding beyond the 'common-sense' one of the nature and causes of individual differences is important in the workplace in at least two ways. Firstly, the management of people is likely to be more skilful if managers are better equipped to comprehend and predict the behaviour of others. Secondly, it can be used to make better decisions about people's suitability for posts.

Personality

Freudian concepts, for example, can help managers and employees to consider what may be occurring beneath the surface of their own and others' behaviour. Organizations are designed and managed on the assumption that people act rationally. Freud's view, as we have seen, suggested that people's behaviour often falls short of this ideal. One of the ways this can occur is through the operation of defence mechanisms, which protect individuals from threats to their self-esteem. This means that defensive behaviour can be triggered by an event or by other people who threaten an individual's sense of self-worth.

The increased threat to our self-esteem at work caused by pressure for performance, fear of failure and the presence of authority figures means we may utilize the most powerful of defence mechanisms – projection – to protect our egos. This enables us to externalize any difficulties we may be having at work; for example, we can blame poor supervision or unhelpful colleagues rather than accept the part personal inadequacies have played. By projection we can offload unacceptable feelings of inferiority and inadequacy.

Two features of projection increase the difficulties of individuals using this defence mechanism. Firstly, if we project difficulties on to other staff we will not only blame them for our problems but will also tend to treat them with contempt or even hostility. This obviously may cause a deterioration in relationships. Secondly, projection makes it very difficult for individuals to perceive that their own inadequacies have contributed to their current problems. This means people may resent and ignore advice or counselling from colleagues or superiors.

The workplace is also where we are likely to meet higher levels of formal authority than experienced at school or college. Any conflicts people have had with previous authority figures, such as teachers or parents, are likely to be transferred to the workplace if they were not resolved at the time. So according to Freud we can unknowingly transfer our feelings towards earlier authority figures to our current managers and supervisors. Additionally, Freud believed that people are largely unaware of the intensity and ambivalence that may be locked up in their feelings towards authority figures. When transference occurs individuals may cope with these feelings by 'acting out'. This means that a relatively minor event in adult life can cause a quite disproportionate amount either of hostility or affection to be displayed or experienced in the presence of an authority figure. Doctors and psychiatrists are regularly faced with patients experiencing inappropriate feelings towards them through transference. Managers ought similarly to be aware of this possibility.

Both the social learning variables we described earlier offer interesting insights into behaviour in the workplace. David McClelland claimed that by adding two further personality dimensions, the need for power (N-power) and the need for affiliation (N-aff), he would be able to identify the relative importance of each variable to high job performance in particular types of management (McClelland and Burnham, 1976). People who are high in N-ach, for example, set themselves very high standards of personal performance. A surprising consequence of this is that though they make very good entre-preneurs, they do not make particularly good managers. This is because they feel they are the most competent person to do a job and tend not to delegate as often as they should. In addition, McClelland demonstrated that effective managers are higher in N-power than N-aff (McClelland and Boyatzis, 1982). In short, they enjoy the exercise of power more than they enjoy being liked by colleagues and subordinates. However, he found that managers had also to possess a considerable amount of self-control to be effective. Without self-control a high need for power channels energy into attaining personal rather than organizational goals. For example, a manager may suppress information which indicates the line of action he or she has chosen is incorrect (Fodor and Smith, 1982).

There is a good deal of evidence to suggest that locus of control is related to a wide range of organizational variables: occupational level; income; perception of job characteristics; perceived autonomy; perception of working conditions; job satisfaction; occupational advancement; and performance (Mitchell et al., 1975; Kimmons and Greenhaus, 1976; Evans, 1973). In terms of these variables this research indicated that organizations are best staffed by internals. They tend to perceive their workload as manageable and so tend to experience less stress. Furthermore, they perceive a connection between their effort and their performance, and so are more easily motivated and more satisfied with their jobs.

As we saw, an individual's locus of control, though believed to be stable enough to be considered as an aspect of personality, is not completely fixed. This means that if organizations allow people more control over their work, job satisfaction and motivation are likely to be increased and stress reduced. As we shall see later, one theory of leadership (path goal theory) and a theory of motivation (VIE) focus on increasing an individual's perceptions of control. Similarly, an important approach in designing work to increase motivation and job satisfaction involves using groups, which are afforded a greater degree of autonomy over the way work is performed.

Eysenck, as we have seen, suggested an individual's standing on the introversion–extraversion dimension reflected how 'stimulus-hungry' he or she is. The significance of this for workplace behaviour is that individuals differ in the sort of work environment they are constitutionally best equipped for. Introverts appear to be able to cope with jobs which provide low levels of stimulation. On vigilance tasks, where attention has to be focused for long periods of time on a single stimulus source, a radar screen for example, most people are subject to a *performance decrement*. As we pointed out earlier, signals are missed and signals which did not occur are reported. Introverts, however, display far less deterioration over time in performance on vigilance tasks. Conversely, extraverts tend to prefer and be better at jobs where the work is complex and varied (Sterns *et al.*, 1983). Knowing an individual's position on this dimension can therefore help predict what kind of tasks he or she will prefer and perform well.

The neuroticism–stability dimension essentially indicates an individual's emotional stability. Therefore jobs like selling, which routinely involve a good deal of rejection, may not be suitable for people scoring high on the N scale. Rejection would reinforce the low opinion that high scorers tend to have of themselves and could ultimately lead to depression.

Intelligence

Because occupational status is a fundamental form of achievement in any industrial society, and the basis of most other aspects of consumption, we might assume that such status is determined by an individual's intellectual capacity. But access to professional and managerial occupations largely occurs through achievements in higher education. This means we first need to consider the relative importance of intelligence in gaining access to higher education. In fact, social class and the type of school an individual attends are better predictions of his or her chances of going on to higher education than intelligence (Halsey, Heath and Ridge, 1980). The relationship between intelligence and occupational status therefore is not a simple or direct one.

What intelligence does seem to do is set a threshold for entry into occupations which makes access to higher-status jobs difficult for people with low scores. Large-scale research on army recruits in the Second World War found that the median IQ scores increased and the range of scores decreased with increasing occupational status. Thus, the median score for accountants was 128 with a range from 94 to 154 while the median score for labourers was 88 with a range of scores from 46 to 145 (Harrell and Harrell, 1945). Some researchers have argued that even this relationship can be questioned. They argue that this simply reflects the way the concept of intelligence has been operationalized. Psychologists, they argue, have, wittingly or unwittingly, developed intelligence tests to measure an individual's ability to function in high-status jobs. In other words, part of what has come to be meant by intelligence is the likelihood that an individual can function at certain levels in the occupational structure.

If there does not seem to be a simple association between measures of occupational intelligence and status, what relationship does IQ have with actual performance in a job? The average correlation between test scores and some measure of job performance appears to be about .3 (Kline, 1980). However, the relationship between the two seems to vary according to whether the job is professional, intermediate (e.g. clerical) or routine. Performance in professional jobs appears to have little to do with intelligence test scores. As we suggested earlier, intelligence seems merely to set a minimum level below which entry into an occupation is difficult. Above this level, however, performance in a job is unrelated to intelligence. Fiedler and Leister (1977a) have argued that effectiveness is determined not only by a manager's intellectual capacity but by a number of other personal attributes and aspects of the work environment. They suggested that poor relationships between manager and staff, a manager's lack of experience and motivation and his or her ability to cope with uncertainty all reduced the strength of the relationship between intelligence and effectiveness. This implies, for example, that the knowledge which comes with experience has to be present before the intellectual ability to manipulate information can be used to predict a manager's effectiveness. Fiedler and Leister (1977b) have supported this by demonstrating that the relationship between IQ and managerial effectiveness dropped from .36 with experienced managers to .15 with inexperienced ones.

In intermediate occupations, where there is a wider range of intelligence than in professional and managerial jobs, a fairly strong relationship between test scores and measures of job performance has been observed. In routine jobs, however, there again appears to be little relationship between the two, presumably because the reduced variety and autonomy and increased automation of routine work leaves little opportunity for intelligence to affect the level of performance. However, despite a good deal of research to suggest that IQ is not a powerful predictor of job performance, there remains a widespread belief among managers that intelligence is directly related to high and low achievement in the workplace, which ensures that IQ tests continue to be included in selection procedures for a wide range of occupations.

ASSESSING INDIVIDUAL DIFFERENCES AT WORK

Personality and intelligence are just two of the attributes that can influence selection decisions. Taking decisions about the suitability of applicants for a

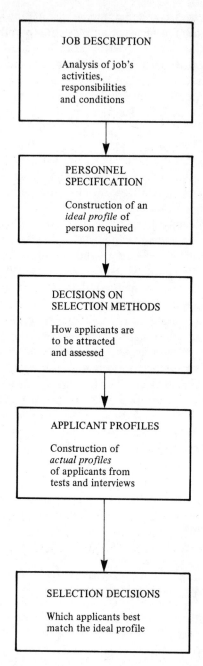

Figure 3.7 *Stages in the selection process.* Adapted from G.M. Bolton (1983) *Interviewing for Selection Decisions.* Windsor: NFER-Nelson.

post represents the end point in a *selection process* that usually involves assessing a wide range of attributes. The stages in the selection process are outlined in Figure 3.7.

A classic framework for translating job descriptions into personnel specifications is known as the seven-point plan (Rodger, 1952) which divides individual differences into the following areas:

(1) physical make-up. Are there defects of health or physique that are occupationally relevant?
(2) attainments. What type or level of education is required? What occupational training and experience is necessary?
(3) general intelligence. How much general intelligence is required?
(4) specific aptitudes. What special aptitudes such as mechanical, mathematical or verbal ability are necessary?
(5) interests. What interests, intellectual, practical, artistic, social or physical are required?
(6) disposition. How acceptable does the applicant for a job need to be to others? What personality attributes are important to job performance?
(7) circumstances. What domestic circumstances are relevant, for example does the applicant need to be mobile?

By using the seven-point plan, or other similar frameworks, it is possible to construct a fairly clear picture of what sort of person is required to fill a given job. The next stage is to decide what methods are to be used in assessing applicants. These include using application forms, references, interviews, situational exercises (simulation of tasks or jobs which test key abilities or aptitudes) and tests. Having decided what method, or mix of methods, is appropriate, the search begins for individuals whose *actual profiles* match or come nearest to the *ideal profiles*. Here we will examine two of the most commonly used methods to construct actual profiles: interviews and tests.

Interviews

Though the most widely used method in the selection process, the interview is considered by many to be of little use in predicting actual performance in a job (e.g. Eysenck, 1953). Critics of its use as a selection tool claim it is subject to the same problems which reduce our capacity to perceive and judge others accurately in all situations, namely:

(1) impression formation. We tend to make judgments about others very quickly and tend to ignore information which later contradicts our first impression;
(2) halo effect. If we perceive certain key traits we tend to judge all other aspects of the individual according to whether we have judged the person favourably or unfavourably on these traits;
(3) stereotypes. Ready-made generalizations about members of social categories can distort judgments about individuals;
(4) limited capacity. The number of evaluative categories we use when judging others tends to be very limited;

71

(5) idiosyncrasy. The categories we use may reflect our own interests and attitudes.

In addition to these general problems the interviewer faces a number of specific difficulties. For example, judgments about a candidate can be affected by the quality of the previous candidate. This is termed the contrast effect. Also, with a large pool of candidates an interviewer can come to view the task as primarily a rejection procedure. This means the interviewer searches for a reason to reject a candidate. Negative information about candidates therefore becomes disproportionately weighted. In addition, the nature of human memory means the first and last candidates will be remembered more vividly. The first candidate benefits from what is termed the primacy effect, the last candidate from the recency effect. Finally, interviewers tend to delude themselves about their interviewing skills and their ability to assess individuals, and so rarely take into account the above defects.

In reply to these criticisms, advocates of interviewing have defended the method on a number of counts. They point out that it often serves more than just an assessment function. The task of an interviewer can include a public relations function, representing an organization to applicants and in a way helping to attract them. If talented candidates are scarce this function may even become more important than assessment itself. Supporters of interviewing suggest that it is an effective method of gathering certain types of personal information that would be difficult to acquire from application forms. Also they claim that interviews can be improved by increasing interviewing skills (Taylor and Sniezek, 1984). Like other social skills, effective interviewing depends on the ability to progress smoothly through the encounter, sensitivity to cues and developing a rapport with another person. These in turn are assisted by having an agenda of items that enables the ideal profile to be systematically related to the applicant's written evidence. For instance, one frequently used agenda employs this sequence: technical aspects of current job, human aspects of current job, selected items of previous jobs, education and training, personal and domestic topics and dealing with applicant questions about the job.

Progression smoothly through an interview is also assisted by the behaviours outlined in Table 3.1. Training programmes are available which enable interviewers to practise these behaviours. Feedback, through audio or audio-visual tapes of practice interviews, is combined with the comments of instructors and other trainees to produce changes in an individual's performance.

Finally, proponents of the interview argue that decisions about the suitability of the interviewee can be improved by taking them in a more systematic manner. One way this can be done is by using a *rating scale* to quantify the degree to which applicants match the ideal profile on each of the areas of the seven-point plan, an example of which is given in Table 3.2. Producing tables like this one considerably clarifies the relative advantages of each candidate. Applicants can be either accepted or rejected on the basis of calculations of a total score, or on a selective basis where some attribute is

Table 3.1 *Key interview behaviours*

BEHAVIOUR	EXAMPLE	COMMENT
Open question	Why did you leave your first job?	Used for opening up an area for discussion
Closed question	You need to give a month's notice in your present job?	Used to clarify details or give an anxious candidate an easy question to reduce his or her nervousness
Advisement	Let's move on to your time at university	Used to guide the thoughts and feelings of the candidate
Reflective listening	So you're saying that you've achieved everything you can in your present company	Used when attempting to capture the thoughts and feelings behind what the candidate has said. Also a powerful method of conveying acceptance. Is possibly the most difficult interviewing skill
Interpretation	You seem to enjoy having to respond quickly to difficulties	Used to communicate the interviewer's perspective on what the candidate has been saying
Process disclosure	I feel you are not being as open as you perhaps could be	Used occasionally by the interviewer to reveal how he or she is reacting to the candidate at that moment, thus giving the candidate a chance to comment on the interviewer's reaction
Biographical disclosure	Yes that happened to me when I moved down from the north	Used to reduce the asymmetry and formality of the interviewer — candidate relationship

considered or has emerged in studies as more important than others. Decisions made in this way also make the risks of a decision more explicit and can indicate where training for a new recruit is necessary.

Tests

Critics of the interview are usually advocates of the psychometric test. The British Psychological Society (1981) defined a psychometric test as 'an instrument for the quantitative assessment of some psychological attribute or attributes of an individual'. Tests have been used to distinguish between individuals on a number of attributes: (1) general intellectual ability; (2) aptitudes; (3) interests; (4) personality.

A test usually consists of a series of questions or items to which people

Table 3.2 *Example of a rating scale using the seven-point plan. Candidates are ranked on a five-point scale where (5) = fully matches the specification, (4) matches very well, (3) matches fairly well, (2) matches in some respects but with important omissions and (1) does not match specification. The candidates were interviewed for the job of home help organizer in a Social Services Department.*

		CANDIDATES		
		A	B	C
PHYSICAL MAKEUP				
Essential:	Fit, active, 25–40, work well under stress	4	5	3
Desirable:	28–35, fluent speech	Health needs examining		Poor appearance
ATTAINMENTS				
Essential:	Good level of general education	5	5	5
Desirable:	Home Help Organizer Diploma/ Certificate in Social Services			
GENERAL INTELLIGENCE				
Essential:	Think quickly and clearly	5	5	3
Desirable:	Ability to relate to and communicate effectively orally and in writing with a wide range of people			Poor communication skills
SPECIAL APTITUDES				
Essential:	Ability to plan and deliver instructional sessions	5	4	2
	Respond sensitively to people and situations			Doubt about ability to plan
Desirable:	Quickly establish rapport and relationship with clients			
	Ability to distinguish fact from opinion and fantasy			
INTERESTS				
Essential:	Social welfare and the needs of the elderly, handicapped and mentally ill	5	3 Little empathy for handicapped	1 Too concerned about salary
Contra-indication	Instrumental attitude			
DISPOSITION				
Essential:	Sympathetic, ability to form good relationships with manual staff and clients	5	3 Little ability to lead	5
Desirable:	Ability to cope with crises			
CIRCUMSTANCES				
Essential:	Driving licence and car owner	5	3 Lives 25 miles from district	1 No car
Desirable:	Reside locally			
	TOTAL	34	28	20

respond either by indicating their preferences, as in the case of personality tests, or by attempting a solution in the case of aptitude or intellectual tests. Their responses are then scored according to some predetermined format. A good test will provide a table of results which enable an individual's score to be compared with the scores of the general population. For occupational assessment, tests often provide norms for particular occupational groups, so that individuals can be compared to the relevant sub-population. For example, the score on a mechanical aptitude test of an applicant for an apprentice's job can be compared with the range of scores for apprentices who successfully completed their training.

Tests have two technical criteria to meet before they are useful in occupational assessment: *reliability* and *validity*.

The concept of reliability addresses two questions. Firstly, is the measure self-consistent? In other words, to what extent does each test item measure the same variable? This is sometimes termed *internal reliability*. Secondly, does the test yield the same score for an individual on retesting (assuming the trait or ability is itself stable)? This is often called *test–retest reliability*. Internal reliability can be calculated by correlating scores for each question with those for each other question. The average correlation indicates the extent to which questions are measuring the same thing. Alternatively scores on one half of the test can be correlated with scores on the other half. Test–retest reliability is measured by establishing the extent to which scores obtained on two administrations of a test are similar. To reduce the chances of subjects remembering their answers from the first sitting, the interval between testing sessions should be at least a month. Some tests have 'parallel forms', that is, two versions of a test, to remove the risk of subjects remembering previous answers.

Normally we would expect test scores to possess test–retest reliability and not be subject to fluctuations. Reliability coefficients (in other words the correlation between test scores at time one with test scores for the same group of subjects at time two) of about .7 are usually expected in tests used in occupational assessment.

The validity of test scores is equally important. A test is said to be valid when it measures what it purports to measure. This means that differences between individuals' scores actually reflect differences on the variable being measured. Firstly, if a test looks like it measures what it claims to measure it is said to have *face validity*. This is important because if applicants can see that a test seems to be measuring relevant attributes they are more likely to cooperate with the tester. Face validity therefore increases the acceptability of tests in the selection procedure. Secondly, when scores on a test correlate well with scores on other tests of the same attribute it is said to possess *concurrent validity*. For example, if scores for a group on a new IQ test correlate well with their scores on other IQ tests we can be reasonably confident that the new test is measuring intelligence. Concurrent validity does not, however, imply *predictive validity*, the ability of a test to predict real-life performance. The predictive value of an aptitude test used in employee selection would be its ability to predict some aspect of job performance. Finally, it is sometimes difficult to find a measure against which a test's predictive value can be assessed. In these situations the test's *construct validity* is measured instead. This involves generating a number of hypotheses about the test variable as a construct or concept and then finding evidence to support or reject these hypotheses. For instance, to demonstrate the construct validity of a measure of job satisfaction we might hypothesize that high scorers would have less absenteeism, be less inclined to leave the organization and show higher levels of job performance. Low scorers should be absent more often, should be more likely to leave and demonstrate poorer work performance than high scorers.

Test usage is becoming increasingly popular in Britain, since many senior managers see tests as a way of greatly reducing error in selection decisions (Edwardes, 1984). Nevertheless, while tests are seen as more objective than interviews, testing does involve considerable problems of procedure and interpretation. The reliability and validity of a test can be seriously undermined by the practical realities of administration in the workplace. When standardized administration procedures are not followed the utility of test scores is reduced. Similarly, as with interviewing, if insufficient rapport with the candidate is established his or her willingness to participate fully in the procedure is greatly reduced.

While the poor administration of tests may produce scores lacking reliability and validity, an inability to interpret scores properly is even more of a problem. Statistics rarely speak for themselves, and test scores, like interview data, can only be a starting point when assessing individuals. They have to be interpreted, not only with information provided by the authors of the test but also with other sources of evidence concerning the applicants' education, attitudes and interests. Blind acceptance of test scores without adequate consideration of these other aspects of the applicants' abilities can result in serious injustices.

To protect both the integrity of psychometric tests and the interests of test subjects, test usage is at present restricted by the British Psychological Society to trained individuals. The value of tests and the information they provide in assessment procedure is, therefore, less likely to be compromised.

FURTHER READING

Eysenck, H.J. (1981) *A Model for Personality*. New York: Springer-Verlag
Eysenck, H.J. (1985) *Decline and Fall of the Freudian Empire*. Harmondsworth: Viking.

Eysenck, H.J. and M.W. Eysenck (1985) *Personality and Individual Differences*. New York: Plenum Press.

Feffer, M. (1982) *The Structure of Freudian Thought: The Problem of Immutability and Discontinuity in Developmental Theory*. New York: International University Press.

Goldstein, G. and M. Hersen (eds.) (1984) *Handbook of Psychological Assessment*. Oxford: Pergamon Press.

Kets De Vries, M.F.R. and D. Miller. (1984) *The Neurotic Organization*. London: Jossey-Bass

Kline, P. (1984) *Psychology and Freudian Theory: An Introduction*. London: Methuen.

Kline, P. (1986) *A Handbook of Test Construction*. London: Methuen.

Lefcourt, H.M. (1982) *Locus of Control: Current Trends in Theory and Research* (2nd ed.). Hillsdale, N.J.: Lawrence Erlbaum.

Lynn, R. (ed.) (1981) *Diversions of Personalty: Papers in Honour of H.J. Eysenck*. Oxford: Pergamon Press.

McClelland, D.C. (1975) *Power: The Inner Experience*. London: Wiley.

McClelland, D.C. (1984) *Motives, Personality and Society: Selected Papers*. New York: Praeger.

Miller, K.M. (1975) *Psychological Testing in Personnel Assessment*. Aldershot: Gower.

Rotter, J.B. (1982) *The Development and Applications of Social Learning Theory: Selected Papers*. New York: Praeger.

Shackleton, V. and C. Fletcher (1984) *Individual Differences: Theories and Applications*. London: Methuen.

Woolman, B.B. (ed.) (1985) *Handbook of Intelligence: Theories, Measurements, and Applications*. Chichester: Wiley.

4

Motivation and Job Satisfaction

In the years following the Second World War, western industrialized societies experienced increasing prosperity and relatively full employment. Developments in housing, welfare and education policies both reflected and fostered the rising expectations of people in post-war society. In this context employers were faced with a workforce which could, if dissatisfied, change jobs relatively easily. This led to an interest in what creates a stable and well-motivated workforce, and in particular to an interest in the concepts of *motivation* and *job satisfaction*. Nowadays, though relatively full employment is no longer a feature of the labour market, because of its practical implications (particularly productivity and labour turnover) interest in motivation and job satisfaction has persisted. Indeed, there are still a great many occupations where employers experience difficulties in obtaining skilled staff, where the demand for such types of labour is high and the problems of attracting and maintaining a stable workforce continue.

In this chapter we will examine research which has sought to identify the conditions which create a motivated and satisfied workforce.

NEEDS AT WORK

Motivational theories can be divided into two categories, termed *content* and *process*. Content theories assume that all individuals possess the same set of *needs*. These theories tend to be heavily prescriptive in nature, since by assuming people have similar needs they are also recommending the characteristics that ought to be present in jobs. Process theories, on the other hand, stress the differences in people's needs and focus on the cognitive processes that create these differences.

Content theories

Although content theories are based on the assumption that we can attribute a similar set of needs to all individuals, theories within this category differ in their accounts of what these needs are. Maslow (1954) outlined what is perhaps the most influential of the content theories. He suggested there was a *hierarchy of needs* up which people progress. Once individuals satisfy a need at one level in the hierarchy, it ceases to motivate their behaviour; instead they are motivated by the need at the next level up the hierarchy. Thus, at first individuals are motivated by physiological needs such as hunger and thirst. If conditions are such that these needs can be satisfied, security needs such as the need for shelter and protection become the major influence on an individual's behaviour. A favourable environment allows an individual to progress from behaviour activated by these *deficiency needs* to behaviour which reflects what Maslow termed *higher-order needs*.

As can be seen from Figure 4.1, this progression ultimately leads to behaviour motivated principally by the need to realize one's full potential, which Maslow termed the need for *self-actualization*. Maslow, however,

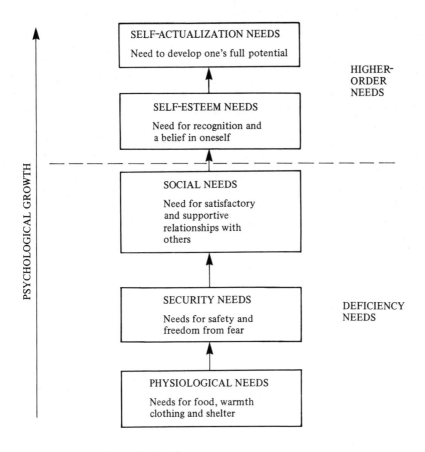

Figure 4.1 *Maslow's hierarchy of needs.*

believed that because of the uneven distribution of satisfying work only a small proportion of the population reached this level. Thus, self-actualization is for most of us a need which will motivate our behaviour throughout our lives.

Although not originally intended as an explanation of motivation in the workplace, Maslow's idea of a hierarchy of needs has, nonetheless, been enthusiastically adopted by many management theorists. It was seen as offering a number of predictions about what motivates people in societies offering relatively full employment. When jobs are scarce, employees are motivated solely by deficiency needs. When jobs are readily available, and deficiency needs are easily satisfied, social needs become important motivators in the workplace. This means organizations will have to provide opportunities for employees to satisfy their social needs, for example by providing company sports and social facilities. Once social needs are met, intrinsic aspects of work, the amount of challenge, responsibility and autonomy it offers become increasingly salient to employee motivation. Thus, the theory suggests that employees will always tend to want more from their employers. Having satisfied their subsistence needs they strive to fulfil security needs. When jobs are secure they will seek ways of satisfying social needs and if successful will seek the means (increased autonomy, participation, responsibility) to the ultimate end of self-actualization.

Though many found the idea of a hierarchy of needs appealing, we should stress that the notion has not much empirical support (Wahba and Bridwell, 1976). In fact, Maslow had not intended his ideas, based on his observations of patients, to be used as a theory in the traditional sense of the term. Consequently he provided no operational definitions of the variables he described, which has made measurement of their relative strengths difficult.

What Maslow's ideas have done is to make one basic, important point: in prosperous societies the need for self-actualization becomes a key motivator.

One content theory which does provide reasonably reliable measures for the needs it proposes is known as ERG theory (Alderfer, 1972). This suggests that individual needs can be divided into three groups:

(1) existence needs, which include nutritional and material requirements. At work, working conditions and pay would fall into this group;
(2) relatedness needs, which are met through relationships with family and friends and at work with colleagues and supervisors;
(3) growth needs, which reflect a desire for personal psychological development.

Alderfer's theory differs in a number of important respects from Maslow's. While Maslow proposed a progression up a hierarchy, Alderfer argued it was better to think in terms of a continuum, from concrete (existence needs) to least concrete (growth needs); and he believed it was possible to move along it in either direction. This means that if, for example, fulfilment of growth needs is difficult *frustration regression* occurs causing individuals to concentrate on fulfilling their relatedness needs. Unsatisfied needs therefore become less rather than more important, whereas Maslow assumed the opposite.

The two theories also differ as regards the importance to individuals of satisfied needs. Whereas Maslow argued that when satisfied a need becomes less important to an individual, research based on Alderfer's ideas has found that relatedness or growth needs actually become more important when satisfied (Wanous and Zwany, 1977). This means, for example, that team working arrangements which satisfy relatedness needs can continue to motivate employees and are not necessarily superseded by growth needs. Employers, according to Alderfer, are in this sense more easily able to satisfy the needs of their employees. In general, tests of the two theories have tended to favour Alderfer's predictions.

By breaking Maslow's and Alderfer's broad variables up a number of more specific needs can be identified which can offer clearer insights into the nature of motivation in the workplace. Mumford (1976) suggested that workers have:

(1) knowledge needs, work that utilizes their knowledges and skills;
(2) control needs, which are satisfied by the provision of information, good working conditions and high quality supervision;
(3) psychological needs, such as the needs for recognition, responsibility, status and advancement;
(4) task needs, which include the need for meaningful work and some degree of autonomy;
(5) moral needs, to be treated in the way that employers would themselves wish to be treated.

Mumford's assumption, therefore, was that employees did not simply see their job as a means to an end but had needs which related to the nature of their work.

A second theory which makes the same basic point is known as Herzberg's *two-factor theory* (Herzberg *et al.*, 1959). The original research for this was based on interviews with 200 accountants and engineers using what is known as the critical incidents technique. This involves asking interviewees to talk about occasions when they felt either particularly satisfied or particularly dissatisfied with their jobs. Two sets of incidents seemed to emerge from these interviews. One involved achievement, advancement, recognition, autonomy and other intrinsic aspects of work. Because these represented sources of satisfaction they were called *motivators*. The second set of incidents concerned working conditions, salary, job security, company policy, supervisors and inter-personal relations. This set, termed *hygiene factors*, were described as sources of dissatisfaction by the sample. Job satisfaction and dissatisfaction therefore appeared to be caused by different sets of factors. The presence of motivators in the workplace caused enduring states of motivation in employees. Their absence, however, did not lead to job dissatisfaction. Hygiene factors, on the other hand, produced an acceptable work environment though not increased satisfaction or involvement with a job; their absence (e.g. low pay), how-ever, caused job dissatisfaction. Thus motivators reflected people's need for self-actualization while hygienes represented the need to avoid pain (Table 4.1).

Table 4.1 *Herzberg's two-factor theory of motivation.*

MOTIVATORS	HYGIENES
Responsibility	Supervision
Recognition	Salary
Promotion	Company policies
Achievement	
Intrinsic aspects of the job	Relationships with colleagues

As well as describing employees' needs, the theory goes a stage further and indicates how people's jobs can be redesigned to incorporate more motivators (Table 4.2). And not surprisingly, a theory which describes both what motivates employees and how jobs can be changed to achieve a well-motivated workforce, has attracted a great deal of interest both from managers seeking ways of motivating staff and academics testing Herzberg's propositions.

Table 4.2 *Herzberg's principles of vertical job loading.*

Principles	Motivators involved
Increasing employees' autonomy while retaining accountability	Responsibility and achievement
Increasing the accountability of employees for their own work	Responsibility and recognition
Providing employees with a complete natural unit of work	Responsibility, achievement and recognition
Making performance feedback available to employees	Recognition
Introducing new and more difficult tasks to employees' work	Growth and learning
Assigning employees specific or specialized tasks at which they can become expert	Responsibility, growth and advancement

Support for the two-factor theory has been mixed, however. The independent effect of motivators and hygienes has been questioned, and at least one study has demonstrated that both can be related to job satisfaction and dissatisfaction (Schneider and Locke, 1971). By using accountants and engineers, who have fairly lucrative occupations, Herzberg may have introduced a middle-class bias into his research. A wider sample of the working population may have produced a somewhat different list. The validity of the critical incidents technique has also been questioned. Firstly, it has been argued that people tend to externalize explanations of failure and internalize explanations of success. In other words, interviewees would tend to relate their successes to the exercise of their personal initiative, but see their problems at work as a reflection of other people's or organizational inadequacies. Thus the two distinct sets of factors could simply reflect this tendency rather than a genuine division in the motivational properties of the incidents interviewees talked about. Secondly, there may well be a gap between what people are prepared to admit motivates them and what actually motivates them. This could account, for example, for pay appearing as a hygiene factor.

Despite criticisms of the ideas of Maslow, Alderfer and Herzberg, their notion of a self-actualizing or growth need has had considerable influence on management theory and to an extent on management practice. Before these content theories were popularized there were two 'models of man' on which management theory and practice could be based. There was the model of *rational economic* man and that of *social* man. The former would expend effort to the extent that it was in his or her economic interests to do so. The latter searched for affiliation and supportive relationships in the workplace, and thus effort was significantly influenced by the collective workrate. (Later we shall see how these different approaches to human motivation have produced very different approaches to the design of work and the style of supervision employed in a workplace.)

One notable attempt to illustrate the connection between different models of motivation and managerial practices was made by Douglas McGregor in *The Human Side of Enterprise* (1960). He pointed out that a consequence of assuming people behave like rational economic beings is the belief that they require either reward or coercion to motivate them. McGregor called this model of motivation theory X. Autocratic managerial styles are the logical result of translating theory X into managerial practice. Instead, McGregor advocated managerial strategies based on theory Y, which uses the self-actualizing model of motivation proposed by Maslow and Herzberg. Theory Y has at its centre *complex man* possessing a bundle of social and self-actualizing needs who, given the appropriate conditions at work, can show high levels of responsibility and self-direction. Complex man does not avoid responsibility, but because of the routinization of work and high levels of external supervision is generally provided with a working environment which offers little opportunity to exercise or develop it. The role of management from this perspective, then, is to create the conditions in which this reservoir of hitherto untapped human resources can be utilized.

Process theories

What all process theories have in common is an emphasis on the role of an individual's cognitive processes in determining his or her level of motivation. One major process theory, *equity theory*, assumes that one important cognitive process involves people looking around and observing what effort other people are putting into their work and what rewards follow for them and comparing this ratio with their own. Individuals can also compare their effort–reward ratio to one which they experienced at another point in time. Equity theorists assume that this *social comparison process* is driven by our concern with fairness or equity. We perceive effort and reward not in absolute but in relative terms (Adams, 1965). When people perceive others enjoying a similar ratio of inputs (effort, qualification, skill level, seniority) to outcomes (pay, advancement, fringe benefits) to themselves, they experience equity. When people perceive a ratio of inputs to outcomes that either favours other people (underpayment) or themselves (overpayment) they experience inequity, which is assumed to be a sufficiently unpleasant experience to motivate either changes in behaviour or perceptions, or both (Table 4.3).

Table 4.3 *The conditions of equity and inequity described by Adams (1965).*

	MYSELF	**YOURSELF**
EQUITY	Inputs (100) / Outcomes (100)	Inputs (100) / Outcomes (100)
INEQUITY (Underpayment)	Inputs (100) / Outcomes (100)	Inputs (100) / Outcomes (125)
INEQUITY (Overpayment)	Inputs (100) / Outcomes (125)	Inputs (100) / Outcomes (100)

In one notable experiment, Adams and Jacobsen (1964) tested a number of predictions from this theory. To induce equity and inequity in people they set up a fictitious publishing company and advertised vacancies for students to do proofreading. One group of students was told that they were not qualified to earn the going rate but would still be paid it. Theoretically this should induce feelings of inequity. Another group was told they were not qualified to earn the going rate and would earn a lesser rate, which should be experienced as equitable. Finally, a third group was told they were qualified to earn the proofreading rate and would earn it. This again should be experienced as equitable. Results supported equity theory predictions: not only did the first group produce better quality work, they also worked harder than either of the other groups.

Most subsequent studies, however, have found that predictions from equity theory are supported best in conditions of underpayment, since the threshold for experiencing overpayment is high and feelings of overpayment do not appear to last very long (Carrell and Dittrich, 1978). This is perhaps because we find it easier to rationalize why we should be overpaid than underpaid.

Additionally, if the feeling of underpayment is shared by enough people in a workplace collective industrial action can occur. Managers involved in wage-setting therefore have to be careful to avoid setting wage rates which cause people to feel underpaid relative to others within the same plant (internal inequity) or to comparison groups outside the organization (external inequity).

Although rates of pay are a common cause of perceived inequity, and thus industrial disputes, conflict can be caused by perceived inequity in what is termed the *effort bargain*. Employers and employees may have quite different ideas about the intensity of labour that constitutes 'a fair day's work'. Employers naturally feel that, having paid the wage, they should decide what is a suitable level of effort from workers. Workers for their part fear that if the employer has control of effort intensity he may be tempted to increase it arbitrarily to an inequitable level, which they will resist if they have the power to do so.

Baldamus's classic study *Efficiency and Effort* (1961) remains the most thorough analysis of what is involved in the effort bargain. He points out that in a stable employment relationship the two sides will in effect have struck a bargain, in which the employee's total effort is exchanged for pay and other returns. He draws attention to the fundamental role of 'custom and practice' in industrial relations in determining an equitable effort–reward ratio. A variety of factors will affect effort, the pace and intensity of work, and the individual worker's experience of fatigue and monotony. Reward is comprised chiefly of pay but convivial working conditions, job security, interesting work and reasonable supervision may be involved as well. With so many factors the effort bargain can only be established over time by custom and practice.

In addition, he suggests the effort bargain is potentially unstable. When established there will be a balance between effort and reward. Should any of the elements change, however, the relationship may begin to be perceived as inequitable by one or both of the parties. Baldamus defined situations in which the wages–effort exchange deviates from previously accepted standards, under the notion of 'wage disparity' which he suggests is 'the very centre of industrial conflict'. Of course, workers may fail to notice any change that has taken place, or they may be aware of it but be unable to do much about it, or they may accept the change as equitable. During periods of high unemployment, for example, workers' expectations tend to adjust to their reduced labour market power, and they may put up with conditions they would previously have found unacceptable. Nonetheless, if an effort bargain is disrupted it may lead directly to conflict as one side or the other attempts to force a renegotiation. Moreover, Baldamus adds, modern industry is dynamic: managements are continually looking for higher productivity, workers' opinions on a fair return for their effort may change, and there are changes in the wider environment which have an impact within the firm. Inflation, for example, undermines the effort bargain by tipping it in the employer's favour, because it reduces the value of wages while the employee still puts in the same effort.

The key role of employees' perceptions of their jobs is underlined again in the valence instrumentality and expectancy (VIE) theory. This explanation of employee motivation has been popular since the publication of Vroom's study *Work and Motivation* (1964). He argued that what was crucial to motivation at work was the perception of a link between effort and reward. Perceiving this link could be thought of as a process in which individuals first calculated whether there was a connection between their effort and their performance (expectancy), then the probability that valued rewards (valences) would follow from high performance (instrumentality). The *motivational force* of a job can be calculated if the expectancy, instrumentality and valence values are known. (Figure 4.2).

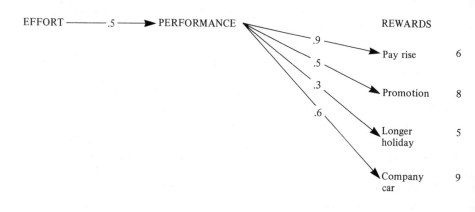

Figure 4.2   *The VIE model of motivation. In this example the individual perceives only a 50 per cent chance of increased effort leading to increased performance. She has ranked four rewards on a +10 to –10 scale and has estimated the probability of increased performance producing each of these desired rewards. The motivational force of the job – the effort she is willing to expend on it – is calculated by adding the products of the valence x instrumentality calculations and multiplying the total by the expectancy value. Thus (.9 x 6) + (.5 x 8) + (.3 x 5) + (.6 x 9) = 16.3 and 16.3 x .5 = 8.15. This figure can be used to predict some criterion of job performance – a supervisor's assessment, for example, or if available, more reliable measures, such as sales figures for sales staff.*

The motivational force of a job is attenuated by the individual's abilities, traits, role perceptions and opportunities. This implies, for example, that although a person might be motivated to perform a particular task well, he or she may be restricted from doing so by his or her abilities. In addition, opportunities for the exercise of effort also vary and thus affect the impact of an individual's motivational force on his or her achievement. Recession, for example, makes the task of selling more difficult whatever an individual's motivational force.

In summary, VIE theory stresses the rational–cognitive aspects of an individual's work motivation. The theory predicts that jobs which produce low levels of motivation will be those where aspects of job performance are out of the worker's control. In machine-paced assembly tasks, for example, we would find that expectancy and instrumentalities have low values. In fact, one of the desired outcomes may even be machine breakdown (Beynon, 1984).

VIE theory is supported by studies which attempt to predict the tasks on which an individual will work most and least hard. Prediction coefficients for this type of study are usually between .5 and .6 (Matsui et al., 1977). Attempts to use VIE measures to predict which person will work hardest in a group or on a particular task are less successful, producing coefficients of .3 to .4 (Prichard and Sanders, 1973). In one study, however, though the validity coefficients averaged out at .52 for the group, individual coefficients varied from −.08 to −.92. Thus, for some students, behaviour could be predicted quite well from the VIE measures whereas for others they were unable to predict performance (Muchinsky, 1977). This has prompted some researchers to suggest that when VIE measures are not predictive of behaviour, unconscious or irrational processes have motivated individuals (Miner, 1980). There does not seem to be any reason, however, to suggest behaviour not predicted by VIE measures is irrational. As we saw earlier, social rationality is highly complex; the subjects who performed best in the Adams and Jacobsen experiment did so because they felt they were being overpaid relative to their qualifications. Our perceptions and calculations are therefore not solely concerned with the future, predicting the value of our own efforts; we also look sideways at others and often alter our performance according to internalized norms about what is fair and unfair in terms of effort and reward.

The main contribution of both types of process theory has been to highlight the effects of cognitive and perceptual processes on objective work conditions. It suggests that managers need to pay attention to four main aspects of their subordinates' perceptions:

(1) they need to focus on the crucial expectancy values; employees must perceive a link between their effort and their performance. This may mean improving training so that effort is utilized more efficiently, providing guidance and ensuring sufficient support for high performance is available, for example by ensuring adequate machine maintenance;
(2) managers should determine what outcomes an employee values. It may well be

that employees value recognition and praise more than they do economic reward;
(3) they need to link the reward that subordinates value to their performance, since this reflects the simple psychological truth that people are likely to repeat a response if they have been rewarded for doing so;
(4) managers finally need to ensure that wage rates are not set at a level which employees perceive as inequitable.

Knowledge of results and goal setting

Imagine you are set an essay question by a tutor, you are a highly motivated student, you read around the question and carefully prepare an answer. What happens to that essay after you have handed it to your tutor can determine whether you remain highly motivated. Similarly at work, what happens after a particular response may be important to the maintenance or enhancement of motivation. What is required in both cases is what is termed knowledge of results. Management theorists have, for some time, pointed to the motivational properties of this type of feedback to employees, and have explored ways in which information systems in organizations provide it (e.g. Nemeroff and Cosentino, 1979).

Despite a wealth of research highlighting the positive motivational benefits of knowledge of results, many organizations still provide employees with little or no information about their performance. Often this is because information systems tend to be designed for management functions (accounting, planning, production) and use data that may be incomprehensible to employees.

In some organizations knowledge of results is provided only where performance has fallen below some optimum level. In such cases of 'management by exception' managers exert their authority only when performance is poor, and appear on the shopfloor only when something has gone wrong (Clegg and Fitter, 1978). This is because many managers are reluctant to feed back positive information since they feel that they would be congratulating staff for doing what they are paid to do. Feedback in these contexts therefore tends only to occur when output is significantly less than satisfactory and management comes under pressure to improve it.

To harness the motivational properties of information, feedback needs to be relatively rapid. Daily or weekly summaries of performance are more useful than quarterly or annual. The system should be capable of providing information that is valid to employees, it must be capable of distinguishing, for example, the effects of faulty machinery and employees' efforts, allocating output correctly to each shift, and be in units that are understood by employees.

It should be stressed that though an information system that provides comprehensible, unbiased and frequent summaries of an operator team or department's performance has considerable positive motivational and learning consequences, implementing such a system often involves wider organizational issues. For example, it can affect the relationship between shopfloor employees and supervisors since employees are given wider access to data which the latter may resent.

The positive motivational consequences for employees of accurate inform-ation on work performance being available can be further enhanced by a practice known as goal-setting (Locke, 1968). Goals direct effort, and provide guidelines for deciding how much effort to put into each activity when there are multiple goals. To be effective the goal or goals need to be made reasonably specific. One study of a group of lumberjacks found a dramatic improvement in performance following a specific goal being set. The lumberjacks were responsible for felling trees, loading them on to lorries and delivering them to the mill. Before the goal-setting experiment lumberjacks were simply asked to do their best and on average lorries were being driven to the mill with only 60 per cent of their maximum capacity. They were then requested to load lorries up to 94 per cent of their maximum legal load. The lumberjacks considered this goal difficult but reasonable and even though it was made clear that there were neither rewards for meeting the goal nor punishments for failing to reach it the average loads went up to 94 per cent of maximum capacity and remained at this level. The increased loads produced savings in maintenance, replacement and fuel costs (Latham and Blades, 1975).

Although knowledge of results and goal-setting are not general theories of motivation they offer the most specific advice to managers dealing with the day-to-day problems of motivating staff. Firstly, managers can harness the motivational properties of knowledge of results by providing clear and frequent feedback to staff, particularly when positive. And secondly, managers are able to increase motivation by setting specific and reasonable goals. This is best achieved by allowing staff to take part in and influence the goal-setting process. Participation in goal-setting can both increase staff's commitment to the goal and make it less likely that unreasonably high goals, which are counter-productive, are set.

SATISFACTION AT WORK

Few concepts in the applied behavioural sciences have attracted as much interest as job satisfaction. Many popular and academic writers have become increasingly critical of the work performed by a large proportion of the working population, seeing in the workplace a part of society which had neither kept pace with improvements in living standards nor accommodated the rising expectations of the post-war period. Factories were, they argued, often dirty, noisy, dangerous places which offered little satisfaction for the needs we described in the preceding section. And clerical work too often lacked any intrinsic satisfaction, even though this was due to the routine nature of the work and declining status and pay rather than to poor conditions. Managers found themselves facing the behavioural consequences of this central problem in the experience of work: costly levels of staff turnover, absenteeism and poor industrial relations.

What is job satisfaction?

If people claim to be satisfied with their jobs, what do they mean? They are usually expressing something more like a feeling about their job rather than their thoughts about it. Locke (1976) attempted to capture the affective nature of job satisfaction in his definition 'a pleasurable positive emotional state resulting from the appraisal of one's job or job experiences'.

Behavioural scientists have argued that it is useful to distinguish two types of feeling people have about their jobs: *global* and *facet*. Global job satisfaction reflects an individual's overall feeling towards his or her job. But in addition, people may express feelings about particular aspects or facets of their jobs. For example, they may be upset by an overbearing supervisor but be fairly happy with their salary and workmates.

Breaking the global concept up into its constituent facets can be done conceptually or statistically. In the conceptual approach, researchers can either use their own hunches and investigations about what the significant facets in a job are, or adopt a particular theoretical framework which specifies a set of facets in advance. Sometimes the specific nature of the organization or occupation in which the job satisfaction research is being conducted means the former is preferable. For example, in an attempt to identify the causes of low job satisfaction in nursing, Wallis and Cope (1980) found that the relevant facets of job satisfaction for nurses included the feeling of being needed by patients, the way hours of work are organized, the adequacy of the in-service training received, and the pay compared to others working outside the hospital.

The statistical method of deriving facets involves using techniques, such as factor analysis, to reduce large quantities of questionnaire data to a few general dimensions. Many of the 'off-the-peg' questionnaires available to people doing job satisfaction research have been developed in this way.

Some researchers, while deriving measures of facets of job satisfaction, also like to combine these to produce a global measure. This raises the question of whether the predictive validity of a global job satisfaction measure can be improved by weighting facets which subjects have indicated are important to them. In some cases there appears to be a clear justification for doing this. For example, in the study of nurses' job satisfaction cited above, the feelings nurses experienced on the occasions when they thought they had 'got through to patients' were found to be very important to their overall level of job satisfaction. However, in practice weighting does not seem to improve the ability of a global job satisfaction measure to predict behaviour (Mikes and Hulin, 1968). This seems to be because people are already implicitly weighting the importance of a facet when they give a rating of their satisfaction of that aspect of their job. For example, if people indicate that they are highly satisfied or highly dissatisfied with their rate of pay, the chances are that pay is important to them. On the other hand, if people indicate that they are neither satisfied nor dissatisfied with their supervisors it is probably the case that supervisory style is not an important component of their job satisfaction. In other words, getting a person to weight the importance of a facet adds little new information and so does not improve the predictive validity of global job satisfaction measures.

Theories of job satisfaction

In this section we will examine two widely used theories in contemporary job satisfaction research. One theory stresses the individual, subjective nature of job satisfaction. It assumes that individuals can differ in their perceptions and experience of similar jobs. The other proposes that there are important objective features of the jobs people do which give rise to job satisfaction. Both provide important insights into either why some jobs are experienced as satisfying while others are not, or why some individuals find particular types of work dissatisfying while their colleagues doing identical jobs are satisfied with their work.

(1) Variance theory

Variance theory is based on a simple idea: if you want x from your work then you are satisfied to the extent that it provides you with x. The major problem for variance theorists is defining what it is that people want from their jobs. One way of solving this is to borrow concepts from motivation theory so that variance in what is wanted and what is available from a job occurs, for example, in the extent to which self-actualizing needs can be fulfilled (Schaffer, 1953; Porter, 1962). This means that by borrowing from motivation theory some researchers can specify in advance the variations in work satisfaction that employees report in their jobs. Another approach assumes that the relevant variances depend on the nature of the work and thus differ from occupation to occupation. This provides a more flexible framework with which to analyse problems of low job satisfaction within occupations. Exley (1977), for example, was asked to locate the sources of considerable job dissatisfaction reported by customs officers. She assumed that the relevant facets of job satisfaction in customs and excise work could not be specified in advance. After a systematic interviewing programme she was able to identify the facets of job satisfaction for customs officers. Similarly, Wallis and Cope (1980) were not prepared to specify the facets of job satisfaction in nursing until they had analysed data from a series of interviews with nurses.

Either approach, specifying in advance the relevant facets of job satisfaction or identifying them through investigation, enables researchers to establish whether there are significant individual differences present in reported levels of job satisfaction or whether there is a high degree of consensus among staff about what aspects of work lead to high levels of satisfaction and dissatisfaction. By identifying what aspects of a job give rise to high and low levels of satisfaction, managers are better placed when considering what changes can be made to improve job satisfaction.

(2) Job characteristics

If variance theory suggests the causes of job satisfaction are subjective, the job characteristics model suggests the opposite: the causes of job satisfaction are to be found in the objective characteristics of a job. This view was first outlined by Hackman and Oldham (1975). These researchers argued that jobs differ in the extent to which they involve five core dimensions:

(1) skill variety. The extent to which they require the use of a number of different skills and talents;
(2) task identity. The extent to which they require the completion of a whole, identifiable piece of work;
(3) task significance. The degree of impact they are believed to have on other people inside and outside the organization they are situated in;
(4) autonomy. The extent to which they provide freedom, independence and discretion in determining such things as work pace, work breaks and allocation of tasks;
(5) task feedback. The extent to which they provide clear and direct information about the effectiveness of performance.

They suggested that if jobs were designed in a way that increased the presence of these core dimensions, for example by combining tasks and opening feedback channels, three critical psychological states can occur in employees termed:

(1) experienced meaningfulness of work. This is determined by the level of skill variety, task identity and task significance;
(2) experienced responsibility for work outcomes. This is determined by the amount of autonomy present;
(3) knowledge of results of work activities. This is determined by the amount of feedback present.

According to Hackman and Oldham, when these critical psychological states are experienced work motivation and job satisfaction will be high. Furthermore, behavioural outcomes, such as the quality of work and attendance, may also be improved. Hackman and Oldham did, however, include one personal attribute in their theory termed *growth need strength* (GNS) which they believed moderated the extent to which the critical psychological states could be experienced. If an individual has little need for growth it is unlikely that he or she will experience the critical psychological states strongly. The relationship between the theory's concepts is illustrated in Figure 4.3

Hackman and Oldham constructed the job diagnostic survey (JDS), a questionnaire completed by employees to provide measures for each of their variables. They believed that it was possible to combine these measures to

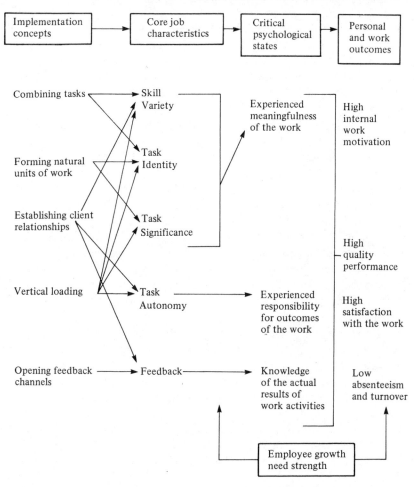

Figure 4.3 *Hackman and Oldham's job characteristics model.* From J.R. Hackman, G.R. Oldham, R. Janson, and K. Purdy (1975) 'A new strategy for job enrichment', *California Management Review*, 17, 57–71.

produce what they termed the motivating potential score (MPS), for a job using the formula:

$$MPS = \frac{\text{Skill variety} + \text{Task identity} + \text{Task significance}}{3} \times \text{Autonomy} \times \text{Feedback}$$

Since the first three core dimensions contribute to the same critical psychological state, they are averaged. As scores on measures of the other two dimensions are multiplied and not added, low scores on either produces a low MPS value. If no autonomy or feedback are present the MPS value is zero.

Thus, the theory encompasses not only job characteristics and job satisfaction but also work design principles, psychological states and motivation. The scope of the theory has made it popular with researchers who find the combination of a clear specification of variables and inter-relationships between them and a measuring instrument readily available for them particularly attractive.

The initial test of the theory by Hackman and Oldham (1976) generally supported it. They found the core job dimensions of skill variety, task identity and task significance did combine to predict the level of experienced meaningfulness of a job, and the three critical psychological states predicted job satisfaction and motivation reasonably well. The one internal variable, growth need strength, did moderate the relationship between the critical psychological states and the personal work outcomes; individuals with a high score reported higher job satisfaction after experiencing the critical psychological states. Hackman and Oldham did not however manage to find the expected relationship between autonomy and feedback and their corresponding psychological states. They were also not able to show strong predictive validities of critical psychological states for objective outcomes, absenteeism and work performance.

Since the original test of the theory, further research has also tended to provide it with only partial support. The moderating effect of GNS on the relationship between the critical psychological states and attitudinal and behavioural outcomes has been fairly well supported (Evans, Kiggundu and House, 1979). The relationship between job characteristics and job satisfaction has also been found in a number of studies. Orpen (1978). for example, studied clerical workers in a South African government department and used the model's principles to modify core job dimensions. After six months the clerks in the redesigned jobs displayed lower levels of absenteeism and reported higher levels of job satisfaction and motivation compared to a control group. He was not able to find any increase, however, in the experimental group's performance. Partial support is also found in Kemp et al. (1983). The careful design of this study of four shift groups at two sites within the same company enabled the effects of site, shift and job characteristics to be separated. A clear relationship emerged between job characteristics and job satisfaction, but not between job characteristics and measures of motivation and performance.

In addition to receiving only partial empirical support, the job characteristics model has also been criticized on conceptual grounds. For example, Wall (1980) pointed out that it fails to take account of a range of contextual variables which affect job satisfaction, motivation and work redesign, such as technology, supervisory style and managerial practices. However, despite these criticisms, its clear specification of objective job characteristics and critical psychological states coupled with the availability of measures for them has meant concepts derived from the model have become central to current research in job satisfaction, motivation and work redesign.

Correlates of job satisfaction

As well as the two theories we have just examined, there have also been attempts to establish whether specific variables such as age, sex or occupational status are predictive of differences in job satisfaction. Weaver (1980), for example, found occupational status correlated significantly with job satisfaction. Managerial, technical, professional and self-employed groups all reported higher levels of job satisfaction than blue-collar workers. Status appears to be the only personal variable which does correlate with job satisfaction. We might, for instance, expect age to correlate with job satisfaction (since older workers have a historical basis for comparing their current rewards), but it appears to account for only about 1 per cent of the differences in scores on job satisfaction measures. Similarly, differences in job satisfaction between males and females are negligible once other variables such as education and status are controlled for.

Sociologists have suggested that out-plant factors can be linked with job satisfaction. One classic study of car assembly workers in Luton found that though they performed repetitive, semi-skilled work at individual work stations they expressed a general satisfaction with the work (Goldthorpe, Lockwood et al., 1968). During interviews the assembly workers expressed what the researchers described as a calculative, instrumental orientation to work tasks, workmates and the company. The researchers tentatively linked this instrumental attitude to work to a number of out-plant factors. Workers tended to be young and married with high financial commitments. Luton was a new community and so had a population with no familial links there. Generally the assembly workers had experienced downward social mobility relative to their fathers who had been skilled men. These out-plant factors, the researchers concluded, might in turn cause the assembly workers to construe the term 'job satisfaction' not as 'deriving pleasure from a job' but as 'the practicality of a job'. If the wages were relatively high, which they were, the job was seen simply as a means to a high standard of living.

The Luton study is a useful reminder to psychologists that explanations of job satisfaction which focus exclusively on in-plant variables ignore a whole range of important contextual variables which might cause different groups of workers to construct different meanings as to what constitutes a satisfactory job.

Behavioural correlates of job satisfaction

So far we have discussed the meaning of job satisfaction and the ways in which it has been explained or predicted, but for most researchers the key issue is the practical one: what are the implications of job satisfaction for workplace behaviour? The common-sense assumption is that if people are content with their work, this will be reflected in behaviour favourable for the organization. In short, the behavioural correlates of job satisfaction should be higher work performance, lower absenteeism and lower staff turnover. This highly plausible assumption was what fuelled a good deal of the managerial interest in the concept in the first place. Yet, as we shall see, an enormous amount of research focused on the practical implications of job satisfaction has failed to establish a strong direct link between job satisfaction and workplace behaviour.

One problem which researchers using job satisfaction measures to predict workplace behaviour have encountered is one that is common to all attitude–behaviour research: an attitudinal measure as general as job satisfaction cannot be expected to predict specific behaviours. More specific attitudinal questions have been found to have a higher predictive validity. This implies that more specific job satisfaction questions relating, for example, to aspects of task performance would yield stronger correlations between job satisfaction and workplace behaviour.

Another problem facing researchers is the set of 'intervening variables' that stand between job satisfaction and the behaviour they are trying to predict. Correlations between *absenteeism* and job satisfaction, for instance, have been found to be moderate, usually no higher than $-.35$. The relationship seems to be affected by a series of intervening variables. One ingenious demonstration of this fact is seen in a study by Smith (1975). During his research a heavy unexpected snowstorm occurred in an area in which the company he was studying had an office. He was therefore able to compare attendance in this office with another office within the same company. The snowstorm produced an attendance of 70 per cent compared to 96 per cent in the unaffected office. He found that job satisfaction measures were able to discriminate between those who made a special effort to get through the snowstorm to get to work and those who did not. This meant that the job satisfaction–attendance relationship increased dramatically in the snowstorm office compared with the unaffected office; for example, a measure of satisfaction with career prospects correlated as highly as .6 with attendance.

An elaborate model of the job satisfaction–attendance relationship was proposed by Steers and Rhodes (1978). They suggested the relationship is moderated by a string of variables including: pressures to attend (economic, normative, organizational) and ability to attend (illness, family, transportation problems). Their model implies that an individual may have a high level of job satisfaction but often be absent through little ability or pressure to attend.

A similarly complex, indirect and weak relationship appears to exist between job satisfaction and *staff turnover*. The relationship between the two in statistical terms is slightly more substantial, around $-.40$ (Michaels and Spector, 1982). Once again, though, intervening variables appear to reduce the relationship between the two. Mobley (1977), for example, outlined a model of the relationship which suggested that dissatisfied individuals begin by thinking of leaving, then form the intention to search for another job. This leads to the appraisal of alternatives relative to the present job and finally a decision to leave or stay. In a test of the model, Mobley, Horner and Hollingsworth (1978) found that for a sample of hospital employees, the strength of the relationship declined in the way the model predicts; job satisfaction correlated −.54 with thinking of leaving, −.54 with intention to search, −.49 with intention to leave and −.21 with actual turnover.

Finally, the relationship between job satisfaction and *productivity* is the one that has been of most interest to management. Research here suggests that for a number of reasons the relationship is far from straightforward. It has been argued that the relationship varies in strength between different types of job. Since a stimulating job allows holders to experience job satisfaction when they perform well, the relationship between the two variables should be higher in more interesting jobs. However, results of studies testing this hypothesis have not been sufficiently consistent to support it in all circumstances (Ivancevich, 1978).

Some researchers, on the assumption that the most significant source of satisfaction at work is doing a job well, have suggested the relationship is conceptualized better the other way round: high productivity leads to high job satisfaction (e.g. Wanous, 1974). The implications of this for management seeking higher productivity are quite considerable. The common-sense view suggests management should concern themselves with their employees' job satisfaction to achieve high productivity. The reverse view, that high performance leads to high job satisfaction, if true, means management simply need to reward past levels of high performance to increase productivity.

The strongest implication of much of the research is that the two variables, job satisfaction and output, are virtually independent of each other. There seem to be at least two possible reasons for this. The first is that in many jobs, variations in satisfaction cannot lead to variations in productivity. In machine-paced assembly work, for instance, the speed of the production line is constant whatever the level of job satisfaction of people working on the line. Secondly, even when correlations do appear, as Porter and Lawler (1968) have suggested, the association may be spurious, since both may be associated with another factor. In other words, job satisfaction and productivity may well have largely separate causal paths; one set of factors (e.g. investment in technology) determines productivity, another set (e.g. perceived equity of rewards) produces job satisfaction.

Though much of the interest in job satisfaction research stems from a practical concern with increased productivity, managers as we have seen, have not been provided with easy answers to questions about the nature of the satisfaction–performance relationship. Attempts to increase performance have now been set in a more broadly based theoretical and practical context than job satisfaction. This wider context which includes changing the organization and design of work will be examined in Chapter 8.

FURTHER READING

Arkes, H.R. and J.P. Garske (1981) *Psychological Theories of Motivation* (2nd ed.). Monterey, Calif.: Brooks/Cole.

Gruneberg, M.M. (1979) *Understanding Job Satisfaction*. London: Macmillan.

Howarth, C. (1984) *The Way People Work: Job Satisfaction and the Challenge of Change*. Oxford: Oxford University Press.

Orpen, C. (ed.) (1985) *Job Satisfaction*. Amsterdam: Elsevier.

Satinoff, E. and P. Testelbaum (eds.) (1983) *Motivation*. London: Plenum Press.

Vroom, V. and E.L. Deci (1970) *Management and Motivation*. Harmondsworth: Penguin.

SECTION TWO

GROUPS AND WORK

In the last section the fundamental unit of analysis was the individual employee. While the psychological properties people bring to the workplace are obviously important, by the early 1930s psychologists realized that several important workplace phenomena could not be satisfactorily explained if the individual employee remained the basic unit of analysis. These psychologists suggested that to advance the understanding of workplace behaviour the focus of research would have to shift from individual to group processes.

What had prompted this realization was the Hawthorne studies, a series of experiments conducted by a group of psychologists in a large electrical components factory over a fifteen-year period. The studies suggested that work groups were a fundamental unit of social organization which possessed properties that existed independently of their members. Perhaps the most important conclusions of the Hawthorne researchers were that groups were capable of causing profound changes in their members' perceptions, beliefs, attitudes and behaviour.

The results of the studies were popularized by a management writer, Elton Mayo, who believed management had a lot to gain from an increased awareness of the social dynamics of the workplace. He believed there was a fundamental paradox between the technical accomplishments of modern industry on the one hand and the social incompetence he claimed existed amongst managers on the other. Thus, Elton Mayo and a group of his colleagues began what became known as the human relations movement. They believed that their research and writing offered management the opportunity of increasing their behavioural sophistication, and therefore their effectiveness.

Because much of the initial material produced by the human relations movement was based on a rather paternalistic social ideology, in which managers were assumed to act on rational criteria while workers were seen as motivated by unconscious social 'sentiments', much of it is now discredited. Nonetheless, Mayo and his associates did establish the agenda for what social aspects of the workplace merited detailed attention. In this section we have used the agenda the human relations movement provided but expanded it where recent developments in the behavioural sciences have added items of interest to it.

In Chapter 5 we examine the nature of social interaction. Since much of a manager's time is spent interacting with other people an analysis of what occurs during social encounters is particularly useful, especially if it offers insights into why some individuals are better than others at dealing with people. This analysis thus provides a basis for training programmes which develop the social skills required for successful performance in a job.

The social group, as we suggested above, is a fundamental form of social organization and an analysis of its structures and processes is essential to an adequate understanding of workplace behaviour. In Chapter 6, in addition to examining the effects of group membership on individuals we consider in some detail the research and the movement that began the interest in work groups: the Hawthorne studies and the human relations movement.

Leadership in the workplace was another traditional concern of the human relations movement. The view of human relations writers was that supportive leadership leads to high performing workgroups. In Chapter 7 we summarize and comment on the vast amount of leadership research undertaken by behavioural scientists to test this and other propositions about what constitutes effective leadership. We conclude with a discussion of the various leadership training programmes that have been developed.

In Chapter 8 we close the section by describing and evaluating research of behavioural scientists involved in the humanization of the workplace. Although behavioural scientists began with a narrow focus on motivation and job satisfaction, many have broadened the scope of their research to include all technological and social features of the workplace that affect the quality of working life. Research now includes the effects of changes in job content, provision for group working, style of supervision and the amount of participation and decision-making present. We conclude by considering what progress has been achieved in providing environments at work that fulfil the human needs of employees.

5

Social Interaction

In the first section we examined attributes of individuals such as personality and intelligence which can be referred to when explaining or predicting behaviour. Though individual differences are undoubtedly important, it is now time to consider other complementary perspectives. In this chapter we will examine the basic processes underlying the activity between people in everyday social settings. The concepts of *dramaturgy* and *social skill* will be central considerations here. The former highlights the expressive and symbolic aspects of social interaction. Writers who have explored the dramaturgy of everyday life have argued that the statistical systems of exploration and classification involved in the study of individual differences are static, and so cannot capture the dynamic and creative aspects of our social activity. The concept of skill, you may remember, embraced both cognitive control of actions and automated behaviour. This implies that we may be unaware of the considerable cognitive achievement our automatic social responses represent. The concept also forces us to consider what kinds of modelling and categorization are involved in social interaction and so helps explain, for example, how changes in social competence occur over time and why some individuals perform better than others at jobs which involve social skills.

DRAMATURGY AND IMPRESSION MANAGEMENT

A central theme of this perspective involves our ability to engage in *impression management*. The social world is seen as a stage on which 'actors' constantly create and recreate their social selves according to their conceptions of what it is to be a social person (de Waele and Harré, 1976). Interactions between actors are characterized by each monitoring his or her own performance and the performance of others. Personality, from this perspective, is the internal resources an actor can draw upon to construct a 'social face'.

Harré (1979) used the term *persona* to describe the social face we present to others. He saw persona production as a kind of intellectual puzzle. Actors have somehow to select the correct persona or range of personas for a given situation. To do this actors have to be able to recognize, create or define the social situation they are in and possess some knowledge of the rules of behaviour within it. Being able to recognize a solution does not guarantee that actors will give good performances, however. They may be able to define a situation correctly, for instance, but not have an adequate supply of personas to draw upon to act appropriately within it.

Goffman (1971) has also attempted to capture the creative and expressive aspects of our social behaviour. He particularly emphasized the symbolic aspects of our self-presentational activity. He saw social encounters as comprising a manipulation of both *sign activity* (verbal and non-verbal behaviour) and *sign equipment* (props such as clothes). Actors manipulate these symbolic aspects of social interaction in order to project definitions of themselves on to situations. This self-definition is termed a *personal front*. Social interaction involves a constant monitoring of our own and other people's personal fronts. To do this, we make comparisons between what Goffman called *the given* and *the given off*. The former are the more controllable aspects of sign activity, particularly verbal behaviour; while the principal source of the latter, less controllable, portion of sign activity is an actor's non-verbal behaviour. Of course, other people are not unaware of being monitored and will attempt to control these aspects of their own sign activity. We, in turn, are aware of the possibility of this kind of manipulation.

When we monitor others we also expect a correspondence between the *appearance* and *manner* of the other's personal front. Our appearance is determined by our choice of sign equipment, such as style of dress. Our manner indicates the part we want to play during an encounter and is the result of our sign activity, for example, the tone of voice we use. Though we constantly monitor the personal fronts of others, it remains true that we rarely, if ever, attempt to discredit the definitions people present of themselves. Goffman suggested this is because there is a moral obligation or social rule that we should accept other actors' self-definitions. Breaking this rule by damaging the integrity of another person's front severely disrupts interaction and is likely to cause considerable embarrassment.

Goffman argued that individuals often project fronts for tactical reasons without really believing in them. For example, at work a front may be adopted in order to gain some reward, such as a coveted appointment or promotion. Assuming the individual doesn't drop the front, it may be some time before the individual believes it has anything to do with what he or she feels is 'the real me'.

The adoption of particular fronts is often encouraged by organizations. This is because fronts symbolically convey and dramatically highlight information which might otherwise be unapparent. The formal suit of the executive, for example, gives the impression that tasks will be carried out in a similarly reliable and discreet manner. Goffman claimed that there were at least two disadvantages of preferred fronts as far as organizations were concerned. Firstly, some executives will get their jobs because they 'look the part' rather than through genuine managerial talent. Secondly, getting on in an organization may be determined by the extent to which individuals can manipulate their sign activity and sign equipment to imitate the personal fronts of their organizational superiors. In both cases, impression management can become more important in the struggle for authority, status and power than competence and accomplishment.

According to Thompson (1961), impression management in the workplace involves at least four personal fronts:

(1) superior. Impression management here is concerned with the projection of competence, sincerity, poise and activity;
(2) subordinate. Employees in subordinate roles have to project loyalty to company and superiors, deference and dependability;
(3) specialist. Those engaged in specialist positions have to symbolically convey dedication to their speciality and disinterest in the organizational power game. They therefore appear incorruptible, concerned only with the truths revealed by their speciality;
(4) lower participants. Employees with little or no chance of moving up the hierarchy have to display activity even when there is little or no work to do. Though loyalty is not expected, compliance is. By projecting innocence and limited competence they can maintain their aura of compliance when they transgress rules and legitimately reduce their contribution to the organization.

Thus, from the dramaturgical perspective, much of an individual's activity at work or in other social situations involves symbolically conveying through sign activity and sign equipment aspects of the personal front he or she has adopted. However, it has also been pointed out that side by side with the expressive, self-presentational goals of social interaction that Goffman, Harré and others highlight, social situations also usually involve more specific task-related goals such as selling, negotiating or interviewing. Therefore, the likelihood of successfully attaining a goal in a social situation depends upon a dynamic combination of interpersonal skills (chiefly impression management) together with the more straightforward technical skills. This combination we would define as *social skill*.

SOCIAL SKILL

The skills that we deploy in social situations appear to involve developing understandings of three aspects of social interaction: the social situations we must interact within, the person(s) with whom we interact and the components of the 'interactional work' which enable us to attain our goals in social encounters.

Understanding social situations

Understanding the nature of a social situation is essential to a competent social performance in it. If we are unable to perceive what behaviour ought to be used in a particular social situation, we are unlikely to achieve whatever goals we may have been pursuing. How, then, do individuals develop a comprehension of situations? This has proved difficult to answer. Social scientists have to be careful not to develop inadequate conceptual frameworks to describe social situations, or they risk creating a gap between the characteristics of situations as described by social researchers and as experienced by people themselves. Argyle *et al.* (1981) have suggested that we should characterize situations as discrete entities, each having its own goals, rules, elements, concepts, settings and roles.

(1) Goals

Social situations, as we have already proposed, provide opportunities for the attainment of goals, both expressive and task-related. Individuals often pursue more than one goal and these can interfere with or assist one another. For example, a supervisor may pursue an expressive goal (to be accepted as an approachable person) and a task goal (such as coordinating group activity). An important part of social skill is balancing the demands of expressive and task goals.

(2) Rules

Perhaps the most important aspect of any social situation is the rules which guide individuals' goal-directed behaviour. Argyle *et al.* (1981) defined rules as the shared beliefs which dictate which behaviour is permitted, not permitted, or required. In social situations our understanding of the rules regulates our conduct, enabling us to respond to cues and predict the likely effect of our actions. Hence social situations seem to contain two clusters of rules (Argyle *et al.*, 1981). One cluster contains universal rules present in all social situations, such as: use a common language or signalling system; make interaction pleasant (e.g. do not embarrass others); and prevent aggression (e.g. be polite). The second cluster applies to specific social situations, for example, do what the doctor says when in the surgery. Poppleton (1981) analysed the rules which appeared to apply to selling. He found both the universal rules and situation-specific rules: show mood control; listen to objections; do not get into lengthy arguments. Another classification of the rules operating in social situations suggests there are:

(1) interpretative rules. These provide criteria for interpreting and labelling events in the social world. For example, interpretative rules operating on football terraces define what constitutes 'provocation' from a supporter of the other team;
(2) prescriptive rules. These indicate what ought to be done in response, once a situation has been interpreted and understood. In this sense, prescriptive rules also reflect the moral concerns and values of participants in the situation;

(3) non-generalizable rules. These are 'one-off' rules created on the spot when routines produced by the more stable rules are interrupted. Non-generalizable rules reflect the fact that social situations are often quite complex, and established rules can rarely cover all the variations and possibilities.

Breaches of prescriptive rules are often seen as 'mistakes' by other participants and usually call for an 'explanation'. For example, if a football supporter is too violent and breaches rules about acceptable levels of violence, his behaviour might be explained by other supporters by labelling him a 'nutter' (Marsh, 1982). Breaches of rules in occupational contexts, such as selling or negotiating, drastically reduce the chances of a successful outcome to an encounter. In the legal and medical professions a breach of a rule by a practitioner may mean the end of his or her career.

Though the action of rules has proved important for the study of social activity, the impact of rules on situations varies. Brenner (1982) provided a useful classification of the extent to which rules govern behaviour in situations. He suggested situations could be *closed*, *defined* or *open*. Closed situations have a fully rule-guided character. Ceremonial or ritual situations such as weddings or auctions are closed situations. Defined situations are also rule-guided but involve a certain level of ambiguity about how participants' goals are to be realized. Social skills are therefore crucial to success in defined situations. Rules in open situations have less of an impact on activity, since neither fixed goals nor prescribed interactional routes are present. Informal evenings at home with your family or friends are 'open situations'.

(3) Repertoire of elements

The attainment of goals in situations appears to involve a specific repertoire of 'acts' or 'elements'. Each situation defines a specific repertoire of elements as meaningful and others as inappropriate. Elements can be divided into verbal categories, verbal contents, non-verbal communication and bodily actions. For example, in negotiations the verbal categories would include: offer; accept; and reject. Verbal contents would contain information and settlement points. Non-verbal elements would include: looking; frowning; and smiling. Bodily actions would involve various body postures and perhaps walking out. Knowing the repertoire of elements appropriate to a situation is crucial to a skilled or competent social performance in it.

(4) Concepts

We acquire skills by actively abstracting concepts which appear to have some explanatory utility for the system we are attempting to integrate with. Concepts provide us with the categories which enable us to reduce the complexity of incoming stimuli. In Chapter 1, we cited an account of a production manager whose goal of increased efficiency was achieved by conceptualizing the costing and production system and making cross-references between them. Concepts are also the basis of our comprehension of social situations, other people and social interaction. Professional social skills like selling, supervising, interviewing, negotiating and psychotherapy each involve a specialized set of concepts in addition to the general stock of concepts.

(5) Environmental settings

Environmental psychologists have explored for some time the effects of the physical layout of furniture, barriers (e.g. filing cabinets), the amount of privacy, personal space and crowding on psychological variables such as arousal, interaction, self-evaluation and aggression. For example, props are often used to divide offices up into 'pressure' and 'semi-social' areas. The pressure area, usually around the desk, is where formal interaction 'in role' occurs, with the occupant of the office taking the lead. The 'semi-social' area, perhaps around a coffee table, provides the opportunity for less formal interaction. Skilled managers are able to select the area of their office most appropriate for the type of interaction they expect to have during a meeting (Korda, 1976). Similarly, a skilled selection interviewer uses the semi-social area to obtain biographical information from a candidate and can further reduce the formality of the situation by sitting at right angles to the candidate rather than directly opposite (McHenry, 1981). Props can also symbolically convey information about personal attributes such as status, competence and affluence.

(6) Roles

Social interaction occurs within the context of a social world structured by the relations in which people stand to one another. Such a structure means that we are able to see order in other people's behaviour, and to predict their likely responses. This in turn reflects the fact that much behaviour involves people enacting social *roles*; for we would define a role as the normal way for people to behave in given situations. At home, for example, the relations of marriage and parenthood give rise to the familial roles of wife, husband, father, mother, son and daughter. At work, the division of labour and distribution of authority create roles like supervisor, manager and worker.

The most important aspect of this structure of relations is the *expectations* that others have of appropriate behaviour within a role. In fact, roles are defined by *the set of expectations that others have of the role incumbent's behaviour*. Some expectations are made explicit by legislation; for example, parents must feed their children and protect them from physical and moral danger. Mixed with whatever legal expectations exist are the cultural assumptions about appropriate behaviour within a role. Both legislation and cultural assumptions are subject to modification.

It is often difficult for us to recognize the profound effect that roles have on our behaviour or that they are part of an external social structure, defined by other people's expectations. This is because we experience social roles not as something external to ourselves, but as personal properties. We manage to translate the set of external expectations about our behaviour in a role into a corresponding set of psychological properties such as beliefs, values, attitudes, prescriptions (I ought to) and proscriptions (I ought not to).

This is referred to as *internalization* of expectations, and it can result in major changes in an individual's behaviour. Roles are internalized during *role episodes* which refer to the whole of the process of perceiving others' expectations of us. These involve: (1) the initial expectations of others of what behaviour is appropriate in a role; (2) communicating these initial expectations to the new occupant of a role. In the workplace this may involve formal procedures such as training or induction courses, or can occur informally by observing others occupying similar roles; (3) developing a set of initial assumptions about what behaviour is expected; (4) testing one's own initial assumptions about appropriate role behaviour by performing tasks; and (5) feedback from others on the extent to which the performance matches their expectations.

Finally, we must distinguish between the role itself and *role behaviour*. The main point here is that, though the role itself is structured (like the script in a play), behaviour in a role can be modified by the expressive concerns of individuals (like an actor interprets a part). A new manager, for example, may want to be the most popular or the most innovative in the firm. In this way, roles provide an arena for the interplay of the practical requirements we have to meet and our own expressive concerns.

Comprehending other people

In our discussion of general skills in Chapter 1, we saw that skilled individuals develop a *model* or inner representation of the dynamics of the system they are interacting with. This enables them to predict future states of the system and responses of the system to their actions. Their models were based on conceptual categories developed to translate 'raw data' from sources into 'action-relevant inputs'. The categories contained in their models meant that skilled workers could quickly 'read the face of the system' by sampling information from time to time, and so update their models of the state of the system. Therefore, in social interaction we need to construct 'models' of others in order to predict their reactions. In some work-related situations, such as selection interviewing and psychotherapy, constructing a model of the candidate or patient is the principal goal of the encounter. In other situations, supervising or selling, for example, developing an adequate understanding of the member of staff or customer plays an important part in determining the effectiveness of an individual's performance.

Though comparison with skilled activity is useful, since it makes us consider what categories or 'sampling strategies' people use, there are some important differences between social and practical skills. Firstly, the uncertainty presented by people can be very considerable, because individuals can change and they differ in terms of their attitudes, beliefs and goals. Secondly, we have to include in our model what model the other person may have of us.

How, then, do we build these models? People we interact with provide us with a continuous flow of data, both verbal and non-verbal. Language is the symbolic system through which a great deal of our practical and expressive activity is achieved. Argyle's work, however, has demonstrated the importance of 'non-verbal channels' as a source of information about the feelings and attitudes of others towards us. Even when contact occurs through speech alone, as when talking on the telephone, we use features of speech such as accent, changes in tone, pauses and variations in tempo to complement our understanding of the speaker and what he or she has said (Singleton, 1983).

Our attention across verbal and non-verbal channels is as selective and organized as perception in other skilled activities. What we attend to is determined by the 'categories' we use to model others. These, in turn, are often related to the purpose of the encounter. The categories you would employ to model someone you have just met at a party are likely to be different from those employed by a supervisor to model a new subordinate. Whatever categories are employed, much of our attention will be directed towards non-verbal aspects of the other's performance since these also provide us with feedback about our own performance.

There are a number of potential sources of non-verbal information provided by others during social interaction. The most important source is the *face*. As Argyle (1983, p.33) stated, 'the face gives a fast-moving display of reactions to what others have said or done, and a running commentary on what the owner of the face is saying'. We are able to identify with reasonable accuracy eight emotions and cognitive reactions from the faces of others: happiness; surprise; fear; sadness; anger; disgust; contempt; and interest. We should, however, not forget that the face muscles are under voluntary control. This means that though a rich source of emotional and attitudinal data is available, facial expressions are very often a mix of wanted and unwanted movements, for example, a polite smile in the bottom half of the face and a frown in the top half.

Gaze performs a number of non-verbal communication functions. We gather information from the faces of others with brief gazes aimed mainly around their eyes. The gaze of other people provides an important additional source of information about their attitudes and feelings towards us. High levels of gaze can indicate a range of feelings towards us from love, through interest, to hate. Argyle and Cook (1976) reviewed gaze studies and found high gaze from another person could indicate the other is: interested in you; of low status; attempting to dominate you; extravert; and not embarrassed. In some contexts, correctly decoding gaze is extremely useful. For example, Goodfellow (1983) described how the skilled teacher could decode the slightest gaze from a pupil to detect whether anything was amiss, whether the pupil was being mildly mischievous or malicious. Decoding gaze becomes less accurate in encounters between people from different cultures, because the use of gaze varies considerably across cultures (Watson, 1970). This means gaze can become the source of considerable embarrassment and misunderstanding in cross-cultural encounters. Negotiators involved in selling to foreign clients need to be able to decode correctly the level of gaze being received and display the appropriate level of gaze within the context of a particular culture.

Additional sources of non-verbal information include *body posture* and *body movement*. Though these do not usually provide specific information about the attitudes or emotions of others towards us, they can indicate their general emotional state or mood. In some contexts where a person is being judged (such as a selection interview), they may attempt to suppress indicators of mood, and here *non-verbal leakage* can provide an indication of how relaxed, anxious or confident the person is. Skilled interviewers can use leakage, such as excessive lower body movements, to make a guess about the nature of the candidate's feelings on a subject, and if necessary return to the subject later in the interview (McHenry, 1981). Mood is often contagious. An awareness of the role played by body posture and movements in conveying information about mood is important in professional contexts since it reduces the risk of contagion occuring. The salesperson, for example, needs to be aware of the mood being signalled by his or her body posture or movements when dealing with customers. If it is not positive it is likely to be 'caught' by customers (Potter, 1983). The selection interviewer similarly needs to be careful he or she does not catch the mood (particularly anxiety) of the candidate.

Appearance often provides us with a rich source of information about others, particularly when little other information is available. Although aspects of the other's personal front are highly controllable, they are nonetheless often assumed to be an important source of information about attitudes, allegiances, status or class. In addition, appearance can be used in an active mode to convey highly specific messages. On the football terraces, for example, minor differences in the way scarves are tied, the precise type of footwear and the length of the trousers people wear all contribute significantly to the models football fans construct of each other (Marsh, 1982).

Personal construct theory

Given all these potential sources of information, how do we make inferences about others? As we suggested earlier, the *filtering and selection* from amongst these inputs is determined by the categories we employ. This was the basic assumption of Kelly's (1955) personal construct theory, which has provided behavioural scientists with a novel way of exploring how individuals comprehend situations and others. Constructs are 'bi-polar adjectives' with which individuals organize their perception of the world and provide it with meaning. Examples of the type of constructs used in daily interaction are intelligent–dull, rejecting–accepting, autocratic–democratic, stable–unstable and promotable–unpromotable. Marsh's (1982) study provided some more specific examples of the way football supporters examine the appearance of other fans and model them using constructs such as loyal–disloyal and hard–soft.

Summarizing research on the way individuals construct others, Adams-Webber (1981) found:

(1) people exhibit stable idiosyncratic preferences for using particular sets of constructs in characterizing themselves and others;

(2) people are consistent over time in the number of different constructs they employ to describe people they know;

(3) if they are able to obtain more information about others, people's construct systems develop in terms of a gradual shift of emphasis from a primary concern with appearance, social roles and behaviour to a predominant interest in personality;

(4) the personal meaningfulness of any construct used by an individual will depend partly on the contexts in which the individual typically applies it;

(5) the personal meaningfulness of any construct also depends on its implicative potential, the number of specific inferences an individual can make from a particular construct to other related constructs within his or her own system.

According to personal construct theory, the structure and content of an individual's construct system is what determines his or her ability to make a variety of distinctions between people and their personalities. The simplest feature of a construct system which can be considered is how *elaborate* it is. The more constructs an individual can employ in a situation the more able he or she will be to make inferences about the other's personality and motives. The more elaborate a construct system is the more an individual is able to construe an interaction from different perspectives and make inferences about the attitudes of others involved. (Neimeyer and Hudson, 1985). Professional social skills such as interviewing, selling or negotiating are supported by a stock of valid constructs enabling relevant predictions to be made about other participants. An individual's preference for particular constructs may reduce the validity of models constructed of others. For example, if a selection interviewer's construing of candidates is dominated by very idiosyncratic constructs such as 'plays rugby–does not play rugby', 'will come to the pub at lunchtime–won't come to the pub at lunchtime', the validity of selection decisions will be drastically reduced.

Constructing other people adequately is also facilitated by what Kelly (1955) termed *commonality*, namely the extent to which there is overlap or similarity between the constructs and construing processes of oneself and others. This is because similarity between one's constructs and those of another person make it easier to understand their psychological processes. Commonality has been found to be a good predictor of friendship formation among groups of individuals (Duck, 1973).

Having an overlap or commonality with other people's construct systems does not always guarantee comprehension. A person may possess very similar constructs and construing processes to others but may still make little or no attempt to understand them. At this more complex level, where we have to take into account people's motives and wishes, comprehending the other involves what Kelly termed *sociality*. This is the deliberate attempt to subsume the construing processes of the other into one's own construct system. Sociality does not necessarily involve commonality. A manager, for example, may be able to subsume a subordinate's construct system without their respective construct systems being similar. Commonality, however, as we have already suggested, does increase the probability of success of attempts to subsume the construct system of others.

Kelly saw sociality as the key to viable social relationships; 'to the extent that one person construes the construction processes of another, he may play a role in a social process involving the other person'. In occupational settings, sociality is essential to skilled social performance. In selling, for example, sociality enables predictions to be made about what aspect of the product or service will be most attractive to the customer (Potter, 1983) and anticipate his or her information-processing capacity (Moorhouse, 1983; Poppleton, 1981). In supervision sociality provides a supervisor with an idea of how subordinates will treat instructions. Sociality is not always one-way or asymmetrical; most social situations, particularly in professional settings, involve some degree of mutual construing. But not everyone is aware that mutual construing occurs in social encounters. Some people model others often quite elaborately but do not comprehend that others are also modelling them. Some people model others but assume others have a fixed and fully established model of them. The hallmark of social skill is when we actively develop models of others while assuming that they are actively modelling us.

As we have seen, personal construct theory suggests that we actively construct models of one another. It also suggests this process can go wrong. We have already seen that lack of commonality, sociality and adequate constructs reduce the probability of a valid model of the other being constructed. There are two other ways in which a model's validity can be reduced: *pre-emption* and *circumspection*. Pre-emption, the cutting short of construing processes, is seen when there is lack of time, willingness or capacity to construe others. When construing is pre-empted the model is constructed out of stereotypes and ready-made generalizations. In contrast to this, circumspection involves the excessive construing of others and a consequent failure to commit oneself to a particular view of or lines of action with them. Circumspection is triggered by the uncertainty and ambiguity which other people's behaviour or personalities contain. Attempting to cope with this uncertainty can, as with neurotic thought, cause individuals to become 'preoccupied with' or 'lodged in' construing. Social skills depend on an ability to strike an appropriate balance between the pre-emptive and the circumspective construing of other people.

Interactional work

The concept of skill is particularly helpful when examining the 'interactional

111

work' which constitutes much of our social life and through which our practical and expressive goals are attained. Like other skilled work, interactional work possesses a hierarchial structure, and therefore offers a number of possible units of analysis. Words form up into sentences, sentences construct social acts (demanding, asserting, complying, rejecting, etc.), social acts build up into episodes (a group of social acts characterized by some internal homogeneity such as an introduction) and episodes form encounters (interviews, sales negotiations, team briefings, etc.). This building up of encounters out of words is termed *concatenation* (Harré, 1979). Achieving goals in social situations therefore depends on the ability to build up and progress through social encounters. As we shall see, some progress has been made in describing how this is achieved.

Open sequences

If we use Brenner's (1982) typology of situations described earlier, we can consider the skills required for competent interaction in different types of situation. We can begin with those situations he termed 'open' which seemingly involved neither prior goals nor specific interactional routes for participants. For example, simply talking to friends in a chance encounter usually involves no specific objectives or sequences of interaction. In these situations discourse is relatively unplanned, lacking forethought or organization (Ochs, 1983). Sequences of interaction occurring in open situations involve what Jones and Gerard (1967) termed *reactive contingency*, that is, each participant simply responds to what the previous contributor has said.

Even in these seemingly 'open' situations it is possible to discern some rules operating to shape sequences. At the simplest level, participants have to coordinate their contributions. *Turn-taking* is achieved using principles acquired at the earliest stages of the development of interactional competence. Young children capable of only one- or two-word utterances take turns to make their contributions which to the annoyance of many a parent they tend to repeat until the other participant has acknowledged what they have said. Schieffelin (1983), for example, found 30-month-old children attending to each other's contributions and sustaining interactions of over twenty-five turns. In adulthood, the conventions for indicating a desire to retain, obtain or hand over the role of contributor are usually so well learned that we are unaware of them. Analyses of interaction show individuals signal a willingness to hand over the role of contributor by pausing, gazing at each other at the end of a contribution or asking a question. Gaze at the end of a contribution is used not only to signal a willingness to hand over the floor but also to gain feedback on how others have reacted to a contribution. Keeping the floor involves not pausing, not looking at others at the end of sentences, using certain gestures and raising one's voice. To take the floor, a participant needs to listen for what Sacks *et al.* (1974) described as 'transition relevance space'. At these points in the interaction an individual uses particular grammatical constructions as 'place-holders' which give him or her time to construct a well-formed proposition (Duranti and Ochs, 1979).

In addition to turn-taking, participants in conversations also appear to adhere to other rules: (1) quantity: contributions should be as informative as possible without providing too much information; (2) quality: contributions should be true or have sufficient evidence to support them; (3) relevance: contributions should be relevant to what has preceded them; and (4) manner: contributions should be clear, unambiguous and organized (Grice, 1975).

Orderliness also appears at the level of the social acts performed by contributors. Clarke (1983) discovered that subjects could rearrange into the correct order cards containing single contributions taken from informal sequences of interaction. More importantly, they could do the same for a set of cards on which the various social acts constituted by these contributions had been written. The orderliness subjects detected among social acts was between pairs such as question–answer, offer–accept, request–comply and reject– reason. These sequences are known as *two-step* sequences. The ability of his subjects to recognize orderliness in interaction at the level of both social act and sentences led Clarke to suggest that there was a 'grammar' or 'syntax' of social acts analogous to that of languages. One such rule, which enables people to perceive orderliness, reflects generally held beliefs about sustaining harmony in social interaction. For instance, if an individual is to sustain a pleasant exchange, he or she must provide a reason after refusing an offer because of a general belief that offers should be accepted, even when acceptance involves inconvenience.

Although two-step sequences are observable in many interactions, there do not seem to be regularities in associations between two-step units in most situations. Sequences of more than two acts are generated by the persistence over time of an individual's goals. In the relatively unplanned discourse of open situations, the goal of a participant is often simply to establish and sustain what are termed *discourse topics* (a concern or a set of concerns). If an individual wants to sustain a discourse topic he or she needs to match a contribution to the preceding utterance of the other person. This produces sequences termed *topic-collaborating sequences*. If, however, an individual wishes to continue the flow of discourse but change the topic, the previous contributor's last utterance can be used to create a new discourse topic. These sequences are termed *topic-incorporating sequences*. New discourse topics can also be introduced by 'breaking and entering', that is, by creating discontinuities in the dialogue. This can be done either by introducing a new discourse topic which has already appeared in the 'discourse history' or negotiating a completely new discourse topic (Ochs and Schieffelin, 1983). The skills required to sustain or negotiate new discourse topics in open situations include: securing the other's attention; articulating utterances clearly; providing sufficient information for the other to identify objects, people or events (referents) included in the discourse topic; providing sufficient information for the other to understand the relationships between referents of the discourse topic; locating and attending to sources of misunderstanding ('repair work'); and shaping utterances taking into account what is termed the other's 'presupposition pool', an estimation of what the other person understands ('recipient design').

Defined sequences

Interaction in defined situations, such as between incumbents of organizational roles, involves more than merely attempting to draw on each other's presupposition pools to sustain discourse topics. At least one participant will invariably have an objective. This may be to provide the other with information, sell the other something or make a selection decision. Utterances are, therefore, preceded by more forethought and planning than in 'open' situations, and discourse is relatively planned. One feature of this is the *four-step* sequence, produced by a goal of one participant persisting after the other's response, as in the following example:

A	Interviewer: (question)	Why do you want to leave your present job?
B	Candidate: (inadequate response)	I would rather not go into that.
C	Interviewer: (accounts for question)	I think we really do need to know why you have decided to leave our major competitor.
D	Candidate: (adequate response)	I felt the company no longer offers me the challenges I'm looking for.

Here, the interviewer's goal of ascertaining the candidate's reason for leaving persists from A through B to C. Sequences structured by the goal of one participant only possess what Jones and Gerard (1967) termed *asymmetrical contingency*, one participant responding according to the objectives of the other.

In encounters between individuals occupying specific roles, it is usually the case that both participants have goals. Encounters in these 'defined' situations, as Brenner (1982) pointed out, may still be relatively underidentified for participants in a number of ways. The precise nature and variability of the other's objectives or initial construction of the situation may not be known. No routine sequences of interaction are built into defined situations so a strategy for dealing with the encounter has to be worked out. This means participants have to establish a '*working consensus*' of what type of situation they are involved in. This then provides the stable ground on which they can base a strategy for interaction (McCall and Simmons, 1966).

The ambiguity and unstructuredness that still reside in defined situations make social skills an important determinant of effectiveness in them. To establish a working consensus of a situation individuals need to be able to construe the construing processes of others. As Singleton (1983, p.291) pointed out, 'in the case of social skills reality is not only physical events, it is also the schemata in other people's minds which control their attempts to communicate'. An individual, therefore, must be able to detect, absorb and recreate the schemata or models which lie behind the initial statements of other participants. As we saw in the last section, the complexity of an individual's construing was related to his or her ability to construe a situation from another's point of view. In selling, for example, the ability to imagine being the customer enables a salesperson to understand the customer's needs. Establishing a working consensus of a situation is also assisted by a degree of commonality between the participants' construct systems. An individual's willingness to share constructs increases the likelihood of this commonality between constructions of a situation being achieved. By sharing constructs, individuals allow others to check to what extent their models of the situation map on to each other. If, for example, a manager's and subordinate's constructions of a situation do not map on to each other reasonably well interaction is unlikely to get very far, and some form of conflict or opposition may ensue. Sharing constructs allows the other to accept, elaborate, modify and return the model until the models map on to each other sufficiently well for a working consensus of the situation to have developed.

Having established a working consensus, participants can develop a strategy for dealing with the encounter and for achieving their objectives. At this stage skilled communication requires the same skills as those required in 'open' situations. To move nearer to our goals our contributions must possess good recipient design. The skilled communicator is sensitive to cues provided by the listener which enable utterances with good recipient design to be constructed. Increasing sensitivity to these cues is now central to training programmes in many areas where professional competence depends on social skills. For example, sales training once consisted of requiring salespeople to rote learn scripts. In other words, training was based on an implicit model of simple asymmetrical contingency in interaction – a one-way communication from the salesperson to the customer. Nowadays, however, sales training emphasizes the importance in successful selling of sensitivity to cues from customers. In selling, as in other areas where professional social skills are employed, an accurate estimation of the listener's ability to process information is crucial. The skilled salesperson is able to provide screened and selected information at a pace which matches the customer's ability to assimilate it. One device known as 'checkback', where agreement is sought from a customer (e.g. 'don't you agree?'), enables the salesperson to ensure that he or she is working at the same pace as the customer. If checkback indicates that a customer's pace has been exceeded, the salesperson would need to engage in 'repair work', locating and attending to the points when the customer was lost. Checkback is also thought to increase the commitment of a customer to the salesperson's objectives.

Listeners can also be lost by asking what are known as *closed questions* which require simple definitive responses. The importance of avoiding these closed questions has been stressed in situations as diverse as selling (Potter, 1983) and psychotherapeutic interviews (Barker, 1983). The closed question often creates a hiatus which allows listeners to disengage from the discourse. A further way listeners are lost is when statements threatening their self-esteem or self-concept are used. This means *tact* is an important component of social skill, since it protects the feelings of listeners and so retains their attention. Argyle (1983, p.51) defined tact as 'the production of socially effective utterances in difficult situations'. In selling, for example, a salesperson needs to transform 'do you have the authority to order?' into 'do you normally decide on the ordering or do you leave that up to someone else?'

Tact is also a component of a crucial skill in professional and occupational settings, namely dealing with objections. In modern complex organizations people's objections and grievances often stem from real conflicts of interest, and may not be readily handled even by tactful negotiation. But in many cases objections that result from disappointments or misunderstandings can be resolved. Loveridge (1983) described a sequence for handling grievances in line management: search; probe; handle; and restructure. For example, a subordinate claims she is not able to use her skills fully. By searching and probing on the basis of her statements, her supervisor establishes that the source of the grievance is actually her feeling that she should have been promoted by now. Handling and restructuring involve carefully readjusting her expectations in line with a more realistic time-scale for acquiring the experience necessary for competence in a promoted post. In selling, one commonly used sequence for handling objections is: welcome; restate; overcome; and continue. For example, an objection is welcomed by the salesperson: 'I can understand how you feel, Mr Jones.' It is restated to enable the salesperson to confirm precisely what the objection refers to: 'You're unhappy about using the magazine because you don't believe it is reaching 25,000 potential customers.' The salesperson can then overcome the objection by giving more information: 'As I mentioned earlier our circulation is fully controlled so we can guarantee who is receiving it.' If the customer accepts this response the salesperson returns to the point before the objection occurred.

This ability to progress smoothly through an interactional sequence in pursuit of a goal appears to be crucial at all levels of interaction in social encounters: sentences, social acts and episodes. The generally held beliefs about sustaining harmony in social interaction and presenting pleasant fronts operate at all these levels. Thus, entire social encounters, particularly in defined situations, need to have the practical purpose of the meeting sandwiched between episodes in which a harmonious social relationship is established, for example by recalling the last meeting, and then re-established, perhaps by arranging a future meeting. This gives rise to the common five-episode structure for encounters: greeting; establishing relationship; central task; re-establishing relationship; and parting (Argyle *et al.*, 1981). All these episodes are themselves built up out of two-step and four-step sequences. The central task containing the practical purpose of the encounter, may itself be comprised of a number of smaller episodes. For example, the central task in a sales encounter often involves: (1) gaining the interest of the customer; (2) identifying the customer's needs; (3) selling the benefits of a particular item or service to the customer; (4) overcoming the customer's objections; and (5) clinching the sale. Argyle and Lydall (in Argyle, 1983) found that high selling sales staff were those who by developing a good rapport with the customer could move smoothly through the episodes involved in the central task and were thus more likely to clinch the sale.

Like other skilled activity, then, social skills involve a smooth progression towards a goal. This means that responses should be well-timed and in the correct order. An appropriate sequencing of responses for socially skilled behaviour ultimately depends on the validity of the models we construct of the people we interact with and of the social situations in which we find ourselves.

FURTHER READING

Adams-Webber, J. and J.C. Mancuso (eds.) (1983) *Applications of Personal Construct Theory*. London: Academic Press.

Argyle, M. (ed.) (1981) *Social Skills and Work*. London: Methuen.

Arnoff, J. and J.P. Wilson (1985) *Personality in the Social Process*. Hillsdale, N.J.: Lawrence Erlbaum.

Bannister, D. (ed.) (1985) *Issues and Approaches in Personal Construct Theory*. London: Academic Press.

Bannister, D. and F. Fransella (1986) *Inquiring Man: The Psychology of Personal Constructs* (3rd ed.). London: Croom Helm.

Cook, M. (1984) *Issues in Person Perception*. London: Methuen.

Ditton, J. (ed.) (1980) *The View from Goffman*. London: Macmillan.

Goffman, E. (1971) *The Presentation of Self in Everyday Life*. Harmondsworth: Penguin.

Phillips, K. and T. Fraser (1982) *The Management of Interpersonal Skills*. Aldershot: Gower.

Singleton, W.T. (ed.) (1983) *Social Skills*. Lancaster: MTP Press.

Stewart, V. and A. Stewart (1981) *Business Applications of Repertory Grids*. Maidenhead: McGraw-Hill.

6

Group and Inter-group Behaviour

Much of our social interaction takes place in a group context, and we will now go on to discuss the effects of group memberships on social behaviour. Groups can be considered in terms of the *structures* they develop, the *processes* they involve and their *interaction* with other groups. In this chapter we will examine these three aspects of groups, and conclude with a discussion of a series of classic experiments in work groups, the *Hawthorne studies*, which, as we shall see, has had a profound influence on management thinking.

Before considering the effects of group membership on social behaviour we should first ask the question: how and why do groups form? Although there is no straightforward answer to this, at least two main assumptions about the basis of group formation have been put forward. Some writers stress the *functional* reasons for the existence of groups such as joint action on a task; face-to-face interaction; or mutually dependent relationships. Others have emphasized the *psychological* processes that cause groups to form; the perception of a shared social identity; and attempting to fulfill needs for affiliation and supportive relationships. In real-life groups we can often see a predominantly functional basis of formation, or a psychological basis; or, as is often the case, a mixture of the two.

Fiedler (1967) has provided a useful typology of work groups based on the nature and intensity of the interaction they involve:

(1) interacting groups. Members are interdependent and need to cooperate and coordinate their actions to accomplish the group task;
(2) co-acting groups. Members work together on a common task but do so relatively independently;
(3) counteracting groups. Individuals work together for the purposes of negotiating and reconciling conflicting demands and objectives. Performance is measured by the acceptability of the solution to group members.

This typology reflects the extent to which group members' behaviour is determined by group structure and processes. The impact on members' behaviour, values and attitudes of interacting and counteracting groups is far greater than in co-acting groups because of the increased intensity of interaction they involve.

GROUP STRUCTURE

The structure of a group reflects the basis of group identity – and indeed the very fact that we can speak of a group at all rather than merely a number of individuals. For structure reflects the established patterns of behaviour that are distinctive within a particular group. Structure constitutes a distinctively *social* aspect of group life, and may act as an objective constraint on members' activity. One important aspect of structure consists of the different *categories of membership* that the different individuals making up the group occupy.

(1) Early on in a group's history a *group leader* will often emerge because he or she is perceived by other members as the most competent at the functional requirements of the leadership role. The division of status and authority between leaders and followers that this implies is an important dimension of group structure. Bales and Slater (1955) suggested these functional requirements were related both to the group's task and to the group's socio-emotional requirements. Behaviours associated with the task include, coordinating, initiating contributions, evaluating, information-giving, information-seeking, opinion-giving, opinion-seeking, and motivating individuals. Behaviours associated with the group's socio-emotional requirements include reconciling differences, arbitrating, encouraging participation, and increasing interdependence among group members. One individual may be perceived by the group as capable of meeting both the socio-emotional and the task requirements of the leadership role. In some groups, however, two leaders may emerge, each with perceived competence in one of these leadership functions.

(2) Group *members* can be defined as individuals who have accepted group goals as relevant and recognize an interdependence with other group members in the achievement of these goals. Acceptance of group goals is associated with an individual's needs (subsistence, dependence, affiliation, dominance) and the extent to which his or her social identity is derived from membership of the group. Individuals can also decide whether to accept group goals on the basis of a rational estimation of the utility of group membership.

(3) Sometimes, however, an individual's personal goals conflict with the group's goals; and if he or she is not prepared to modify his or her personal goals, dissatisfaction with the group becomes almost inevitable. The individual is then identified as a *deviate*. Group members will usually attempt to increase the deviate's acceptance of group goals. Indeed, persuading a deviate to accept group goals can absorb a considerable proportion of a group's time.

(4) If deviates resist group pressure and continue to reject group goals the group will eventually give up on them and they are left alone by other group

members. They become *isolates*. Though they may be tolerated because their output is required, they are unlikely to be included in activities which do not directly involve the task. In extreme cases group members may seek not only the psychological isolation of such individuals but their physical isolation too.

Groups have their most significant impact on our behaviour through the operation of *norms*. Indeed, many social psychologists believe that behaviour in groups can only be understood in relation to the norms that are operating within it, since they represent the *expectations* within the group for appropriate behaviour of group members. As these expectations are external to each member norms are thus part of a group's structure. It is often hard for individuals to realize the impact that the expectations of others have on their behaviour (as it was in the similar case of roles, discussed in Chapter 5) because norms become part of their psychological make-up, affecting their attitudes, values, beliefs and behaviour.

A group's norms do not occur by accident, they represent the interaction of social, historical and psychological processes, and they are thus resistant to change. In Chapter 4, for instance, we discussed an example of the historical development of group norms when considering the effort bargain at work, which we saw emerged from a normative consensus about what constitutes a fair ratio of effort to reward. Although norms are generated out of the practical activity of groups, and are embedded in their experiences and history, when necessary groups can also generate norms very quickly.

If a group suddenly faces very different demands or the novel conditions are such that it is necessary to form a new group, then the ability to generate norms quickly may well be essential to the group's survival. Industrial disputes provide a number of examples of sudden changes in circumstances. For instance, in the 1980 steel strike the unions involved had no previous experience of strikes and thus of strike organization. The norms structuring the activities of the various newly formed groups (local picket cells, picket control groups and the various levels of the strike committee) had to be established quickly in order to carry out the numerous activities (e.g. fund-raising, dealing with the media, striker welfare, support services for pickets) necessary to maintain and enhance the strike.

The principal way in which group norms are absorbed is through observation. At work, for example, a new employee will estimate the norms for attendance, workrate and dress from the group's modal behaviour, that is, how most people in the group behave. Group members also observe the extent to which an individual's behaviour matches the group's norms. Norms usually include a degree of tolerance and specify a range of acceptable behaviour, known as the *zone of acceptance*, so that members will only take action if another member's behaviour falls outside this range. For example, in the Hawthorne studies which we will be discussing in greater detail later in the chapter, the norms included: (1) not 'rate-busting' (turning out too much work); (2) not 'chiselling' (turning out too little work); (3) not 'squealing' (telling the supervisor anything detrimental to the group). Anyone who deviated from these norms was either subjected to sarcasm and ridicule or to a physical penalty – a harsh blow to the upper arm – known in the plant as 'binging'. These sanctions generally ensured conformity to group norms. Groups thus wield an enormous amount of power over their members.

GROUP PROCESSES

We turn now to the *process* of interaction within groups, which refers to the manner in which group action is constructed on a continuing basis. Unlike structure, process emphasizes changes in the flow of activities; indeed group processes indicate how structures become established and how over time they may change. Process also points to the subjective perceptions of group members and their active involvement in group life.

Cohesiveness

Cohesiveness can be defined as the complex of forces which gives rise to the perceptions by members of a group identity. The cohesiveness of groups has a major impact on their functioning. Its most important effect is on the *potency* of group norms, that is, the extent to which norms determine behaviour within a group. The cohesive work group can develop norms that present management with major problems, for example by enforcing conformity to a workrate far below what is considered acceptable by management. Equally, they can be a great asset to management, for example, by having norms which prescribe a willingness to put in additional effort when required. Not surprisingly, then, sources of group cohesiveness are of considerable interest.

A proportion of any group's time will be spent on what are termed *process issues*, such as getting to know other members and resolving any interpersonal difficulties. And if the problems arising from process issues are successfully dealt with, the group will be a reasonably harmonious and cohesive social unit. The *stability* of group membership plays an important part in a group's capacity to resolve process problems, and if changes in membership are infrequent these problems will be reduced to a minimum and group members can concentrate on task performance. Thus, frequent changes in membership increase the time spent on process issues, and may disrupt the development of group cohesiveness. The stability of groups in the workplace can involve wider issues. Clegg and Fitter (1978), for example, describe how the management of a confectionery company attempted to improve the very low levels of job satisfaction among their workforce by stabilizing membership. Demand for the firm's product was seasonal, and traditional management policy had been to lay off staff and employ staff according to demand. But this undermined the cohesiveness of work groups which depended on the stability of membership. Thus management recognized that they had to adopt a policy of evening out production over the year.

The *attractiveness* of group membership is also an important ingredient in the creation of a cohesive group since the more attractive a group is to its members, the more they will desire its continued existence and work to make it a cohesive social unit. The attractiveness of a group is partly determined by its *composition*. Members of a group have to get along with each other, which may be difficult if they are very different in status, values, attitudes, abilities or interests. At the same time, if group members are too similar, some of the benefits of group cohesion will be lost. For example, if members all have similar views, a range of alternatives is unlikely to be considered. Moderate heterogeneity in a group balances the requirements of cohesion and productivity (Hackman, 1980). Group attractiveness is also influenced by the extent to which its members are *dependent* on it either to satisfy their psychological needs or to achieve their goals (Cartwright and Zander, 1968).

As we will see when discussing inter-group behaviour, a group's relationships with other groups have an important effect on cohesiveness. *Competition* with other groups causes a group member to perceive other members as more similar than they actually are (Turner, 1982). This increases solidarity within the group and the willingness of group members to cooperate with one another.

While the primary importance of cohesiveness, as we stated earlier, lies in determining the impact of a group's norms on its members, membership of such groups has been found to have a number of other important effects on group members and group functioning. Perhaps the most important of these is the beneficial effects a cohesive group has on its members' psychological state. In fact, this aspect is utilized by psychotherapists who treat their patients in groups. Positive identification with a cohesive group enhances an individual's self-concept and self-esteem, while supportive inter-personal relationships reduce anxiety and satisfy a range of ego needs. These benefits do not, however, always occur. Inexperienced psychotherapists may, for example, not be able to prevent one member's self-esteem being damaged if they are victimized by other members of the group. However, most therapists feel the benefits of using cohesive groups outweigh the potential disadvantages.

Synergy

If we consider decision-making within groups, or committees in organizations, the common-sense view of committees is that they take a great deal of time to produce poor quality decisions. Much of the research on groups, however, reveals the opposite, that in most conditions groups outperform even their best member (Hill, 1982). This phenomenon of groups has been termed synergy, and is demonstrated by group exercises like 'Lost on the Moon' (Hall, 1971). This begins with each member being asked to imagine being lost on the moon and having to decide on the priority of items he or she would include for the journey back to the mother ship. The members are then asked to achieve a consensus of opinion on the ranking of items. When a consensus has been achieved individual and group rankings are compared to a ranking produced by NASA experts. The group's ranking is usually superior to any of the individual rankings. This and similar exercises are used widely in management training since they provide a quick method of demonstrating the synergistic qualities of groups, and thus indicate both the invalidity of the common-sense view of groups and their decision-making potential.

Synergy occurs because discussion within groups generates more alternatives than individuals, tends to eliminate inferior contributions, averages out errors and supports creative thinking. This means groups invariably have the edge over individuals in situations where accuracy is a priority, errors are expensive and time is relatively cheap.

Groupthink

One notable disadvantage of groups which are too cohesive is that their decision-making ability can be drastically reduced by what Janis (1972) termed groupthink. He defined this as 'a deterioration of mental efficiency, reality testing, and moral judgment that results from in-group pressures'. In other words, the pressures for conformity that can arise in highly cohesive groups may cloud members' judgment and their ability to reach correct decisions.

Interestingly, Janis illustrated this notion with a detailed analysis of the ill-fated attempt by the Kennedy administration to invade Cuba. Janis claimed the decision which instigated the Bay of Pigs fiasco in 1961 was the result of groupthink. He claimed all the symptoms of groupthink were present in the advisory group, comprised of President Kennedy, his cabinet and other senior staff, which took the decision to invade. They became convinced of their *invulnerability* – they assumed that since they were all exceptionally able they could not possibly fail. They believed that the 1,000 Cuban exiles, outnumbered 140 to 1, really could beat Castro's army. Group discussion was characterized by a collective *rationalizing away* of information contrary to the group's beliefs. The group also believed they were *morally correct* in what they were doing, thus giving them a right to interfere with Cuba's sovereignty. This belief stemmed in part from the inaccurate *stereotyping* of the Cubans that occurred within the group – they believed, for example, that the Cuban people would flock to the support of the exiles. Janis argued that *self-censorship* prevented people in the group from expressing dissent since group members feared being seen as disloyal. This process was reinforced by what he termed *mindguards* who protected the group from information and individuals that would disrupt the consensus.

Janis believed, however, that groupthink was not inevitable even in cohesive groups. Members of such groups can avoid it by actively searching out

123

information, irrespective of whether it is contrary to the group's opinion. The group can also assign the role of 'devil's advocate' to one member to ensure alternative solutions are proposed and discussed. When trust is present in cohesive groups, conflict does not damage relations between members and will ultimately yield more productive solutions.

Group polarization

Another common-sense assumption about groups is that they are inherently more conservative than individuals when it comes to taking decisions that involve risks. Again research evidence appears to undermine this. A substantial number of studies show that groups tend to make more extreme decisions compared to the same decisions made alone by the individual group members (Lamm and Myers, 1978). Since the group seemed to shift towards risk in its decisions it was called *risky shift*. More recently, however, a number of studies have demonstrated that groups could also show the opposite tendency, a *caution shift*. Nowadays it is generally accepted that what is termed group polarization, the tendency for group decisions to be more extreme than those of individuals, is responsible for both sets of findings.

Why should groups produce more extreme decisions than individuals? One suggestion is that there is a *diffusion of responsibility*, where individuals, feeling that they will not be held wholly responsible for a decision, are willing to take riskier decisions. Another explanation is that *social comparison processes* are operating (Goethals and Darley, 1977). Here group members, attempting to present themselves in the best light, not only endorse the predominant cultural value but, by comparing their views with others, attempt to endorse it at least as much as everyone else. Thus group decisions become more extreme in the direction of the prevailing social attitudes. This would explain, for example, why groups tend to take riskier business decisions but more cautious decisions about whether an individual should marry. In the former, as entrepreneurial qualities are valued in a wider context, each member will adopt an entrepreneurial stance to ensure the approval of other members, in the latter, caution stems from beliefs about the dangers of broken marriages. The most recent explanation proposes that *information exchange* and *persuasive arguments* are a major cause of the polarization of views in groups (Burnstein, 1983). In juries, for example, a juror starts off with a fairly moderate view about the defendant's innocence or guilt. After listening to the information and arguments presented by other jurors he or she becomes convinced of the defendant's guilt or innocence. In other words, group discussion creates a bandwagon which everyone eventually will jump on.

It is no doubt the case that all four processes operate in groups to produce the polarization phenomenon.

Group decision-making in organizations

As we have mentioned, decisions in occupational and organizational situations are very frequently taken within a group context. Meetings, committees, project teams and so on are important decision arenas. Similarly, at the very highest level, decisions can frequently be traced to a senior corporate group. Even though organizations typically have chief executives who exercise the largest single influence, a plural executive system is still the locus of much of the real power.

This means that the processes discussed above take on a major significance (particularly since a common-sense understanding of groups, as was also mentioned, is not a very reliable guide). The overwhelming advantages of group-based decision-making that were summarized in terms of synergy – the breadth of experience brought to a problem, the benefits of discussion, emergence of new ideas – may be offset in certain circumstancces by phenomena like groupthink and polarization. Hence, it is vitally important that people in organizations remain aware of the potential problems, and of the group processes that can cause both excessive conformity or highly extreme decisions to emerge.

INTER-GROUP BEHAVIOUR

Groups do not exist in isolation, they are usually embedded in a network of relationships with other groups. At work, for example, there are a variety of groups representing different functional, professional, departmental and economic interests. Though not inevitable, it is often the case that when such divisions between groups become salient, conflict follows. An analysis of the reasons for increased competitiveness in inter-group behaviour is important, because if we know what processes are involved we are more likely to be able to derive feasible solutions to inter-group conflict. In the wider arena of public policy, where issues such as racial or sexual discrimination occur, this could mean the difference between success and failure in reducing inter-group divisions.

Two main explanations of inter-group conflict have emerged, and they reflect the two different bases of group formation we identified at the beginning of this chapter. The first stems from the assumption that groups form for functional reasons (Sherif and Sherif, 1982). Functional theorists believe that if groups have a functional basis, group conflict must be the result of a group perceiving another group as a threat or a potential threat to its goal attainment. For example, if a firm's management pursues the goals of low unit costs and high volume, while labour seeks higher wages and shorter working hours, then according to functional theory inter-group conflict is highly likely.

The second explanation is known as *social identity theory*, which assumes groups form through the perception of a shared social identity (Tajfel, 1978; Turner, 1982; Miller and Brewer, 1984). Social identity theorists argue that an individual's self-concept is made up from his or her personal identity which derives from a unique combination or personality and intelligence traits together with an identity created by membership of various social groups. They argue further that our self-evaluation, and thus our self-esteem, are a function of the *positive distinctiveness* (attributes which are valued by members and are thus used to make comparisons between one's own and other groups) we perceive in the groups to which we belong.

The implications of group membership for an individual's self-evaluation mean that when people perceive positive distinctiveness in other groups they can do one of three things: (1) join the outgroup; (2) redefine the elements of the status comparison so as to change their own perception of negative distinctiveness into positive distinctiveness (e.g. 'Black is beautiful'); or (3) compete to change the relative position of the outgroup on the significant status dimension(s). The third strategy will lead to conflict between the two groups when the status dimension is a valued resource such as power or money.

The competitiveness involved in inter-group behaviour is reinforced by the effects of ingroup membership on the perception, attitudes and ultimately behaviour of ingroup members. The perception among individuals of membership of a common group causes members to stereotype themselves. They see themselves as less differentiated than they actually are on dimensions such as goals, personality traits, status, motives, attitudes and values. This process, termed *depersonalization*, enables ingroup members to perceive themselves as a cohesive social unit. This depersonalization of ingroup members does not occur to the same extent as it does to outgroup members who are seen as completely undifferentiated (Park and Rothbart, 1982). The need for a positive social identity also means that ingroup members are likely to perceive larger differences between themselves and outgroup members than actually exists (Allen and Wilder, 1979). In addition, there is likely to be what is termed *ingroup favouritism*, ingroup members tending to favour each other over outgroup members. This can get to the point where it is unjustified and unreasonable and becomes *ingroup bias*. At this point perception of the outgroup has little basis in truth. Ingroup members tend to remember only negative information about the outgroup. Attributions about the outgroup also tend to be made on the basis of 'illusory correlations', that is accidental pairing of events which are perceived as supporting inferences about the outgroup.

How, then, is inter-group conflict resolved? A functional theorist would argue that the solution of inter-group conflict lies in contriving conditions in which shared goals can be perceived. This is based on the assumption that *superordinate goals* will create a *superordinate group*; an example of this would be reducing conflict between managerial groups by drawing attention to outside competition and thus a threat to the shared interest of survival. A modification of functional theory suggests it is not so much the practical goals which members seek to attain that is the basis of group formation but the social interaction that task-related activity necessarily involves. This modification has produced a solution to inter-group conflict known as the *contact hypothesis*, which predicts that increased social interaction between ingroup and outgroup will break down the inter-group division. An example of this approach is the desegregation of schools in the United States by bussing schoolchildren of one ethnic group to school, where they mix with children of another group. In a famous series of studies testing the functional and contact hypotheses, two groups of boys in a summer camp were made to compete in a number of events, resulting in a considerable amount of inter-group hostility. In the final series of events, groups had to work together to achieve common goals in one event and join forces to compete against a group from outside the camp in another. Both the cooperative task interaction and the threat from outsiders reduced the inter-group hostility that had been established (Sherif *et al.*, 1961).

Though in some instances increased contact and the perception of super-ordinate goals can successfully reduce inter-group divisions, social identity theorists claim that in many cases this is unlikely to occur, and even where it does, the change in attitudes is not necessarily transferred to other situations. Thus at work, for example, the presence of rewards contingent on management and labour working together for a common goal can provide individuals with precisely the justification they need for their cooperation with the outgroup, so leaving their private attitudes to the outgroup unchanged. For social identity theorists one solution lies in increasing the availability of social identifications that cut across existing divisions, thus enabling superordinate social groups to emerge. Appeals to identify with the nation or the organization, and the use of slogans and symbols to reinforce this, are examples of attempts to create superordinate social identifications.

Unfortunately, individuals' group-based perceptions seem to remain intact even when new social identifications are contrived that cut across existing boundaries. Social identity theorists believe that a history of conflict at the societal level leads to a general belief that boundaries between groups are immutable. Secondly, the biases in social perception caused by group membership (e.g. self-stereotyping, accentuation of differences between ingroup and outgroup) mean that the chances are that the new social identifications will not be perceived (Miller and Brewer, 1984).

For social identity theorists the answer lies in uncovering what factors in situations trigger inter-group behaviour rather than inter-personal behaviour. The salience of group memberships seems to be related, firstly, to how secure the status differential is between the groups; if it is secure its salience will not, in most situations, be high. Secondly, within a specific setting, the relative proportion of members of each group seems to influence the salience of group memberships; equal distribution seems to reduce the likelihood of inter-group behaviour. The most hostility between groups seems to occur between a minority group with a positive self-image and a majority group with a negative self-image (Moscovi and Paicheler, 1978). Finally, Wagner and Schönbach (1984) found that low self-esteem on the part of the individual can enhance the importance of group identification as a means of achieving positive social identity. The greater the importance of a particular group to an individual's self-esteem the more likely he or she is to respond according to the norms of that group in various social situations.

In many situations, however, individuals clearly have a choice between inter-group and inter-personal behaviour. In negotiations, for example, the relationship between the parties built up over a number of years is often highly valued by each party. At the same time, at an inter-group level, each negotiator is a representative of a group which seeks to achieve distinctive objectives and this usually serves to force groups apart. In one study by Stephenson (1981) it was clear that the necessity of having to treat others as members of a separate group caused considerable embarrassment during negotiations. Indeed, Stephenson suggests that one key skill in negotiation is the ability to enhance inter-personal or inter-group aspects of the situation. He found that by highlighting the inter-personal content of the negotiation, for example by invoking the personal relationships and friendships between parties, the negotiation was more likely to result in a compromise solution. Conversely, increasing the importance of the inter-group division, for example by meeting in separate rooms with occasional contact between a nominee from each group, was associated with victory for one side only.

In sum, then, functional theorists can indicate how conflict can be reduced, but only in the range of situations in which intense goal differences are not present. To account for conflict which still occurs, particularly where inter-group behaviour is involved in a wider social context, it is social identity theory which provides the necessary conceptual framework. However, at present, social identity theory provides no solutions to inter-group conflict, a fact which serves to remind us of the salience of our group memberships in society and the enduring effect they have on our perceptions, beliefs, attitudes and behaviour.

HAWTHORNE AND THE HUMAN RELATIONS MOVEMENT

The emphasis on social interaction and group dynamics that we have been exploring in this and previous chapters reflects very much the modern concerns in the study of behaviour at work. But during the early stages of its development, in the 1920s, occupational psychology relied heavily on a crude 'mechanical' model of human behaviour. Individuals were regarded as acting in isolation and responsive only to 'rational' economic and physical stimuli. A great deal of research was preoccupied with ways of increasing workers' productivity.

There was a consensus among the researchers and managers of the day that an individual's workrate was determined by factors such as temperature, humidity and illumination. Other aspects of the work stituation, such as payment systems, patterns of rest breaks and the length of the working day, also played a part in determining a worker's output. The demand for scientific research into the effects of these factors led to the founding of the National Institute of Industrial Psychology in Britain and the Psychological Corporation in America.

However, in the late 1920s this picture was to change radically; and we will conclude by looking at the research which is normally credited with having brought about this transformation, the so-called Hawthorne experiments.

In 1927 the Western Electric Company invited a group of researchers from Harvard University to help the management continue their investigation of factors affecting worker productivity at their Hawthorne plant near Chicago. What prompted this invitation was some rather curious findings which had emerged from studies that had taken place in the plant over the preceding three years. The company wanted a definitive answer to a seemingly simple question: what is the relationship between illumination and productivity levels? A group of engineers from the American Academy of Sciences was hired to provide the answer. They ran a series of studies which manipulated illumination levels and recorded output. To their surprise they found that output seemed to increase both in control groups where illumination was constant and in experimental groups when illumination was lowered. In one study illumination was cut to an amount which represented the amount of light available on a moonlight night, but output was maintained and the employees reported no eyestrain and claimed they actually felt less tired than when working under bright lights.

The Harvard researchers assumed the failure to relate illumination and output could be attributed to the fact that the engineers were not systematic enough and only took one variable into account. They believed that if they selected a small group of workers and placed them in a separate room away from the disruptive influences of other employees and departmental routine, they would succeed where the Academy of Sciences' researchers had failed.

The researchers began their first series of experiments, the so-called relay assembly test room experiments, with a group of six female employees. They selected women who reported they would be happy to work together, and who were equivalent in the level of skill they possessed so that differences in performance could not be attributed to a skill difference within the group. They also chose a routine task, assembling telephone relays, which required no machinery, so that an individual's output would be determined by her performance alone. The women were placed in an observation room with one other person, an observer, whose task was to record output data and maintain a friendly atmosphere in the room.

The researchers then set about posing the questions that were typical of the day: what is the effect of temperature, humidity, health, number of rest breaks, length of working day, method of production and payment system on output? They manipulated these variables in a long series of experiments, changing the pattern of rest breaks, hours worked, etc. and monitoring the effect on output. What the studies showed were major increases in output achieved by the group under virtually all conditions. Even when original conditions were restored production frequently still went up, and this of course totally contradicted the predictions of the 'rational man' model of behaviour.

Though the relay assembly experiments continued for five years, quite early on the experimenters reached a tentative explanation of their striking results. This is now recognized as a turning point in the development of psychology applied in the workplace; and it continues to exert an influence on management theory and practice some sixty years later. What the experimenters gradually realized was that none of the variables which were commonly associated with increases in productivity could explain their findings. What had come into existence in the relay assembly test room was a *social system*. As Elton Mayo, the person responsible for popularizing the results and developing the implications of the research into a social and managerial philosophy, put it, 'what actually happened was that six individuals became a team and the team gave itself wholeheartedly and spontaneously to cooperation in the experiment' (1943, p. 73).

In other words, the women had become a social group demonstrating the kinds of process which we discussed earlier in this chapter. This does not however explain why their output norms were high. To do this the experimenters pointed to what had become known as the *Hawthorne effect*. In fact, nowadays it is more common to distinguish two Hawthorne effects. The first effect is that the mere knowledge of being an experimental subject changes behaviour from what it would otherwise have been. This distortion in behaviour can easily undermine the value of social scientific research. The second is produced by friendly supervision; the observer in the relay assembly experiment had become a trusted friend of the women, allowing the new social organization to develop which, in turn, had imbued their working lives with new meaning.

The Hawthorne studies continued for twelve years and included a mass interviewing of 21,000 Western Electric employees, observation of a group of men in a bank wiring room (discussed in Chapter 10) and extensive personnel counselling. What was so important about these studies was that though some British industrial psychologists had drawn attention to similar findings (Myers, 1924; Cathcart, 1928), here for the first time was a large body of evidence shaking the settled managerial convictions of the time that workers were wage-pursuing automata (Bendix, 1956). The social organization of the workplace and its implications for effective management were spelled out to a large audience. Thus managers were urged to use the studies to master the nature of the social reality they operated in:

We have failed to train students in the study of social situations; we have thought that first class technical training was sufficient in a modern and mechanical age. As a consequence we are technically competent as no other age in history has been; and we combined this with utter social incompetence. (Mayo, 1943, p.120)

The Hawthorne studies marked the beginning of the human relations movement, a tradition in management which stresses the importance of social factors at work. For human relations theorists, the role of management is to provide organizational environments in which employers can fulfil the social needs of their employees, thus providing work with the meaning that routinization has taken out of it, and tap the employees' desire for cooperative activity. This can be done through team-building, supportive supervision, increased communication and opportunity for participation in decision-making and counselling. Thus, human relations theorists assume that, to the extent that managements have insight into the skills to manipulate these social factors, they will be able to harness their employees' social needs to managerial ends.

We will not devote more space here to an account of this vitally important school of thought, because in a sense much of what is discussed in this and certain other chapters reflects human relations interests. The application of group dynamics, the concern with leadership, and accounts of work motivation and satisfaction, dealt with elsewhere in this book, are all central issues in human relations research.

However, it is appropriate finally to indicate some of the adverse reaction that this approach has attracted. A number of criticisms of the Hawthorne studies have appeared (Rose, 1975; Rice, 1982) and of the human relations movement in general (Braverman, 1974; Hill, 1981). Carey (1967), for example, argued that the studies were so flawed in terms of the experimental methods employed that their conclusions cannot be regarded as supported from the evidence. In one sense, though, this does not matter. The vitality of the Hawthorne studies now stems not from any academic merits but from their all-round influence on the management process.

For this reason, much of the criticism of the human relations movement has focused on its impact on *management practice*. And here Bendix's noted *Work and Authority in Industry* (1956) has been highly influential. Bendix argues, for example, that Mayo and his colleagues were too preoccupied with group processes, often to the exclusion of organizational factors like the impact of managerial power, and wider social factors in the labour market. Sometimes this put the research in rather a dubious ethical position, since the managerial motives for commissioning the research tended to be ignored. Sometimes, too, it led the researchers to adopt paternalistic attitudes towards workers: workers were regarded as being irrationally motivated by social and affectual interests. In contrast, management were seen to act on the basis of rational economic criteria reflecting the drive towards efficiency. Secondly, Bendix and others have pointed out that in reality human relations ideas have found only limited acceptance. In particular, the claim that they have 'superseded' previous mechanical models of man is very much overstated. In fact, the basis of managerial control in industry, as represented by modern methods of production control, remains those very same mechanical models. And thirdly, even where these ideas have been influential the claim that they represent a new 'humane' approach is likewise largely untrue: they really represent simply another strategy of organizational control. Bendix, for instance, argued that the human relations movement has provided a new 'verbal dress' for managers who have little sympathy for its message, and who pursue the traditional authority-based relationship between themselves and their employees.

That said, however, the human relations movement has affected certain specific areas of management, such as personnel practices and management training, even if this is far less true in the central areas of managerial responsibility. Moreover, there has been an enduring influence on modern thinking about the managerial role, and about the directions in which that role might be reformed and made more progressive. As we will see in following chapters – in Chapter 7 on leadership and Chapter 8 on work redesign – the pervasiveness of these ideas has ensured that human relations has had some influence on managerial policies, albeit not as much as the Hawthorne researchers once envisaged.

FURTHER READING

Belbin, R.M. (1981) *Management Teams: Why They Succeed or Fail*. London: Heinemann.

Fisher, B.A. (1980) *Small Group Decision Making: Communication and the Group Process* (2nd ed.). London: McGraw-Hill.

Napier, R. and M.K. Gershenfeld (1985) *Groups: Theory and Experience* (3rd ed.). Boston: Houghton Mifflin.

Olsen, S.A. (1981) *Task Oriented Small Groups: Research, Theory and Methods*. Monticello, Ill.: Vance Bibliographics.

Palazzolo, C.S. (1981) *Small Groups: An Introduction*. London: Van Norstrand.

Patten Jr., T.H. (1981) *Organizational Development through Teambuilding*. Chichester: Wiley.

Tajfel, H. (ed.) (1982) *Social Identity and Inter-group Relations*. Cambridge: Cambridge University Press.

Tubbs, S.L. (1984) *A Systems Approach to Small Group Interaction* (2nd ed.). New York: Random House.

7

Leadership

Why can some managers and supervisors gain the best efforts of their staff while others are only able to obtain a moderate amount of cooperation, or even attract open hostility? Obviously organizations are keenly interested in the answers to this question. Their hierarchical structure means that organizations continually have to face the problem of selecting and training people to assume positions of authority over others. At every level in organizations and in every department there will be groups of subordinates under the control of superordinates – in other words, there will be leadership situations.

The term leadership, however, often conveys a rather more glamorous image than that of the mundane world of work. Leaders like Napoleon, Gandhi and Churchill emerge from a broad political context rather than an occupational setting. Authority is vested in them because of their personal gifts and abilities and the charismatic qualities they possess, or at least so we imagine. The example of such leaders gave rise to the earliest attempts at psychological research on the topic: the so-called *trait* theory of leadership. This assumes that certain people are born with a set of key personality characteristics, or traits, which make them 'natural leaders' – indeed, this view of leadership is sometimes termed an 'implicit' theory, or the 'great man' theory of leadership.

As we shall see, the search for these traits has proved relatively fruitless. Another approach has been to study not what sort of person the effective leader is but what he or she actually does. In other words the *behaviour* of leaders becomes the focus of interest. This research has given us a reasonably clear idea of the main dimensions of leadership behaviour. What has been more difficult is the discovery of strong relationships between these dimensions and organizational variables such as productivity, job satisfaction and staff turnover. The recognition that no one pattern of leader behaviour, or leadership 'style', produces high effectiveness has led to the view that certain styles are effective in particular situations but inappropriate in others. We will examine two theories which attempt to predict which styles 'fit' which situation. We will conclude the chapter by examining some of the attempts to translate these insights into what makes a leader effective into leadership training programmes.

LEADERSHIP AS AN ATTRIBUTE OF THE INDIVIDUAL

At first sight the relationship suggested in the heading of this section seems plausible and confirmed by personal experience. The relationship seems further supported by the study of great leaders throughout history. This view of leadership implies that leadership resides in traits or attributes of the individual. In any situation where leadership is appropriate the person with the largest number of desirable traits emerges as the leader. In organizations this would represent an ideal state of affairs for the selection process. Having located the traits and developed measures for them, personnel selection would become a fairly simple and mechanistic affair.

This traditional view of leadership would also suggest a list of variables we would expect it to be associated with. These could be grouped under such headings as physical (height, weight, age, appearance), personality (dominance, self-esteem, aggressiveness), motivational (need for power, need for achievement), status (socio-economic, popularity) and abilities (IQ, experience, inter-personal skills). All of these and many more besides have been correlated against leadership variables.

The search for associations between the personal attributes of a leader and measures of his or her effectiveness dominated leadership research for the first half of this century. In a major review of the trait studies, Stogdill (1948) found enough cumulative evidence to conclude that the average leader was higher than subordinates in intelligence, scholarship, dependability in exercising responsibilities, activity, social participation and socio-economic status. The inconsistency of much of the research results, however, forced Stogdill to a conclusion that proved to be a major turning point in leadership research: 'the evidence suggests that leadership is a relation that exists between persons in a social situation, and that the persons who are leaders in one situation may not necessarily be leaders in other situations'. Stogdill did not rule out the possibility of trait variables explaining some of the differences in the effectiveness of leaders. He regarded their omission from any model of leadership as being as unacceptable as the study of them to the exclusion of all other classes of variable.

More recently, critics of trait research have pointed out that even where correlations do emerge, interpretation of them is far from straightforward. For example, an association between assertiveness and leadership does not tell us whether assertiveness caused the individual to become a leader or the leadership position caused the assertiveness. Even if we had a positive correlation between a trait and leadership variables, where we knew the trait variable was causally prior, we would still be left with a 'partial explanation'. We would not know how or why this particular variable operated to increase leadership effectiveness.

One variable that we would expect to be related to success in leadership is IQ. Organizations consistently prefer to employ bright rather than dull managers. Some studies have found correlations of IQ with leadership effectiveness as low as zero, though the median result of such studies is a small positive correlation of .2 (Fiedler, 1982). The discrepancy between the results of these studies has encouraged some researchers to attempt to explain the absence of a stronger relationship in the data. We have already encountered one such attempt in Chapter 1 when we discussed Fiedler's hypothesis that a series of 'screens' (intervening variables) moderated the effect of a leader's intelligence on his or her effectiveness. Another researcher, Ghiselli (1963) suggested that there is a curvilinear relationship between the two variables. Correlations are reduced if relationships between variables are not linear. To test this idea he sorted a sample of managers into high, medium and low IQ groups. He found that managers in the high and low bands were less likely to achieve success in their management positions. This implies that an optimum level of intelligence is where IQ is high enough for managers to be competent but is not too high, which itself may carry disadvantages – for example, very high IQ levels may be seen as threatening by superordinates or as intimidating by subordinates.

The plausibility of an 'implicit' theory of leadership has meant that interest in trait research has persisted in spite of Stogdill's evidence and conclusions and subsequent criticisms. Recent trait studies, however, have broadened to include the skills, values and needs that leaders possess. Bass (1981) surveyed factorial studies published since 1945 and found twenty-six factors common to more than three studies. The most frequently occurring factors he found were those which described inter-personal, intellectual and technical skills of leaders. The second most frequent were those concerned with how leaders related to their groups, particularly the methods used to motivate and coordinate group activity. The least frequently occurring were factors which related to personal characteristics such as dominance and emotionality. This implies that successful leadership is best understood as resulting from the possession of a set of social skills, rather than personality characteristics.

In the work context, it has often been assumed that attaining a managerial position and being successful in it is not so much a reflection of intellect or personality but more the systematic mapping of the motivational make-up of managers on to organizational life. Research has focused on uncovering what these attitudinal and motivational factors are and to what extent they are related to success in the leadership role. Three large-scale studies provide some tentative answers to these questions. Bass et al. (1979) surveyed over 3,000 middle managers. Respondents were asked to rank eleven life goals. A clear set of preferences emerged, the most preferred goals reflecting self-actualization needs (self-realization and independence). A middle band related to affection, security and competence. Least preferred were prestige and wealth. Though all managers had emphasized 'higher-order' needs, the goals dealing with assertiveness and accomplishment were more often emphasized by faster-climbing managers, whereas those dealing with comfort were chosen by those with slower rates of promotion. Similarly Hofstede (1978), using factor analysis to identify underlying motivational dimensions in the ranking of life goals by 65,000 IBM employees, found two factors that explained 54 per cent of the variation in rankings. One factor stressed comfort rather than accomplishment, the other stressed assertiveness and leadership as opposed to service.

Two contrasting lifestyles were identified by Bray, Campbell and Grant (1974) after studying the progress over eight years of 400 managers in a large American company. These reflected motivational differences in the sample similar to those found in the other studies. They described those who tended to gain in occupational interests and in whom self-actualization needs seemed pre-eminent as 'enlargers'. These individuals were less concerned with friends, parents, family and recreational or social activities than with work. They were more likely to move away from their home towns and stressed the importance of innovation and change in their approach to organizational problems. This contrasted with the 'enfolder' in whom the 'lower-order' security and comfort needs were strongest. They were more likely to stay in their home base and maintain long-term friendships. They were much less likely to engage in self-improvement activities but did not lose their interest in recreational and social activities to the same extent as the 'enlarger'. Bray, Campbell and Grant found these differences were associated with rates of advancement, 'enlargers' being more successful than 'enfolders'.

What may seem surprising is the lack of evidence suggesting that a need for money and wealth is a key component of the motivational make-up of successful managers. Some managers do in fact express a strong interest in pay. The evidence suggests a manager's position in an organization determines the extent to which wealth is a dominant need. Interest in pay tends to be stronger lower down the managerial hierarchy, whereas intrinsic aspects of work and a spiralling search for challenge seem to motivate successful senior and middle managers.

THE EMERGENCE AND MAINTENANCE OF LEADERSHIP

Although leadership positions in formal organizations are assigned to individuals on the basis of experience, seniority or expertise, there are many situations at work where leadership emerges without formal sanction. There are many individuals in the workplace who lack formal status but who nonetheless are perceived as leaders. Many researchers have been interested in how these people acquire leadership roles in groups. The examination of group interaction reveals that the people who become leaders tend to participate early on in group discussion (Hollander, 1978; Sorrentino and Boutillier, 1975). Being the strong silent type is not a successful strategy. Initially the person who emerges as leader is the individual who does the most talking. The quantity of a person's contributions seems to indicate to other group members his or her intention to take a leadership role. The quality of contributions, however, dictates whether the individual remains acceptable as leader since it determines the extent to which an individual is seen by other members as competent and contributing to group goals (Sorrentino and Boutillier, 1975).

Group members seem to look for two types of competence. Firstly, they look for what is termed *socio-emotional* competence. People who are perceived as possessing this are those who appear to be aware of and can influence group relations and cohesion. Secondly, groups identify the level of *task competence* in individuals, people who appear to be able to contribute to the problem-solving capacities and effectiveness of the group (Bales and Slater, 1955). Some researchers have suggested that this broad division can be further broken down into a number of more specific competencies. One study found five types of competence were displayed by naval officers: task achievement; skilful use of leadership; management control; advising and counselling; and coercion. All types of competence other than coercion predicted whether a person would emerge as leader (Winter, 1978).

An interesting distinction has been made between actual and perceived competence. This distinction is similar to that made by Goffman (1971), who argued that the maintenance of the correct 'personal front' enables relatively incompetent individuals to be perceived as competent. Price and Garland (1981) manipulated perceived competence by informing subjects that the leader was either highly competent or relatively incompetent. This had a marked effect both on the willingness of subjects to comply with the requests of the leaders and on the ratings of the leaders' effectiveness, subjects being less willing to comply with leaders perceived as relatively incompetent and rating them as less effective.

Emergence as a leader has also been associated with the extent to which individuals are able to behave with *spontaneity*. People who initiate a wider range of activities within the groups or attempt to develop wider opportunities for individuals to participate are more likely to emerge as group leader. The converse of spontaneity is *contagion*, the extent to which an individual is influenced by others. The skilful leader is able to balance the needs for spontaneity and contagion. Indeed, an individual emerging as group leader is related to the perception by group members of an appropriate balance between the two in his or her behaviour. Unsuccessful initial attempts at leadership may be the result of too much spontaneity and too little contagion, for example, attempting to take the group off in a direction which is not acceptable to group members. On the other hand, the individual who displays no contagion may be seen by group members as simply pursuing the dictates of self-interest.

Having gained the leadership role, a leader may need at some point to initiate activity that does deviate from group norms. This is made possible by earning what are termed *idiosyncrasy credits* (Hollander, 1958; Michener and Lawler,

1975). The leader acquires these by being perceived as displaying competence on the group task and conformity to group norms. Maintaining credits is crucial to survival in the leadership position. It appears that once individuals have acquired the leadership role they may have less latitude to deviate from particular role obligations (Hollander, 1961). This seems to be because leaders have to negotiate with group members a trade-off between being allowed to deviate from general group norms (e.g. hours of work) and conforming closely to other norms such as promoting group cohesion and task performance.

The research on leadership emergence supports the view that what is important is not so much what people are but what they actually do. In the next section we will examine some attempts to identify the key dimensions of leadership behaviour.

LEADERSHIP STYLE

Consideration and initiating structure

In 1945 Shartle instigated the Ohio State University Studies to investigate the nature of leadership behaviour and its relationship to various criteria of leadership effectiveness. He and his associates began by collecting a list of 1,800 phrases which described leadership behaviour. These were then placed into nine different behavioural categories. Of the initial items only 150 fell into only one category. These items formed the first questionnaire designed to assess aspects of leadership behaviour (Hemphill, 1950). Two independent factors emerged when data collected by using the questionnaire was subjected to factor analysis (Halpin and Winer, 1957).

The inter-correlations producing the first factor, *consideration*, were among items like 'exhibits concern for the welfare of group members', 'appreciates good work', 'is easy to approach', 'responds to suggestions' and 'obtains approval of actions'. The inter-correlations producing the second factor, *initiation of structure*, reflected associations between such leader behaviours as 'maintains standards', 'meets deadlines', and 'defines in detail objectives, methods of work and roles'. Two tests, one for subordinates, the leader behaviour description questionnaire (LBDQ) and another for supervisors, the leader opinion questionnaire (LOQ) were then constructed to provide measures of supervisors along each dimension.

The identification of these two dimensions of leadership behaviour and the development of measures enabling supervisors to be measured on each prompted a great deal of research assessing their reliability and validity. A classic study of the effects of interactions between the scales on two organizational variables, grievance rate and turnover rate, established that quite complex relationships existed between the scales and these organizational variables (Fleishman and Harris, 1962). Some of the results are illustrated in

Figure 7.1 As the graph indicates, being low in consideration generates most grievances and is not compensated for by being low in structure. For supervisors medium in consideration, grievance rates were determined by their level of structure. In general a supervisor's level of consideration is positively related to employee satisfaction with the organization and to measures of group and organizational cohesiveness. Initiation of structure, on the other hand, in general negatively correlates with absences, grievance and staff turnover.

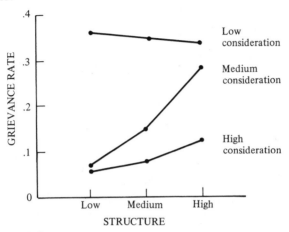

Figure 7.1 *The interaction between structure, consideration and grievance rate.* From E.A. Fleishman and E.F. Harris (1962) 'Patterns of leadership behaviour related to employee grievances and turnover', *Personnel Psychology*, 15, 43–56.

It rapidly became clear, however, that the effects of consideration and structure on the variables of productivity and job satisfaction were moderated by intervening variables such as the type or size of the work unit. For example, an early study by Fleishman and Harris (1955) found that merit ratings for supervisors by their managers were positively related to their level of structure in manufacturing departments but negatively related for supervisors in service departments. Similarly, Schriesheim and Murphy (1976) found that the supervisor's initiation of structure was positively related to subordinates' job satisfaction in large work groups but negatively related in small groups. A number of other aspects of the workplace – the nature of the task, skill differential between supervisor and subordinates – also appear to alter the relationship between effectiveness and the two types of behaviour. At present we do not have a complete understanding of how the relationship between a leader's behaviour and his or her effectiveness is modified by organizational variables.

Some researchers have pointed out that though assumed to be conceptually distinct, empirically the scales used to measure initiating structure and consideration do not appear to operate independently. A number of studies have shown that the scales can correlate with each other. In other words, managers who are high on one scale tend to be high on the other (Schriesheim, House and Kerr, 1976). This has lead to the claim that we can also describe leaders along one general activity factor, termed *motivation to manage vs laissez-faire management*. Laissez-faire or inactive managers are unwilling to accept responsibility, give directions or provide support. They tend to act not so much on their own initiative but in response to specific requests from their staff. There is some evidence that the level of a leader's activity is an important explanatory variable (Bass *et al.*, 1975). Inactivity in leaders is consistently negatively related to productivity, subordinate satisfaction and group cohesiveness (Stogdill, 1974).

While some people have suggested that the Ohio dimensions can be collapsed into one general activity factor, others have stressed the very opposite, that two dimensions are not enough. Bass (1981) argued that by using only two factors much specific information about a leader's behaviour is thrown away. For example, a moderate score on the initiation of structure dimension may mask certain specific difficulties a leader has, such as maintaining work standards. To counter this, some techniques of factor analysis have produced as many as twelve factors describing leadership behaviour. In practical applications, such as counselling, selection or leadership training, where information about a manager's leadership style is required, it may well be important to have available a more detailed description of leadership behaviour.

One of the main problems in interpreting the results of research using the Ohio dimensions is that much of it is of the concurrent correlation type. This means data on leader behaviour and organizational variables are collected at one point in time. We are not able to tell from the results whether high performance has caused high consideration or vice versa; each is equally plausible. This makes studies of the effects of changes in leadership behaviour and organizational variables over time particularly valuable. Unfortunately these studies are few and far between. One series of studies, however, has collected data on leader behaviour, subordinate satisfaction and production at different points in time and across a wide variety of industrial settings (Greene, 1975, 1979). The results suggest that considerate leadership was causally antecedent to increased subordinate satisfaction. But it also seems that changes in the productivity of the subordinates resulted in changes in leadership behaviour. An increase in productivity caused an increase in consideration and a decrease in initiation of structure. In other words there is an *interaction* between leadership behaviour and group output variables. Leaders affect the behaviour of their staff who, in turn, affect the behaviour of their supervisors.

However, despite methodological problems, there are two reasons why initiation of structure and consideration remain the most widely used concepts in leadership research. Firstly, the availability of a reliable and easily administered measure for them means data on the leadership style of individual or groups of supervisors can be gathered quickly. Secondly, the validity of the measures – their ability to account for some of the variance in organizational variables such as productivity and staff turnover indicates that the Ohio researchers have identified two key dimensions of supervisory behaviour.

Democratic vs autocratic leadership

An alternative to the Ohio dimensions of leadership behaviour was developed at another American university, the University of Michigan. These 'Michigan studies' now amount to over 500 surveys, involving over 20,000 managers and 200,000 non-supervisory employees. The dimension at the heart of these studies, democratic–autocratic leadership, is perhaps the most complex construct in the leadership literature. It refers to the way in which decisions are taken, whose needs in the organization are met, what characterizes the relations between leader and follower and how much coercion is present in the relationship between leaders and subordinates.

Many of the studies have used the framework developed by Likert (1961) to capture these aspects of leader–follower relations. Likert proposed four 'systems' of relationships in large organizations which reflected an organization's position on the democratic vs autocratic dimension:

(1) exploitative autocratic
(2) benevolent autocratic
(3) consultative
(4) democratic

Leadership in systems 1 and 2 emphasizes the *legitimacy* of managerial authority, for example, by providing no opportunities for consultation between staff and management. Relationships between leaders and subordinates are formal in system 1. Managers will treat subordinates in an aloof, cold and in extreme instances hostile manner. The chief distinction between systems 1 and 2 involves the nature of control. The benevolent autocrat prefers to control by using rewards, the exploitative autocrat uses more coercive and punitive methods of control. Power in systems 1 and 2 organizations is concentrated at the top with no consultation with subordinates.

The emphasis of leadership in systems 3 and 4 is on the creation of supportive, friendly inter-personal relationships based on trust, participation and two-way communication between follower and leader. The organizational goals of high output and high standards are no different to those in systems 1 and 2 but in systems 3 and 4 the aim is to achieve these objectives by team working and the leader's encouragement of the group members' best efforts, for example by obtaining and making constructive use of subordinates' ideas on improving work methods. Subordinates are also able to influence or determine their performance targets during group goal-setting sessions. In order to study organizations with these different systems of management, Likert developed a measure known as the profile of organizational characteristics (POC). This included the range of variables embraced by the democratic vs autocratic dimension – how decisions are taken, whose needs are met, what characterizes the relations between leaders and subordinates and how much coercion is generally present in the leader–subordinate relationship. Likert was thus able to establish what position an organization occupied along the autocratic vs democratic dimension.

Drawing attention to the autocratic–democratic dimension has however led to a critical problem of leadership and management. This is the apparent conflict that exists between the democratic ideals widespread in most Western industrialized nations, and the practices of work organizations. It seems paradoxical to many people that most organizations within countries claiming to be democratic are autocratic. As Daniel Bell (1948) put it,

> the problem of leadership is shaped by the fact that while we live in a society of political democracy almost all basic social patterns are authoritarian and tend to instill feelings of helplessness and dependence . . . our factories, hierarchical in structure, are, for all the talk of human relations programs, still places where certain men exercise arbitrary authority over others. (p.375)

Likert was completely in favour of system 4 management. His prescription to organizations to move towards system 4 was not just a political campaign. He claimed that such a shift had a positive impact on organizational effectiveness. These effects could occur in any type of industry and range from improvements in employee motivation and job satisfaction to increased productivity. Research had produced correlations of the POC measure with organizational performances ranging from .3 to .6. Likert found that a period of five years may be required for improvements to appear. One organization in a study of three continuous process plants was able to produce immediate savings of a quarter of a million dollars by autocratically imposing cost-saving measures. However, Likert argued that the stoppages and staff losses this resulted in ultimately cost the firm twice that amount (Likert, 1977a). In eleven commercial organizations that had been encouraged to shift towards system 4, before and after studies showed productivity increases of between 15 and 40 per cent. Where control groups were used no similar improvements were found. These improvements continued if the shifts towards democratic arrangements were maintained (Likert, 1977b).

One problem that the Michigan researchers face is that their ideas were developed and tested before the recession at a time when growth and success were the norm for large organizations in Western societies. Currently, change, stress, failure and conflict in organizations have produced conditions that are distinctively different from the period in which the Michigan researchers introduced their arguments. To what extent organizations are willing to experiment by moving towards more democratic styles of leadership in current conditions is, at present, unclear.

Participative vs directive leadership

Although this dimension overlaps with the autocratic vs democratic dimension it is worth including since it relates specifically to the extent to which supervisors direct or consult. At one end of the dimension supervisors attempt to equalize the distribution of power in decision-making using consultation, participation and delegation. This can range from a supervisor involving subordinates in the decision-making but ultimately taking the decision him- or herself, through consulting and achieving a consensus decision, to delegating the entire responsibility for making a decision to the group. Moving up the other end of the continuum entails an increasing portion of the decision-making being taken by the supervisor. This dimension characterizes one key aspect of leader behaviour – decision-making – which may have important effects on group or organizational climate and effectiveness.

Though a useful conceptual contribution, empirically the distinction has proved less useful. Few individual managers have fixed styles of decision-making. Vroom and Yetton (1973) found on asking several thousand managers to indicate their decision-making style in dealing with a variety of situations that only about 10 per cent of managers displayed fixed tendencies to be either directive or participative. Similarly, Bass and Valenzi (1974) found neither extreme reported with any frequencey by subordinates. Consultation, the middle ground in the dimension, was the style reported with the most frequency.

If managers do not stick to one style of decision-making, what makes them decide to consult rather than direct? One variable involved is the skill differential they perceive between themselves and their subordinates. If a manager has reservations about the competence of staff to achieve objectives or their commitment to organizational goals, he or she is likely to use more direction (Rosen and Jerdee, 1977). Conversely, where the differential is less because subordinates are highly qualified, highly educated or highly skilled, managers adopt participatory styles of leadership (Maher, 1976; Bass et al., 1975).

One of the major criticisms of the participative approach to leadership is that it can be much slower and more expensive than directive leadership. In some organizations rapid decision-making may be essential because of the very short time perspectives of the business. Market research firms, for example, are often required to turn a client's brief into an interview schedule, collect and have ready data by the end of the next day. These organizations therefore may need to use a directive style of leadership. The choice of decision-making style may also be influenced by the nature of the technology utilized in the organization. Woodward (1965), for example, found companies using short time-span, batch process as opposed to continuous process production believed directive leadership fitted their technology better than participative leadership.

An interesting approach to the problem of deciding what decision-making style is most appropriate to a particular situation has been developed by Vroom and Yetton (1973). This approach includes both descriptive and prescriptive elements. It enables managers to describe the characteristics of the situation and then derive what style of decision-making he or she ought to adopt. The manager begins by answering seven questions:

(1) Is there a quality requirement such that one solution is better than another?
(2) Does the leader have sufficient information to make a high-quality decision?
(3) Is the problem structured?
(4) Is the acceptance of the decision by subordinates critical to effective implementation?
(5) If the leader were to make the decision by himself is it reasonably certain that it would be accepted by subordinates?
(6) Do subordinates share the organizational goals to be obtained in solving this problem?
(7) Is conflict likely between manager and staff in the preferred solution?

The response to these questions allows what Vroom and Yetton call the 'feasible sets' of leadership styles to be derived:

AI   you solve the problem or make the decision yourself using information available to you;

AII you obtain necessary information from subordinates then decide on the solution to the problem yourself. Subordinates are not asked to generate or evaluate alternative solutions;

CI   you share the problem with relevant subordinates individually, getting their ideas and suggestions, and make a decision which may or may not reflect your subordinates' influence;

CII you share the problem with your subordinates as a group collectively obtaining their ideas and suggestions. Again you make the decision yourself;

GII you share the problem with your subordinates and attempt to reach a solution. You do not try to influence the group to adopt your solution and you are willing to accept and implement any solution which has the support of the entire group.

The relationship between the decisions and the feasible sets is illustrated in Figure 7.2.

Vroom has buttressed his ideas with some empirical support. In one study (Vroom and Jago, 1978), ninety-six managers were asked to describe their leadership style in a number of situations. They were also asked to describe the quality and acceptance of the solution in each situation. The results indicated that the effectiveness of the solution, particularly subordinates' acceptance of it, declined the more the model's rules were violated.

Underlying the Vroom and Yetton model is the assumption that there is a strong relationship between the acceptance of a decision and the level of participation by subordinates in it. Whenever quality and acceptance of decisions are important, participation is indicated in the feasible set of leadership styles (Field, 1979).

The assumption that there is a strong positive relationship between the

QUESTIONS

1	2	3	4	5	6	7
Is there a quality requirement?	Do I have sufficient information to make a high quality decision?	Is the problem structured?	Is the acceptance of the decision by subordinates critical to effective implementation?	If I make the decision myself is it reasonably certain that it would be accepted by my subordinates?	Do subordinates share the organizational goals to be obtained in solving this problem?	Is conflict likely in preferred solutions?

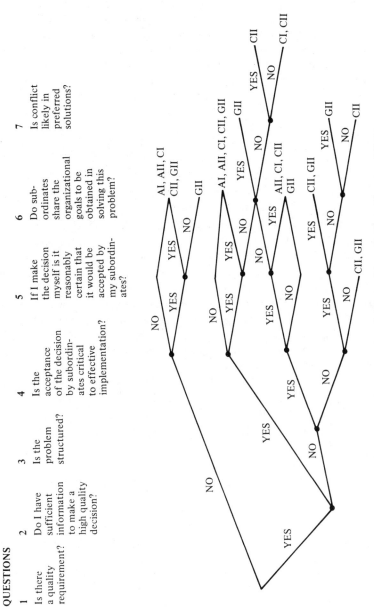

Figure 7.2 *Decision tree for identifying appropriate decision-making style.* From Vroom and Yetton (1973) © 1973 by University of Pittsburgh Press.

quality and acceptance of a decision and the amount of participation by subordinates in it stems from evidence suggesting participation harnesses positive motivational and group dynamic effects. Decision quality, for instance, is thought to draw on the group dynamic phenomenon, *synergy*, discussed in Chapter 5, which produces group decisions usually of higher quality than the average group member (though sometimes not as good as the best group member). At the individual level, participative leadership is thought to increase the 'ego involvement' of subordinates with the organization, and their 'psychological entry' into the organization and its decisions. Most of the available evidence does in fact support the relationship between subordinate acceptance of decisions and participative leadership styles (Bass, 1981). In addition, there is some evidence to suggest that as well as improving decision quality and subordinate acceptance of decisions, participative leadership can also lead to increased satisfaction with the job and supervision.

A major problem for participative leadership is the ease with which group members can perceive it as manipulation. Some research indicates staff in organizations which are attempting to adopt participative methods of decision-making do perceive it in this way and feel they have actually lost some of their power (Richbell, 1976). There are also some issues which raise basic questions of power and interests, redundancies, for example, where participation would be difficult if not impossible. Furthermore, the handing over of decision-making power to staff may not be greeted with equal enthusiasm by all supervisors since it may blur role definitions and reduce the differential in status between staff and supervisor which can make many supervisors feel uncomfortable (Clegg and Fitter, 1978). Though recent EEC legislation now makes it obligatory for companies to give an account in their annual report of the progress made in installing participative decision-making procedures, the types of decision companies are prepared to have taken participatively remain for the most part very limited.

Task-oriented vs relationship-oriented leadership

Stogdill's review of the trait literature encouraged a recognition of the part situational variables played in the explanation of leadership effectiveness. Although much of the subsequent empirical research included situational variables, little theoretical development occurred to assist in the explanation of results of this more broadly based research. However, the publication of Fred Fiedler's *A Theory of Leadership Effectiveness* (1967) ended this atheoretical phase of leadership research. Fiedler presented an elaborate theory that attempted to account for the contingent nature of leadership effectiveness.

Fiedler began by distinguishing leadership behaviour from leadership style. Leadership behaviour is the specific response a supervisor makes in a particular situation. Unlike most other researchers Fiedler believed that leadership style – consistencies in the pattern of responses across different situations – was a relatively fixed feature of individuals which reflected a supervisor's motivational make-up.

He proposed that leadership style is fundamentally characterized along a dimension termed task-oriented leadership vs relationship-oriented leadership. He developed an instrument, the least preferred co-worker (LPC) scale, which provided a measure of an individual's position on the dimension and by implication his or her motivational make-up. The LPC score is derived by a supervisor describing on a number of bipolar adjectival scales the person they have found the most difficult to work with. Thus, a supervisor would rate the least preferred co-worker along eight point scales like friendly–unfriendly, intelligent–unintelligent. A high score is obtained by placing the least preferred co-worker towards the positive end of each scale. Fiedler interprets the high-scoring supervisor as an individual who is concerned with establishing good interpersonal relations, more considerate and lower in anxiety. High scorers are also more 'cognitively complex' since they are able to separate out evaluations of the least preferred co-worker's job performance from evaluations of his or her personality and ability. The high scorer acquires self-esteem not through the intrinsic satisfaction of a job well done but through the recognition by others of his or her competence. A low score is acquired by denigrating the least preferred co-worker, describing him or her as unintelligent, lazy and unfriendly. This is thought to reflect a lack of concern with personal relationships and by implication more concern with the task. The low scorer is presumed to be less cognitively complex than the high scorer, being unable to differentiate work performance and personality. Successful task performance is the principal source of satisfaction for the low scorer. Both high and low scorers are concerned with the task and inter-personal relationships. The high-scoring supervisor is concerned with the task in order to achieve successful relationships. The low-scoring leader is concerned with inter-personal relationships in order to achieve successful task performance. Fiedler argued that low-scoring and high-scoring leaders differ in behaviour most when the satisfaction of their needs is threatened.

Fiedler's second task was to construct a satisfactory method of describing and measuring leadership situations. An important feature of leadership positions, he argued, is the extent to which the authority of the leader is legitimized by the organization. Does the leader have the power to hire and fire? Are there large differences in status and rank? This feature of leadership situations he termed the leader's *position power*, and a checklist was devised to provide a measure of it.

The second feature of leadership situations which he sought to describe was the *task structure*. Some tasks are routine, and have one route to a single solution, while others are less straightforward. He classified task structure using four dimensions: goal clarity, the degree to which the goal requirements are clearly ascertainable; decision verifiability, the degree to which it is possible to know whether a solution is correct, goal path multiplicity, the number of

147

possible routes to the goal; and solution specificity, the number of possible solutions.

The third feature of the situation that Fiedler built into the model was what he called *leader–group relations*. If leader–group relations were good the leader was accepted, group members were loyal and communication easier. Fiedler devised an instrument (the group atmosphere score) which yielded a measure of leader–group relations.

These three aspects of the work situation Fiedler presumed captured the essential features of leadership situations. Research on a large number of work groups in a variety of work settings showed that the relationship between a supervisor's style and his or her effectiveness was mediated by the leadership situation. Thus the final task for Fiedler was to describe and explain the interaction between leadership style, the leadership situation and the leader's effectiveness.

In order to identify the pattern of this interaction Fiedler simplified his concept of a leadership situation by combining the three measures of it (position power, task structure and leader–group relations) into one representing the *favourability* of the situation to the leader. To do this Fiedler assumed that the most important determinant of situation favourability was leader–group relations followed by task structure and position power. He then divided each of these three measures into two on the basis of the median point that had been identified for each scale by his research. By combining each of the three, now dichotomized, dimensions in their order of importance he created a dimension comprised of eight (2 x 2 x 2) octants representing situational favourability. Thus, according to Fiedler the most favourable situation was one in which leader–group relations were good and task structure and position power were high. Conversely, the least favourable situation for a supervisor was one in which he or she faced poor leader–group relations, low task structure and low position power.

Fiedler then plotted each of his research studies by placing them on the horizontal dimension according to what octant they fell into and plotted them on the vertical axis according to the correlation found between the supervisor's LPC score and his or her team's effectiveness.

To summarize the interaction between leadership style, situational favourability and effectiveness, Fiedler drew a line connecting the median correlations of studies in each octant (Figure 7.3). Fiedler found that low LPC leaders were most effective when the situation was either highly favourable or highly unfavourable.

In situations of moderate favourability high-scoring supervisors performed best. This represented an important correction to the prevailing human relations view that relationship-oriented supervision was always preferable.

Fiedler explained his conclusions by arguing that since high and low LPC leaders seek to satisfy different needs, situations that threaten the satisfaction of those needs will trigger very different behaviours in each. In situations of low

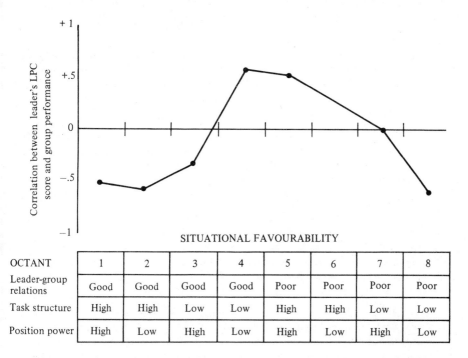

OCTANT	1	2	3	4	5	6	7	8
Leader-group relations	Good	Good	Good	Good	Poor	Poor	Poor	Poor
Task structure	High	High	Low	Low	High	High	Low	Low
Position power	High	Low	High	Low	High	Low	High	Low

Figure 7.3 *The relationship between situational favourability and leaders' LPC score. The bow shape was formed by joining the median correlation for studies in each octant between LPC scores and group performance.* From Fiedler (1967).

favourability the group is best served by directive and structuring leadership and the needs of low LPC leaders are more likely to produce these behaviours. In jobs where there is a low level of task structure, for example where the goals are not clear or the number of possible routes to a solution is high, directive and structuring leadership may be welcomed by group members in order to reduce their frustration and anxiety. Conversely, highly favourable situations where jobs are routinized, the position of power is high and leader–group relations are good, provide an environment in which the low LPC leaders' needs are not threatened, enabling them to relax and becomes less structuring.

Highly favourable situations produce very different behaviours in a high LPC supervisor. Since there are already good relations they become more involved and structuring which, since the task is already highly structured, is likely to be resented by group members.

In situations of moderate favourability where conditions are mixed the relationship-oriented high LPC scorer performs better since it is in these positions that inter-personal relations play an important part in determining the work group's productivity.

The hallmark of any good theory is the number of specific and testable predictions it is able to generate. Fiedler's theory produces a large number of predictions, many of which predict results that we would not expect on the basis of common sense. For example, we would expect increased experience to be associated with increased effectiveness in a leader. Correlations between the two do not confirm this (Fiedler, 1970). Fiedler (in Fiedler *et al.*, 1975; Fiedler, 1982) points out that the absence of a relationship can be predicted using his theory. The effect of experience on the effectiveness of a leader would depend on the LPC of the leader and the initial level of situational favourability. The high LPC leader will benefit from experience since it would make the situation more favourable. The effects of increased experience in conditions of low situational favourability for the low LPC leader is to reduce effectiveness since it changes the situation to one in which their behaviour is least effective. Converse predictions for high and low LPC leaders occur if situational favourability is initially moderate. Some evidence is available to support these predictions (Fiedler, *et al.*, 1975).

Research has supported other predictions derived from the model. One review of 178 studies testing various predictions derived from the model concluded that despite numerous exceptions the majority of the studies supported it (Strube and Garcia, 1981). Critics of the model, however, have argued that a distinction has to be made between studies that are relevant tests of the model and those that are less relevant to it. Schriesheim and Hosking (1978), for example, argued that relevant studies are those that test all eight octants and use adequate sample sizes in each to provide the necessary statistical power to results. They claim that at present there are not enough studies testing all eight octants simultaneously to provide the model with sufficient empirical support.

Given the scope of the model it is hardly surprising that it has received mixed support. There is no doubt, however, that there are some specific problems with the model. Some studies have shown LPC scores are not as fixed as Fiedler envisaged and may not be independent of group performance (Katz and Farris, 1976). This implies that changes in group performance may lead to changes in a leader's style. Group performance may also affect leader–member relations (Vroom, 1976). However, Fiedler's attempt to explain the nature of leadership effectiveness represented a considerable advance in leadership theory, and his basic finding that the effectiveness of a leadership style was contingent on the situation remains the view that most behavioural scientists still subscribe to.

Path–goal theory

Path–goal theory is an attempt to integrate theories of leadership, motivation and job satisfaction. It utilizes aspects of the Michigan and Ohio studies, Fiedler's contingency theory and the VIE theory of motivation (see Chapter 4). Path–goal theory began in the late 1950s but did not attract much attention until it was popularized by Evans (1970) and House (1971). Though now considerably modified, the apparent promise of the theory has allowed it to continue exerting considerable influence in leadership research, even in the absence of clear empirical support.

Path–goal theory begins by assuming that leaders must be capable of displaying four types of behaviour:

(1) initiation of structure;
(2) consideration;
(3) participation;
(4) goal setting.

Like Fiedler's theory, path–goal theory is a contingency theory. But while Fiedler specified three factors mediating the effect of leader behaviour on leadership effectiveness, path–goal theory specifies a much broader range of variables. In fact the list of contingency variables suggested by path–goal theory includes any relevant characteristics of subordinates and environment. We have already seen that an important subordinate variable is level of skill or ability; others might reflect motivational and personality characteristics such as the locus of control, need for affiliation and authoritarianism. Environmental variables would include Fiedler's task structure, authority system, type of organization and amount of performance feedback. What integrates the leadership behaviours and the contingency factors is VIE motivational theory. This theory assumes people are motivated if they perceive connections or 'instrumentalities' between their effort, performance and the attainment of valued rewards. This implies that the effective leader is the leader who is able to modify these key perceptions in subordinates. By providing the appropriate leadership behaviour given the nature of the staff and leadership situation, supervisors can influence the clarity of subordinate perceptions of paths to goals, the desirability of goals and the link between effort and goal attainment.

As well as dealing with the perceptions of links between effort and reward, a leader needs to behave in a way that makes subordinates believe he or she is instrumental in goal attainment. Therefore, leaders seen as assisting in attaining valued ends are more likely to be accepted. In practice, this means providing assistance, coaching, guidance and rewards. It can also mean consulting and standing up for subordinates by defending their interests.

Which of these behaviours is selected is decided by what seems most likely to lead to the attainment of valued rewards by subordinates. For example, considerate leadership is expected to correlate more highly with productivity and job satisfaction in structured situations. Initiation of structure is more appropriate in unstructured situations. Similarly, if subordinates are self-actualizers they are likely to need participative leadership, whereas authoritarian subordinates would require initiation of structure in order to be satisfied with their job and leader. When the leader is able to display the correct leadership behaviour path–goal theory predicts rises in motivation, job satisfaction, satisfaction with supervisors and performance.

By combining path–goal variables a large number of predictions can be derived. For example, combining two styles of leadership and three levels of task structure produces six predictions. In view of this, researchers have tended to concentrate on consideration, initiation of structure and levels of task structure. Some predictions of path–goal theory have been supported. Greene (1979), for example, classified the work of a sample of engineers, scientists and technicians according to the amount of structure present in their work. Initiation of structure was positively correlated with subordinate job satisfaction and performance if low task structure was present. If the task was highly structured, initiation of structure was negatively correlated with subordinate job satisfaction and was not predictive of performance.

A wider range of path–goal predictions was tested in two studies by Schriesheim and de Nisi (1981). The first study was based on 110 employees working for a medium-sized bank, the second on 205 employees of a medium-sized manufacturing plant. The task variables used by the researchers included task variety, feedback and whether the job involved dealing with other people. Path–goal theory predicted that initiation of structure would increase job satisfaction when individuals perceived their jobs as varied, low in feedback and involving little contact with other people. Conversely, for routine jobs where feedback was already present and subordinates dealt with other people, initiation of structure would be redundant and would actually reduce job satisfaction. Schriesheim and de Nisi's results confirmed these predictions.

Generally, however, support for path–goal theory has been mixed. Research has provided strongest support for path–goal predictions which have either used consideration as a predictor or job satisfaction as a criterion (the variable being predicted). However, despite mixed support, path–goal theory continues to attract considerable attention from behavioural scientists. It is seen by many researchers as more flexible than Fiedler's theory since the range of contingency variables it embraces is potentially much larger. In addition, combining contingency variables offers behavioural scientists a large number of specific hypotheses to test. Finally, what makes path–goal theory especially attractive to many researchers is the logic of VIE theory it incorporates which provides a solid theoretical basis for making predictions about the effect of various leadership styles in specific work situations.

LEADERSHIP TRAINING: FROM THEORY TO PRACTICE

Sensitivity training

Leadership research has provided us with a composite picture of effective leaders. They are the individuals who are sensitive to key contingency variables and so can alter their leadership style accordingly. They are able to initiate, maintain and enhance expectations of success within their work groups. Their decisions are accepted because they are perceived as competent by other group members. As we have seen, effective leaders are continuously negotiating their role with their subordinates. In this context group members exchange their compliance in return for the leader meeting their needs.

In order to meet the group's needs a leader must first be able to perceive them. Therefore, the development of leaders' sensitivity to subordinates' needs has been a key area in leadership training. A number of techniques have been developed to do just this. The best known of these, the T-group (T for training), has been the subject of much controversy since it was developed in the late 1940s. A T-group consists of about twelve trainees and one trainer. The usual factors such as agendas and work roles which guide interaction in the workplace are absent. The task of the trainees is to interact and then at points analyse what has occurred in the group, for example, what roles have emerged, who is participating and who is becoming dependent on whom. The trainer throws the burden of keeping the interaction going almost entirely on the group, intervening only occasionally to reflect on what is occurring in the group or to encourage participation.

Trainers believe that this sequence of interaction, analysis and feedback promotes:

(1) an increased self-awareness;
(2) an increased awareness of the needs of subordinates;
(3) an increased desire to share information;
(4) an increased desire to reach decisions participatively;
(5) a shift towards less formal styles of interaction with subordinates;
(6) a reduction in assertive and directive leadership behaviour.

A number of studies of the effects of T-groups suggest that the experience does, in general, produce the desired outcomes (Bass, 1981). However, a number of behavioural scientists have doubts about the use of T-groups. Some critics claim the technique is simply *unethical* because it may invade individual privacy, disrupt an individual's defence systems and pressure group members to conform. In addition trainees may be required to assume that the trainer's values are superior to their own. While some people undoubtedly find T-groups a powerful psychological experience, the emotional stress involved can produce 'casualties' in the group, trainees sometimes actually requiring psychiatric help afterwards. In reply to these criticisms trainers claim that the benefits of T-group training make the small amount of stress and damage it may cause acceptable (e.g. Cooper, 1975).

A second problem for trainers is demonstrating that the learning which occurs in the group is *transferrable* to the workplace. Some critics have suggested that trainees can have difficulty perceiving a link between the learning of abstract social-psychological concepts and practical problems in their workplace. In response to this trainers are increasingly complementing the T-group activity with exercises such as role-playing based on trainees' current work problems. Following the failure of trainees to transfer their learning back to their workplace one trainer went a stage further and decided to move into the compnay as a consultant. This enabled him to join formal work group meetings within the plant. From this vantage he was able to explore the use of authority, communications, inter-personal relations and role definitions in real day-to-day work problems (Bamforth, 1965).

In an effort to reduce the variability in the effects of T-groups caused by differences in the skill of trainers, standardized and self-administered sensitivity training techniques have been developed. These typically involve group problem-solving exercises followed by feedback and discussion. A widely used example of this is 'Lost on the Moon' (Hall, 1971) described in Chapter 6. Though not as powerful an experience as a T-group, the exercise, particularly when combined with audio-visual feedback, similarly gives trainees an indication of the way they respond in groups and of the impact of their behaviour on other people.

Leader match training

Fiedler's contribution to leadership theory has been immense and attempts have been made to translate his insights into a leadership training programme. You may remember that the distinctive difference between Fiedler's contingency theory was in his conceptualization of leadership style. Path–goal theory assumes, in principle, that it is possible for a leader to change the leadership style according to contingency variables. Fiedler however assumed leadership style was a reflection of relatively permanent personality and motivational variables. If this is correct it would be easier to teach leaders how to change the situation than change themselves. Fiedler and Chemars (1984) developed a training programme called leader match training based on this assumption. The first stage of the programme is the assessment of where a trainee is on the task-oriented–relations-oriented dimension. This indicates what sort of situations each leader is likely to be effective in. The trainee is then taught how to assess the favourability of a work situation and how to change the situation to suit his or her leadership style. Support for this approach comes from twelve studies in which performance evaluations of trainees were taken from two to six months after the course (Fiedler and Mahar, 1979). Performance ratings of 423 trained leaders were compared to ratings of 480 leaders in control groups. The results indicated leader match trainees had significantly higher ratings than control groups.

The value of leader match training, however, is doubted by a number of researchers. We have already seen that the notion of fixed leadership styles has been questioned. In addition the 'match' between leadership style and leadership situation was based on the median correlation of effectiveness and style in the original studies. In some octants along Fiedler's dimension of situational favourability the median result masks a considerable range in the size and direction of correlations between leadership style and effectiveness. Thus, some behavioural scientists claim that Fiedler's contingency theory is at present not sufficiently proven for it to form the basis of a specific training programme.

Rational training

Other contingency theories assume flexibility in leadership style. Vroom and Yetton's model, as we have seen, provides rules for leaders to assist them in choosing between participative and directive styles of leadership. They have developed a programme known as rational training. This, they claim, enables trainees to understand the cause of discrepancies between their own way of approaching leadership problems and that prescribed by their model. Trainees are encouraged to focus on:

(1) the situations in which they are prepared to behave participatively, and those in which they are directive;
(2) whether they are more concerned with the development of their staff or working within time constraints;
(3) whether they are more concerned with decision quality than decision acceptability;
(4) which Vroom and Yetton rules they are adhering to and which they are violating.

Vroom and Yetton's model and the training associated with it operates primarily at the cognitive level; it sensitizes managers to a range of variables and helps them conceptualize the leadership problem. Support for their approach has, in general, been mixed. One study, for example, found that while managers who had been through their training programme enjoyed greater acceptance of their decisions by subordinates there was no effect on the quality of their decisions (Vroom and Jago, 1978).

Skill training

Much leadership training is now based on skill theory. Leadership skills such as information-gathering, interviewing, counselling, negotiating, motivating, and using feedback are assumed, like other skills, to be organized hierarchically with a cognitive component ultimately governing the behavioural responses. The leadership trainer therefore divides the training programme equally between developing the ability of trainees to develop adequate cognitive models of their staff and work situation and developing the behaviours associated with the skill through practice and feedback. For example, to improve trainees' skill of motivating staff the trainer would spend a day exploring theories of motivation with trainees using motivational theories to identify the possible 'blocks' in organizations which reduce the inclination to work and 'boosters' which improve motivation.

In the next stage the trainer role plays a member of the trainee's staff and is interviewed by the trainee who uses the conceptual material acquired in stage 1 to guide the interview. This is followed by a feedback session in which the trainer and other trainees comment on the effectiveness of the interview in terms of how effectively the subordinate's current motivational state was diagnosed and to what extent the interview would have increased his or her motivation. Further practice interviews are arranged for the trainee on the basis of these comments and suggestions, and the procedure is repeated until the trainee's performance is considered satisfactory.

In conclusion, we have explored a range of attempts to develop training programmes out of the leadership theories available. Human relations theorists have established a tradition which emphasizes an increased awareness of self and of group dynamics. They would argue that the relationship-oriented style of leadership which emerges from an increased sensitivity to group dynamics is preferable and more effective. In contrast, contingency theorists assume that a leader's effectiveness is the result of an interaction of a leader with a situation. They train supervisors to analyse their own behaviour and leadership situation and to change aspects of either to produce a better fit. Skill theorists bring the insights of skill theory to the traditional human relations perspective by developing a leader's ability to comprehend his or her staff and using these macro-cognitive changes to develop the micro-behavioural responses involved in skilled leadership. Each will persist and continue to be developed, and in their different ways contribute to achieving the broad aims of the human relations movement set out some fifty years ago, to increase social skill and insight into the social dynamics of the workplace among supervisors and thus reduce the level of social incompetence in the management of organizations.

FURTHER READING

Adair, J. (1983) *Effective Leadership: A Self Development Manual.* Aldershot: Gower.

Bennis, W. and B. Narious (1985) *Leaders.* New York: Harper and Row.

Blake, R. and J.S. Mouton (1986) *Executive Achievement.* London: McGraw-Hill.

Brannen, P. (1983) *Authority and Participation in Industry.* London: Batsford.

Guest, D. and K. Knight (1979) *Putting Participation into Practice.* Farnborough: Gower.

Hunt, J.G. (ed.) (1984) *Leaders and Managers: International Perspectives on Managerial Behaviour and Leadership.* Oxford: Pergamon Press.

Hunt, J.G., U. Sekaran and C.A. Schriesheim (eds.) (1982) *Leadership Beyond Establishment Views.* Carbondale: Southern Illinois University Press.

Irwin, R. and R. Wolenik (1985) *Winning Strategies for Managing People.* London: Kogan Page.

Mant, A. (1983) *Leaders We Deserve*. Oxford: Martin Robertson.

Pedler, M. and T. Boydell (1985) *Managing Yourself*. London: Fontana.

Pedler, M., J. Burgoyne and T. Boydell (eds.) (1986) *A Manager's Guide to Self-Development* (2nd ed.). Maidenhead: McGraw-Hill.

Whetton, D.A. and K. Cameron (1984) *Developing Management Skills*. Glenview Ill.: Scott, Foresman.

Williamson, J.N. (ed.) (1984) *The Leader-Manager*. New York: Wiley.

Wright, P.L. and D.S. Taylor (1984) *Improving Leadership Performance*. London: Prentice-Hall.

8

Alternative Work Design

The expectations that we have of employment in a modern industrial society include social rewards as well as purely economic ones. Yet, leaving aside adequate economic returns, the human needs of people in work are very often frustrated by jobs, many of which make little or no allowance for individual commitment or the exercise of skills and initiative. This is widely perceived as constituting a serious problem. The human and social problems of dissatisfaction experienced in work may in turn lead to economic problems for employers. Poor productivity and quality of output, the 'withdrawal' from work manifest as absenteeism and labour turnover, as well as various types of industrial conflict, like strikes and sabotage, have all been linked with low levels of worker motivation. However, there is an equally widely shared conviction that management's goals of performance can be reconciled with workers' interest in more satisfying and fulfilling work.

The attempt to organize work along more humane and democratic lines has long been a concern of social scientists and socially aware employers. And social psychology has made a contribution to these efforts which goes back at least to the Hawthorne experiments in the 1920s. The 'discovery' of socio-psychological factors in work marked the beginning of the human relations movement, which developed very fully theories about employee behaviour in work groups. Indeed, in different ways the theories of motivation and group dynamics that were reviewed in the last four chapters have all been concerned with the question of appropriate occupational rewards and appropriate work settings. Recently, however, much of this interest has focused on the problem of changing the actual jobs that people perform, and in this chapter we will be looking at these central issues in the redesign of work.

Wall (1982) has defined work redesign as the attempt 'to organise the work of individuals or groups in such a way as to provide greater complexity with respect to one or more of the following characteristics: variety, autonomy and completeness of task'.

THE TECHNIQUES OF WORK REDESIGN

Two basic approaches to the redesign of work involve rotating the jobs that workers do and enlarging individual work tasks. Job rotation does not actually mean changing the work itself, but it permits a greater variety for individuals by moving them between jobs. In practice, managers often use this method without necessarily having a formal system of rotating workers at regular intervals. They may simply ensure that particularly unpleasant or monotonous jobs are shared, and that certain workers are not allocated to them permanently. Secondly, job enlargement involves merging a number of simplified tasks to form a single task with an extended range of work. In mass assembly industries, for instance, this often means that cycle times (i.e. the time taken to complete a single cycle of a repetitive task) are not allowed to fall below some stipulated minimum level, so there is a limit placed on the extent to which jobs can be subdivided.

However, each of these methods is thought to be inadequate as a basis for genuinely humanizing work. Job rotation merely redistributes existing work, and job enlargement involves regrouping unit tasks rather than seeking to improve the work itself. At best, it has been argued, these methods make cosmetic changes. At worst they may bring about an actual deterioration in working conditions. For example, if job rotation is used chiefly to create a more flexible workforce, workers may find themselves being moved from job to job without being consulted. This may disrupt the rhythm of work, and even threaten job security if workers become interchangeable. Similarly, the enlargement of jobs sometimes merely results in an intensification of work. People often cope with monotonous jobs by mentally 'switching off' to some extent, but work that involves a whole series of repetitive tasks may require much closer attention. The most unpleasant and taxing jobs are often those that are monotonous and also demand high levels of attention.

The 'enrichment' of work

There are however other methods regarded as more meaningful ways of redesigning work. Two of the most important ones are *job enrichment* and the provision for *group working*. The basic purpose of job enrichment is to introduce responsibilities or additional tasks into a job which genuinely do make it more of a complete occupation. Many routinized production jobs can be enriched by the inclusion of tasks such as machine maintenance, elements of inspection and quality control, or machine-setting. It may also be possible for workers to arrange to obtain their own materials, or to deal with communications with other departments. Changes like these can enhance workers' skills and enable them to deal with complete tasks rather than highly fragmented ones. Thus, instead of similar degraded tasks being combined together, genuine job enrichment means that a certain amount of planning and control is

159

introduced into the work – tasks which otherwise would have been the responsibility of supervisors or specialist groups of workers.

Secondly, group working has many potential advantages. There are manifest social and psychological gains in working cooperatively with others, rather than on isolated tasks; also many of the requirements of job enrichment can be built into the group context. Group tasks by their very nature tend to be based on complete operations and involve greater complexity and variety than fragmented tasks. Groups can be self-regulating, reducing the need for supervision and increasing members' perception of control. Furthermore, it is relatively easy to allow for job rotation and the fair allocation of tasks within a group system of working – indeed it can be beneficial to allow group members to arrange this for themselves.

Some widely publicized projects have utilized group-based methods. For instance, certain aspects of car assembly have been rearranged from the straight-line system to a 'dock' system, with workers responsible for clusters of tasks. Such an approach was used in axle production at Renault's Le Mans plant and in engine assembly at Saab–Scania, both of which achieved substantial increases in cycle times and levels of group responsibility.

The car assembly plant built by Volvo at Kalmar in Sweden is probably the best known of all work redesign programmes. Starting from scratch on a greenfield site, Volvo designed a revolutionary method of car production which in effect combined the features of line and dock assembly. Work groups were located in assembly bays, and the car bodies were mounted on self-propelling skips guided by a conductive tape which moved in and out of the bays. The technology allowed work groups to call up cars from the main track to be worked on, after which they would be sent back out into the plant. Group tasks involved complete assemblies on identifiable sections of the car.

Such a technology satisfied practically all the requirements of job enrichment. People worked in groups, and to a degree controlled their own pace of work rather than it being dictated by the assembly line. Most workers learnt more than one task; work groups also had responsibility for complete tasks and for things like initial quality checks and ensuring supplies of materials. In this way Volvo succeeded in giving a human face to a type of work that is universally regarded as being alienating in the extreme. Over the years good economic results have been obtained from Kalmar, and it has proved to be the catalyst for other similar plants. In addition, the company is also justly famous for its broader progress towards more democratic working methods (Gyllenhammar, 1977).

The socio-technical systems approach

The application of group theory to the work situation has been greatly advanced by the researchers of the Tavistock Institute of Human Relations. Their distinctive approach, developed in a series of classic studies in the British coal-mining industry and later in the Indian textiles industry, stressed an active involvement on the part of researchers in diagnosing firms' problems and proposing long-term solutions.

The Tavistock's interest in work groups began in the late 1940s when one of their researchers, Eric Trist, investigated the reasons for the failure of mechanization in coal-mining to bring about improvements in productivity, and for the poor state of industrial relations in the industry. Before mechanization, coal had been extracted manually by small teams of miners. Each shift team worked a section of the coalface, miners shared all the tasks in the coal-getting cycle (cutting, removal, and advancing the seam), and teams were paid in a lump sum which would be distributed according to group consensus. These shift teams became highly cohesive social units, with strong emotional bonds developing between members which helped them deal with the dangerous and difficult conditions in which they worked (Trist and Bamforth, 1951).

However, the arrival of new technology (conveyor belts and coal-cutting machinery) transformed the old methods, and also seemed to require a different set of social relationships. With the new method, each shift consisted of a large group of miners under a supervisor, a novel role in coal production. The team was divided into specialists and performed only one phase of the work. An elaborate pay structure led to a status hierarchy developing among miners; and these divisions were compounded by physical separation as miners worked on greatly extended seams. The severe production and industrial relations problems caused by these changes included coordination difficulties as shifts were unable or unwilling to clear work left by the previous shift, and problems of control due to miners' resentment of being supervised.

Trist recognized the central problem of the impact of technological advances on traditional group working practices. Any solution would have to involve 'the general character of the method so that a social as well as a technological whole can come into existence' (Trist and Bamforth, 1951). This line of thought led to the concept of work organization as a *socio-technical system*. It implied that the work setting has to be seen in terms of two inter-related systems: a social and a technical system, each with its own independent properties. Further, the optimization of one system could occur at the expense of the other, and of the system as a whole. But while optimizing the overall system does usually mean sub-optimal states for each component, ideally the costs would be balanced out so that no one system carried them all. (Whereas what had occurred in mining was that optimization of the technology had led to a severely sub-optimal state in the miners' group relationships.)

Using this concept, Tavistock researchers designed a 'composite' method, which still utilized the new technology but modified the working arrangements. Groups of miners were divided into three shift-teams. Each miner acquired the skills in all phases of the work cycle, miners could choose what shift they worked on and the task they wanted within each shift. The pay structure was dismantled and replaced with a shared productivity bonus. These modifications reduced the coordination and supervisory problems, as well as satisfying miners' socio-psychological needs for more meaningful work and satisfactory relations with other miners.

The first direct application of Trist's socio-technical principle came with research conducted by A. K. Rice in an Indian textile mill (Rice, 1958). As with the mining study, mechanization had disrupted an established work pattern. The introduction of automatic looms had deskilled jobs and turned workers into machine-minders, the effects of which had nullified any expected productivity gains. In this context, Rice helped to introduce a group working system, later extending it to non-automatic weaving. Both systems were based on small groups of workers, self-regulating and self-led, responsible for clusters of looms, and performing all the tasks of weaving. This resulted in steady improvements in output and quality of cloth. Rice also stressed the very high value that workers placed on these cooperative working arrangements. Once they had been given the opportunity to reorganize themselves into secure groups, workers showed great determination in making the new system successful.

The model of production as a socio-technical system provided a framework within which Rice included a broad range of factors. For example, he noted that workers' attachment to the group system was strengthened by elements of Indian culture, particularly the tradition of collective working in family-based cottage industries. In addition, the enhancement of work had meant that jobs became more demanding, and Rice was very clear about the responsibility of management to provide adequate training and technical support for the new groups.

Interestingly, in his follow-up study, conducted some fifteen years after Rice's original research, Miller (1975) confirmed the importance of these aspects of the work context. Miller found that in automatic weaving production had reverted to individual methods, while in the non-automatic sheds the group system had survived remarkably intact. He explained this by the different impact of increased work pressure on the two production systems. Workers' strong attachment to the groups made them resilient over the long term, but under excessive pressure some of the groups had been unable to adjust. Here, a failure of management to continue to provide support and protection for the groups had accounted for the collapse of group working.

Tavistock principles can be applied in their fullest form not on mining and textiles projects but on new, 'greenfield' sites where the technology is not already established. As Rice (1958, p.250) pointed out, innovation is all too frequently obsessed with the technological side, while the human aspects are only considered as an afterthought, or when changes have been resisted. The concept of production as a socio-technical system implies that *both* subsystems are equally important.

For example, Klein (1981) has described the design of a new plant for the confectionery company, Trebor. Because of strong company interest in the human side of work, she was able to examine the social consequences of particular layouts and equipment with the design team. This resulted in the building of an impressive factory, with single-status facilities, pleasant surroundings, and a group-based production process. As Klein was at pains to emphasize, however, the different groups involved (architects, equipment suppliers, management) were not always in harmony; and the involvement of a social scientist was no automatic guarantee of a humane environment being achieved. Amid the 'welter of activities' a number of potentially important choices as to how work might be organized were lost. Nevertheless, it remains true that the work process is more likely to be optimized where choices can be made which adapt the social as well as technological aspects.

Autonomous work groups

The great virtue of the Tavistock approach, based as it is on an open-systems model of organization, has been in extending the range of variables that are seen to affect workers' attitudes and performance. It has thus greatly increased the *scope* of work redesign. In classic studies like those of Trist and Rice we see wider factors, such as the culture and the key role of management in managing group boundary conditions, being taken into account. But although the socio-technical approach has been extremely useful and influential, it has not evolved into a general theoretical framework. The practical concerns of investigators have usually caused them to focus on the particular workplace under investigation, and to adopt 'action' methods in order to intervene at each stage to try to improve different aspects of performance. These factors have made it difficult to define variables and the inter-relations between them, and have proved harmful in setting out more general guidelines for the design of work. In short, the breadth of socio-technical theory has been achieved at the cost of precision (Klein, 1979).

Recently, however, psychologists have been concerned to develop precise definitions of group variables. They have proposed 'autonomous work groups' as a useful model, both theoretically and for the practical purpose of introducing changes in the workplace. This is seen as a compromise between the very narrow job characteristics model, based on individual motivation, and the much more diffuse socio-technical systems (Kemp *et al.*, 1983).

The autonomous work group needs to be distinguished from the more ordinary co-acting group, where the main impact of membership on individuals is through higher levels of interaction (see Chapter 5). The crucial difference between the two types of group is the means of *control*. Co-acting groups are controlled externally, whereas autonomous work groups are to a large extent self-regulating, either removing the need for supervisors or greatly reducing it.

For example, Kemp *et al.* (1983) investigated job design on a greenfield site,

163

where they were able to use several control groups so that plant and shift factors could be eliminated. Groups of eight to twelve operatives had been established, and responsible work roles included job allocation, the resolution of local production problems, organizing work breaks, contacting other departments and training new recruits. When compared with control groups, the researchers were able to show that greater job satisfaction, perceptions of higher job complexity and improved leadership style were successfully established in the experimental groups. However, workers' commitment to the firm and their work motivation remained the same. In other words, this carefully designed experiment showed both that beneficial changes may be brought about, and also that the effects are rarely simple when a broad range of variables is measured.

THE CONSTRAINTS ON WORK REDESIGN

Since the 1960s numerous programmes of work redesign have been initiated. The most widespread and systematic developments have undoubtedly been those in Scandinavian companies, such as Volvo, Saab-Scania and Norsk-Hydro, but other major companies like ICI, Phillips and Fiat have also pursued work redesign as a central element of employee policy. Moreover, individual case studies have often shown impressive results. Changes in working conditions and improvements in various criteria of performance and worker satisfaction have all been reported. However, this apparently sound body of research and practical application is now being assessed much more critically.

Part of this criticism has arisen from a re-evaluation of the *evidence*. Although the record is impressive at first sight, under scrutiny the research methodology of many case studies turns out to have been seriously flawed (Kelly, 1982). For example, there have been tendencies to report only positive findings and to accept managerial assessments of success rather than seek objective measures. There has often been a marked failure to allow for a 'novelty effect' – the possibility that improvements in workers' satisfaction may arise out of the newness of change rather than changes in the working arrangements themselves. Thus, few experiments verify whether improvements are sustained over the long term. Related to this, the problem of 'compensatory rivalry' occurs if other plants within a company, or other departments, get to hear of a particular job redesign project, and their own performance suffers because they feel they have been overlooked. Obviously this may lead to the performance of the experimental group being artificially inflated. Finally, a further drawback is that it may be impossible to isolate the effects of job redesign if, as sometimes happens, a whole package of changes is implemented at one time. Volvo's Kalmar project presented a good example of this. Although we stressed the technological changes involved, in fact working conditions in the plant – noise levels, cleanliness, safety and general facilities – were also vastly improved over those in conventional car plants; and these factors may equally have accounted for the success of the experiment (Wedderburn, 1978).

A second general criticism concerns the *influence* of job redesign. Again, the record of research and the support of major companies is superficially impressive. Furthermore, there has been a wide acceptance of work humanization at the level of public policy. Several European governments, Britain's included, as well as international bodies, have supported initiatives in this direction. Nonetheless, the true impact of all this, it is suggested, has been far less significant (Wall, 1982). Many of the programmes have in fact never progressed beyond the experimental stage, and have often been discontinued after a short period. Similarly, many schemes have implemented cosmetic changes, despite claims of far-reaching job enrichment. Child, who on the whole is well disposed towards attempts to humanize work, has concluded rather pessimistically; 'The scale and scope of experiments in job redesign and work restructuring remain extremely limited. There are many minor developments masquerading under the label of job enrichment, but there are possibly no more than 100 or so European schemes that really enrich jobs significantly' (1984, p.43).

In this context, Guest, Williams and Dewe (1980) discovered a yawning gap between workers' and managers' perceptions of job redesign. These researchers found, in a scheme management regarded as having been very beneficial, that only about half of the workers involved were even aware of any change having taken place, and of these only a small proportion identified the change as being positive and significant. The implications of such a finding for studies that fail to elicit workers' opinions (and many do not) are obviously very damaging.

One of the main reasons why so much research in this area has not conformed to sound methodology is because many case studies have been carried out by paid consultants. Even research conducted by academics is often part of a consultancy exercise and so is far from being independent. Under such circumstances, where management calls the tune, researchers may be under great pressure to short-circuit proper empirical procedures, and to come up with positive findings, to persuade companies that the exercise has been worthwhile. This gap between theory and practice can only be explained by taking seriously into account the *context* in which work restructuring experiments are conducted. In other words, the full range of group variables, as well as wider environmental factors, have to be considered.

The work group context

The more detailed experiments that occupational psychologists have developed include a range of factors which can influence work design, and which determine whether any benefits will be sustained (Slocum and Sims, 1980; Wall, 1980; Kemp *et al.*, 1983).

(1) First level managerial practices. It is clear that the behaviour of supervisors is critical in determining the value of autonomous work groups to an organization and to group members. Drawing on the leadership behaviour dimensions of 'initiating structure', 'consideration' (see Chapter 7) and 'tolerance of freedom', Wall and Cordery (1982) argued that if autonomous work groups are to be successful – indeed if the groups are to enjoy a measure of true autonomy – then supervisory practice has to change in the direction of more freedom, less initiating structure and more consideration.

(2) Task. The group task has to be motivationally engaging, otherwise the members as a whole may still exhibit the same pattern of withdrawal from work and low commitment that often characterize performance in routine and repetitive work.

(3) Group composition. While the group has to possess task-relevant skills, these alone are not usually sufficient for effective performance. To utilize pooled resources, process problems also have to be minimized. We saw in Chapter 5 how cohesiveness within a group can be undermined if members are too dissimilar in status, values and abilities. Hence, effective personal and work outcomes are more likely with moderate heterogeneity in group members.

(4) Norms and performance strategies. Discussions of how work can be accomplished can cause anxiety in group members and this too can lead to group process problems. Members may avoid discussing appropriate ways of performing group tasks, and develop strategies either as an habitual response or by accident. Autonomous work groups may, therefore, need to be encouraged to develop norms which support the exploration of various performance strategies.

(5) The general work setting. Good group design, in terms of task, composition and supervisory practices, can be reinforced or undermined by a number of contextual factors. For example, the reward system and the performance targets need to be planned appropriately. Effective task behaviour must be adequately rewarded, and performance targets must be both challenging and realistic, if good work group design is to be enhanced. Management also has a key role in ensuring that teams are provided with enough information to enable members to distinguish between flexible performance targets and targets which act as real constraints on behaviour. Without such detailed information, the group may develop ways of working based on inaccurate perceptions of an organization's requirements. Finally, the pattern of relationships between a group and other groups may affect the outcome of autonomous working arrangements. A balance has to be achieved between integration and differentiation: too much integration of effort between

166

groups may lead to a loss in group identity; too much differentiation may result in damaging levels of competition.

The organizational context

In addition to the immediate context of work groups, the economic demands for profitability in organizations, and established technological practices, impose very powerful constraints on what may be done to improve work. Much of the work humanization literature, it has been suggested, has overlooked or underestimated these realities of organizations.

Job design An important though often unacknowledged factor constraining work re design is the process by which work is designed in the first place. Particularly with complex mass assembly, the production jobs that workers perform have to be seen not as discrete tasks but as the final link in a long chain, beginning in the original design phase and continuing through product and process development. In these early stages little or no consideration will have been given to the human needs of the workers who will eventually carry out production. As Child (1984, pp.38–9) has pointed out, 'heavily capitalized mass production plant . . . has generally imposed the greatest constraint upon work restructuring.' Inflexible production processes, where individual tasks are highly integrated, can prevent all but the most superficial of changes in the assembly stages. (In car assembly, for example, the design patterns within the vehicle, known as 'the build', mean that workers' tasks have to be performed in strict sequence.)

Furthermore, while we may assume that programmes of work redesign are based on human criteria, in reality the reverse is often the case: the rationale of job design may continue to constrain attempts to humanize work. Thus, in a survey of work design programmes in Europe, Lupton and Tanner (1980) found that production engineers initiated the majority of projects, and efficiency-related goals were uppermost. This was despite the fact that projects were mostly publicized in terms of the benefits for workers.

Organizational power structures Organizational hierarchies in reality are structures of deeply entrenched power, and this has also proved to be a major constraint on work humanization. The attempt to transfer control to shopfloor jobs may well threaten the status and security of managers and supervisors who presently exercise that control, and in several instances where apparently promising schemes have been abandoned it has been because of the wider repercussions for organizational power. Indeed, as Wall (1982) has pointed out, to the extent that work redesign really is significant, we should expect it to cut across the existing divisions of power.

One of the commonest causes of failure in programmes is resistance from supervisors. An early experiment carried out in the Norwegian company Norsk-Hydro clearly illustrated this problem. The firm's intention was to enrich workers' jobs by the inclusion of some basic supervisory tasks, which would also allow the foremen to devote more time to forward planning.

167

However, the foremen perceived the changes rather differently. They saw the bread and butter elements of their jobs being taken over by workers, and being compensated by some vague activity, planning, of which they had little experience. Consequently, the foremen resisted the scheme in its early stages and, faced with their disapproval, management called it off. However, by this time the workers had begun to respond positively to the changes, and were disappointed when they had to return to the old ways of working. Thus, at the end of the day, management were back where they started, but with a suspicious supervisory group and a disgruntled workforce.

The constraint of organizational power is also frequently the explanation behind the common paradox of projects being abandoned because they are 'too successful'. The strict demarcation of power within organizations means that even seemingly small changes may be widely disruptive. Thus Blackler and Brown (1980) described a project involving the dock assembly of trucks (where the stationary vehicle is assembled on a chassis by a team of workers) at Volvo's Arendal plant. The project was initially given a high priority; plant-wide changes were implemented to attempt to make it a success, and in the early stages production and quality levels were comparable with the conventional assembly line. However, when the researchers conducted a follow-up study some three years after, production had reverted to conventional methods. As far as they were able to ascertain this was simply due to a hardening of opinion against the new methods among senior managers: 'their main objections were more emotional than rational. Dock methods involve a loss of immediate control by management; this factor we felt weighed more strongly with some individuals than did the potential commercial advantages available from the system.'

A similar case involved the introduction of flexitime into an office. The arrangement was started on a trial basis in one section, and quickly became popular as employees began to exercise a degree of control over how work was organized. They would meet informally and arrange timekeeping to cover the work and also to suit their own interests. Management, however, became alarmed as they felt their traditional authority was slipping away; and when there were signs of other employees wanting the same conditions, the scheme was hurriedly cancelled.

EVALUATING WORK REDESIGN

How, then, should we assess the possibility of the meaningful redesign of work? Should these methods be dismissed as ineffective, or perhaps even as a management 'con trick'? Clearly, if the above criticisms are to be treated at all seriously, work redesign cannot be taken at face value. For one thing, despite the claims often made, jobs are rarely if ever redesigned at the expense of *managerial control*. Indeed, restructuring may itself be used as a tactic of control. Schemes may convey the impression that firms are concerned with the welfare of their employees, while management remains only marginally committed to change. Similarly, the use of consultants as 'independent experts' may confer legitimacy on schemes, while consultants are still acting on management's initiative. Another way in which these methods may be used as a means of control is in undermining trade union organization. Job redesign schemes should allow for workers to participate in planned change, yet they may really be intended as a means of diverting workers' grievances away from their trade union representatives.

In this vein, the efforts to humanize work are seen to serve an *ideological* purpose, rather than necessarily being a part of management practice. They represent a body of ideas that may be called upon if management is being held up to public criticism, and that is favoured by certain sections of management (like personnel and public relations) concerned with a firm's outward image, yet with little real impact on the work process. Moreover, as with all systems of ideas, interest in them ebbs and flows with circumstances. Thus, work humanization is essentially seen as a product of the years of full employment when employers had to compete for labour. Recently there has been a sharp decline in the number of projects initiated and in the interest shown by companies. The charitable view of this is that work humanization has been making 'slow progress'. But more critically it has been suggested that employers' concern peaked in the 1960s and early 1970s. With the current high levels of unemployment, labour market power is running strongly in their favour, and, quite simply, employers no longer need work humanization either as a means of attracting labour or as a justification of their policies.

However, in spite of all these criticisms there remains a certain amount of guarded optimism concerning work redesign. The gains looked for are more modest and specific, but they are nonetheless positive. For example, Roberts and Wood (1982) have argued that rather than ask whether these methods are capable of transforming work, it is more important that trade unionists and workers should take the initiative and begin to make serious attempts to bargain over job redesign.

In terms of the more usual approach to job redesign, under managerial initiative, we are now able to define appropriate conditions very clearly. If, in the past, this has been used as a cheap alternative to making real improvements in working conditions – which of course mean capital expenditure and may involve acknowledging trade union demands – it is now accepted that meaningful work redesign itself requires adequate resources. The careful design of projects, assessment of possible repercussions, and the sustained backing of all levels of management are basic requisites. If this kind of commitment is forthcoming, it has been argued, improvements in worker satisfaction and performance can be brought about. Thus, while the evidence is not conclusive, it is at least suggestive of some positive changes (Kelly, 1982).

Finally, it can be stressed that the work restructuring programmes which have been building up since the 1960s have left behind a certain residue of change in management practice. Even if this has not been dramatic, there are indications that the designers of jobs and work systems are at least aware of the arguments against fragmented, highly repetitive work; and there are some signs of a shift away from strictly Taylorist methods towards an emphasis on overall systems of work organization.

FURTHER READING

Bailey, J. (1983) *Job Design and Work Organization*. Englewood Cliffs, N.J.: Prentice-Hall.

Clutterbuck, D. (ed.) (1985) *New Patterns of Work*. Aldershot: Gower.

Cooper, C. and E. Mumford (1979) *The Quality of Working Life in Western and Eastern Europe*. London: Associated Business Press.

Davis, L.E. and A.B. Cherns (1975) *The Quality of Working Life*. London: Collier-Macmillan.

Kelly, J.E. (1982) *Scientific Management, Job Redesign and Work Performance*. London: Academic Press.

Knights, D., H. Willmott and D. Collinson (1985) *Job Redesign: Critical Perspectives on the Labour Process*. Aldershot: Gower.

Robertson, I.T. and M. Smith (1985) *Motivation and Job Design: Theory and Practice*. London: Institute of Personnel Management.

Weir, M. (1976) *Job Satisfaction*. Harmondsworth: Penguin.

SECTION THREE

THE SOCIOLOGY OF WORK

The focus in earlier parts of this book has been on the psychological processes acting on individuals and their immediate environment in work groups. Factors in the social and economic environment – the wider context in which work is carried out – were not really considered in their own right. In the chapters in Section Two, where we examined motivation in work, the improvement of work group experiences and job satisfaction, we took for granted the reasons why these alternative forms of work organization were needed in the first place. However, it is now necessary to retrace our steps and consider more thoroughly the nature of work in modern industrial society. We turn to a *sociological* analysis of work, for it is sociology which is concerned with the broader structural and processual factors affecting behaviour.

An important theme helping to set out the different topics discussed below is that of the *division of labour*. This complex process reflects the many ways in which the productive work performed in society has historically become differentiated and apportioned. Within the work situation itself, the strict divisions between different jobs is the basis of control and efficiency in modern organizations, although it has also produced the kind of fragmented, routine jobs that are associated with many of the problems of industry. On another level, the division of labour has produced the occupational structure. The divide between different professions and crafts has always been characteristic, even during pre-industrial times, but in a modern economy we find an enormously complex system of occupations reflecting the vast number of different jobs available. Finally, other aspects of the social division of labour reflect the fact that certain groups of people (differentiated by factors like sex and ethnic origins) typically are found in certain types of work.

Following this general schema, in Chapter 9 we begin by looking at the basic forces that shape work, and the chief characteristics that define it in an industrial economy like our own. This rests on an examination of the classical writings on work of Marx and Weber, which provide the basis of much modern thinking. Other important variables, notably technology and skill, are located within this framework.

Modern forms of administering work, under the approach developed here, are seen essentially as structures of control and authority. Hence the problem of workplace conflict is an integral part of this approach, and an account of conflict follows in Chapter 10. Industrial sociology has usually confined itself to the study of informal conflict based on work groups, leaving trade union action to be the subject matter of industrial relations. To some extent, however, this is an artificial distinction – especially for an applied discipline like behavioural studies – so both types of conflict are explored here.

In Chapter 11 the focus is extended to include occupational variation. A full account of the changing occupational structure is beyond our scope. What we do look at, however, are a number of occupational groups selected for their prominence and social visibility. We examine the labour market situation of manual workers, the nature of white-collar work, and the professions.

The employment situation confronting women is described in Chapter 12. Here, instead of looking at forces that shape and structure jobs, we look at a particular group filling those jobs. Female employment has attracted much interest recently, and we focus on the broad patterns of discrimination against women at work, as well as some of the more active ways in which women participate in employment.

Finally, in this part of the book, Chapter 13 discusses the 'new technology' of microelectronics. In one way this follows on directly from the sociological account of technology in Chapter 9. However, the impact of new technology on the work process has attracted massive interest recently and merits study in its own right.

9

The Control of Work

Questions about the nature of work in modern society have to begin by asking about the largest concentrations of employment and the types of work that most people do. A cursory examination of the occupational skills structure shows what is perhaps an obvious point, namely that 'lower-level' jobs, in services and industry, constitute the main groupings of employment. Low-grade service jobs comprise about 27 per cent of total employment, and low-grade manual jobs about 22 per cent. These are jobs primarily with a low content of skills and consequently relatively poor pay. The upshot of this is that the experience of work for a great many people is of jobs which are uninteresting, and which almost always offer little in terms of a career or hope of advancement.

Of course, this picture needs to be qualified; certainly there is a great deal of *variation* in work. Although the largest single categories of employment are unskilled manual and low-grade service work, many people have satisfying professional or managerial jobs, while others exercise technical or manual skills. There is also an important subjective element. People experience work in different ways; and what may be an unrewarding job, done out of pure necessity, to one person, might be perfectly satisfactory to someone else. Also, in a time of high unemployment and deep industrial recession, it can be argued that people's expectations of work change: in such straitened times perhaps many people regard any job as a good job.

Nonetheless, it remains true that as far as objective factors are concerned, a high proportion of work probably affords little in the way of individual fulfilment or hope beyond the immediate present. In order to understand why the typical factory or office job involves routine operations and few skills and is intrinsically unrewarding, we need to develop an analysis of the forces shaping the jobs performed by the bulk of employed people.

Of the various ideas we will need to take into account in a sociological analysis of work, the theory of *alienation* developed by Karl Marx is of central importance. The notion that modern conditions of work produce alienated labour has long been influential, both directly on our understanding of work and in terms of the alternative theories it has evoked. Recently there has been a great resurgence of interest in Marx, and in particular we now have a much more detailed understanding of his analysis of work as a '*labour process*'.

Another of sociology's founding fathers, Max Weber, has also attracted renewed interest. Weber's influence on the whole of the discipline of sociology has been immense, and one of his main contributions was his analysis of bureaucracy. This will be discussed later, in Chapter 13, but behind his theory of bureaucracy lay the conviction that this particular form of organization represented the most rational expression of economic order, and Weber's ideas concerning the *rationalization* of labour are pertinent to our discussion here.

In this chapter, then, we shall first examine the basis which exists in classical sociological theory for an analysis of the work process. We will then briefly turn to historical developments, and to the rise of modern systems of work organization. We go on to single out *technology*, which has often been regarded by industrial sociologists and other commentators as having had a distinctive impact on industrial growth. Here we discuss the classical 'political economy of mechanization' as well as the later sociological study of technology. Finally, as might be expected, these critical perspectives have led to a good deal of debate and disagreement, and we will conclude by examining an important current debate in the sociological analysis of work which concerns the nature of *skills*.

MARX, WEBER AND THE CRITIQUE OF LABOUR

Alienated labour

It is important to know how Marx developed his ideas on alienation, as this is a concept which has subsequently been much misunderstood and misused. In particular, it has become commonplace to stress individual experiences, and to equate alienation loosely with feelings of 'dissatisfaction' with work, or indeed any social situation. Marx's usage was very different. For him, alienation was a concrete process of social change, although one which certainly affected people's subjective experiences.

Central to Marx's approach was a 'materialist' view of labour as the basis of human society. The transformation of the natural world through shared labour, initially out of the physical needs for survival, brings the social and cultural world into existence. This is true of all societies, but in advanced ones labour is carried out under definite 'relations of production', and here the institutions of political power shape the forms of useful collective work. Within capitalist class relations, in particular, the creation of a material and social world becomes a distorted and degraded activity. Human labour becomes alienated labour, an idea Marx first put forward among his early writings in the '*1844 Manuscripts*' (1975, pp.279–400).

What constitutes the alienation of labour?

Firstly, the fact that labour is *external* to the worker, i.e. does not belong to his essential being; that he therefore does not confirm himself in his work, but denies himself, feels miserable and not happy, does not develop free mental and physical energy, but mortifies his flesh and ruins his mind. . . . His labour is therefore not voluntary but forced, it is *forced labour*. It is therefore not the satisfaction of a need but a mere *means* to satisfy needs outside itself. Its alien character is clearly demonstrated by the fact that as soon as no physical or other compulsion exists it is shunned like the plague. (1975, p.326)

Marx set out a number of dimensions of alienation, describing the impact of class relations on work and on the wider human community. Firstly, workers are divorced both from the *product* of their labour and from the *process* of production. In other words, the product and the manner in which work is performed are controlled by the employer by virtue of his ownership of capital. The fact that labour is 'external' to the worker, a mere means to an end, follows from this. These economic factors have social consequences in that *people become alienated from themselves*. The forces that strip work of its creativity in effect remove from it the truly human element, reducing workers virtually to the level of animals which produce only out of instinct or for immediate need. Also, a broader social alienation occurs: *people stand in an instrumental relationship to one another*, defined in terms of the economic power they command rather than their worth as human beings.

Marx contrasted the might of capital – the huge accumulation of private property, the development of a central state, the private ownership of cultural and artistic products – with the impoverishment of the mass of working people. Lacking control over their own labour, the material things people themselves have created confront them as a hostile entity. They become subject to the industrial and technological systems others have designed and built, and they are powerless in the face of market forces. Alienation thus produces the unequal and polarized society in terms of which Marx viewed modern industrial capitalism. He saw in 'this whole system of estrangement' a supreme irony. For at just the point in history where the powers of science and industry conferred a degree of mastery over society's traditional enemies – the natural world (disease, shortage of food) and fear of superstition – so the class divisions in capitalism negated these achievements for the majority of people. Humankind fell victim to itself.

The labour process

Until fairly recently, a commonplace criticism of Marx had been that he gradually abandoned his earlier 'humanistic' concern with alienation for the strictly 'economic' analysis found in his later writings, notably in *Capital, Volume One*. However, it now tends to be acknowledged that he did not reject the idea of alienation. Rather, he focused more narrowly on 'the act of production within labour' and developed an account of alienation within the work process. We shall briefly explore some of the main ideas from this approach (for more detailed accounts, see Friedman, 1977, pp.10–19, and Thompson, 1983, pp.38–64).

At the heart of Marx's theory of the labour process – and for him the defining feature of capitalist society – was the emergence of the wage relationship and of labour as a *commodity*. When labour itself is bought and sold on a market of exchange, it becomes a cost of production, an object of commercial investment, and this underlines the dehumanization of work. Commodity-status also points to the essential insecurity of much modern employment. Certain things can improve a person's chances of a job (qualifications, trade union protection) but in the end society provides no natural right to work.

However, labour is unique in being an active human commodity. While it contains great potential for productive work, workers may resist their exploitation. In this context, Marx suggested that the exchange between capital and labour is not a simple exchange of wages for work. Rather it has two aspects: the employer first buys the *labour power* of the worker, expressed as an agreement to work for a certain time; and it is then the employer's responsibility to convert this potential into real labour – to set employees to work, in other words. The notion of labour as a 'variable' or 'potential' input to production draws attention to the struggle for control of the labour process, and to the employer's motivation to intensify the use of labour.

Thompson (1986) has identified four key features of labour process theory. Firstly, the employment relationship as the basic producer of wealth occupies a privileged position in analysis. The employer–worker relationship is the basic class relationship, and changes here provide the main 'motor' of change in the rest of the economy and society. Secondly, the employment relationship is highly dynamic. Competing capitalists have to seek ever greater rates of profit, and hence the labour process will continuously be transformed in pursuit of greater productivity. Thirdly, capital is compelled to increase its control over labour. The means of control are often very complex, forms of control exist outside the labour process, and the degree of control over labour is never total – nonetheless, a generalized 'control imperative' within the work process does exist. And fourthly, the employment relationship is a relationship both of production and of exploitation. Hence, although it contains aspects of cooperation, conflict remains an endemic and structural feature.

In sum, Marx's analysis points to the divisive nature of the capitalist labour process. Pre-capitalist work processes, he pointed out, were limited in their productivity and in the extent of the control of any ruling group by the need to rely upon handicraft skills. Effort and efficiency were subjective factors held in check by the worker. In pre-industrial society, where people had control of their working lives to a much greater extent, the historical record shows that a much greater value was placed on creative leisure, and work and leisure were closely integrated (Marx, 1974, p.381). However, all this began to change under a capitalist economy. The alienation of labour from production then became the root cause of industrial conflict, representing the real basis of broader social conflicts and the massive inequalities of wealth and power that characterize modern industrial societies.

Weber and rationalization

Modern thinking on work has also been greatly influenced by Max Weber, whose ideas on rationalization have implications that are similar in many ways to the Marxist idea of alienation.

Weber regarded the spread of rational, goal-oriented behaviour as the central dynamic of western capitalist societies. In the transition from pre-industrial society, religious and mystical paradigms for coming to terms with the world declined and gave way to secular forms of explanation based on empirical science; this culminated in the market economy and the rise of industrial capitalism. In particular, the impact of rational criteria on economic action was for Weber the decisive factor which distinguished modern industrial capitalism from more traditional forms of society.

> In the last resort the factor which produced capitalism is the rational permanent enterprise, rational accounting, rational technology and rational law, but again not these alone. Necessary complementary factors were the rational spirit, the rationalisation of the conduct of life in general, and a rational economic ethic. (Quoted in Lee and Newby, 1983, p.189)

This 'spirit of rationality', which pervaded economic and social life, was especially apparent in the ways in which work was administered and organized. Rationality here refers to the use of formal procedures (capital accounting, systematic management, corporate planning, etc.) in the control of economic enterprises. The point Weber emphasized was that only formal administration provided the basis for operations to be *calculable*. Being able to plan ahead with some degree of certainty is an essential requirement when large amounts of resources have to be committed. Both the massive level of provision in the modern state and the increasing size and complexity of modern industry require that organizations meet forecasts and perform predictably. This would be so, Weber argued, whether in a capitalist market economy or a centrally planned socialist one.

Calculative logic was not, however, the only attribute of a modern society. Here Weber contrasted *formal* with *substantive* rationality. Formal rationality referred to the calculation of economic means, discussed above, while substantive rationality referred to the persistent intervention of human ends and values. The two rationales were 'always in principle in conflict', since human needs are not necessarily met by rational calculation (Weber, 1964, p.185). This viewpoint was the cause of an undercurrent of profound pessimism in Weber's thought, for although he stressed the effectiveness of rational administration, he believed that this mode of action would inevitably spread to and rule all areas of social life. In this, Weber was author of a fundamental criticism of modern society: the fear of all 'ultimate values' eventually becoming submerged in a society dominated by the cold logic of formal decision-making.

The spread of formal rationality entailed 'the complete appropriation of economic resources by owners' (Weber, 1964, p.247). The calculability of large-scale enterprise and the autonomy of workers were, Weber stressed, polar opposites. To the extent that formal rationality was enforced, the worker had to be completely excluded from any role in the authority structure of the firm. For Weber, this was the upshot of inevitable technical developments. Technical efficiency depended upon managements having 'extensive control over the selection and modes of use of workers'; any 'rights to participate in management' in practice led to 'irrational obstacles to efficiency' (p.247).

> From a historical point of view, the expropriation of labour has developed since the sixteenth century in an economy characterized by a progressive development of the market system, both extensively and intensively, by the sheer technical superiority and actual indispensibility of a type of autocratic management oriented to the particular market situations, and by the structure of sheer power relationships in society. (1964, p.247)

For Weber, then, rationalization in the modern world meant the transformation of human relationships into impersonal exchanges under the compulsion of technical rationality. The normal, spontaneous qualities of human society are obliterated as work organizations concentrate on the *means* to achieve economic goals, while the goals themselves may become increasingly meaningless. Rational conduct ultimately produces a society that

> is bound to the technical and economic conditions of machine production, which today determine the lives of all the individuals who are born into this mechanism, not only those directly concerned with economic acquisition, with irresistible force. Perhaps it will so determine them until the last ton of fossilized coal is burnt. (Weber, quoted in Salaman, 1981, p.59)

Conclusion

The notions of alienation and rationalization together point to the problems of productive work being increasingly degraded and overshadowed by the institutions of capital. This is not to say that the theories of Marx and Weber were always in agreement. There remain deep divisions between them. Nonetheless, the similarities in their conclusions were also striking. They both sought the causes of the development of capitalism in the dynamics of production, and distinguished capitalism as a specific way of appropriating labour within distinct institutional forms. Both too gave full credit to capitalism's unleashing of enormous productive powers, but at the same time saw deep-rooted conflict between rational and irrational forces. The trend in recent studies of industrial organization has been to return to these sources. As Hill has remarked, new perspectives owe a great debt to Marx and Weber 'because they have successfully structured the agenda of what is held to be worth discussing' (1981, p.vii).

EMERGING FORMS OF WORK ORGANIZATION

One of the most important concepts to have emerged in recent sociological analyses of work is that of *control*. Here it is suggested that conflicts of interest between employers and employees bring about a fundamental problem of the control of labour. From this it follows that work is often designed for the chief purpose of facilitating control, and that the historical development of forms of work organization is to be understood in terms of employers' strategies to secure control in changing circumstances. Thus, Salaman (1979, p.23) has suggested that renewed interest in the classical writings of Marx and Weber in large part reflects their concern with the 'processes of control and legitimation' in work organizations.

Of course, controls inside the workplace cannot be divorced from wider legitimation of managerial authority that derives from the ownership of capital. The threat of dismissal to workers is the ultimate sanction behind managerial authority. The freedom to dispose of assets (which may involve threats to close a plant, or to transfer production) can also be decisive. Nonetheless, the authority delegated to management by virtue of the legal rights of ownership is not in itself normally sufficient. In addition, there are important structural controls of labour which derive from the basic form of work organization, the modern factory.

The factory system

Throughout the seventeenth and eighteenth centuries, in Britain, the system of production of the feudal and mercantile era underwent radical transformation, culminating in the Industrial Revolution of the 1780s. Independent producers in agriculture and in handicraft industries came under the sway of capitalists, and production was being organized on an increasingly large scale. Marx, for example, identified 'two ways' into industrial capitalism. One saw the expansion of small workshops, as master craftsmen began to take on larger labour forces, rather than merely apprentices to renew the ranks of the craft. In the other, merchants began to extend their trading activities into production, particularly in the domestic system where craftspeople working from cottages would be organized and supplied by a merchant-turned-employer (Dobb, 1963, p.123). Both paths led to the development of the factory as the fundamental form of organizing production.

The emphasis placed on control is not of course to deny the purely economic and technical advantages of the factory system. Vastly improved economies of scale were possible, as was the later application of machinery and the new power source, steam. Also, in the developing markets of the nineteenth century, goods of a comparable quality and specification were in demand, a type of output only possible where methods could be standardized. Yet, as Marglin (1974) has pointed out, it was only as this system gradually came to predominate, and technical improvements were diverted exclusively into it, that its economic advantages came to the fore. The prime motive behind the *initial* development of the factory system was enhanced control.

The very fact of work being performed in organizations is itself a control of labour and the basis of other controls. In the preceding domestic system there were limits on the extent to which work could be regulated. With individual tasks dispersed over different households, and even communities, cottage systems were only capable of developing fairly rudimentary forms of control, and employers were often more interested in the profits to be gained from trading off occupational communities (supplying them with materials and selling the finished products) than they were in organizing production itself. But with the advent of the factory all this changed. When workers were gathered under one roof, their activities could be much more tightly controlled: tasks could be assigned, output accurately measured and times of attendance checked.

In this sense the appointment of a special group directly to oversee the labour process – *supervision* in other words – has always been a central element of the factory system. The early labour masters were powerful figures, responsible for recruiting and organizing workers. Later on, as Gospel (1983, p.98) notes, 'The foreman of the late nineteenth and early twentieth centuries was very much the master in the workplace and was the key figure in labour management.' In more recent times supervisors have lost these powers. The power to hire and fire and to fix wages has been taken over by managerial specialisms, such as industrial relations and personnel. But although their direct control over workers has been eroded, supervisors still play a significant part in the control of labour within modern systems of management. The expanding management structure has absorbed supervision, and the occupation itself has become diversified and developed its own hierarchy.

In terms of the industrial discipline that could be imposed, a *division of labour* was also crucial in forging the link between efficiency and control. The splitting up of work into specialized functions, organized by department and section, raised the productive powers of labour at the same time as it enabled the central control of the labour process. Most observers of the early factory system were surprised by the extreme fragmentation of work, which was qualitatively different from anything that had gone before. Marx spoke of the worker being transformed into a 'detail labourer', with the factory itself becoming the 'collective labourer' where tasks were integrated. Before Marx, Adam Smith had focused specifically on the division of labour as the basis of economic prosperity. Indeed, he begins *The Wealth of Nations* with a detailed account of the productivity gains attendant on 'a proper division and combination' of operations. 'The different operations into which the making of a pin, or of a metal button, is subdivided, are all of them much more simple, and the dexterity of the person, of whose life it has been the sole business to perform them, is usually much greater' (1982, p.113). However, Smith had mixed feelings about this form of work organization: while he marvelled at its contribution to productivity, he was not blind to the less desirable social consequences. He saw, as did Marx, that the fragmentation of work was the chief cause of labour becoming a degraded activity – a fact no less true of the 'manufactories' of the eighteenth century than of today's assembly lines.

Modern management and Taylorism

Another aspect of work organization that reflects the class nature of production involves the *intensification* of work. Marx, on this point, distinguished the 'formal' from the 'real' control of labour. Nineteenth-century capitalism inherited a labour process based on artisan production, and in the early factories previously independent craftsmen became wage workers. Marx referred to this as formal subjugation, because at this stage labour still retained its craft nature. Real subjugation arose, Marx suggested, when capital began transforming work itself from its archaic forms (Brighton Labour Process Group, 1977; Elger, 1979).

The Factory Acts of the 1840s and 1850s were an early impetus to labour intensification. Previously there had been very little legal control of employment conditions; but the Acts placed a limit on the length of the working day, and on other abuses like the use of child labour, which encouraged employers to concentrate on raising productivity. Marx notes that employers' interest in *efficiency* greatly increased from that time forward (1974, pp.442–51).

Still, for most of the nineteenth century the means to increase productive intensity had not progressed much beyond the basic controls of the factory itself. During the last quarter of the century, however, modern methods of the systematic control of labour came into use. These originated in the scientific management movement pioneered by the American, F.W. Taylor. Beginning in the 1890s, Taylor developed a 'science of work', the methods of which involved the detailed study of work processes with a view to increasing efficiency and labour productivity. Tasks were carefully observed and broken down into component actions, which were then measured on the basis of standard times – hence the more popular name of 'time and motion' study.

The far-reaching effects of scientific management, or 'Taylorism', for work in contemporary society have been widely recognized. Weber, for example, spoke of the Taylor system as the pioneer of the application of rationalized methods of work (1964, p.261). More recently, Braverman in his influential study *Labor and Monopoly Capital* (1974) has been particularly important in drawing attention to the general principles of scientific management that

Taylor set out, and to their implications for the 'degradation' of work. (For discussion of Taylorism, see also Clegg and Dunkerley, 1980, pp.87–98, and Mouzelis, 1975, pp.79–87.)

Firstly, Taylor recommended the most detailed division of labour that was practically possible: relatively complex tasks should be split up into the maximum number of sub-tasks. More significantly, he insisted that the skills which had built up within a workforce – skills of hand and eye, knowledge and experience – should be absorbed within the management function and converted into formal procedures. Management should assume 'the burden of gathering together all of the traditional knowledge which in the past has been possessed by the workmen and then of classifying, tabulating, and reducing this knowledge to rules, laws, and formulae' (quoted in Braverman, 1974, p.112). Taylor also recommended the 'divorce of conception from execution'. All thinking about work – planning, the securing of supplies, maintenance of equipment, etc. – should be managed by a specialist staff. The worker should simply have to execute the task in hand, or become an 'operator', to use the modern term. Thus Taylor stressed that, 'All possible brainwork should be removed from the shop and centred in the planning or laying out department' (Braverman, 1974, p.113). Abercrombie and Urry (1983) have usefully summarized the 'Taylorist strategy for capital', and the manner in which it transformed existing labour practices, as follows:

> . . . as long as workers knew more than their managers, then management would have to persuade the workers to cooperation. This could clearly be seen in relation to piecework – since management did not know how long in fact it took to do each piece of work; it was rational for workers to . . . restrict output. Taylor realised that the only long-term solution to this from the viewpoint of capital was to devise a new system of capitalist control that would overcome the rational tendency for workers to restrict output . . . this could only be achieved by transforming the very form of knowledge possessed by workers. (p.101)

The advantages to employers of adopting such a strategy are overwhelming. Labour is cheapened by reducing its skilled component, the flexibility of labour is increased by simplifying tasks, and there is a great potential for generally streamlining production. Unnecessary tasks can be eliminated, physical layouts improved and work speeded up. Taylor himself conducted thousands of consultancy exercises in his time and often achieved notable increases in output and productivitiy. Above all, with work designed by staff specialists and integrated within a production plan, management's control of production was intensified in a way which hitherto had not been possible.

Not least important was the *ideological* aspect. Systematic measurement and methods of standardizing tasks, it was claimed, made this a 'scientific' study of work. Standards of effort were argued to have been arrived at by purely rational methods. At bottom this claim was spurious because, as critics have pointed out, work study is always dependent upon agreed notions of what is a fair and reasonable pace of work (Baldamus, 1961; Braverman, 1974, p.86). Nevertheless, managerial authority has been legitimized to an important degree by the 'neutral' language of scientific management.

Finally, it is important to consider the *historical context* in which scientific management was introduced. Allied to industrialization in the United States, there was a rapid growth in the size of the economy and labour force. America industrialized on the basis of the then new technologies, like steel, chemicals and mass production. Littler (1978, 1982) points to the labour crisis created in these new industries as workers entered jobs lacking any traditional standards of pay and effort. In this fluid situation, scientific management represented an employers' initiative to establish a formal system of discipline, one which they very definitely controlled.

Littler has also stressed that Taylorism was chiefly important for extending *direct* managerial control. Up to the 1880s, the most common form of shopfloor organization was based upon the authority of sub-contractors and supervisors. Labour masters, gang bosses and foremen were powerful figures in the early factory system, recruiting workers and organizing payment and discipline. However, with economic growth, these personal and informal methods of control became a barrier to efficiency. Taylorism helped to eliminate such systems of internal contracting, and provided a form of industrial discipline that enabled owners to employ labour directly.

Like all aspects of industrial development, these methods were adopted unevenly. Their concrete impact varied widely, and other methods that modified Taylor's original system were developed. Yet Taylor's doctrine was taken up enthusiastically in the United States, and by the 1920s and 1930s had spread to continental Europe and Britain. In important respects, this started the process of diversification into specialist functions, such as production control and industrial engineering, which laid the basis of modern management as a rational system of administering work.

TECHNOLOGY AND WORKPLACE BEHAVIOUR

So far we have seen how a wide range of developments account for the rise of industrial societies. They include the spread of market relationships and the growth of the money economy, the organization of work in the shape of the factory system, employment as the dominant relationship of production, and generally rational modes of thought and action. Of all such preconditions, however, the one that is linked most directly with industrialism itself is technology. This is because advancing technology can be identified with the high rates of *change* that are a defining feature of modern societies. It was essentially the Industrial Revolution, and the first development of machinery which came with it, which brought about the rapid pace of innovation we are now familiar with. Since then the specifically *technical* aspect of change has continued to provide a powerful symbol of conditions that we think of as 'modern'; and sociologists have been particularly interested in this variable as a way of explaining workplace attitudes and behaviour.

In the way social scientists use the term nowadays, technology is not simply restricted to the hardware of production systems. (This is in contrast to common-sense usage, where the term usually does conjure up the image of some complex machine or device.) Instead, technology is used to refer to entire technical processes. Thus, for example, we might speak of a mass production technology, like car assembly, or a continuous-flow process technology, such as chemicals or oil refining. In these cases the hardware component (machinery, automation equipment, plant) would be included, but also the skills and know-how involved are taken into account, as is the type of work organization within which the hardware is applied. These other considerations are vitally important, since the application of machinery can have very different implications in different circumstances.

A second important point, to be followed up later in the section, concerns the notion of *technological determinism*. This refers to arguments which appear to be saying that technology is the determining cause of particular conditions or behaviour in work. Social scientists have rightly criticized such arguments, their main point being that technology itself cannot be the independent cause of anything: it is the manner in which techology is applied, and the motives and actions of groups which control technology, which are decisive.

As a result both of the complexity of technological processes and of the active role of social elements, several different and often contrasting viewpoints have come to characterize the study of technology.

Technology and the labour process

Commentators on the early industrial scene, like Marx and Adam Smith, perceived the close link between technology and the way in which work is organized. The imposition of the factory system, with its concentration of the labour force and intricate division of labour, actually made possible the development of machinery. Complex and skilled craft work had to be reorganized along rational lines before it could be mechanized. Hence a dynamic relationship exists between work structuring and mechanization, the one progressing under the impetus of the other. Both Marx and Smith had mixed feelings about the factory system, recognizing that the massive increases in the productive powers of labour seemed to go hand in hand with the subjugation of people to work. Marx in particular was preoccupied with mechanization (1974, pp.351–475); and his critique remains the basis of many more recent attacks on modern technology (e.g. Levidow and Young, 1981, 1985). He believed that the fiercely competitive nature of capitalism compelled employers to force up productivity, and that mechanization was their chief means of doing this.

In its most fundamental form the emergent conflict between technology and labour rested on the so-called 'organic composition' of capital. By this Marx meant that the economy, composed of technical capital (machines, plant, equipment) and human capital (living labour), was constantly changing. He believed, further, that the overall trend favoured an expanding technology. Although modern economics would disagree with this – recognizing that industrial economies are becoming increasingly capital-intensive, but not accepting that this necessarily occurs at the workers' expense – Marx did believe that over the long term capital intensification diminished the contribution of living labour.

Marx detailed a number of aspects of the 'strife between workman and machine'. Machinery was the great leveller, reducing any special techniques and skills needed in work, so that human labour was rendered interchangeable and easy to substitute. In this is found a central theme of labour process theory, that capitalist work organization has a long-run tendency to produce 'homogeneous' labour. Not only did machinery displace labour, it created actual unemployment. Marx thought that the rate at which labour was displaced by machinery would always outpace the rate at which new work was created via general economic expansion. Hence the tendency of capitalism to generate a 'reserve army' of unemployed people was in large part attributed to technological advances. Marx also stressed the enslavement of workers to machines, particularly in terms of the perpetuation of working hours. This is because machinery, especially complex machinery, runs the risk of becoming obsolete even before it is worn out. Hence employers will be anxious to have it used intensively to extract its full value before obsolescence takes over.

In short, Marx believed that under pressure of existing class relationships machinery played a key role in the alienation of labour. Much of this still rings true, and is especially consistent with the social and economic problems of today's recession. Modern ideas about the 'capital-deepening' effects of new technology have led to fears that economies are now so capital-intensive and productive that mass unemployment has become a structural feature. We also find concern being expressed about changing patterns of work. The change to highly intensive forms of shift- and rota-working, such as in complex plant like continuous-process technology and large mainframe computers, seems to pay little heed to the social and physical needs of workers. Set against these forms of labour displacement, deskilling and work intensification, however, there are some far more positive views of technology. Perhaps the most influential of these has been put forward by the American sociologist, Robert Blauner, in his study *Alienation and Freedom* (1964).

Blauner and the functional view of technology

Blauner's actual research, which goes back to the early 1960s, may seem outdated in relation to the fast-moving subject matter of technology. Indeed, the purely empirical value of his research was always rather limited, based as it was on secondary analysis of workers' attitudes, and with case study and anecdotal materials included on a highly selective basis. But Blauner's account of technology remains influential for other reasons. What it represents is a theory of a widely popular and prevailing view: the functional view of technology as a liberating and energizing force. It emphasizes the potential, particularly of the most advanced forms of automation, for 'upgrading' the skills and occupational status of those who work with it.

Blauner contrasted the 'existence of critically different types of work environments in modern industry' with the Marxist notion of diversity within manual labour being eliminated, and working conditions as a whole becoming increasingly degraded. He conceived a model linking the degree of alienation that workers experienced with the conditions of the particular work situation: 'In some industrial environments the alienating tendencies that Marx emphasized are present to a high degree. In others they are relatively undeveloped or have been countered by new technical, economic and social forces' (1964, p.5). Blauner chose four industries to cover different types of technical system. These were printing, which represented a craft technology; textiles, which typified a machine-minding technology; automobiles as typical of mass assembly; and chemicals to represent continuous-process technology.

From his findings worker alienation, firstly, seemed at a minimum in craft technology. Print workers' trade skills and powerful union organization gave them a high degree of job security, as well as control over their jobs. Because they were able to see work through from start to finish they could perceive meaning in their own contribution. In contrast, both machine-minding and mass assembly technologies maximized alienation. Textile workers were powerless in the face of constant work pressure, and lacked any choice over the pace and methods of work. In car plants the nature of work was consistently alienating. The production line dominated all aspects of the work situation. Car workers' jobs were repetitive and meaningless, they were isolated from co-workers, and the work itself gave no feelings of pride or self-esteem.

For the process workers, however, alienation declined once more to a low level. These workers were often technically qualified and their jobs involved the monitoring of entire operations. Whilst routine for much of the time, their work carried freedom and responsibility, so they tended to identify strongly with their jobs and the efficient running of the plant. As Blauner put it, 'the responsibility for automated production confers a new sense of dignity and worth on manual employment – a possibility not foreseen by many students of alienation, who assess manual work by the yardstick of traditional craftsmanship' (p.165).

The distinctive aspect of Blauner's argument, however, was that the four industries had been chosen to reflect the historical development of technology. The craft occupation (printing) was intended to characterize a pre-industrial system of production, while machine-minding and mass assembly technologies (textiles and cars) represented mature industrialism. Most importantly, the automated process technology was held to be representative of future trends in advanced industrial society.

The long-term implications are that unskilled, machine-dominated work will progressively give way to manual work typified by complex technology, and thus alienation will decline from a peak in the traditional industrial society. Hence, Blauner made his well-known assertion that the progress of alienation can be charted as an inverted U-curve.

> . . . with automated industry there is a counter-trend, one that we can fortunately expect to become even more important in the future. The case of the continuous-process industries, particularly the chemical industry, shows that automation increases the worker's control over his work process and checks the further division of labour and growth of large factories. The result is meaningful work in a more cohesive, integrated industrial climate. The alienation curve begins to decline from its previous height as employees in automated industries gain a new dignity from responsibility and a sense of individual function – thus the inverted U-curve. (p. 182)

Technological development is therefore seen ultimately as a positive force. The progressive elimination of alienating working conditions, and their replacement by work which is socially integrating, is not only possible within the present industrial economy, it is happening more or less spontaneously under the normal course of industrial evolution. Alienation is regarded as an intermediate and passing phase of industrial society, rather than its culmination as in Marx's theory.

Criticisms of Blauner

Blauner's sophisticated argument essentially gave substance to the widely held belief that technological advances are somehow linked with positive progress. He dealt with the Marxist critique of technology extremely effectively – and not by rejecting Marx. Blauner allowed the truth of Marx's argument, but defined it as a special case of his own much broader theory.

As Gallie (1978) points out, Blauner's research reflected a view of the pattern of technological development that had become well established by the 1960s. This held that, up to the inter-war period, the 'mature' industrial economies had been dominated by mass production industries characterized by Taylorist methods and routine manual labour. But with the growth of highly automated process technologies these trends were being reversed. 'This technological revolution', writes Gallie, 'appeared to have quite fundamental consequences for the nature of work and the character of the business enterprise' (p. 7).

Nonetheless, Blauner's thesis has been subject to detailed criticism, both on theoretical grounds (Eldridge, 1971; Hill, 1981, pp.90–9; Salaman, 1981, pp.89–98) and by research which has challenged his findings (Nichols and Beynon, 1977; Gallie, 1978).

Certainly the break with the classical tradition of Marx and Weber is clear enough. As we saw in Chapter 9, they both conceived of deep processes of change within the capitalist economy. In contrast to this, for Blauner alienation became a function of technology – a factor confined to the circumstances of the work situation, and not implicated in class relationships or in the broader structure of industrial authority. The restricted meaning attributed to alienation stripped the concept of much of its radical force. True, Blauner did clearly define factory work as being alienating. But he has been criticized for concluding on quite limited evidence that work in continuous-process plants was intrinsically rewarding. The findings of several empirical studies since Blauner's have cast doubt on the simple link between technology and alienation he suggested, particularly for the critical case of the process industries. For example, Nichols and Beynon's (1977) study of a British chemical plant revealed the existence of much low-grade, unskilled work. They also found that pressure on labour costs caused job insecurity, conflict and the degradation of skills. This was in sharp contrast to Blauner's claim that, because labour is both a small part of total costs and critical for production, workers in high-technology industries would be subject to few of these pressures. Similarly, in his major study of British and French oil refinery workers, Gallie (1978) discovered:

> The work of most of the operators was substantially less advantageous than Blauner suggested, and the most common attitude towards work in our refineries was one of indifference. It is extremely doubtful whether automation leads to the overcoming of alienation in work in any profound sense of the word. (p. 296)

Hence the claim that technology has any inbuilt evolutionary trend towards less alienating conditions has been challenged.

Sociological explanations of technology

Blauner was not the only writer to be concerned with the influence of technology on work. Since the 1950s, a growing body of literature has examined the relationships between technology and a range of industrial behaviours: patterns of industrial conflict, workers' integration into firms, and workers' attitudes. It is in this use of technology as an explanatory variable accounting for work-related behaviour that Blauner's argument – quite apart from any of the specific failings noted above – has influenced a much wider debate. Two well-known studies, both of which lend some support to his thesis, were those of Woodward (1965) and Wedderburn and Crompton (1972).

In Woodward's noted 'south-east Essex' study the climates of industrial relations in different firms were compared with the technical systems used, emphasizing the improved relations in the process industries.

> Industrial relations certainly seemed to be better in process industry than in large batch and mass production, but it is not safe to assume that the good relationships

were due to the large number of specialist staff employed . . . there were a number of contributory factors: less tension and pressure, smaller working groups, and smaller spans of control, for instance. (p. 55)

Wedderburn and Crompton studied a large chemicals complex, and their findings also stressed that employees in continuous-process plants had relatively favourable attitudes towards work, got on well with their supervisors and enjoyed some autonomy. However, this was not extended to any broader 'moral' attachment to the firm. Although process technology gave a more convivial work environment, the harsh realities of employment were still present. Process workers 'retained a calculative involvement with the company' and were a group of workers 'directly experiencing conflicts of interest between themselves and their employer which had to be bargained about' (Wedderburn and Crompton, 1972, p.151).

These findings lend qualified support to the idea of process technology providing superior conditions, as Blauner contended, and this being favourably reflected in certain of workers' attitudes. But they lend no support to any sweeping notion of a 'new' industrial working class emerging as the product of such conditions. In the plant Wedderburn and Crompton studied process workers were militant and critical of the company. This conflict was attributed to the traditions in what was a strongly working-class area, and the researchers took the view that technology was only one among many possible factors that explain behaviour.

. . . there is no simple association to be postulated between expressed attitudes and behaviour. . . . The general norms of the community, the nature of the influence and leadership offered by the trades union, as well as the constraints of the immediate work situation, all contributed in the final event to a very complex interplay of forces. (p. 142)

It has also been argued that technology implies too narrow an explanation of attitudes and behaviour. This centres on the sociological debate in the late 1960s and early 1970s about the alleged technological determinism of research like that of Woodward and Blauner. Major critics were Goldthorpe, Lockwood *et al.* (1968) in their influential *Affluent Worker* study. These researchers argued that attitudes towards work were not shaped by factors (especially technology) internal to the work situation. The problem of understanding how people assign subjective meanings to work situations is extremely complex, and must be seen in the context of adjustments and responses to wider factors than merely those within work. They argued that attitudes were underpinned by 'orientations to work' – stable beliefs and values which originated in workers' past experience, and which they brought into the work situation. Their study of car assembly workers at the Vauxhall plant at Luton showed that while being dissatisfied with the work itself, workers still wanted to retain their jobs and were uncritical of the company. The researchers explained this by arguing that workers had developed a distinctive *instrumental orientation* towards work.

Their attitudes were shaped by their own definition of work as a source of secure and comparatively high income, but of little intrinsic interest or worth. Work had become a means to other ends – the enjoyment of family life, leisure pursuits and so forth. With low expectations of their jobs, and alternatives in their private lives to compensate, these workers were apparently satisfied with jobs that were objectively highly alienating.

Other empirical studies have demonstrated that working conditions, and people's responses to them, can vary independently of technology. Child (1978), for example, showed that the climate of industrial relations in an American car plant was not determined by the alienating technology of mass assembly. The plant changed from being notorious for strikes to having relatively harmonious industrial relations. However, it was a softening of management's approach to discipline, together with changes in workers' expectations in the face of rising unemployment, that altered the situation. The technology of course remained a constant factor. Similarly, Gallie's (1978) study referred to above concluded that 'the nature of technology *per se* has, at most, very little importance' for the social integration of the workforce (p.295). Industrial relations patterns, particularly the markedly more militant attitudes of French process workers, could only be explained by contextual factors: the structures of power in the industry, managerial and trade union strategies, and wider historical and cultural factors in French and British society.

So, while technology remains important, it is misleading to see it as a prime cause of working conditions. Any narrow focus on technology must be avoided by emphasizing the interests of the groups involved and the social elements in the context of work. There are three main considerations here: (1) technology is developed in the first place to meet specific requirements; (2) managements have the freedom to choose among different technologies; and (3) even when implemented there remains a degree of flexibility over the use of technology. Put simply, it is people who develop, select and implement technical systems, and they do so under the constraints of relations of production.

Conclusion

This said, the idea of progress through technological renewal, central to Blauner's thesis, is still highly influential. Technology is readily accepted as a powerful force for change, and the notion of automation eventually placing the worker in control of the work process is both appealing and plausible. This type of explanation from technology remains persuasive because it allows a measure of optimism about the future of work. Based on science, technology is continually developing and thus contains a range of possibilities.

So, any impression of a closed debate about the influence of technology on work and on wider social change would be quite misleading. Interestingly, the recent applications of microelectronics have once again raised the issue of technology and alienation. A number of writers (e.g. Crompton and Reid,

1982) have speculated that the new 'flexible' computer systems could allow the possibility of reversing earlier trends towards routinization. They suggest precisely the same cycle of the early degradation of conditions, followed by improvement, that Blauner postulated with his inverted U-curve. Thus in much the same way as the process industries in the 1960s sparked off debate, a new debate on the relationship between technology and work is being opened up – although an account of this will be deferred until Chapter 13.

THE 'DESKILLING' DEBATE

If technology has been singled out as a key factor in explaining industrial behaviour, we should not forget the broader pattern of workplace experiences. Recently, labour process theory has had a major impact on sociological debates, focusing particularly on the notion of *skill* in work. We referred above to Braverman's account of Taylorism. However, the publication of *Labor and Monopoly Capital* sparked off a major debate concerning the true impact of these forms of work organization. The controversial view Braverman put forward was that the contemporary labour process is characterized by a progressive 'degradation' of work. He focused particularly on craft and trade skills, seeing modern systems of management like Taylorism as methods of degrading and deskilling work. Zimbalist, one of Braverman's main supporters, has summarized this as follows:

> There is a long-run tendency through fragmentation, rationalization and mechaniz-ation for workers and their jobs to become deskilled, both in an absolute sense (they lose craft and traditional abilities) and in a relative one (scientific knowledge progressively accumulates in the production process). Even where the individual worker retains certain traditional skills, the degraded job he or she performs does not demand the exercise of these abilities. Thus, the worker, regardless of his or her personal talents, may be more easily and cheaply substituted for in the production process. (1979, p.xv)

Braverman mainly intended his argument as a correction to a view which had become the accepted wisdom in organizational psychology and sociology, namely that Taylor's ideas had been 'superseded' and no longer determined management methods. This orthodox view held that the human relations movement (discussed in Chapter 5) heralded a much more sophisticated approach to the design and management of work, one which recognized the human needs of workers and supplanted the coercive Taylorist methods. Braverman's answer was that this was merely wishful thinking, a confusion between what academics were prescribing and what employers were doing. In his view a visit to any modern organization would show that, far from being superseded, Taylorist methods are in fact *institutionalized*. They have been refined over a long period and form the basis of most modern systems of production control.

This interpretation of Taylorism was by no means original. For example, Braverman quotes the noted management writer Peter Drucker, who pointed out that while human relations has had a fairly limited influence, Taylor's methods determine 'the actual management of the worker and work' (1974, p.88). Bendix (1956, p.319) also stressed that the main impact of human relations has been as a management ideology, while scientific management represents the practice. And Marxist writers before Braverman have viewed Taylorist methods as an 'employers' offensive' (Cliff, 1970). Braverman's contribution, though, was to make a timely intervention when the shortcomings of certain conventional explanations were becoming obvious.

The critique of Braverman

His thesis was not received uncritically, however, and the decade following the publication of *Labor and Monopoly Capital* saw a growing critique of his work (e.g. Elger, 1979; Littler, 1982; Littler and Salaman, 1982; Wood, 1982; Storey, 1983). This can be briefly summarized as follows.

Firstly, it was argued that Braverman's thesis is an *oversimplification*. He suggested that general and progressive deskilling typifies the capitalist labour process, whereas no such simple pattern can be discerned in the changing distribution of skills. Taylorism is only one of the control strategies that managements have at their disposal, and alternative strategies may lead to workers retaining a measure of control over production. Here, Friedman (1977) suggested that *'responsible autonomy'* could be contrasted with strategies of direct control like scientific management. The former strategies rely upon accommodation between management and workers; and Friedman suggested that a trend towards such forms of control could be detected in practices like job enrichment (see Chapter 8) and in declining competitive pressures on labour.

Secondly, the 'universal deskilling' thesis attributed to Braverman was held to be historically inaccurate since *reskilling* also occurs. In effect, Braverman had an idealized romantic image of the craftworker as a survivor from the pre-industrial past, implying that skills exist merely as a residue from those times. However, it has been pointed out that technological development is constantly bringing into existence new skills, specialisms and indeed entire occupations. Thus, if capitalism itself can create new skills, there can be no simple process of deskilling.

Thirdly, Braverman offers no analysis of, nor seems to reserve any place for, *workers' resistance*. Hence he has been criticized for having a schematic model of class relations, and for assuming that the employing class is all-powerful and the working class totally passive. What is being emphasized here is the need to reassess the significance of actions like strikes, sabotage and output restriction, which have hitherto been regarded as rather limited defences adopted by workers, or as simply troublesome for efficiency. On the contrary, these are important elements shaping the relationship between workers and employers. Thus, critics such as Cutler (1978) have argued that the point of production is an important locus of class struggle, and the employment relationship must be conceived of as an interaction between the two classes.

Fourthly, the possibility of worker resistance means that skills themselves should not be seen as purely technical abilities: in important respects *skills are socially created*. Wood (1982, p.17), for example, has stressed that it is the legitimacy of skills that is decisive. It is not sufficient merely to possess a skill; practitioners have to be accorded a degree of prestige by society at large, and this is crucially determined by their power to protect skills. In contrast to this dynamic view, Braverman had a rather superficial understanding of skill, simply as technique, so that by ignoring the occupational status of particular jobs he denied this vitally important social aspect.

In sum, his critics have accused Braverman of taking a 'one-dimensional and unilinear' view of changing work organization. They argue that any uniform transition from skilled craftwork to rationalized labour is at variance with the historical record. Rather, industrial capitalism generates technologies which hold out the possibility of skill creation, and workers themselves are an active force in grasping and developing these opportunities.

Deskilling reassessed

While these criticisms are certainly persuasive, they are perhaps somewhat uncharitable to Braverman. The exclusive focus on him has created the impression that deskilling was 'his' idea alone. Yet it is misleading to detach Braverman from the mainstream of Marxist thinking of which he is a part. Other writers have also focused on the concept of skill quite independently. For example, the British Marxist writer V.L. Allen (1975) argued that skills are crucial as they represent the only 'capital' possessed by workers, and the degrading of skills represents a decisive new stage in worker alienation.

In its own right, *Labor and Monopoly Capital* was a deliberately polemical book, and not meant to satisfy the methodological criteria of social science. Braverman wrote within the same tradition of political economy as Marx, and with Marx he shared a selective emphasis on the 'objective' aspects of class relationships. (In the whole of Marx's *Capital*, for example, there is very little mention of workers' resistance or of trade union organization.) It may also be true that Braverman's critics have distorted his argument somewhat. Braverman did allow for more complexity than the 'crude deskilling thesis' (Wood, 1982, p.18) which is usually laid at his door. Rather ironically, too, empirical research by Braverman's critics has sometimes supported his position. Crompton and Reid (1982), for example, found overwhelming evidence of deskilling amongst clerical workers, although they themselves supported the argument that Braverman's thesis needed refining.

Others have defended the deskilling thesis in more specific terms, notably Zimbalist (1979), Hill (1981) and Thompson (1983).

These writers suggest that an even more complex relationship exists between the various types of managerial control than Braverman's critics have allowed. Thus, responsible autonomy should not be regarded as an *alternative* to direct control, as Friedman argued it was. Rather, managerial strategies which share control with workers usually operate *within* an overall strategy of direct control. (A similar point was argued in Chapter 8, where it was stressed that a detailed evaluation of job redesign programmes has revealed their limited impact.) Both Hill (1981, p.34) and Thompson (1983, p.136) have argued that the case for 'responsible' strategies being equated in importance with those based on direct control is not sustainable. On the contrary, the long-term trend is clearly that of a shift towards direct control in the central areas of industrial employment.

The criticism that Braverman overestimated the impact of scientific management has also been challenged. While there certainly were barriers to the diffusion of Taylorist methods, and methods other than Taylor's were developed, it would be mistaken to lose sight of the broader pattern of change because of these variations. Thus, Hill (1981, p.31) used the term 'rationalized management' to indicate the growth of formal labour policies and bureacratic structures. Similarly, Thompson (1983, p.126) refers to 'systematic management' to mean the same general trend towards bureaucratic control. Any slowness in the development of such systems was confined mainly to Britain, and may well have reflected our decline as an industrial power; but in the United States and Germany, these principles of work organization spread early and rapidly (Abercrombie and Urry, 1983, p.102).

The debate probably comes down finally to a difference between the (mainly Marxist) writers who argue for a long-term secular trend towards the degradation of work, and other writers who argue that the changing nature of work is essentially a spontaneous and uneven process. These positions are difficult to reconcile. It is hard to impose a single interpretation on anything so complex as industrial and occupational change. Moreover, the dilemma may be unresolvable in any practical way, since it ultimately rests on more fundamental debates within the social sciences.

What is perhaps more important is to emphasize the deeper understanding of work that the deskilling debate has led to. The clear focus on skills has given a contemporary account of alienation: that of labour being progressively 'disqualified' from the production process, as modern systems of control diminish workers' expertise. The significant amount of research that has come out of the critique of Braverman also represents a major advance. This has focused attention on the historical development of forms of work organization, as well as on current realities of work.

Still, it remains clear that any comprehensive account of work must cover the areas referred to by Braverman's critics. Consideration of the *active* role that workers play, particularly in terms of resistance to control, and the industrial conflict which arises from this have made a valuable contribution to the emerging sociology of workplace relations. It is to an account of this that we turn in the next chapter.

FURTHER READING

Burawoy, M. (1979) *Manufacturing Consent: Changes in the Labor Process under Monopoly Capitalism*. Chicago: Chicago University Press.

Edwards, R. (1979) *Contested Terrain: The Transformation of the Workplace in the Twentieth Century*. London: Heinemann.

Friedman, A. (1977) *Industry and Labour: Class Struggles at Work and Monopoly Capitalism*. London: Macmillan.

Gorz, A. (ed.) (1976) *The Division of Labour*. Hassocks, Sussex: Harvester Press.

Littler, C.R. (1982) *The Development of the Labour Process in Capitalist Societies*. London: Heinemann.

Littler, C.R. and G. Salaman (1984) *Class at Work*. London: Batsford.

McKinlay, J.B. (ed.) (1976) *Procssing People: Cases in Organizational Behaviour*. London: Holt, Rinehart and Winston.

Storey, J. (1985) 'The means of management control', *Sociology*, 19, 193–211.

Thompson, P. (1983) *The Nature of Work*. London: Macmillan.

Wood, S. (ed.) (1982) *The Degradation of Work?* London: Hutchinson.

Zimbalist, A. (1979) *Case Studies on the Labor Process*. London: Monthly Review Press.

10

Conflict and the Employment Relationship

INTRODUCTION

We have seen how, from the workers' point of view, rationalized labour practices can mean a very constraining and potentially unstable working environment. However, the emphasis on structural constraints and formal controls provides only a partial view. Relationships between workers and managements are much more complex, involving struggle on the part of workers, as well as degrees of cooperation and consent. Workers have certain resources even in the most restrictive circumstances: the power to disrupt production, to withhold cooperation, and the practical abilities and skills upon which employers depend. If production is to go ahead at all there has to be some minimum level of cooperation between management and workers, and workers require some autonomy if their initiative is to be counted upon.

Still, there can be a sharp discrepancy between the degree of freedom and dignity that workers believe they deserve and the control that employers think is necessary for their authority to be maintained. Therefore, resistance to control on the part of workers, and the conflict which follows from this, remain a constant feature of the labour process.

Dimensions of industrial conflict Workers' opposition to the constraints of the workplace can vary in a number of different ways. To begin with, the level on which conflict occurs can be based on actions taken by individuals, action taken by work groups, and action at the level of workers' organization, namely the trade union. Secondly, conflict may be formal in the sense of being openly recognized by the parties involved, and perhaps institutionalized as part of an established bargaining procedure; or it can be informal, and confined to a sphere of covert activity outside the organization's authority structure. And thirdly, conflict may be spontaneous or it may be organized.

To an extent, these dimensions occur as patterned forms of conflict. Thus the resistance of individuals would normally be classified as being both informal and spontaneous. Similarly, resistance based on work groups is also usually informal, although it shows a degree of organization in the sense of providing a collective response even if not a pre-planned one. Trade union organization provides a very important basis of opposition, preventing any single group of workers from becoming isolated. Essentially the formal recognition of a union *legitimizes* workers' resistance, and this can immeasurably strengthen their bargaining position.

Having made these distinctions, however, it is important not to oversimply them. The different dimensions of conflict overlap and interact in a sometimes bewildering variety of ways. For example, types of worker resistance which derive from spontaneous, unofficial initiatives on the part of groups of workers often benefit from a degree of tacit legitimacy, in the sense that those in authority may 'turn a blind eye' to various workshop practices. Conversely, while a trade union provides the basis for claiming legitimacy of action, official industrial disputes may still not actually enjoy widespread legitimacy. The extent to which workers are able openly to contest issues can vary a great deal, depending on factors like prevailing public opinion and the attitude of the particular employer.

Range of industrial conflict While it is possible to take the view that collective trade union action is of a different kind from initiatives taken by individuals or small groups of workers, most social scientists nowadays would probably accept that these forms of conflict stem from the same root causes in the commodity-status of labour and the constraints of managerial authority. And, indeed, on close inspection there does prove to be an overlap between different levels of conflict.

The great complexity in patterns and forms of industrial conflict that these diverse dimensions point to has often been noted (Eldridge, 1968, p.19; Hyman, 1984, p.55). As an individual response conflict may occur where workers, finding themselves at odds with their work for whatever reasons, may respond by taking time off or by leaving the job after a relatively short period. Thus, high rates of absenteeism, lateness or labour turnover usually indicate a 'withdrawal' from the work situation. Industrial sabotage is also seen as a similar reaction to a work situation experienced as disagreeable. As well as conflict individually expressed, there is collective conflict involving the solidarity of the workforce.

The great diversity of industrial conflict means that it often takes the form of a *tactical* response. Interests will be mobilized in pursuit of explicit objectives, and the parties involved will use forms of resistance which seem most appropriate. For instance, if workers and their leaders regard an all-out strike as a measure of last resort, they may wish first to test management's resolve with less drastic action such as an overtime ban, or with subtle forms of non-cooperation which affect output and quality. Similarly, in the case of a plant under threat of closure, a strike would make little sense if the company intended moving the stock and machinery elsewhere. The occupation of the site would be more likely to add to workers' bargaining strength.

Conflict initiated by management can also be a tactical response in changing circumstances. Thus, for example, if the market for a firm's products is buoyant and it can sell all it makes, management would normally be reluctant to provoke action that would disrupt output. Supervisors and personnel officers will be instructed to tread carefully when dealing with workers. However, if demand falls collective action poses less of a threat, and may even be beneficial. A strike of limited duration can improve a firm's financial position by saving on wages. Thus, in times of slack demand it is not uncommon to find managements tightening up on industrial discipline.

In this chapter these various aspects of industrial conflict will be explored, essentially by examining the three principal levels of conflict: individual and group conflict (which are here classed under workplace conflict) and broader industrial conflict based on trade union action.

WORKPLACE RESISTANCE

The point-of-production resistance of workers has often been interpreted as being a problem of poor communications, of managers and workers unable to understand each other's points of view, or as some other type of human relations difficulty. However, Salaman (1979) has recently drawn attention to the dialectic between managerial control and workers' resistance as a vital, if often neglected, aspect of class conflict. This suggests that individual and group resistance has a *structural* aspect and stems from a clash of real material interests. Nonetheless, it is a structure which is dynamic and changing. In this sense, for example, the employment relationship was visualized by Goodrich (1975) in his classic study of the British mining industry in terms of a 'frontier of control', the boundaries of which continually shift as one side or the other gains ascendancy. Workers or management may control some aspect of operations, but the struggle may simply shift to another level or another area. As Thompson (1983, p.124) points out, control reflects 'the degree of power management has to direct work', and this is always relative to the counter-vailing power possessed by workers.

In reality, a perpetual struggle for control in work is not always obvious or observable. The tactics workers adopt are often versatile and frequently covert, so that an intimate knowledge of a particular place of work might be needed in order to be aware of resistance going on. Nor does resistance have to be manifest to be effective. The threat of resistance being offered if some change were to be initiated may be enough to maintain the *status quo*. For example, skilled workers may enjoy considerable autonomy by virtue of their employer's reliance on their skills – so much so that the employer gives little thought to attempts to rationalize work or deskill jobs.

Spontaneous resistance and sabotage

A form of activity which clearly comes under the heading of subtle and covert resistance is industrial sabotage. This is a response from workers who are perhaps seeking a respite from a tedious job, or who wish to defy what they regard as an oppressive management. Sabotage can break the rhythm of work and it can give workers the feeling of having some control over their work situation, however slight. Highly constraining technologies, like assembly lines, can produce in workers a desire to 'beat the system', while other acts of sabotage may simply be a by-product of pressures for output. The removal of safety devices to speed up production, for instance, is often done with the tacit connivance of supervisors.

Industrial sabotage has been a neglected area of research, despite its being one of the commonest forms of worker resistance. However Taylor and Walton (1971) have provided a sociological framework of analysis. They argued that although sabotage is usually regarded as irrational or even pathological behaviour, careful investigation shows that 'in many cases the meanings which inform sabotage are explicitly intentional'. A knowledge of the *context* in which acts of sabotage occur – the lack of alternatives available to workers, the frustrations that build up over time – often shows sabotage to have been an understandable response.

Taylor and Walton note that sabotage can be difficult to define: at one end it merges with informal practices which become almost part of normal procedure, 'neither openly demanded nor openly questioned', while in extreme cases sabotage may be identified with explicitly political violence. Indeed, it is possible to argue with Taylor and Walton's own definition: 'rule-breaking which takes the form of conscious action or inaction directed towards mutilation or destruction of the work environment'. Here, they use the common-sense idea of sabotage as a 'spanner in the works', yet several of their own examples do not fit readily into such a definition. Not all acts of sabotage 'mutilate or destroy' the work environment, some merely cause delays and confusion. Nor does sabotage necessarily break rules in any simple sense. Rules themselves may conflict with one another, and sabotage may break one (usually formal) rule whilst fulfilling some other informal expectation.

Work groups and work cultures

The collective resistance of workers is also a feature of much informal action in the workplace. Given the power of the managerial hierarchy to dispense or withhold rewards, open acts of defiance expose individuals to reprisal. But resistance which is both group-based and informal can be very difficult for management to pin down. The example of sabotage, discussed above, was a case in point. Although covert, sabotage is not necessarily just an individual

199

response. Taylor and Walton noted that 'often the active or passive cooperation of hundreds is observable'.

Work groups may generate distinctive 'cultures of resistance' based on informal relations of friendship, or on some shared occupational identity such as a craft ethic (Salaman, 1979, pp.163–6). In any case, work groups often develop common values and a sense of their own history. They may also share distinctive ways of communicating, such as a repertoire of sayings and in-jokes. This culture – frequently the expression of past struggles with management – can form an effective basis of unity and continuing resistance to formal control.

A classic study of work group resistance, which we first discussed in Chapter 5 above, is found in the famous Hawthorne research (Roethlisberger and Dickson, 1943). The management at the Hawthorne plant had been frustrated in their efforts to raise production in a section where electrical assemblies were wired up – the so-called Bank Wiring Room – and the researchers were called in to try to resolve this problem. The researchers discovered the existence of a strong group culture which enforced an output norm. Workers in the section perceived management's standards – arrived at by Taylorist methods – to be outside their control and liable to be raised arbitrarily. Consequently they restricted their output to a level they regarded as reasonable, one that did not undermine their own pay and job security, and that the slower members could keep up with. The Hawthorne researchers stressed the pressure that groups can bring to bear on members to conform to common norms. In this case positive sanctions involved acceptance in the friendship cliques, while negative sanctions meant ridicule and ostracism for anyone who broke ranks and tried to 'bust' the agreed work rate.

The prevailing view of such work group resistance has often been that it stems from workers' misunderstanding of management's intentions. Indeed, such disapproval is implicit in the very notion of workers 'restricting' output. Lupton's noted study *On the Shop Floor* (1963) traced the widespread acceptance of this biased view to the Hawthorne research and the human relations movement which followed it. These interpreted output restriction in terms of the *social* requirements of sustaining a group structure. Workers' desire for group membership, and their supposedly affectual motives, were contrasted with management's rational criteria based on technical efficiency. (The focus of the human relations school has always centred on the possibility of reconciling these social and technical rationales.) However, as Lupton points out, the conflict of interest may well be genuine, not merely an irrational response by workers. Workers' behaviour, he argues, is really a response to *managerial control*, and is best understood as a counter-attempt to assert workers' own control (1963, p.6).

The point has been made more generally by Eldridge in his historical survey of workers' resistance (1971, pp. 45–64). He suggested that in the early stages of the industrial system, tactics like machine-breaking by agricultural labourers may indeed have reflected a clash between workers' 'traditionalistic outlook' and the new methods of technical efficiency. But as industrial capitalism developed, the basis of conflict shifted to one of 'competing rationalities'. The struggle to exert control increasingly brought managements and workers into conflict over issues related to the work itself: bargaining over piecework rates, the rules of shop practice, the pace and intensity of work, and so on. Thus, conflict reflects workers' coming to terms with the rational procedures of employment, and learning to fight back using employers' own categories of time and money.

Some celebrated empirical studies of work groups have argued that so-called restrictive practices usually reflect the attempt by workers to impose their own definition of a fair day's work. Lupton's own research, in an electrical components firm, showed how an equitable balance between wages and effort can develop on the shopfloor. Not only workers but supervisors too colluded to 'fiddle' earnings and work allocation in a complex piecework system. The 'fiddle' was 'a quite stable adjustment of the discrepant goals of management and workers' (1963, p.197). Similarly, Donald Roy's well-known studies also showed the conscious manipulation of payment systems. In one case, Roy (1952) observed that output restriction stopped short of the point where management would have retimed jobs and cut the piece rates; in another (1954) study operators, inspectors and supervisors cooperated in informal practices to 'fix' a fair job rate.

Manual workers are not the only occupational group to have to cope with imposed controls. Professionals and white-collar employees nowadays increasingly find their status and conditions under attack. As a result, it is possible to see in such groups the collective responses normally associated with shopfloor workers. Pettigrew's (1973) study of the implementation of a computer network in a large retailing firm provides a good example of group solidarity amongst employed professionals. The programmers in the company initially had a good deal of control over the computer installation, which provoked management to cut down their influence. The programmers responded in a variety of ways – by attacking the competence of the 'dilutees' whom management brought in to fragment their work, and by habitually withholding their most important resource: information. They kept details of programs in their heads, and always explained procedures in highly technical jargon. Their varied and imaginative tactics grew out of a strong collective identity developed in the face of the hostility they encountered from management.

Finally, the ways in which employees can adapt systems of managerial control depend to a large extent upon the *work context*, particularly the room for manoeuvre allowed by factors like market pressures, technology and work organization. Patterns like the 'fix' and the 'fiddle' were developed by skilled workers, in piecework systems where considerable discretion was retained on the shopfloor. Similarly, professional groups possessing key skills can often rely on employers' dependence upon them. Where this kind of space exists, informal relationships need not always subvert formal goals. Indeed, workers can adapt in ways which support the organization (Fox, 1971, p.33). Instances in which workers take the initiative to get a job done reflect cooperative elements in the employment relationship. However, in work situations under much tighter constraint, or based on work-pacing technology like the assembly line, there is far less scope to manipulate managerial control. In such cases workers' resistance may be defensive and more obviously oppositional.

INDUSTRIAL CONFLICT AND INDUSTRIAL RELATIONS

The forms of industrial conflict whereby workers' interests are mobilized on a broader front include strikes and other kinds of industrial action, and here the role of trade unions as workers' official representatives comes into play. Of course, in reality there is a continuum between these and more informal types of conflict. A great deal of strike activity turns out, on closer inspection, to be spontaneous and based on resistance by specific groups of workers. Likewise, the strength of any union in the final analysis rests on the resolve of workers to oppose managerial control at the point of production. This was well demonstrated, for example, in Huw Beynon's famous study of a Ford car assembly plant, which gave a detailed account of the two-way relationship between official trade union activity and the shopfloor resistance of workers (Beynon, 1984). Still, in focusing on the *collective* character of disputes, we are moving to a level of analysis that includes the wider framework of economic and political changes. Outside the confines of the work organization, factors like public opinion, the state of the economy, and government policy on industrial relations cannot be ignored.

Conflict in the employment relationship has had an important influence on theories of industrial relations. The orthodox approach to the subject of the 1950s and 1960s essentially involved a *pluralist* perspective. It viewed management, on the one hand, and workers organized and represented by trade unions, on the other, as both possessing roughly comparable resources of power. Their interests were seen as being conflictual in some degree, but the pluralist model implied that the terms of the relationship were negotiable. As Alan Fox, a major proponent and later critic of pluralism, has put it, 'The pluralist does not claim anything approaching perfection for this system . . . [but the] imbalances of strength between employers and unions . . . are not seen as so numerous or severe as generally to discredit the system either from the union's point of view or the management's' (1977, p.136).

More recently, however, the weaknesses of this approach have been recognized. To view workers and employers as equal partners in an agreement lacks any sense of the sharp inequalities of power dividing them. But more importantly, since the late 1960s, the 'return' of industrial conflict as a major issue in workplace relations has created serious difficulties for this analysis. A pluralist perspective sees conflict essentially as a temporary breakdown in job regulation, which means that the emphasis is very much on the resolution of disputes in collective bargaining. So while the model could certainly account for conflict, high rates of strikes and evidence of a powerful opposition of interests between employers and workers could not be accommodated. The scale of many more recent industrial disputes, together with the manner in which they have been regarded by workers, employers and the state, have made explanations based on pluralism seem less and less plausible.

The failure of conventional pluralist ideas prompted the emergence of what Hill (1976) has called the 'new industrial relations' based on a 'sociological and radical perspective'. The main exponents of this approach – writers like Hyman, Beynon and Fox – all take conflict to be a major structural component of employment; although we should also note that sociology in fact has a longer tradition of exploring the distinctive problems of explanation and under-standing associated with industrial conflict (e.g. Eldridge, 1968).

Interpreting industrial conflict

At least two main aspects of the sociological approach can be singled out. Firstly, it sees industrial relations as part of a totality of social relations. It is necessary to consider the social context of industrial relations as well as the labour process; and here the new sociology of work, discussed in the previous chapter, is of central relevance. Above all, a sociological view of *power and control* is essential. Thus a unifying theme of the 'new' industrial relations, to quote Hill (1976), is 'the conviction that order and coherence in industry and society rest on relations of dominance and power, and that in modern industrial societies, particularly capitalist ones, power disparities are long-term, structured and not susceptible of much modification'.

A second important feature of sociological explanations of industrial conflict is that they assume conflict to be a reasoned response of one form or another. Even where it at first appears to be a rather pointless reaction there is invariably found to be some rational element, which means that conflict must be classed alongside other forms of purposive *social action*. This approach, pioneered by Weber (1964, pp.88–115), has been widely applied in studies of industrial conflict. Viewing behaviour as social action means that explanations of events must be 'adequate at the level of meaning'. Or, as Eldridge has put it, 'adequate description for sociological purposes involves the attempt to delineate the meaning people attribute to their behaviour, and to the situations in which they find themselves' (1968, p.17). The basic focus of interest here is the different versions of events that industrial conflict is likely to produce. What the workers might think is a lively practical joke, management may regard as disruption or sabotage; what workers might see as an intensification of their labour, management may regard as an improvement in flexibility, and so forth.

Therefore, as impartial observers, it is important that we take account of all definitions of the situation, and are prepared to understand events as the participants themselves experience them.

Implied in this approach is a definite change of emphasis from pluralist-type accounts. The latter involved a narrow focus on the formal institutions of industrial relations. But the sociological approach argues that this is inherently abstract and artificial, as if decisions taken within the negotiating arena somehow independently shape the course of events. Instead, it is recommended that the motives and actions of the groups involved in workplace relations should be the main focus of attention. It is how they perceive and define events, and how their consciousness forms and changes, that is ultimately decisive.

A sociological model of industrial conflict

In the accounts of industrial action one reads about in newspapers or sees on television, the cause of a dispute will usually be attributed to the issue over which work relations broke down. Most of us therefore tend to think that strikes are brought about by specific disagreements – over pay, for example, or over alleged misconduct by workers or managers. However, a sociological explanation needs to be more holistic than this, and it is not normally sufficient merely to regard the events leading up to a strike as its cause. Following Eldridge (1968, pp.19–23), we can distinguish different 'causal levels' on

Table 10.1 *Causes of industrial conflict.*

Causal factors	Level at which applied	Type of explanation provided
(1) Precipitating	Confined to each specific cause of conflict	Necessary to account for the immediate causes of conflict
(2) Background	Locally within a particular place of work. 'Custom and practice'	Sufficient to account for the nature of conflict within a particular place of work
(3) Contextual	Structure of wider society, particularly socio-economic inequality and power	Sufficient to account for broader relationships between groups in conflict

which behaviour is structured. The events that immediately precede a strike are more accurately defined as the factors which serve to *precipitate* the ensuing conflict. But in addition there are issues which form the local *background* to any given dispute, and other factors which constitute the broader societal *context* of conflict.

Thus it is possible to discern three main levels of causality in this model of industrial conflict. Firstly, there is the immediate cause, which is necessary to bring about the specific instance of conflict but which does not provide the sufficient conditions for conflict in general to occur. Secondly, there is the background to the dispute, or the rules of 'custom and practice' which constitute a sort of local social structure within a place of work. Superimposed on them, at the third level, is the wider social structure (Table 10.1).

A classic study which serves as a model analysis of how these levels of explanation may be linked up is provided by Gouldner's *Wildcat Strike* (1955). This traced the course of an unofficial stoppage in a small gypsum mine and a factory in which the mineral was processed into plasterboard. The plant, a major source of employment in a small community, for years had been operated under what Gouldner termed an 'indulgency pattern' of management. Here, the relationships between managers and workers were tolerant and friendly, and involved loyalties and commitments over and above the mere exchange of wages for work. However, the corporation that owned the plant regarded it as being inefficiently run and took steps to introduce a regime of tighter discipline. New machinery was brought in which meant an unpredictable pace of work. All in all, the 'indulgency pattern was subjected to a crippling attack, and workers' hostility rapidly mounted' (p.28). As events came to a head, there were changes in the supervisory structure, with popular supervisors demoted and unpopular men promoted. Finally, a quarrel broke out between the union steward and a production engineer, who was himself closely associated with the efficiency drive and the focus of much of the tension. It was this which sparked off the strike.

By dwelling on this complex chain of cause and effect, Gouldner indicated that the strike could only be understood against the background of changes in the employment relationship. The employer's intention to re-take certain areas of discretion was seen by the workers as the contravention of a rule, the indulgency pattern, which was regarded as fair and legitimate by most people in the plant, including many in supervision and management. Thus the strike came as no surprise to those involved. The researchers, the workers, management and union officials all 'saw it coming' and regarded the strike as a wholly understandable outcome.

While Gouldner described an 'everyday' strike, Lane and Roberts's *Strike at Pilkingtons* (1971) gives an account of a dispute that attained national fame – a seven-week stoppage at the glass-making company in 1970. Their approach was similar to Gouldner's in attempting 'to see the strike through the eyes of its different groups of participants' (p.18). But the Pilkington dispute could not have been anticipated (although there were issues that precipitated it – pay levels were perceived to be low and the initial walk-out occurred over a wages error). The main point Lane and Roberts stressed was the dynamism of the strike itself. Once under way, sections of the workforce were 'drawn in' and the strike became a liberating experience for many of those involved in organizing it. Crucially, a rift developed between a local strike leadership and the trade union's national officials. The union, notoriously moderate and bureaucratic, repudiated the strike and made several attempts to engineer a return to work (including alleged collaboration with the employer). This produced a deep sense of betrayal amongst workers; and the 'civil war' between rank-and-file workers and the official union was essentially what turned the strike into a protracted struggle.

Lane and Roberts argued that strikes are not difficult to explain. They are 'normal events', arising almost naturally out of the circumstances of the employment relationship itself: 'A wildcat can break out in perfectly normal conditions, and the structure of the relations between employers, trade unions, governments and workers guarantees that some strikes will grow from small beginnings into mightly struggles' (p.241).

This brings us to consider the broader *context* of industrial conflict. Factors operating at this level are remote from the event itself, yet they predispose different groups of people towards certain kinds of action and hence define the limits of other causes. The key factor put forward as the underlying cause of conflict is the distribution of wealth and power, reflecting the deep class divisions of our society.

Within the workplace inequality and conflict are inextricably bound up, irrespective of the relationship between particular managements and work-forces. Because wages are part of the employers' costs, which they must seek to minimize if they are to survive, workers experience a ceaseless downward pressure on their standards of living. It is only by exerting upward pressure themselves, using whatever means are at their disposal, that workers are able to sustain wage levels and general conditions. Thus the returns going to labour and capital are not simply allocated by the hidden hand of the market, they stabilize only as the outcome of conflict. Work organizations (as we shall see in more detail in Chapter 13) are power hierarchies in which 'lower participants' – manual and white-collar employees who make up the bulk of the employed population – find themselves continuously under the control of others. Sociologists have argued that this sharply divided authority itself provokes conflict (Dahrendorf, 1959). In order to sustain authority structures, managers are obliged continually to assert the power of their position, which inevitably calls forth resistance on the part of workers.

The social response to strikes

Although industrial conflict occurs across a wide range of behaviour, there can be little doubt of the massive amount of attention focused on one of its forms: strikes. This partly reflects the fact that strikes are a dramatic form of conflict (or at least they can be portrayed as dramatic events), and partly it reflects the fact that public opinion in Britain is firmly fixed upon strikes. Repeated surveys have shown that a large majority of people remains convinced that Britain is much more strike-prone than other industrial countries, that strikes cause severe economic disruption and that they are a major contributor to the country's industrial decline (Taylor, 1980, p.13).

This is important because public opinion has a crucial influence on the climate in which industrial relations is conducted. Yet the manner in which strikes are perceived needs some explaining. Indeed, as industrial relations experts have frequently pointed out, albeit with almost no effect, the popular view bears little relation to the known facts (Turner, 1969).

Table 10.2 *International comparisons of work stoppages 1974–83*. From *Employment Gazette* (London: HMSO), April 1985, p. 150.

	Average striker-days per 1,000 employees		
	1974–78	1979–83	1974–83
United Kingdom	380	500	440
Australia	690	590	640
Canada	990	750	860
Irish Republic	700	730	720
Italy	1410	1190	1300
Spain	1030	970	1000
Belgium	240	130	210
Denmark	90	110	100
France	210	120	170
Germany (FR)	60	10	30
Japan	130	20	70
Netherlands	10	30	20
Norway	70	50	60
Sweden	30	250	140

Table 10.2 compares stoppages in fourteen major industrial nations. (The differences in definitions adopted by different countries would not affect the broad pattern of international comparison, although we should be sceptical about small variations between countries.) These data do lend some support to the prevailing public opinion. The figure for Britain falls within a band of figures for countries (Australia, Canada, Ireland, Italy and Spain) which can be regarded as relatively strike-prone, albeit the number of days lost in Britain is the lowest in the group. Moreover, Britain's recorded striker-days are high

compared with some other European countries, particularly France and Germany. Nevertheless, we can see straightaway that these figures give the lie to any simple notion of Britain being excessively strike-ridden. We fall roughly in the middle of this overall ranking.

In addition, the impact that strikes have on production tends for numerous reasons to be exaggerated. We have already mentioned that strikes need not be damaging to individual firms; and while it is true that the economy as a whole can be damaged by certain groups of workers (e.g. power workers, miners and transport workers), relatively few groups actually have this kind of muscle. Also, strikes are responsible for an almost negligible amount of lost time compared with total hours worked by the employed population. Causes of lost production other than strikes, such as sickness, industrial accidents, and more recently of course unemployment, affect output much more seriously.

Why, then, the outcry about strikes? In his thorough sociological analysis of industrial conflict, Richard Hyman (1984) has put forward two main reasons. Firstly, the role of the news media in forming public opinion is very important. Certainly recent research has detected an element of straightforward bias in the reporting of strikes. Managers are often subtly portrayed as the more reasonable and responsible party, and greater authority is attributed to their views, while strikes are seen as 'problems' created by workers. This type of imbalance, it is suggested, reflects deeply rooted divisions of power and wealth in our society. The news media, themselves privately owned and controlled, convey an image of society which supports dominant class interests. From this viewpoint, Philo, Beharrell and Hewitt (1977) have argued that the television news's 'one-dimensional' treatment of industrial relations helps to create a consensual image of society, which 'at its most damaging amounts to laying the blame for the problems of an economy based on private interest at the door of the workforce'.

However, simple bias is not a complete answer; we need to take into account the way in which news is produced. News cannot just be seen as information about events that is transmitted to the public in some unproblematic way; in a very real sense the news is *manufactured*. The raw material of events is processed – selected, edited, dramatized, presented – by the professionals who run the media; ultimately it is their values which influence the version of events the public receives (Edwards, 1979).

In seeking to present strikes as 'newsworthy', media professionals often convey a quite artificial image of industrial relations. News coverage tends to reduce the complex process of strikes down to a single issue. (In terms of the model developed earlier, only the precipitating causes tend to be brought out.) It is only if a strike remains in the news for a long period that anything of its history or underlying causes will emerge – and then only in the 'quality' press, rarely on television or in the tabloid newspapers where most people obtain their information. Hence the demand of workers for jobs with reasonable pay and security may command public sympathy, but it does not find widespread legitimacy, and those on strike may simply appear as troublemakers causing dissent unnecessarily. Employers, by contrast, can call upon powerful ideological forces in our culture to legitimize their interests. They need only announce a general aim of improving efficiency or international competitiveness and their case is virtually made for them.

However, this line of argument still leaves unanswered the question why strikes are presented as they are, which brings us to the second of the points Hyman raised. He suggested the basic reason for the public clamour over strikes reflects their political repercussions rather than any direct economic impact. Strikes, in other words, represent a challenge to *managerial authority*. Even though very few strikes create a real crisis of control in firms, any strike, no matter how short-lived, contains the seeds of a deeper threat to management. As Hyman (1984, p.156) puts it, it is hardly surprising 'that those who exercise managerial authority typically resent this limitation on their autonomy, and are sometimes haunted by the fear that strikes may escalate into an explicit challenge to the minority control of industry'. Managerial authority, and indeed the whole edifice of organizational power, represent the rights of ownership delegated to management. Thus, when the managerial control of labour is thwarted by industrial action, ultimately the employment relationship itself is being undermined. As we have stressed, this is the basis of a capitalist industrial economy, hence we can see why in the final analysis the disruption of authority in industry should be regarded as being so critical.

Conclusion: patterns of industrial action

Finally, on the issue of strike statistics, the data in Table 10.3 reveal several important aspects of industrial relations. The changing pattern of strikes in the period since 1961 falls roughly into three stages. Stoppages in the early 1960s were numerous but tended to be limited in the numbers of workers involved and in duration. This reflected the high level of local organization of the early post-war years: industrial action sprang from the shopfloor, and the preponderance of unofficial or 'wildcat' strikes was a major industrial relations issue. However, during the 1970s this pattern was transformed. The changes were complex, as ever, but there were two important aspects: a shift of union power from plant to national level, and with industry entering the early stages of recession some major struggles occurred. Thus, we can see strikes still frequent, but becoming larger in size and longer in duration.

The pattern changed again in the early 1980s. Strikes remained relatively large, but the numbers have fallen sharply and represent the lowest level of industrial conflict in the post-war years. There can be little doubt that this reflects the very high unemployment experienced so far and the resultant weakened state of the union movement and of labour generally.

In the current period industrial relations is conducted in a very different climate from that of much of the post-war era. The impact of the recession in

Britain has compelled employers drastically to reduce labour costs at the same time as it has effectively shifted the balance of market strength in their favour. As a result, a whole range of measures including stricter disciplinary codes, work reorganization and redundancies have been carried through in large numbers of firms (Hyman and Elger, 1981). In this period of 'realism' the immediate concerns of many workers have moved towards job security.

Table 10.3 *Stoppages of work in Britain 1961–85*. Compiled from *Employment Gazette* (London: HMSO), various issues.

	Number of stoppages	Workers involved (000)	Working days lost (000)
1961	2686	771	3046
1963	2068	590	1755
1965	2354	868	2925
1967	2116	731	2787
1969	3116	1654	6846
1971	2228	1171	13551
1973	2873	1513	7197
1975	2282	789	6012
1977	2703	1155	10142
1978	2471	1011	9405
1979	2080	4583	29474
1980	1330	830	11964
1981	1338	1499	4266
1982	1528	2101	5313
1983	1352	573	3754
1984	1206	1436	27135
1985	887	643	6402

Nonetheless, it would be misleading to 'read off' from the unemployment situation a decline in workers' resolve to take independent action. As the table shows, the level of conflict in the early 1980s fell far below that of the 1970s, but the pattern was certainly not one of uniform decline. In 1979 and again in 1984 enormous numbers of working days were lost to disputes resulting, firstly, from the major strikes mounted by engineering and public sector workers, and secondly, the mineworkers' strike which lasted a bitter fourteen months. In the aftermath of both these outbursts of militancy stoppages of work declined dramatically. But after 1979 levels of industrial action steadily climbed. Following the miners' strike in 1984, industrial action has sunk again, to what seems its lowest point in the period under consideration, though it is still too soon to tell if this will be sustained. At any rate, it would be an exaggeration to speak of a collapse of militancy, or to infer that over the long term workers' resistance cannot be maintained. Much depends on the determination of workers to defend jobs and conditions, and factors like this may alter considerably over time. Above all, the changes and uncertainty of the present period mean that the full extent of the current developments in employment patterns remains very much an open issue.

FURTHER READING

Baldamus, W. (1961) *Efficiency and Effort*. London: Tavistock.

Beynon, H. (1984) *Working for Ford* (2nd ed.). Harmondsworth: Penguin.

Clarke, T. and L. Clements (eds.) (1977) *Trade Unions under Capitalism*. London: Fontana.

Hill, S. (1981) *Competition and Control at Work*. London: Heinemann.

Hyman, R. (1975) *Industrial Relations: A Marxist Introduction*. London: Macmillan.

Hyman, R. (1984) *Strikes* (3rd ed.). London: Fontana.

Nichols, T. and P. Armstrong (1976) *Workers Divided: A Study in Shop Floor Politics*. London: Fontana.

Nichols, T. and H. Beynor (1977) *Living with Capitalism*. London: Routledge and Kegan Paul.

Salaman, G. (1979) *Work Organisations: Resistance and Control*. London: Longman.

11

Divisions of Labour

While most people in a modern industrial economy have to sell their labour, they certainly do not all do so under the same conditions. Over and above the common factors in the labour process (which were discussed in the previous two chapters), there are also wide variations in the kind of jobs available and in the rewards attached to them. This variety in work will be the focus of this chapter; and in order to examine it we need to look essentially at *occupational* themes and at the range of available employment. However, rather than survey the entire occupational structure, or look for wider sources of change in the general distribution of skills, we will take a more selective approach and concentrate on certain of the main occupational areas.

We shall look first at the *labour market* which confronts the manual working class – still the largest section of the employed population in spite of any decline in industrial jobs. The work opportunities open to the bulk of the population and their perceptions of these chances are vitally important for an understanding of modern employment. Secondly, we will examine the nature of *white-collar work*. Here we will be concerned chiefly with 'low-grade' office work, another of the largest job sectors. Interest here will focus on a debate which has exercised the minds of social scientists for more than fifty years: what are the implications for white-collar workers, particularly those in clerical and related occupations, of the declining status of office work? In the third section we look at another occupational group that has attracted much recent attention, namely *professionals*. The reasons for this interest are not hard to find. The professions are the most rapidly expanding group in the occupational structure, and this itself has created uncertainty and ambiguity as regards their work situation. But the professions also have a highly dynamic impact in that many of the new skills crucial in a modern industrial economy are commanded by these occupations. In examining the professions, however, our emphasis changes, and instead of looking at the structures of available jobs, we consider the strategies adopted by professionals actively to influence their occupational status.

As already indicated, this coverage does not by any means take in all occupations – groups like management, skilled workers and technical staff are omissions that readily spring to mind. But the three above are certainly important occupational groups, and in considering them we will be exploring some of the most important debates in the current sociological analysis of work.

THE LABOUR MARKET

In a modern economy the labour market mediates the relationship between employers and employees. A key factor in workers' labour market behaviour is the notion of *choice*. If the market is to distribute labour rationally, the employer must be in a position of maximum possible choice, able to match the requirements of the vacant job with the abilities of applicants. It is also important, from the workers' point of view, to be able to choose the kind of job and the employer they want, since freedom of choice between jobs remains vital to the process of obtaining advantageous employment.

Although labour markets are known to depart from conditions of free choice, they have often been assumed to be essentially rational, and to allow a reasonable amount of free movement of labour and efficient allocation. However, more recently some serious doubts have been raised about this. The basic concepts of 'freedom' and 'choice' seem to be notoriously problematic. How much choice constitutes real choice? What apparent choices really represent people bowing to the inevitable? The concept of choice can also obscure the conflicting interests and power differences in society – in other words, what exists as choice for a powerful group may well appear as constraint to the less well placed. Thus, any sociological understanding of the labour market must dig deeper than a face-value notion of individual choice. It has to take serious account of the structural forces (class, gender, race, etc.) which influence the opportunities open to people and which shape the images of their own opportunities that they develop.

Job choice and work orientations

An influential model of the way in which workers choose jobs was developed by Goldthorpe, Lockwood et al. (1968) in the 'affluent worker' research. The car assembly workers in the study experienced their work as it really was: routine and dead-end. But they had, as it were, made a rational decision to enter a type of employment that offered little intrinsic interest but high pay, since this reflected their underlying 'orientations' to work – in this case an instrumental orientation. The researchers therefore inferred a causal link between prior orientations to work and job choice: people with particular work orientations would seek out employment which gave the balance of rewards they desired and the deprivations they were willing to put up with.

The Luton study was never meant to be entirely representative of the manual working class. It focused on a certain type of worker – unskilled but in well-paid jobs – of which car assembly was a classic example. Nevertheless, the study can be criticized for implying a higher degree of job choice than exists in practice. Criticism comes on two counts. Firstly, the *origins* of work orientations may need to be questioned. To take their existence for granted, as Goldthorpe *et al.* did, is to ignore the possibility that it may be the labour market experiences of workers that cause them to adopt instrumental orientations in the first place. Thus the *voluntary* nature of the acceptance of unskilled work implied in the affluent worker model tended to play down the extent to which market choice for workers is limited by their educational attainment and by the availability of job opportunities, and so assumed a more rational market than may exist. Wedderburn and Crompton (1972), for instance, point out that the Luton sample was chosen to maximize job choice, being in the South-East and based on a mobile, relatively young workforce. Their own study of chemical workers in an area in the North-East, with a much higher incidence of unemployment, showed indications of far more restricted job choice.

Secondly, although Goldthorpe *et al.* wanted to avoid any narrow reliance on production technology to explain workers' attitudes (i.e. technologically 'determinist' theories), it has been suggested that they overemphasized factors external to the work situation. Both sets of factors – structural conditions within work, as well as the perceptions people bring to their employment – need to be taken into account. In particular, the happy coincidence between instrumental attitudes and the nature of car assembly work may simply have reflected adjustments and responses to the work situation. Thus, in an earlier American study of car workers Chinoy (1955) found that attitudes followed a career cycle. Younger people entered the work with a concern for certain intrinsic rewards, particularly prospects and promotion, but with longer service they adjusted to restricted opportunities and their orientations shifted to pay and security. Similarly Beynon (1984), in his noted study of car assembly workers at Ford's plant in Liverpool, also emphasized workers' limited job choice. In a region of high unemployment and declining industries, Ford offered reasonably well-paid employment. But workers' distaste for their jobs and their powerful sense of alienation were not diminished by positive aspects of the work.

A more recent account of the job choices open to workers has been provided by Blackburn and Mann (1979) in their intensive survey of the labour market in a single town, Peterborough. They found that manual workers who possessed the skills or qualifications to enable them to exercise any real choice over their employment were in a small minority indeed. The jobs open to the vast majority of workers were mostly routine and poorly paid, with few differences between them. Moreover, the market was *hierarchical* rather than *compensatory*, thus removing one of the only areas of choice that is sometimes attributed to manual work. Very few jobs offered any chances of exchanging detrimental features (longer hours, poor conditions) for extra rewards (pay, status). The only chance of gaining additional rewards came with simply getting a better job, and this was both rare and outside workers' control.

> . . . the *absolute* level of skill of all but the very highest jobs is – to say the least – minimal. Eighty-seven per cent of our workers exercise less skill at work than they would if they drove to work. Indeed, most of them expend more mental effort and resourcefulness in getting to work than in doing their jobs. From this remarkable result flow two important consequences. In the first place, nobody can choose a challengingly skilled job, no matter how much he is prepared to sacrifice in terms of wages and other work rewards. . . . Secondly, it follows that most workers are objectively capable of acquiring the skills necessary for most jobs; we estimate that 85 per cent of workers can do 95 per cent of jobs. (p.280)

What workers looked for in jobs reflected this highly restricted choice. Blackburn and Mann found little evidence in support of distinctive work orientations. Instead, they found 'weak orientations' in the form of complex patterns of preferences for certain types of work (a leaning towards outdoor work, elements of instrumentalism, a desire for jobs with some autonomy). They concluded that workers retain a sense of the reality of their situation – 'all orientations are confined within the limits of the labour market' (p.282) – whilst at the same time making the best of things by valuing very highly the small differences between jobs that did exist. Interestingly, therefore, the labour market can be seen as at least partially rational, but only if workers' subjective perceptions are taken into account.

Labour market theory and the constraints on job choice

The notion of workers competing equally in an open labour market is an ideal far removed from reality. In practice a great many 'substantive' factors – employers' preferences for certain kinds of worker, their desire not to disrupt established workforces, prejudice and discrimination of all kinds – tend to undermine the allocation of labour on a strictly rational basis. Indeed, as Blackburn and Mann (1979) discovered, in the majority of cases the quality employers look for in workers is their cooperativeness, and this alone would restrict any attempt to select workers rationally on the basis of skills and abilities.

The dual labour market A major 'imperfection' in the market for labour that certain economists and sociologists have drawn attention to lies in the fact that it is not unified. In reality it is divided into distinct segments, and in particular into a primary and a secondary labour market (Doeringer and Piore, 1971). Jobs in the primary market are supplied by large firms that are technologically advanced and profitable. Wages and working conditions are relatively good, levels of unionization tend to be high, and employers are concerned with retaining stable workforces. However, this only applies to part of the economy.

In addition, there are jobs in the secondary sector provided by small firms, usually in low technology industries and very competitive markets. Such firms normally experience great pressures to exploit their workers to the utmost, so wages tend to be low and conditions poor. In short, work in the primary sector provides what usually would be thought of as 'good jobs', found in the skilled trades and in industries like engineering and advanced manufacturing. In the secondary sector are found the 'bad jobs' – or even 'sweated' labour – which tend to be concentrated in the services and in industries such as clothing and food processing.

Internal labour markets A further aspect of market irrationality is that much allocation of labour in fact occurs *inside* firms as a result of the selection of existing employees. To a large extent the division between internal and external labour markets overlaps that between primary and secondary markets. In other words, it tends to be large-scale organizations in the advanced sectors of the economy that restrict opportunities for advancement and training to their own employees.

An internal labour market is favoured in the primary sector because it helps firms to stabilize their labour forces. Production here tends to be technically complex, and firms will normally be locked into highly structured product markets, which leads to demands for stable output and quality. Furthermore, primary labour forces contain high proportions of skilled and experienced workers who are not easily replaceable. By restricting such a major reward as promotion to the established labour force, ties of loyalty can be strengthened. In contrast to this, secondary sector firms, which tend to be much less dependent on skilled workers, and are often too small to operate an internal market, rely much more on the wider labour market as a source of labour supply.

The persistence of a secondary labour market has been underestimated in the past, but in general there are no trends to eliminate these low-grade jobs. Primary sector firms often utilize firms in the secondary sector, sub-contracting work to them in order to keep wage costs down. The presence of such a relationship maintains the division between jobs, preventing any long-term equalization.

The primary and secondary sectors form a stratified labour market mainly because the workers who fill these jobs are themselves segregated. There is, as Marx originally noted, a 'social' as well as a 'technical' division of labour. The latter simply reflects the divisions between different occupations and branches of industry. However, the social division of labour refers to the manner in which different groups of people are allocated to different work. Probably the most widespread form of segregation (one we pay particular attention to later) is based on discrimination between the sexes. Women workers rarely compete with men for the same jobs; they usually have to accept relatively low-grade work with poor prospects. But almost any kind of labour market disadvantage can drive workers into the secondary sector. As workers become older, for instance, they may have to drop out of well-paid primary sector jobs and accept less advantageous work. Similarly, in areas containing large immigrant populations sweated industries tend to flourish. Prejudice on the part of those placed to exert influence over selection, like personnel officers and senior management, helps to guarantee that factors like class, sex, race and age are applied in practice.

It may be argued that this merely reflects workers' true value to employers. After all, the primary sector contains a high proportion of workers with marketable qualities, and these have to be rewarded if firms wish to retain such workers. However, this argument is unsatisfactory for at least two reasons. Firstly, even if the purely rational reasons for allocating workers, either to the low-wage or to the high-wage sector, were removed, much residual prejudice and discrimination would remain. Secondly, the argument ignores the fact that chances to obtain skills are allocated in a discriminatory fashion in the first place. Women and ethnic minorities are often given very limited access to training; also youngsters from middle-class backgrounds have in-built advantages when it comes to obtaining further education and skills.

The flexible firm The utilization of these internal market functions by large employing firms is currently being heralded as the prevailing future employment pattern (Child, 1984, p.265). Highly complex labour structures, coupled with flexible working arrangements and the replacement of traditionally demarcated crafts by multi-skilling, will increasingly be developed within firms. Here a 'core' of primary sector jobs are intended to provide the key skills that firms need, with a 'periphery' variously comprising part-time, temporary, sub-contract and self-employed workers to give the firm the capacity to shed or take on labour as market changes dictate. Thus firms which are basically seeking stable workforces, with as little labour turnover as possible, may at the same time pursue plans to become less reliant on their workers – for example by hiving off areas of production to supplier firms, or by mechanizing to eliminate skills.

Dual labour policies reflect managerial strategies which can differ subtly but importantly from firm to firm or over time. Increasing competitive pressures, and increasing uncertainty in traditional markets in time of recession, have forced firms to consider adopting flexible patterns of employment. Simultaneously unemployment has strengthened management's hand, making labour more willing to adapt to the demands of flexibility. And the new micro-technologies (for which, see Chapter 13) have also begun to play a part in permitting firms to introduce diverse work patterns. According to Yates (1986), employers themselves foresee an increasing shift towards labour flexibility, and that this will enable firms to utilize peripheral workers as a 'buffer' in order to avoid having to resort to redundancies in core labour forces.

This being said, we must add that all these distinctions are to an extent rather limited and static attempts to describe a complex reality. Labour market theory is hotly disputed within the social sciences, with several debates going on. To begin with, there is still disagreement about whether labour markets are truly *segmented* in the sense of particular sectors of jobs being entirely cut off from other sectors. While there clearly are major differences in the work open to different groups of people, this may not amount to fully developed segmentation. The need to refer in such cases to very detailed data on the distribution of rewards and choices between jobs has fuelled both sides of the debate.

Even assuming that labour markets are segmented (as opposed to being merely differentiated), the phenomenon has attracted major differences of interpretation and emphasis. Marxist writers, such as Edwards, Reich and Gordon (1975), have stressed that labour market segmentation is the outcome of the control imperative at the heart of the labour process. Employers' need for control inside the firm, they argue, has to be supported by control in the wider labour market, and in particular by a 'divide and rule' strategy towards labour. In this sense, segmentation encourages rivalry between different groups of workers, preventing the labour force as a whole from attaining unity.

Criticism from other radical writers, most notably from feminists, has stressed that the notion of some abstract form of 'capital' which exploits all workers equally is misleading. Pressures from wider society and from within labour itself, such as the forces of sexism and racism, have an independent effect (Rubery, 1980). Primary sector workers frequently seek to exploit the internal promotion market at the expense of other workers. Thus, for example, sexism from men in general – and particularly from inside the trade union movement – may be as important a factor in discrimination against women as that expressed by employers.

In more mainstream social science, the changing organization of work is seen as a more varied process than that envisaged by radical writers. The wide range of labour policies that employers adopt – not all of which can be reduced to a single-minded desire to control workers – challenges the notion of a fixed capitalist logic. There are also various 'subjective' factors which play a part, most notably the desires of workers for changes such as increased leisure, or for patterns of work which fit in with private activities. This line of argument has strong ties with the critique of labour process theory (see Chapter 9), in which various factors, like 'responsible' patterns of job design, were put forward as alternatives to direct control by employers. The emphasis here is on the Marxist interpretation being a mechanical and one-dimensional view, which implies a far too simplistic relationship of antagonism between capital and labour.

Conclusion

There is no space here to discuss these debates in more detail. However, what does seem to emerge is, firstly, that managements are adopting an increasingly *strategic* approach to labour policy. Whereas in previous times firms might adopt a uniform attitude towards employees, or the presence of some primary jobs may have helped to stabilize the secondary ones, increasingly firms are devoting managerial resources to a more cost-effective and efficient use of labour. Secondly, the broad trend appears to indicate that 'flexibility' will mean a greater proportion of secondary-type jobs, and labour will increasingly be utilized as a mere commodity. As Child has pessimistically concluded, this is an attractive scenario only for employers and a minority of skilled workers, while a 'social problem of enormous proportions attends the rest of society' (1984, p.265).

WHITE-COLLAR WORK

If we turn now from manual work to the other major area of employment, the non-manual or white-collar sector, we at once come up against major problems of definition. Whereas manual jobs tend to be similar as regards the type of work performed and the rewards received – indeed Blackburn and Mann stressed how coherent a category they form – the non-manual sector is extremely diverse and extensive. It ranges across managerial and administrative posts, employment in the professions, in scientific and technical activities, supervision, clerical and secretarial jobs, and jobs in sales and distribution. The differences between these types of work in pay, status and authority are often immense; and as a result, methods of classifying non-manual occupations are beset with ambiguities and inconsistencies.

The reasons for this diversity can be found in the changing occupational structure, itself a product of industrial and commercial development. Economic expansion in the major industrial nations during this century has been heavily concentrated in areas of non-manual employment. The fastest growing industries have frequently been science-based ones which employ a high proportion of professional and technical staff; and added to this throughout industry managerial functions (e.g. work control, planning and product development) have expanded. The commercial and financial sector (banks, building societies, insurance) has also developed, enlarging the clerical workforce, while the growth of state provision in health and welfare has expanded the numbers of lower professionals. As Routh (1980) indicates, virtually all groups of non-manual employees have exhibited a persistent growth over the long term, which has only recently shown signs of levelling off (Table 11.1).

The question of the nature of white-collar occupations is bound up with the contemporary sociological analysis of class. Traditionally, the line dividing manual and white-collar jobs has also demarcated the working class from the middle class. In the nineteenth century the middle classes shared in the ownership of *property* (small businesses, self-employment, and income from investment). Propertyless groups, like clerical employees and supervisors,

Table 11.1 *Percentage of occupied population in occupational groups, United States (1910–70) and Great Britain (1911–71).* From Routh (1980, p. 11).

		1910	1930	1950	1970
	US	1910	1930	1950	1970
	GB	1911	1931	1951	1971
Professional and semi-professional	US	4.4	6.1	7.5	14.2
	GB	4.1	4.4	6.1	10.6
Proprietors, managers, officials	US	23.0	19.9	16.3	12.7
	GB	10.4	10.6	10.6	12.3
Clerical and kindred	US	5.2	10.0	13.3	17.4
	GB	7.3	9.2	12.7	15.7
Sales	US	5.0	6.3	6.9	6.2
	GB	5.7	6.1	5.4	9.0
Skilled workers and foremen	US	11.7	12.9	13.8	12.9
	GB	13.9	15.0	16.8	15.5
Service	US	6.8	6.9	7.4	12.4
	GB	10.4	9.4	6.1	11.8
Semi-skilled and unskilled manual	US	29.4	29.3	30.2	22.4
	GB	41.7	40.9	39.1	24.0

were small in size and enjoyed such status and authority as marked them off clearly from manual workers. Hence they were often regarded as being assimilated into the middle class. However, the patterns of economic growth just referred to, which brought about the expansion of white-collar occupations, reversed this situation and the established property-owning middle class declined in numbers. The growing new white-collar groups derived their class position not from property but from their *employment*. This created a problem for analysis since the factors describing occupations (such as pay, status, authority and career expectations) are complex and not always consistent. As Hyman (1983) points out, this adds to the 'structural ambiguity' of extended white-collar hierarchies.

Moreover, there has been no simple transfer from a class position based on economic ownership to one based securely on employment. Certainly there are higher professional and managerial groups which do enjoy superior occupational rewards. Equally clearly, however, groups like clerical and sales workers do not. The expansion in non-manual work has mostly taken place in these lower-ranked kinds of job. As Abercrombie and Urry point out, 'the numerical growth in salaried employees is especially traceable to a demand for subordinates rather than fully qualified responsible people' (1983, p.53). Furthermore, a high proportion of white-collar jobs has been occupied by women, and the sexual divisions in society have been a major influence in reinforcing the downward pressure on employment conditions. Several writers believe that the diversity and fragmentation of white-collar groups is now such that they no longer constitute a single class. Hyman, for example, stresses, 'The range of internal differentiation in pay and conditions, and the existence of a distinct category of lowly-regarded "women's work", clearly casts doubt on the adequacy of the general category "white-collar employment" as a means of classifying occupations' (1983, p.13). Thus the lower ranks of white-collar and service workers are to be distinguished from managerial and higher professional employees, who comprise the 'new' middle class. The latter have also been dubbed the 'service class', reflecting their responsibility for discharging functions, crucial in a modern economy, of planning, administration and the control of labour.

In sketching out this analysis, however, we have disregarded some major problems. It is difficult imposing a *structure* (of class categories and boundaries) upon what are essentially dynamic *processes*. Moreover, the notion that some groups, like clerical employees, have actually changed their class membership is still hotly debated. While most writers would agree that their distinctive class position has been eroded, there is disagreement about how far this has gone, about how these changes are to be interpreted, and about whether in fact 'deskilled white-collar workers' constitute a 'new' element of the working class alongside manual workers.

Proletarianization (I): the work process

In the nineteenth and early twentieth centuries, many white-collar employees were clearly differentiated from the manual working class. In the words of Lockwood:

> . . . the clerk generally enjoyed a natural status clearly removed from that of the manual worker. His salary, hours of work and holidays were decidedly more favourable; and to be added to these were security of tenure, a greater chance of promotion, and the probability of a pension of some kind. . . . He was somehow a privileged type of proletarian. (1958, p.41)

However, the occupational standing and class position of this largest section of the white-collar workforce have subsequently been threatened, in the sense of the gap between them and the working class growing less – a process referred to as the 'proletarianization' of these groups. Abercrombie and Urry (1983), reviewing the contemporary debate about class, stress that proletarianization is the single issue that has 'dominated the literature' on the topic.

Important evidence of proletarianization has come from data on *earnings differentials*. What the figures show is a marked narrowing of differentials between clerical workers and unskilled manual workers, virtually closing the gap between them. Broadly speaking, up to the 1930s clerks earned about the same as skilled manual workers, whereas now their pay has fallen to the level of unskilled workers. The gap between them and the managerial/higher professional group (the 'service class') has widened. (For analyses of the earnings issue, see Hyman, 1983, pp.5–13; Abercrombie and Urry, 1983, p.114; and Braverman, 1974, pp.296–8.)

As well as the narrow question of earnings, however, the major sociological studies of white-collar employment have explored the nature of the work and other occupational factors. In particular, it is trends towards deskilling and routinization, identified in Chapter 9 in relation to manual labour, that are also held responsible for alienation in the office.

The American C. Wright Mills was probably the first modern sociologist to write at length about the deterioriation of office work. In his classic study *White Collar* (1951) Mills linked two basic processes: the introduction of machinery and the intensification of work.

> As the army of clerks grew, they were divided into departments, specialised in function, and thus, before machines were introduced on any scale, socially rationalised. . . . It was this social reorganization, under the impetus of work load, higher cost, and the need for files and figures, that made possible the wide application of business machines. (p.192)

Mills's concern with the rationalization of office work invited the comparison between office and factory. Changes in work patterns, like open-plan layout and typing pools, led to a workflow that could be centrally planned and closely supervised. The application of 'scientific management' too, he noted, was common in larger American offices by the 1920s. Mills anticipated the full rationalization of office work; certain 'status complications' might delay it, but it was the 'model of the future'.

Another influential account is that of Braverman (1974, Chapters 15 and 16). We noted earlier the stimulus that he gave to the 'deskilling' debate, but Braverman was also noted for extending these ideas into his account of white-collar work. He stressed the 'extraordinary enlargement' of these occupations – in the case of clerical workers rising from being less than 1 per cent of the employed population in the mid-nineteenth century, in both Britain and the United States, to developed labour forces respectively comprising 3 million and 14 million employees by the 1970s (p. 295). As these groups expanded, office work changed 'from something merely incidental to management into a labor process in its own right' (p.304). And like Mills, Braverman emphasized the 'merging characteristics of clerical and production labor'. The need to 'systematize and control' white-collar work brought about mechanization (with the typewriter as early as the 1880s, then a range of office equipment, and most importantly the recent introduction of commercial computing), the growth of a separate hierarchy of office management, reorganization of work to give economies of scale, and the erosion of established white-collar skills (e.g. the replacement of shorthand by audio-typing). The clerical occupations, Braverman stated emphatically, represented a major section of the working class, and any general white-collar category that included higher-level occupations was 'absolutely meaningless' (p.295).

Proletarianization (II): occupational status

Unlike these accounts which tend to be confined to the changing labour process, many British sociologists have given prominence to subjective factors concerned with the *status* of white-collar occupations and the *class consciousness* of the incumbents of these jobs. David Lockwood's pioneering early study *The Blackcoated Worker* (1958) set out three separate dimensions of class position. (1) He referred to the basic economic factors related to occupation (pay, prospects, conditions) as 'market situation'; (2) 'work situation' stressed the nature of social relationships at work; and (3) 'status situation' was the prestige accorded to occupations in wider society (p.15). Lockwood argued that whereas the market situation of clerical employees differed little from that of manual workers, the modern office was still not rationalized to the extent that their respective work situations were identical (e.g. he insisted that office mechanization enhanced clerical work rather than reducing it to mere machine-minding). Moreover, considerations of status revealed radical differences, a 'sheer social distance', between clerical and manual workers. Clerks still retained relative advantages in terms of their middle-class origins and level of education. Indeed, the very fact of clerical 'respectability' being insecure, and based on declining occupational advantages, provoked a powerful desire in clerks to remain aloof from the manual working class. Lockwood concluded:

> the traditional superiority of non-manual work has not been entirely eradicated by the changes of the last half-century, even though it has been more frequently questioned. This is best stated by saying that the loss of middle class status by the clerk is not tantamout to the acquisition of working class status, either from the point of view of the clerk or the manual worker. (p.211)

Two more recent major empirical surveys of clerical employees are those of Stewart, Prandy and Blackburn (1980) and Crompton and Jones (1984). Stewart, Prandy and Blackburn argued that if *career expectations* are significant in an occupation, then any approach which focuses on the job itself (whether in terms of its rewards, social status or the nature of the work involved) will convey a static and ultimately a misleading picture. Furthermore, they discovered significantly high rates of promotion out of clerical work, a finding they used to argue against the proletarianization thesis: 'Clerk is not a well-paid position, or even a highly regarded position, but it is an early stage on relatively lucrative and highly regarded careers . . . the image of blocked mobility and non-increasing incomes is far from accurate' (p.172). However, their study was based only on *male* clerks, which limits the relevance of their findings in an occupation three-quarters feminized.

Crompton and Jones's study focused on 'objective' aspects of the labour process and did encompass male and female clerical employees. While these researchers too discovered high rates of mobility for men, the vast majority of women were seen to occupy routine jobs with little control over the work and very limited career chances. They particularly stressed the role of *computers* in deskilling clerical work, and in a sense they here followed Lockwood. His argument against proletarianization was formed in the 1950s, before the start of commercial computing, while Crompton and Jones suggest that automated data-processing so radically altered the clerical labour process as to be the decisive factor in creating a (female) proletariat. Also, implicitly, they disagree with writers like Mills and Braverman, who believed that the routinization of clerical work was well advanced by the first half of the century (although they agree with them that, ultimately, a white-collar working class has come into existence).

Conclusion

Any attempt to say the final word on the nature of white-collar work is probably premature. These changes in the occupational structure are still taking place, and in any case they touch upon major differences of theory and interpretation within the social sciences. What does seem clear is that restructuring of the industrial economy has accelerated in recent years, and that the occupational changes at the heart of this process are reflected directly in changes within the white-collar labour force. The complex make-up of this category of employees and the strength of the forces that are reshaping it make it difficult to arrive at hard and fast conclusions.

No matter what disagreement there is between social scientists, however, the key issue remains that of the decline in standing of white-collar groups. Questions of the *improvement* of the class position of large sections of the working population – which were very much discussed during the 'affluent' 1960s – no longer seem to be on the agenda. The high-grade work, created for example by some new technology, cannot in any sense be regarded as compensation for the degradation of clerical work, since these jobs are in a fairly small minority Nevertheless, this raises as a separate issue the nature of higher-grade white-collar jobs, an important part of which consists of professional work, which we now consider further.

PROFESSIONS AND PROFESSIONALISM

As we have said, the professions form a major section of the white-collar workforce. The term itself tends to be more meaningful than any general category of 'white-collar work' since even low-ranking groups in the professions still seem to enjoy career prospects and conditions of employment which differentiate them from routine white-collar workers. Nevertheless, the differences amongst professional groups remain important. Established professions (such as law, medicine and architecture) command a much superior status and better earnings when compared with lesser professions (like teaching and social work). Moreover, there are pronounced hierarchies *within* professions – the financial controller of a large corporation, for instance, would receive far higher rewards than an auditor, yet both might broadly be described as accountants.

Characteristics of the professions

This range of variation within professional groups has meant that defining the essential features of professions has always proved difficult. In an influential early study, Goode (1957) called the professions a 'community within a community', stressing the highly distinctive and integrated nature of their occupational cultures. Professionals have a common sense of identity and values, they share a consensus as regards their social role, speak a common language and are lifetime members of their occupation.

What does seem to be of prime importance is the nature of *professional work*. Professions traditionally have enjoyed the high status and material rewards associated with positions of authority, yet they are also involved in the concrete process of work. Sometimes this may in fact be manual work (a surgeon, for example, carries out what is probably quite hard manual work, albeit delicate and skilled); and although most professions are white-collar in nature, there remains a belief that professionals should actually perform the work themselves and not merely delegate it to others. In trying to define professional work the following aspects may be singled out.

(1) Professional work typically has a *service* element – either service to the common good, such as in health or education, or service to an individual client, or in an organization the provision of a staff service to line management.

(2) The professions are *ethical* occupations. Because they employ a complex technical language, and are often involved with matters of critical importance to society and to individuals, there is a need to regulate professional conduct by some code of ethics. The central relationship of trust between client and professional, upon which the legitimacy of professional advice is based, itself rests on the belief that professionals will act purely in the client's interest, and for no other purpose.

(3) The professions tend to be *self-regulating* occupations. Their responsibilities usually involve extensive skills and technical knowledge, for which long periods of training are required; hence professionals themselves prefer to reserve the right to be sole judge of the competence of other colleagues. They determine training requirements, control entry to the profession, and in some cases grant the licence to practise.

The skills of professionals, and their concern with services of exceptional importance, have conventionally been used to explain the superior status and rewards that these occupations attract. However, more recently it has been pointed out that to see professional status merely as a reflection of the intrinsic qualities of professional work is to paint a rather static and misleading picture. For example, Johnson (1972) has argued that accounts which focus on the supposed qualities of professions have never been able to agree a list of 'traits' that are typical of all professions in all circumstances. Similarly, the suggestion that professions serve fundamental social needs (for health, law and order, education, etc.) is also rather doubtful. The alleged 'altruism' of professionals has often been the basis of exaggerated claims about their ethical and progressive role. But, as Johnson indicates, this 'falls into the error of accepting professionals' own definitions of themselves' (1972, p.25).

Instead of regarding professionalism as an inherent quality of a few select occupations, it is best regarded as an *occupational strategy*, whereby groups attempt to gain recognition as professions in order to reap the rewards of the established professions. This view was pioneered by the American sociologist Everett Hughes, who maintained that he 'passed from the false question "Is this occupation a profession?" to the more fundamental one, "What are the circumstances in which people in an occupation attempt to turn it into a profession and themselves into professional people?" ' (quoted in Johnson, p.31). Here the emphasis shifts to the *dynamic* process of groups attempting collectively to upgrade their occupational standing.

Professionalism as an occupational strategy

Although the older-established professions are often taken as the benchmark by which the status of all professional groups is measured, the nature of professional work on the whole has undergone major changes. Indeed, professionalism as a strategy reflects both the opportunities that have arisen for groups to move up in status as well as the threats to the status of existing groups.

C. Wright Mills (1951) pointed out two main aspects of this dynamic situation. Firstly, the established professions themselves have been transformed. The independent practitioner may once have represented the 'model' professional, but nowadays even high-status groups, like architects, accountants and lawyers, are often employees rather than partners in independent practice. Secondly, as we could see from Table 11.1, the professional/technical category has grown faster than any other in the occupational structure. Technological changes and industrial development have meant that many entirely new engineering and scientific skills have appeared. Also, the growth of state provision has greatly expanded groups like teachers and social workers. Such a growth in numbers, as much as anything else, poses the problem for these groups of defining and protecting their occupational boundaries.

Several important tactics for securing occupational control can be singled out. One of the chief preconditions of wider occupational control is that the membership itself should be a united force. Thus, *professional associations* are vitally important in representing and furthering the interests of the profession. In the more powerful professions, the association will regulate training and educational standards, in order to preserve the status of the occupation by requiring a high level of technical knowledge and practical ability. Strict entry requirements also serve to limit numbers and to keep practitioners in short supply. Indeed, it has often been noted that the main function of professional associations lies in keeping the profession an exclusive club.

The occupational strategy represented here differs from but also shares some common elements with the two other major strategies of advancement: the trade union strategy of workers and the career strategy of managers. Mindful of this, Parry and Parry (1976) have defined the professional strategy as a form of 'upward collective mobility'. Thus a profession is a coalition of interests and acts collectively, not unlike a trade union. Nor is it unknown for professional associations to resort to industrial action – though they are usually very anxious not to be associated in the public eye with trade unions. To be more precise, professional associations are closer to craft unions than they are to the large general trade unions, which operate on the principle of including as many people as possible in the particular industry. With craft unions the opposing principles of inclusion and exclusion favour the latter more. (Craft unions are very much concerned with preserving the exclusiveness of the craft via control of apprenticeship, for example.) The professions guard their exclusive nature even more jealously. Yet it is a measure of the success of the professions that, whilst unions are often roundly condemned for using 'restrictive' practices in defence of jobs, the tactics of the professions, which are aimed solely at exclusivity, tend to be readily accepted. In contrast to this, the type of rewards being sought are clearly quite different from those aimed at by workers' associations. The professions provide a setting for members to pursue individualistic career paths and distinctively middle-class rewards, much as do senior organizational members.

Studies have also shown how professional ethics, as well as ostensibly protecting clients, crucially serve the interests of professions. The issue here is the *ideological* character of the professional ethic, rather than the truth or otherwise of professional claims. Indeed, it may well be true that the wider public interest is served by having secure professions, yet it is certainly clear that these forms of control enhance the vested interests of the professions concerned. As Elliot (1972) has argued, the professional ethic resembles a sort of occupational ideology uniting the members of the profession. For example, a practitioner threatened with legal action for alleged incompetence can normally expect his colleagues to close ranks behind him, providing he has not broken the code of ethics. Thus, members of the public often find it extremely difficult to bring a case against professionals unless some gross breach of conduct can clearly be proven. Internal discipline within professions tends to be overwhelmingly concerned with cases where the profession itself might have been brought into disrepute (mostly involving illegal or immoral behaviour) rather than with investigating cases of incompetence on behalf of clients or the public.

A major basis of professional privilege, as Hughes (1975) points out, lies in the claim to superior knowledge. It is a mark of occupations struggling to gain exclusive rights to practice, to self-regulation and so forth, that they will make great efforts to have their claims on knowledge recognized; and it is characteristic of the established professions that they guard their monopoly of knowledge very closely. In daily contact with clients and the public, professionals seek to 'mystify' their knowledge, to make it appear that while long training and experience are necessary, there are other indefinable skills that only members of the profession possess or even understand. Doctors, for example, are often extraordinarily reluctant to discuss patients' illnesses with them, the justification being that it would distress patients or that they wouldn't understand anyway. While this may contain some truth, keeping patients in ignorance undeniably helps doctors to manipulate them. Thus the 'manner' that professionals adopt is an important tactic in maintaining their possession of vital knowledge.

The power of certain professions may extend beyond control of their own occupation. Esland (1980) has stressed that the expertise which professions command confers on them 'a mandate to produce and generate certain kinds of knowledge for society as a whole'. While the public as clients may know broadly what service it requires, in important respects this is defined by the relevant profession, and it is this definition that will decide the actual service received.

> Routine definitions of ill-health, social adequacy, school achievement, degrees of criminality, for example, can be seen as grounded in the specific forms of expertness which at any one time are dominant in society. . . . Many of the dominant categories of thought which permeate our commonsense attitudes – as well as the power to enforce them – are to some extent traceable to the political organization of particular occupations. (Esland, 1980)

Conclusion: variations in occupational control

In the last analysis, of course, there can be no guarantee that occupations will be successful in their demands for professional recognition – or if they have succeeded that they will retain their status over the long term. As a strategy professionalism is by definition open-ended, and many groups will enjoy only a limited form of autonomy, although the groups themselves would not necessarily see it in this light. Occupations which because of their nature can hardly aspire to the status of the senior professions nevertheless can be very jealous of the trappings of professional autonomy that they have acquired. Indeed, for groups that are not already fairly influential professionalism may not be the strategy they choose to adopt. Simpson's (1981) study of the regional press has shown that, as the monopoly structure of the newspaper industry has intensified, journalists have suffered reduced status, and control has shifted increasingly to editorial management. These changes have been reflected in the National Union of Journalists' adopting the more militant stance of a trade union rather than that of a professional association.

The question that remains, however, is how we explain the differences in the progress of different groups along the path of professionalism. Why are doctors, say, capable of sustaining their elite status, while teachers are not? It can be argued that the issue itself is unimportant: certain occupations have simply managed to acquire the totem of professional prestige while others have not. Other writers, however, seek more distinctive explanations. Any such answer clearly must take historical and institutional factors into account. Thus, for example, it has been pointed out that state intervention into an occupation seems to be a major factor explaining why such groups become only marginally professional (Johnson, 1972; Parry and Parry, 1976). The ethics of occupations that have been shaped by government bureaucracy (e.g. teachers, social workers) reflect the rules of the state employing agency, while control over the service being provided resides with the agency – all of which detracts from true professional values.

On a more theoretical level, we can point to two related concepts that help to explain variations in professional autonomy. Carchedi (1977) has drawn attention to the contrasting forces operating on middle-class occupations like professions, some of which degrade and constrain occupational control while others serve to enhance an occupation's market position. The explanation Carchedi gives reflects the extent to which the *'functions of capital'* are being served. If the occupation concerned plays an important role in administrative and control functions crucial to the production of surplus value, it will command the market power that will bring prestige and exceptional rewards. (A good example here would be that of accounting, the exclusive authority of which has grown because of its relation with corporate capital.) However, if a profession has only tenuous links with these fundamental capitalist processes, or if the nature of its work places it closer to the labour function, then occupational prestige will be much more marginal.

Secondly, as well as the salience of the function performed, the rewards accruing to a profession are also determined by the nature of the work involved. Jamous and Peloille (1970) have argued that where a high degree of *indeterminacy* exists in the work of a profession, that is, where tasks are variable and non-rationalized, then the people who control this uncertainty are likely to enjoy high status. Conversely, where such work has been systematized and subject to laid-down procedures, it becomes possible for forces outside the occupation to intervene and control the work process.

To a degree, both these types of explanation still seem to be circular in the way that they distinguish between occupations. One still might want to know why a doctor's job should be indeterminate and salient for capital but a teacher's job not. However, salience and indeterminacy are objective features of the work process in only a partial sense – social and political factors also play a crucial role in creating or failing to create these conditions. At crucial points in their development, elite professions are able to capitalize on the objective conditions of their work situation. In other cases, would-be professions have a self-defeating aspect. Their dilemma, as Jamous and Peloille (1970) point out, is that the pursuit of best practice may mean codifying and mechanizing their own work, thereby shifting control to outside managerial elements. Professionals may literally streamline themselves out of a job. In this sense, therefore, concepts of salience and indeterminacy link strategic factors with the structural constraints on strategy. They point to the crucial act of groups seizing or failing to seize on the objective conditions which their work settings provide in their struggles to exert control over an occupational domain.

FURTHER READING

Abercrombie, N. and J. Urry (1983) *Capital, Labour and the Middle Classes*. London: Allen and Unwin.

Blackburn, R.M. and M. Mann (1979) *The Working Class in the Labour Market*. Chapter 1: 'The working class and the labour market'. London: Macmillan.

Child, J. and J. Fulk (1982) 'Maintenance of occupational control: the case of professions', *Work and Occupations*, 9, 155–92.

Crompton, R. and G. Jones (1984) *White Collar Proletariat: Deskilling and Gender in Clerical Work*. London: Macmillan.

Davies, C. (1983) 'Professionals in bureaucracies: the conflict thesis revisited', in R. Dingwall and P. Lewis (eds.) *The Sociology of the Professions*. London: Macmillan.

Edwards, R. (1979) *Contested Terrain: The Transformation of the Workplace in the Twentieth Century*. London: Heinemann.

Elliott, P. (1972) *The Sociology of Professions*. London: Macmillan.

Friedman, A. (1977) *Industry and Labour: Class Struggles at Work and Monopoly Capitalism*. London: Macmillan.

Hyman, R. and R. Price (eds.) (1983) *The New Working Class? White-Collar Workers and their Organizations*. London: Macmillan.

Johnson, T. (1972) *Professions and Power*. London: Macmillan.

Prandy, K., A. Stewart and R.M. Blackburn (1982) *White-Collar Work*. London: Macmillan.

Smith, C. (1986) *Technical Workers: Class, Labour and Trade Unionism*. London: Macmillan.

12

Women and Employment

INTRODUCTION

So far we have explored some of the ways in which occupational factors and the forms of control inherent in the labour process influence the nature of employment. But the constraints of social structure are evident in another way, in the sense that certain groups of people are typically found to occupy particular jobs or particular roles in organizations. One very important aspect of this social division of labour, and central to any discussion of work, involves the divisions between the sexes. It can readily be shown that all societies distinguish traditionally between the work that men do and the work that women do. However, in modern industrial societies, with their enormously complex structure of occupations and authority levels, the sexual division of labour that is superimposed on this is likewise highly complex.

There are many cogent reasons for wanting to understand the special role that women play in employment, and the role of employment in women's lives. This whole subject involves important aspects of recent social change, as well as the fact that women's experiences in the labour force have either been ignored or have been labelled with simple stereotypes up until quite recently.

Employment versus work An important point to make at the outset concerns the use of the terms 'work' and 'employment'. Usually the two are simply equated, so that to ask someone what work they do is the same as asking them what their job is. In the case of men this confusion hardly matters, since the useful work most men perform is confined to their jobs. But in the case of 'women and work' the distinction becomes critical, and we have to bear in mind the crucial differences between paid and unpaid work. In our society, unpaid work in the home and in the form of child-rearing is sharply distinguished from employment, or work done outside the home for a wage or salary.

The sexual division of labour This division between economic and domestic activities, between paid and unpaid work, marks a major division between the sexes. When the factory system first created economic activity separate from the household, it was women who were consigned to the domestic sphere while men moved into the sphere of employment. The sexual division of labour thus marks a fundamental element of social structure, and one which defines the relations between the sexes in wider society. In the employment sphere it massively influences and ultimately restricts women's choice of jobs.

These structured inequalities originate in and are sustained by a range of factors. Firstly, women's material dependence upon men reflects the low levels of pay they obtain when employed and their reliance on low-grade jobs (two issues we take up later in the chapter). In addition, the state plays an important role in designing taxation and welfare benefits systems which effectively make women dependent upon men as legal heads of households. Secondly, there are the broader processes of socialization and the learning of gender roles. A fact long known, and supported by a mass of research evidence, is that child-rearing practices adopted by parents differ markedly for each sex. They reinforce an active role for boys, while for girls there is an emphasis on passivity, on their own decorativeness and on the importance of emotional rewards.

Thirdly, existing patterns of segregation are greatly reinforced by the education system. In spite of all trends towards equal treatment in modern schools – and what is probably the quite genuine desire of many teachers to liberalize curricula – a high degree of restriction remains. There is always a strong bias towards boys taking the science and girls the arts subjects. Schools are also obviously places where socialization continues. Peer groups and friendship cliques are known to exercise a powerful influence on adolescent children, so that they are internalizing a highly specific image of what they believe is possible and proper for them to aspire to. From around 12 years of age onwards, girls are seriously underachieving in relation to measured IQ. The self-images they acquire in these years cause them to hold back, and increasingly to regard academic achievement as irrelevant in the future they anticipate.

The nature of women's work The division of labour that exists in the workplace is strongly related to these wider divisions between the sexes. When young women first enter the labour market, having been encouraged to take non-technical subjects at school and advised to seek these kinds of job, their occupational placement then reinforces the traditional pattern of female employment. The types of work traditionally open to women frequently reflect their domestic role as wives and mothers. And domestic labour, as Wainright (1984) has pointed out, is seen as something that women perform 'naturally' rather than involving active choice, as in the pursuit of a career or occupation. Moreover, the domination of society by market relationships actually distorts our perceptions of the value of different forms of effort. Effort which commands a price, in terms of wages or a salary, alone enjoys status. But domestic labour, which has no exchange value, is hardly accepted as having any economic function, no matter how socially useful it might be. Thus the identification of women, and women's work, with domestic labour serves to massively undervalue their real contribution.

Each of the above factors – the framework of legislation, the self-images women have, and the exclusion of domestic labour from the rest of the economy – reflect deeply rooted beliefs about women's place in a predominantly male-oriented society. They mean that even where women do work, there exists a sort of 'grand myth' that they are not naturally fitted for employment, or that it is not 'real work' they are doing. Many specific prejudices about women and employment can only be understood against the background of these very powerful beliefs.

PATTERNS OF FEMALE EMPLOYMENT

Labour force participation

The expansion of female employment in the post-war period has been one of the most significant of all recent social and economic trends. In 1985 in the United Kingdom there were 9 million women in employment, comprising 43 per cent of the labour force; and between 1960 and 1980 the workforce

Table 12.1 *Rates of female economic activity 1851–1981*. From Hakim (1980) and 1981 Census of Population (London: HMSO).

	Women above minimum working age (%)	Married women aged 15–59 (%)	Women aged 15–59 (%)
1851	42		
1861	43		
1871	42		
1881	32		
1891	32		
1901	32	10	38
1911	32	10	38
1921	32	10	38
1931	34	11	38
1941	—	—	—
1951	35	26	43
1961	38	35	47
1971	43	49	55
1981	46	57	61

increased by about 2 million due almost entirely to the entry into work of the group that traditionally did not work, namely married women. The projections are that this long period of growth is now levelling off. Nonetheless, it has left women very firmly entrenched in the economy.

Over the entire period of industrialization, however, the proportion of women in paid employment has varied considerably. Hakim (1980) has compiled data on rates of female economic activity (i.e. the proportion of women eligible to work that are in employment) from the national census reports, and some of her data are set out in Table 12.1. The general pattern is one of relatively high activity rates up to 1871, a sharp fall lasting until the period around the Second World War (during which no census was taken), then a steady rise back to the early levels. This, Hakim points out, gives us a longer perspective on the question of the economic role that women are capable of fulfilling. The notion of women entering the labour market in recent years is seen as somewhat misleading; rather, women *returned* to employment after being excluded for the best part of a century.

Explanations of this historical pattern need to take several factors into account. Family labour was frequently used in the early factories, but the rationalization of this system from the 1840s onwards gradually eliminated these forms of organized work, which had survived from the early domestic mode. From the middle of the nineteenth century a combination of factory legislation which banned women from certain types of work, the formation of male-dominated trade unions, and the onset of the first great depression in the 1870s, did much to exclude women from paid work. The economic expansion that took place later, in the 1890s, came mostly in the then new heavy industries – chemicals, steel, engineering – which provided work that women were unable to enter. In contrast to this, the return of full employment after the Second World War drew massive numbers of women into the economy. This period saw expansion in sectors which were both labour-intensive and where women were already established: the welfare state, education, consumer manufacturing, and above all clerical and secretarial work.

Even so, the variation in activity rates that the data show is perhaps not as great as one might have expected. Even at the height of the Victorian era, when there were powerful social pressures against women working, these were mostly confined to 'respectable' (that is to say, married and middle-class) women. But it has always been true that single women and working-class women have had to work. Thus, as the table shows, even at the point of their lowest economic activity, about one-third of women were in paid work, while at the peaks of activity about half were and are working.

However, these changes are much more sharply defined if we take into account factors which affect women's circumstances, such as marital status and age. As the data show, marital status once made a great difference to activity rates, while the marked tendency in recent years for married women to work has nearly eliminated any differences in activity rates between married women and women in general. Table 12.2, indicating age and marital status together, confirms the dramatic changes in activity rates between different age groups. However, these variables only partially represent the stage in the life-cycle a woman has attained – so that, for example, marriage by itself has been shown to have no independent effect on activity rates. By far the most significant factor causing women not to work is the presence of a young child to be cared for. Conversely, among young women with no children, the proportion going out to work often approaches 90 per cent and differs little from that of men.

Table 12.2 *Economic activity of women, by age, and for marital status, Spring 1985.* From *Employment Gazette* (London: HMSO), May 1986, p. 136.

Age	All women		Married women	
	Numbers economically active (000)	Economic activity rate (%)	Numbers economically active (000)	Economic activity rate (%)
16–19	1,156	67.9	37	38.4
20–24	1,571	70.9	592	58.4
25–34	2,301	61.4	1,736	57.9
35–49	3,731	72.1	3,172	71.5
50–59	1,752	58.6	1,385	58.4
60–64	298	18.6	212	19.4
65 and over	149	3.1	71	3.9
All aged 16 and over	10,957	49.2	7,204	52.2

Job segregation

The re-establishment of women in the economy has reflected the increased demands of women for economic independence, yet patterns of discrimination have also continued to be remarkably in evidence. Women have moved into only a fairly narrow band of occupations. Female employment is found especially in unskilled factory work, and large proportions are focused particularly in low-grade service work – in the minor professions (nursing, school teaching), in the manual services (shop work, cleaning, canteen work, laundry work), and in the secretarial and clerical sector. Conversely, women are very poorly represented in 'higher' occupational sectors, such as skilled manual work, the senior professions and management (Huws, 1982).

The pattern of female employment is also vertically distorted. Even in occupations where women are well represented and which offer a career structure, they tend to be confined to the junior levels. Thus, women teachers are concentrated in primary schools, while there are fewer in secondary schools, and only a very small proportion in promoted posts like head of department or head of school. In industry, too, it is common to find entire departments of women workers, perhaps with a woman as immediate supervisor, but with all higher levels occupied by men.

A clear indication of these distorted employment patterns emerges from the amount of part-time work that is accepted by a great many women. In 1985, 44 per cent of female jobs were part-time (a far higher proportion that in almost any other industrialized country) and women performed 85 per cent of all such work. Moreover, in the current recession, this trend is being powerfully reinforced. Between 1978 and 1981, 161,000 female jobs were lost as part of the general unemployment; but these were made up of 232,000 losses of full-time jobs and a gain of 71,000 part-time jobs. As we noted earlier, in Chapter 11, employers have been experiencing the need for more *flexible* labour, and part-time workers provide this very effectively. More recently, as unemployment has stabilized, the shift towards part-time female jobs has proved to be one of the few dynamic sectors of the jobs market. Thus, between March 1983 and December 1985, total female employees increased by 554,000, of which 547,000 (or 98.7 per cent) were part-time; and male employment actually declined by 21,000 jobs. So while there have been no recent gains in male employment, female employment has grown considerably – albeit virtually entirely in the part-time sector.

In some ways, therefore, the availability of this type of work has strengthened women's labour market position. Yet what counts as flexibility to employers almost by definition means a second-class job as far as workers are concerned. Part-time workers are in every sense merely 'hired hands'. They have no real contract of employment, very little job security or entitlement to benefits, and their rates of pay often fall well below those of full-time workers. Of course, this is not to say that women necessarily *feel* resentful of being forced into the part-time sector. A great many married women especially are pleased to have a job which enables them to make a significant contribution to family income and where the hours enable them to fulfil their domestic commitments. But the fact remains that the allocation of women to part-time employment represents a major element in discrimination.

Employment inequalities and legislation

The concentration of women in low-grade jobs largely explains the wide differences between male and female earnings. This is a gap that legislation has gone some way towards closing. The Equal Pay Act 1970, aimed specifically at the ideal of 'equal pay for equal work', confers the right to the same treatment with an employee of the opposite sex who is doing identical or similar work, or work rated as equivalent under a job evaluation study. The other relevant piece of legislation is the Sex Discrimination Act 1975. This attempts to prevent discrimination on grounds of sex particularly at the stage of recruitment for jobs, and over the distribution of training opportunities and promotion.

Table 12.3 *Male and female earnings 1969–1985*. From *New Earnings Survey*, London: HMSO (Department of Employment), various issues.

	(Average weekly earnings of men aged 21 and over and women aged 18 and over, for all industries and services.)		
	Full-time men	Full-time women	Female/male earnings ratio
	(£)	(£)	(%)
1969	24.8	12.1	49
1970	28.9	15.7	54
1971	32.9	18.3	56
1972	36.7	20.5	56
1973	41.9	23.1	55
1974	47.7	26.9	56
1975	60.8	37.4	60
1976	71.8	46.2	64
1977	78.6	51.0	65
1978	89.1	56.4	63
1979	101.4	63.0	62
1980	124.5	78.8	63
1981	140.5	91.4	65
1982	154.5	99.0	64
1983	167.5	108.8	65
1984	178.8	117.2	66
1985	192.4	126.4	66

Before the legislation was introduced, women received just under half the male wage, then in 1970 the gap closed slightly and gradually improved to around 63 to 66 per cent (Table 12.3). This may have reflected other labour market changes, a decline in men's pay, for instance, although there have been indications that the legislation was in fact responsible for this partial narrowing of the pay gap. Since the mid-1970s, however, the earnings ratio has remained stable. Thus the legislation seems to have had an initial impact, probably by eliminating grossly unfair situations where men and women in exactly the same jobs were paid at different rates, but in the broader sense of equalizing women's position in the labour market the effect seems to have been more marginal.

WOMEN'S EXPERIENCE IN THE WORKPLACE

Workplace discrimination

It has proved difficult to legislate effectively in the broader area of job opportunities for women, mainly because discrimination is so embedded in employment practices. Some of the main forms of pay discrimination, for example, occur in ways that legislation is powerless to change. Labour force segregation occurs at the occupational level, but more important is the much more detailed segregation that occurs at the level of firms. The Equal Pay Act was never intended to compel employers to pay men and women doing comparable jobs, but working in separate sections or departments, on the same scale. And the evidence suggests that the legislation simply accelerated the tendency for employers to rationalize workforces, separating male and female employees completely. This enables employers to further consolidate pay differentials by evaluating men's jobs differently, and by awarding them extra payments such as shift allowances, overtime and special bonuses.

The pattern of segregation between male and female jobs is complex and subject to change, both over time and from workplace to workplace. In their survey of a range of female occupations, Craig, Garnsey and Rubery (1983) observed that though complex, segregation was always strictly observed, and invariably the feminization of jobs went with low pay and status. Women's employment was subject to a kind of ghettoized status: once an occupation or a job was defined as 'women's work' many social pressures came into play which then reinforced the distinction.

> There was a time when women were considered unsuitable for jobs handling money, but building society customers are now said to expect attractive young female cashiers. [Pharmaceutical] Dispensing has become so identified as a female job that the chemists had not received any applications from men, despite the general high level of unemployment.

Traditional custom and practice played a major part in sustaining this demarcation: 'women were allocated to particular jobs and excluded from others primarily because this had always been the case, at least as far as the current manager could remember'.

Although the relatively poor earnings of women mainly reflect their containment in low-skill jobs, the discrimination against their occupational skills can also occur at another level. As we pointed out in Chapter 9, skills should not be regarded merely as technical abilities – in a crucial sense they are socially created and depend upon *legitimation*. Thus where women do possess skills, these are often not recognized or accepted. Examples of women's jobs with as much skill or managerial content as comparable male jobs, yet with far less status and pay, demonstrate how women's tacit skills can be utilized by employers without women ever receiving the rewards commensurate with their efforts. Formalization of training plays a major part in this. Formal training schemes and apprenticeships, with a recognized certificate at the end, are frequently reserved for male workers, while women receive informal on-site training and are not then accepted as possessing equivalent skills. Craig, Garnsey and Rubery were particularly interested in such cases as an appropriate place to break into the vicious circle of workplace discrimination. They argued that:

> the jobs now normally performed by women should not all be dismissed as low skilled nor should women workers be assumed to be unwilling to become stable and productive employees. . . . An improvement of the position of women in employment requires as a starting point the reassessment of the demands made on employees in 'women's jobs' and recognition of the skills and abilities and of the effort exerted by female employees.

The structure of workplace discrimination is sustained in many important ways by *sexual stereotyping* – and the extent to which stereotyped attitudes of women's abilities is mirrored in the demarcation between male and female jobs is often quite remarkable. The bulk of work performed by women involves the servicing of needs, e.g. cleaning, the care of children or the sick, the preparation of food – tasks which directly reflect the nature of women's unpaid domestic labour. Certain other feminized occupations, usually middle-class ones, exploit sexuality and glamour (the secretary, the air stewardess).

Once a particular job or occupation becomes established as either 'men's work' or 'women's work', the myths and prejudices about the relative abilities of the sexes become powerful justifications for retaining the *status quo*. Thus the supposed inferiority of women as regards physical strength and mechanical aptitude has long justified their exclusion from skilled manual work. Also, women's supposed lack of 'decisiveness' and willingness to take responsibility are often the justification for excluding them from managerial and supervisory positions. In a similar way, the supposed 'female virtues' such as patience and tenderness have all been given as reasons for allocating women to a whole range of subordinate jobs. The secretary who is supposed to minister to her (male) boss, the canteen assistant who prepares food, the caring professions of nursing and social work, all are heavily feminized and in all of them women supposedly exercise special female skills.

Attachment to work

To emphasize the many ways in which workplace inequalities are imposed and maintained, in other words to focus on the *structure* of discrimination, inevitably paints a rather pessimistic picture of the role of work in women's lives, and some would say a static and one-sided picture. More recently feminist writers and researchers have tried to overcome this problem by concentrating instead on the actual experiences of women at work. Although this approach still reveals facets of discrimination, a much more positive view has emerged of women's commitment to paid work. Women's attitudes and orientations to work, their ways of coping with the problems of the workplace, and their motives for wanting to work all reveal a stronger attachment to work than earlier preconceptions of female employment would have allowed.

Research of this kind has shown that women do have distinctive experiences of work, which challenge the simple stereotypes of their economic role as being unimportant to themselves and their families. It is now clear, for example, that women's earnings are not, nor do women see them as, a purely optional extra to the male wage ('pin money'); women's reasons for working are firmly based on financial need. It is also clear that work outside the confines of the home, in a collective environment, can be a liberating experience for women just as for men. On the other hand, women's attachment to work differs from that of men in a number of significant ways. Husbands still tend to be regarded as the main wage-earners, so that a strong element of the image of men as the 'bread-winners' still survives – a fact we might expect from women's low pay alone. Neither do most women define work as their central role. Women 'construct' their lives as wives, mothers and employees in complex ways, balancing out domestic and employment responsibilities. The responsibilities for home and children are not left behind when women enter work but stay intimately with them; family matters are much discussed at work, for example, while tasks like shopping will be integrated in the working day (Pollert, 1981, p.112).

Martin and Roberts's (1983) interview survey of over 5,000 women discovered that most women now 'accept work as their right' and fully expect to work for most of their lives, only stopping when they have young children (or other dependents) to care for. The survey revealed a number of aspects of women's attachment to work. For example, women are returning to work sooner after the birth of their children. They can expect to spend longer total periods of their lives in work – rising from about 60 per cent for the post-war generation to approaching 70 per cent for young women today; and when women are not in employment they anticipate their return to work and retain strong images of themselves as workers.

The issue of redundancy and unemployment has a particular point to make, in the sense that the loss of jobs to women had been thought to cause few problems because they could always return to the home. Indeed, the treatment of women as a 'reserve' of flexible labour, to be called into employment or laid off as employers and the economy demand, has always relied upon this notion of women readily giving up work and returning full-time to domestic duties. But recent studies of women's redundancy show that the loss of their jobs can be just as damaging in the lives of women and their families as it is in the case of men. Much the same hardship follows from the reduction of earnings, and women resent the loss of independence that in our society depends utterly on having access to a wage or salary (Martin and Wallace, 1986).

Sexual stereotyping at work can also be re-examined from the point of view of women's active participation in work. Stereotypes are not simply cultural beliefs about women as employees, they serve a crucial *ideological* function in assisting the control and oppression of women by employers and men in general. Ideological beliefs, however, are not simply imposed from the outside; they are partially at least accepted by those under control. Only this element of 'truth' makes them effective and plausible. In this context, Anna Pollert's (1981) study of women's manual work in a cigarette factory – the experience of working-class women selling 'generalised unskilled labour power' – discovered powerful stereotyped attitudes held by managers and supervisors. She defined these as male-generated images of female experience, yet they were real for the women workers who had to 'live out' these stereotypes on a daily basis. Thus the supervisors firmly believed that women had an 'aptitude' for the repetitive, monotonous jobs that were typical in the factory. The women themselves rejected the crudest version of this stereotype, but they did accept their work as 'women's work' in the sense of knowing that no man could be persuaded to do it ('I'd like to see one of them do my job for a week!', p.87). Although the women refused to believe in the fairness of low-grade jobs, they did accept the reality of themselves as cheap flexible labour, and of the necessity of this as probably the only way they could compete with men's labour. Pollert also analysed 'factory politics', or the relationship between male supervisors and female workers, and the complex ways in which 'sexual banter and pranks' served to bolster authority in the factory.

> Supervision was sexually oppressive, the manner usually cajoling, laced with intimate innuendo, and provocative jokes, hands placed on girls' shoulders as they worked, imposition mixed with flattery. To survive with some pride, without melting into blushes or falling through the floor, the girls had to keep on their toes, have a ready answer, fight back. They were forced into a defensive–aggressive strategy – but always on the men's terms. They had to collude. And in this they also colluded with the language of control. (p.143)

Thus sexist attitudes were the conventional rules of interaction of the workplace, accepted at a certain level by most of the female workers. But while the women were able to manipulate the rules to their advantage, they had to do this by exploiting their own sex appeal; and these were only 'momentary victories of self-assertion' serving in the long run to confirm their subordinate status.

Women's careers

A further factor indicating the dilemmas that women face in employment is the career paths open to them. Undoubtedly the major problem is that of combining the long-term pursuit of a career with care of a family. The fact that the responsibility for child care falls more or less exclusively on women, coupled with the poor provision by public welfare services for the care of young children, mean that employment and family responsibilities become very difficult for women to combine. Thus, objectives which are usually wholly compatible for men are often incompatible for women. As Table 12.2 showed,

241

labour force participation rates fall sharply for women in their mid- to late twenties, when the majority leave work to have children; and the difficulties of coming back to work after a break in employment are a major cause of a great many women having to return to a worse job than the one they left, or of being unable to retain any seniority rights in their jobs. The possession of a qualification can prevent this downward occupational mobility, but far fewer women than men have recognized trade or professional skills. There are some occupations, like teaching and nursing, which do cater more for women returning to work, although even here any upward career mobility is often halted.

Much sociological research has documented the rigid views that employers hold about the unsuitability of women as long-term employees. But there is also an important inter-relation between the factors limiting women's careers and women's own aspirations. Women often will reject responsibility at work, and the chance of promotion, because these conflict with domestic responsibilities. But such a response may come about because they *anticipate* the employer's prejudice. This then 'justifies' their being overlooked for training and promotion. Employers' beliefs that young women will leave work to raise a family may become a self-fulfilling prophesy, since, faced with few prospects of advancement, some women may indeed come to regard work as being of secondary importance (Crompton and Jones, 1984, p.141).

Informal careers Because gender divisions are structured in highly complex ways, the career chances of women can often only be understood in the context of specific work settings. Indeed, the very notion of 'career' for women can take on a subtly different meaning. Whereas for men careers simply consist of the climb up a defined hierarchy of positions, within an organization or a profession, the complex work histories that women have can effectively put an end to any hopes of this kind of structured progress. If women are to have careers, it quite often means that they have to create a niche in some alternative work situation. A good example of this comes from Attwood and Hatton's (1983) account of the gender, class and age factors that shape the career patterns of women and men in the hairdressing industry. This is sharply divided into primary and secondary markets, ranging from the fashionable and lucrative end of the business, to the lower-status 'shampoo and set trade'. Attwood and Hatton distinguished two very different career paths. 'Getting on' in the industry meant becoming a salon-owner or manager in the fashionable sector, and this domain was dictated by the male stylists. Female apprentices usually lacked the confidence to advance, but some women did create longer-term careers in the secondary sector and some became salon-owners. The researchers stressed the sympathetic relationships that existed between these women and the mainly older working-class women who formed their clientele – a sharp contrast to the extremely competitive and exploitative world of 'fashion'.

Organizational careers More generally, career paths in large organizations are invariably acutely competitive. Career hierarchies rapidly narrow down, and employers often have great difficulty in offering realistic promotion opportunities. With women competing for promotion alongside men, the chances for men would become significantly reduced. So there is often a strong imperative for employers to exclude female employees from the promotion race, as well as an effective collusion between employers and male employees underlining their common interest in excluding women.

Crompton and Jones (1984), in their study of clerical work, stressed that male clerical workers had good career prospects only because the vast majority of female clerks were denied promotion. They explained the very poor rates of female promotion in the banking, insurance and local government settings they looked at by a combination of factors: (1) women tended to be less well-qualified on entry from school and university; (2) far fewer women obtained post-entry qualifications, due both to 'anticipation of their withdrawal from the workforce' and to being discouraged by management; (3) their actual withdrawal from the workforce to have children was of 'enormous significance' in denying them careers; and (4) lack of geographical mobility, due once again to family constraints, also restricted women's careers. The researchers found that men's and women's attitudes towards work were remarkably similar, with little to suggest that employment was of 'secondary' interest to women (p.149). There were however marked differences in attitudes related to just one factor: promotion. Many more men were interested in and expected promotion, and were oriented towards aspects of their work associated with 'promotability' (e.g. seeking responsibility).

> The picture that emerges . . . is that the majority of young women, especially if they are reasonably well qualified, initially approach employment with at least modest career expectations, comparable in many respects to those of men. (p.159) . . . The really significant 'break' in the women's attitudes . . . occurs among the group having made the most emphatic commitment to the domestic role – leaving work to rear a family. Whereas 79 per cent of young, unmarried women express an interest in promotion, this proportion declines massively to 29 per cent, among older women in the second phase of their work cycle. (p.156)

Within the vast majority of organizations there are powerful pressures towards internalized career paths and traditions of promotion from within. The type of long-term commitment this requires means that careers are rigidly structured, making re-entry after an absence extremely difficult. In another major survey, Fogarty, Allen and Walters (1981) looked at the progress women had made in managerial and professional jobs. In the four areas they studied – the civil service, the BBC, manufacturing industry and architecture – the researchers found that there had been a considerable increase in the numbers of women entering promotion paths in junior grades. However, they raised doubts about whether these changes would work through to the top positions, because of the mid-career barriers women face.

> The key finding of the case studies is that (progress through the middle grades) is in fact unlikely and by far the most important reason for this is the continued neglect by employers, and by other agencies such as public authorities responsible for community care for children, of the difficulties of reconciling a career with a family. (p.9)

Women did not 'easily abandon their careers when they have children'. The failure rather lay with employers who refused to accept wider responsibility for providing flexible working times and reinstatement after absence, and who simply defined any conflict between career and family as the employee's problem.

Conclusion

The link between women's abilities and women's work, which seems natural to many, is in fact quite arbitrary, and beliefs about the allegedly inherent capabilities of the sexes can rarely be substantiated. In other countries and at other times women have done the work that nowadays tends to be defined exclusively as male, and vice versa. However, the myths and prejudices about women and employment remain powerful constraints, so that the essential basis of sexual inequality and the allocation of women to inferior work, however that is defined, has hardly changed in recent years, in spite of the hugely increased economic contribution of women. The very high incidence of part-time and low-paid work, combined with the increased proportion of married women working, shows that the domestic role of women, their responsibility for the home and for child care, has not been changed by their entry into work. In other words, as Wainright (1984) has pointed out, women's participation in the labour force constitutes an *accommodation* to the traditional division of labour rather than any *erosion* of these basic inequalities. We have indicated briefly some of the areas within paid work where some progress may be being made. But what is now required to make any meaningful changes in the prevailing sexual division of labour is change on a much broader front, and this must involve the explicit challenges women themselves are making at all levels in the trade unions, the community and political institutions.

FURTHER READING

Amsden, A.H. (1980) *The Economics of Women and Work*. Harmondsworth: Penguin.

Cavendish, R. (1982) *Women on the Line*. London: Routledge and Kegan Paul.

Chiplin, B. and P. Sloane (1976) *Sex Discrimination in the Labour Market*. London: Macmillan.

Chiplin, B. and P. Sloane (1982) *Tackling Discrimination in the Workplace*. Cambridge: Cambridge University Press.

Cockburn, C. (1986) *Machinery of Dominance: Women, Men and Technological Know-how*. London: Pluto Press.

Crompton, R. and G. Jones (1984) *White Collar Proletariat: Deskilling and Gender in Clerical Work*. London: Macmillan.

Gamarnikow, E., D. Morgan, J. Purvis and D. Taylorson (eds.) (1983) *Gender, Class and Work*. London: Heinemann.

Knights, D. and H. Willmott (eds.) (1986) *Gender and the Labour Process*. Aldershot: Gower.

McNally, F. (1979) *Women for Hire: A Study of the Female Office Worker*. London: Macmillan.

Pollert, A. (1981) *Girls, Wives, Factory Lives*. London: Macmillan.

Sloane, P. J. (ed.) (1980) *Women and Low Pay*. London: Macmillan.

Spencer, A. and D. Podmore (1987) *In a Man's World: Women in Male Dominated Professions*. London: Tavistock.

Yeandle, S. (1984) *Women's Working Lives: Patterns and Strategies*. London: Tavistock.

13

New Technology and the Future of Work

The account of technology given in Chapter 9 was concerned with the ways in which social action in work was influenced by advancing production systems. However, these sociological debates in a sense have been overtaken in recent years by developments in the 'new technology' of microelectronics. Many people are convinced of the potential for far-reaching social change contained in these new systems. The so-called microelectronic revolution, based on computerized information networks, programmable industrial equipment, computer-aided design and the like, is expected to transform many areas of social and economic life (Forester, 1980, 1985).

New technology contains both threat and promise. The promise of a powerful new industrial economy coupled with the benefits of a leisure society beckons. Indeed, not to adopt the new technologies is seen as a form of national suicide, since other countries of course will innovate, and some are already far ahead of us in this race. Potential threats arise if, as many people fear, the technology turns out to be a potent destroyer of jobs. Either way, the implications are clearly of central importance in an industrial society such as ours.

As we saw earlier, the approach taken towards technology has often been flexible and open-ended; it has been argued that a range of possible choices is available, and there need be no fixed or inevitable impact on work. Nevertheless, the new technologies are clearly labour-saving, and they have arrived at a time of already serious unemployment. Thus the new technology debate follows hard on the heels of concern over British industrial decline, and public awareness of these issues is directly bound up with the concern over jobs. (This, incidentally, is in sharp contrast to the 1960s debate on the process industries, which occurred at a time of expansion and optimism for the future.)

In this chapter we shall look at some of the main arguments about the effects of new technology on work, in particular the effect on employment levels and on skills. Firstly, though, it is necessary briefly to look at microelectronic technology itself, together with some current applications.

DEVELOPMENTS IN MICROELECTRONICS

Microelectronics is an industry in its own right, the beginnings of which can be traced back to the development of the transistor shortly after the Second World War. This was the first device to use the semiconducting material silicon as a base for electrical circuits, and it replaced the existing vacuum valve. From its inception the electronics industry had needed to miniaturize components, and valve technology had evolved along these lines but always with major limitations. It was the development of semiconductors, however, that proved to be the crucial step towards the miniature components ideally suited to electronics. In the 1950s and 1960s, the transistor market expanded enormously based on consumer appliances, like television and radio, and on the early commercial computers and military uses. New companies and the giants of the established electronics industry both exploited the exciting new technology. Then in the late 1950s, the 'planar' techniques were developed which enabled very large numbers of electrical circuits to be packed on to a single chip of silicon. Since then the industry has evolved at astonishing speed, producing a stream of increasingly powerful and cheaper devices. The microelectronics industry is now fully independent of the electronics industry, with specialist semiconductor firms dominating the basic devices market (Braun and MacDonald, 1978).

The major users of microprocessors are the armaments, telecommunications and computer industries. Enormous numbers of the devices go into modern military hardware, into telephone systems and into computers and other business machines. But while microelectronics serves these major industries, it is the growing range of possible applications which has led to widespread interest in the technology. There is hardly an aspect of work which does not involve information-processing in one form or another. The decline in the cost of equipment and the remarkable capacity of microprocessors to extend the range of automation mean that it is becoming profitable to replace labour by machinery in many industrial and commercial activities. Among the applications currently in use are the following (Table 13.1).

(1) The single most important piece of equipment is the computer. Large 'mainframe' computers are important in administration, for maintaining a basic filing system, but are increasingly used across the whole range of commercial and administrative activities. Visual display terminals provide access to centrally stored information at widely dispersed points throughout the organization. In addition, the new generation of smaller computers, as powerful as the older mainframes and far more adaptable, are coming into use in industry as central processing units in integrated production systems.

(2) Within the service sector the new office technology is spreading very rapidly. One of the best-known applications, the word-processor, has virtually replaced the typewriter in many large offices. Also included is electronic funds transfer in use in banks, communications networks like electronic mail, and

Table 13.1 *User applications of microtechnology.*

Computer-based systems
Mainframe, mini and micro-computers.
Visual display units (VDUs).

Office information systems
Word processors, electronic filing, electronic mail. Electronic funds transfer.
Tele-conferencing. Management information systems (MIS). Computer-aided
design (CAD).

Service sector applications
Electronic point-of-sales (EPOS) systems, computerized stock control. Expert
diagnostic systems. Automated laboratory analysis.

Industrial machinery and automation
Industrial robots. Computer numerical control (CNC) machine tools.
Continuous process monitoring and control. Computer-aided manufacturing
(CAM). Flexible manufacturing systems (FMS).

Industry-specific applications
Telecommunications: computerized exchange equipment, fibre optics.
Printing: photo-typesetting, computerized composition.
Media: electronic news-gathering.

Miscellaneous
Energy monitoring systems. Plant security systems.

---

electronic conferencing systems. Outside the large office, electronic point-
of-sales (EPOS) equipment is used in check-out procedures in retail stores,
where the control of stock and shelving is also being computerized. And in
laboratory analysis (medical, scientific, commercial) automatic testing is
increasingly in evidence.

(3) The range of applications in industry is just as varied, partly because
much existing electro-mechanical machinery can be adapted using microprocessors. In all areas of manufacturing, machines that transform raw
materials now employ programmable controls. There are computer numeric-
ally controlled (CNC) machine tools, the operation of which is controlled by
built-in minicomputers. The CNC lathe is the most familiar example, but again
in the engineering industry the range is very wide. And the application that has
most caught the public's imagination is the industrial robot. Microprocessors
in the robot's control system enable it to 'learn' the series of movements
involved in routine tasks like spot-welding and paint-spraying. In addition, in
plants using continuous-process technology, which may include activities as
diverse as beer-brewing, flour-milling, chemicals and petrochemicals, micro-

electronics can help to monitor and control plant automatically.

(4) Lastly, there are industry-specific applications, particularly those in the 'information industries', such as telecommunications, the news media and printing. They are capital-intensive (especially telecommunications), but their product is information, and in these industries are found some of the most highly developed applications of microelectronics. In telecommunications, for instance, computerized telephone exchanges are replacing existing ones that use electro-mechanical switchgear, and optical fibres will eventually replace copper cable. In printing, currently the industry most affected, many traditional work practices have been completely transformed by computerized equipment for the direct input of copy.

This classification is not intended to be exhaustive, merely to give some idea of the kinds of technology currently being deployed (for more detailed accounts see Ide, 1982, and Child, 1984, Chapter 9). It does however help to illustrate the variable nature of technological change. Different technologies have very different implications for production, and are themselves introduced unevenly. Thus there are certain sectors where the effect will be dramatic, others where it will be attenuated, and others still where there are no immediately obvious uses. Thus the likely impact of the technology on work will need to be considered in some detail.

New technology and management

Before looking at these special problems, however, it will be useful to outline the managerial objectives and purposes behind the introduction of new technology, as there is a growing acceptance that the new systems will also have a major impact on the management task and the structure of organizations. Returning to a theme we explored earlier, in Chapter 11, for a combination of reasons managers nowadays are compelled to act more *strategically* in relation to organizational resources and outputs than they have hitherto. Pressures of competition and receding markets have made it more or less a matter of survival that companies respond positively to these changes – and new technologies have emerged as both cause and effect in this process. On the one hand, they provide improved opportunities for strategic choice across the whole range of management tasks, while on the other companies find themselves having to adopt new technology merely to keep up with competitors who threaten to move ahead in capital investment. Several noted management theorists (e.g. Child, 1984) have stressed how the new microtechnologies contribute to key managerial objectives. Fundamental management problems, such as the control and integration of activities, the provision of fast accurate data, and the improvement of performance, are potentially enhanced by powerful management information systems.

However, it is possible to become too preoccupied with the potential of these systems, and to ignore the practical aspects of their application. As a counter to this specific problem, Buchanan and Boddy (1983) developed case studies in several different manufacturing industries which highlighted the 'realities' of technological change processes. They showed, for example, that rather than change always being sweeping, most innovations were introduced on a piecemeal basis and integrated at each stage with existing equipment. Where electronic controls replaced manual or mechanical ones, intervention by operators was still often needed. And, the impact on performance objectives (cost, quality, workflow improvements, reduction of scrap, etc.) was often ambiguous – that is, different performance measures varied inconsistently, or management sometimes used new technology to make changes that could not be measured in performance terms, and the technologies themselves some- times introduced new functions which were not comparable with previous systems. Therefore, in spite of the novel impact of microelectronics, in other ways there is nothing 'new' about new technology. The impact on work, as with all forms of technology, is complex and reliant on human judgment and decisions.

Perhaps the major question about the effect of computers on managerial patterns has been whether they will cause firms to become more centralized in their power structures, or whether the new systems will encourage a more flexibly and democratically organized firm. Of course, these are not the only possibilities. There are also indications of organization structures becoming polarized, with junior managerial and senior clerical grades being eliminated. The work performed at these levels essentially involves the collation and processing of information for forward transmission, rather than actual decision-making which is a middle or senior management task. Flexible modern computing systems are able to produce information of this kind automatically, so the strong expectation is that considerable losses of employ- ment in junior management will result, although this is still some way in the future.

In practice, the pattern of decision-making, whilst not constrained by any fixed technological choices, has favoured the tightening of organizational control. Thus Child (1984, p.261) has observed that various 'contextual' factors, like a complex market structure or primary task, may force firms to decentralize power to on-the-spot decision-makers. But new technologies sometimes now enable managements to centralize power without losing the flexibility of operations that is vital for effectiveness. Similarly, Robey (1977) detected an interesting pattern in a series of case studies of computerization, where the majority resulted in less democratic forms of management control. But even in the minority of cases computers were never actually used to decentralize power; the existing level of decentralization was merely maintained. Studies like these indicate how new technology tends to be treated as a 'window of opportunity' to support the managerial instinct for centralized control.

250

THE EFFECTS OF MICROELECTRONICS

Employment effects

A fundamental question about new technology concerns its impact on employment levels. There are two distinct viewpoints here, which King (1982, p.29) has distinguished respectively as the 'microelectronics evolutionists and revolutionists'. The first is that new technology will result in a net increase in jobs. Industries like microelectronics, this argument runs, are the industries of the future, and we must embrace them wholeheartedly or face the consequences of national decline. The dynamism of the new industries means that the economy as a whole will be stimulated; and while jobs may be lost in traditional sectors, this is part of the normal process of industrial development and these losses will be more than compensated for by new jobs and additional economic demand created by new technology. Set against this argument is a far more pessimistic view. Even allowing for increased demand, from improved products and equipment using microprocessors, this second view stresses the massive potential of new technology for displacing labour across a range of industries and occupations.

It is no simple matter to prove the truth or falsity of these views. The technological changes to which they refer are far from complete; and in any case, as we have repeatedly stressed, the hardware component of technology is only one element. Just as important are the systems of work organization into which the hardware is introduced. This leaves considerable room for human choice as a determining factor. Nonetheless, some trends are beginning to emerge, and we can at least start to evaluate the initial impact of new technology on employment.

The general outcome of mechanization (and new technology is no exception) is to displace labour. In individual cases this need not apply: new equipment may be introduced to replace worn out or obsolete plant, to improve production, or for some other reason that has no impact on jobs. But the *aggregate* impact of mechanization in a particular industry or occupation is to reduce the labour force. Taking the argument a step further, reduction of jobs need not then result in unemployment. If the economy is expanding the labour displaced by capital investment will normally be absorbed. In times of near-full employment, workers may be redeployed within the same firm if their existing jobs are eliminated or they are usually able to find jobs elsewhere (as happened in Britain during the 1960s). However, at times of economic recession and high unemployment, the chances of finding another job are drastically reduced. It is then that job creation slows down, while technological change is still being channelled into the elimination of jobs.

Because new technology has coincided with economic recession and mass unemployment, it often tends to be assumed that the two developments are linked. However, up to the early 1980s unemployment caused by technology in fact had had a negligible impact. Williams (1984), in her review of the employment effects of new technology, refers to estimates that only 5 per cent of total job losses in manufacturing were actually associated with the use of microelectronics over the period 1981–3.

Yet this is not to deny that the impact may eventually prove to be massive. Many authoritative studies are pessimistic about the long-term direct threat to jobs. For example, Barron and Curnow (1979, p.201) project job losses in Britain due to new technology alone at around 16 per cent of the labour force up to the 1990s. A study commissioned by the European Trade Union Institute (ETUI, 1980, pp.78–85) similarly concluded that throughout Europe the potential for job displacement far outstrips that for job creation. Even the optimistic arguments in such reports are very far from convincing: their optimism stems from faith in unpredictable factors like state intervention and economic upturn, or in standard remedies like increased training, while they concede the near-certainty of greatly reduced employment in particular sectors and occupations. Williams, for example, points out that technological unemployment is expected to accelerate, and any 'overall positive impact' will come from knock-on effects in low-technology areas (like construction and services) stimulated by general increases in demand (1984, p.214). However, the level of service sector employment is now fairly stable; and the build-up of jobs in this sector, particularly evident over the past thirty years, seems to have slowed down. Thus if new technology is about to eliminate jobs on the scale suggested there are no obvious major sources of new employment that we can look to.

To examine these issues more closely, we need to look at the links between new technology and specific areas of work. Three that have been singled out for attention in previous chapters are also pertinent here: manual work, white-collar work and women's employment.

(1) Industrial employment

As mentioned above, the very high rates of unemployment in manufacturing, up to the mid-1980s at any rate, were mainly attributable to familiar economic causes in the deepening recession in Britain and the collapse of economic demand, rather than to new technology. But in a number of specific cases there has already been considerable technological displacement of labour.

In many operations like assembly, testing and maintenance, the potential exists for labour forces to be cut back because work can be simplified to the point of merely inserting an electronic component or replacement part. Thus several major firms, making products like cash registers, sewing machines and typewriters, have greatly reduced their manual workforces with this type of innovation (ETUI, 1980, p.81). Of course, some expansion of employment does take place as jobs move 'upstream' into firms making electronic components and machinery for the firms which fabricate final products. But the fact remains that in such cases a considerable *net* loss of jobs is estimated to have occurred.

In routine assembly operations industrial robots are increasingly being used – the lines of robots assembling car bodies, for example, have become a familiar sight. At present these first-generation machines can do only simple tasks, such as spotwelding, paint-spraying, drilling and some materials-handling. But 'intelligent' second-generation robots, equipped with sensors for vision and touch, will soon be able to perform far more complex assemblies. Accordingly, they will be able to take over a far wider range of jobs, and the huge amount of employment worldwide still concentrated in assembly-type work will come under threat.

Another area of job loss is in some of the traditionally high-skill industries. For example the information industries, printing and telecommunications, are both on the brink of very rapid change. Printing especially presents the major example of the elimination of skilled manual work to have occurred so far. Since the mid-1960s as many as one-quarter of jobs in the industry have disappeared, due to advances like computerized composition and computer-aided equipment for the direct input of copy. Roderick Martin's (1981) study of the newspaper industry in Fleet Street has shown how, by the mid-1970s, a new printing technology was available. The trade unions, while having to accept inevitable job losses, were at first able to retain existing jobs for their members. However, Martin repeatedly stresses the precarious nature of union control over the new technology, because most of these jobs can now be done by workers with no craft training.

(2) Office employment

Two related points bear on the argument here: first the suggestion that office employment is ripe for mechanization, and second that the technology to achieve this is now available. The first point relates to the fact that the productivity of office workers is notoriously low, particularly if factory work is taken as some sort of benchmark. Considered as a *labour process*, most offices are not very efficient. Work study of secretarial and clerical jobs invariably shows quite a small proportion of time spent on directly productive work (typing, filing, etc.). It usually takes longer, for example, to walk to and from a filing cabinet than it does to file a document. When compared with factories, where tasks like materials-handling are usually automated or streamlined, office work is quite loosely organized. Given the continued growth in office employment, therefore, managements have had a strong interest in improving productivity as a way of containing the size of office labour forces.

The relative inefficiency of offices in the past has been reflected in the low rate of investment in office machinery, and this has largely been because the technology necessary for office automation has simply not been available. In some ways office machinery has not progressed very far in the past hundred years. The most modern electric typewriter, for instance, is no different in essentials from the first Remington produced in the 1880s – and most other office equipment only enables paper to be handled more efficiently. The computer represents the first really capital-intensive piece of office equipment. But even here the first generation of commercial computers, introduced in the 1960s, were invariably confined to basic clerical tasks of payroll and accounts.

New technology is set to change all this. The work done in offices is essentially information-handling, and microelectronics is an information-processing technology; it stores, edits and transmits information in radically new ways. Thus, for example, the word processor, with its storage and text-editing facilities, is fundamentally different from the conventional typewriter, and great claims are made for its ability to improve secretarial productivity. In many large office establishments it is common now for a small group of seven or eight people to be dealing with the typing for an organization of 200 or 300. As one report notes, particularly where work is highly standardized very large increases in productivity, of the order of several hundred per cent, have been recorded (Williams, 1984). Similarly, in the main areas of white-collar employment, like financial services (banking, insurance, building societies) and the civil service, the bulk of routine clerical work – checking and recording items, filling in forms, filing etc. – is rapidly being dealt with automatically, possibly leading to large-scale reductions in these jobs by the late 1980s.

(3) Women's employment

A third major concern about the impact of office technology is that women may bear the brunt of change. As we saw in Chapter 12, female employment is heavily concentrated in particular occupations and sectors, and while some of these do not seem directly at risk (particularly in social welfare, education and personal services) much female employment is focused in areas expected to suffer high technological unemployment. Office automation poses perhaps the major threat. About 2 million women in Britain work in routine clerical/ secretarial jobs which are in direct line of fire of the new office technology (West, 1982). In addition, about three-quarters of a million women work in the distributional trades, and much of the work here (like stock control and retail sales) is being rapidly automated.

Despite such indications the overall effect of new technology on female employment is likely to be quite complex. For one thing, women's jobs may prove to be rather resilient to the impact of new technology. Female labour is generally cheaper than male labour and so less likely to be mechanized. Certainly the prime candidates for mechanization – expensive organized labour like car assembly workers, engineers and printers – are rarely female. Given the high proportion of part-time work that women do, they are also more flexible and hence attractive to employers during a time of recession.

Of course, the very fact of employers' treating women as a flexible labour force may undermine their job security. Huws's (1982) survey of some forty establishments in the Leeds area found that a wide range of women's occupations were affected, and she revealed the health problems that are increasingly being linked with new technology. Particularly in women's clerical and secretarial work, Huws found a widespread and marked increase in stress reported, as well as other related health hazards like eyestrain, headaches and tiredness. Her research showed that working at visual display units frequently meant an increase in speed, concentration and monotony of work which led to stress (1982, p.29). Thus, even where the numbers of women's jobs are maintained, the *quality* of those jobs may be adversely affected, and women's work might increasingly fall into the category of cheap and degraded, or even sweated labour.

Skills and work organization

Apart from labour displacement, new technology also has important reper- cussions on the labour process – on skills and on the ways in which work is organized. In Chapter 9, we reviewed the sociological debate in this area and compared models which stress the *deskilling* effect of technology and work organization with those which take a more positive approach and argue that there is no reason to suppose the *regeneration* of skills is any less typical than their destruction. The parallel question arises here in relation to new technology: will the new applications on the whole degrade the skills of workers, or will they create new skills and enhanced opportunities for occupational development?

As before, a definitive answer lies beyond our scope, and in any case implementation is still in its early stages. At the moment, therefore, the emphasis tends to be on examining the detailed impact of applications and the choices that technology leaves open, rather than on seeking evidence for any generalized impact.

For example, the computer itself has created wholly new occupations and employment opportunities. Many thousands of jobs, ranging from unskilled assembly work to the highest level of engineering and systems skills, have been created in the computer industry which simply were not in existence thirty years ago. Certainly this is skill (and job) creation on a grand scale. However, there are also indications of deskilling. If we take the occupation of programmer, in the early days of commercial computing programmers controlled most aspects of machine operations. This was reflected in the level of skill required and in their status and pay. Since then, however, the job has been subject to rationalization. Higher-level work is now in the hands of an elite of systems analysts, while programmers mostly write routine specifications and are apt to be tied to specific types of equipment. Also, developments in programming languages have had a deskilling effect. The original machine languages required a knowledge of mathematics to master, but the new 'high- level' languages are more straightforward to learn (Kraft, 1979).

To take a second example, that of the word-processor, Barker and Downing's (1980) research has stressed the deskilling effect of the equipment on secretarial work. The skills of the secretary, they argue, are bound up with the presentation of the typed page – with layout, justification of margins, etc. – tasks which the word-processor does automatically. On the other hand, word-processing does not eliminate the basic 'keyboard' skill of touch-typing, and the machine itself possesses more functions than a conventional typewriter, so there are new skills being created as older ones disappear.

Crompton and Jones's (1984) study of the impact of computerization on clerical work presents a more straightforward account of deskilling. Traditionally clerical work resembled a craft in the sense of being based on the clerk's special knowledge of the firm's filing system. However, Crompton and Jones show how computerized batch systems for basic clerical tasks, like payroll and accounts, have eliminated this control of information, and now clerical work mainly consists of preparing information to be fed into the computer.

> . . . the value of the clerk to the employer once resided both in a detailed knowledge of clerical work procedures (the clerical 'craft') and also in the fact that, to varying extents, clerical workers have exercised control on behalf of capital. . . . The clerk now typically performs the function of (deskilled) labour, being increasingly peripheral to the performance of the computer and having little or no responsibility for the coordination and completion of the many separate work tasks in the process as a whole. (p.76)

Work restructuring that often accompanies mechanization can also cause conditions to deteriorate. In the application of word-processing, for example, we have encountered several companies in which a typing pool, where the work was organized to some extent informally by the women concerned, went over to a much more closely supervised operation. With some of the more complex technologies, like computer-aided design and expert systems, forms of rationalization may also affect certain relatively privileged professional occupations. In the case of design and drafting, Mike Cooley's research has shown how CAD can degrade draftsmen's jobs. The work of production design is increasingly routinized and fragmented, and the imposition of shift-working and bureaucratic hierarchies often becomes necessary for this expensive equipment to be cost-effective (Cooley, 1981). On the other hand, the professions are renowned for their ability to cushion their members against these sorts of pressure; and in this respect new technology may be no different from other forms of rationalization. Thus it remains to be seen what the outcomes will be in the case of specific professional occupations.

Examples such as these indicate the complexity of deskilling and show the importance of the *work context*. Thus a typing pool in a large organization that has been converted to word-processing will have very different implications for secretarial skills from the case of a word-processor used by a senior executive's secretary, where the machine may enhance status and skills. A great deal depends upon the situations in which the new technologies are introduced; and the purely technical issue, whether or not it is feasible to mechanize a given work process, is by no means the only consideration.

The 'impact' of new technology?

In this connection a number of writers recently have been critical of what they call the 'impact' approach, in which attempts are made to survey or predict the overall effects of new technology. The particular target of their criticism is the type of analysis which proposes a simple relationship between technology and work. Here, new applications are matched with the existing jobs they might affect, often producing a 'hit list' of occupations at risk. The counter-argument the critics put forward is that the implementation of technology has to be seen as a much more complex process, involving social interaction. Any final 'impact' on work cannot be pre-defined; it can only be understood by focusing on the particular work context and the role of human agents. As Sorge et al, (1982) have argued, '. . . the constant reference to microelectronics as having "effects" is not often helpful; this glosses over the importance of industry-specific factors which become ever more important as microelectronics is used in an increasing range of industries, services and occupations'. In essence, therefore, this is an argument against technological determinism.

For example, in his case studies of innovation in engineering, Wilkinson (1983) rejected any idea of CNC machinery having any fixed impact on employment levels or skills. Instead, he stressed that a process of 'shopfloor politics' shaped the work situation; and he found that the collective resistance of employees was often important in safeguarding jobs and protecting skills. Similarly, Child et al. (1984) studied a range of different work settings in the service sector and argued that there is nothing inevitable about the way new technology is implemented. They found that in cases of junior-level employees working with new technologies elements of skill and control were lost, and staff expressed dissatisfaction with the way the technologies impinged on their jobs. However, staff who had a developed professional ethic and a relatively strong organizational position remained in control of the new systems. Child et al. concluded that the effect of new technology upon work depends on the 'workplace power' of incumbents, and where key areas of organizational uncertainty are being controlled technology can serve to enhance status and skills.

CONCLUSION

Whatever the complexities that exist in the relationship between technology and work, however, it would be misleading if by this emphasis we detract attention from the full scope of advanced technologies. For when one accumulates the evidence of areas likely to be affected – in office work, middle management, planning and mass production, as well as in specific industries like engineering and telecommunications – it is hard to avoid the conclusion that the medium- to long-term impact might be very dramatic indeed.

In order to grasp these possibilities, different viewpoints on new technology have been used to describe different 'scenarios' of future events. At one extreme an 'optimistic scenario' of the future casts new technology in a positive light, prophesying an increase in prosperity and an end to the alienating work typical of the industrial economy. The 'pessimistic scenario', in stark contrast, looks to a possible future of mass unemployment and social decay.

A more important consideration, however, concerns the route society will take into the future. One version of the optimistic scenario adopts an extreme *laissez-faire* stance. This stresses that science and technology have produced solutions in the past, that new industries and new products have emerged out of the normal operation of economic market forces, and that there is no reason to suppose that such will not continue. Others, however, including a majority of academic commentators, argue that this is a complacent view, and only massive public intervention will secure the benefits of new technology for society as a whole (e.g. Bell, 1980; King, 1982; Benson and Lloyd, 1983; Stonier, 1983).

The comprehensive account of such arguments provided by Adam Schaff (1982) accepts that 'full automation will, in the long run, largely eliminate work in the traditional sense of the word'. There can be no question of reversing or even slowing down this process, and the pessimistic scenario is forecast assuming society proceeds on its present course.

> . . . if in forty to fifty years from now we have tens, if not hundreds, of millions of *structurally* totally or partly unemployed people in the industrialised countries, they will include women, the elderly, the disabled and predominantly *young* people. To rely on spontaneous adjustment to provide for those millions of people, especially young people, means to doom them to frustration, social pathology and rebellion. (p.354)

The notion of any optimistic scenario emerging naturally is rejected mainly on the grounds that technological change is no longer the product of spontaneous invention. Technology now derives from huge research expenditures by corporations and by governments, hence it is controlled by political forces and central planning. Thus, a future of mass unemployment can only be averted by intervention at the societal level.

Schaff argues this will mean changing from a society based on work to one based on 'occupation'. In other words, having accepted that it will no longer be possible to provide everyone with a job, we must expand those areas which creatively *occupy* people. The sorts of activity Schaff has in mind include, firstly, all 'higher'-level jobs, like those in the professions, management, the arts and media; secondly, the provision for public welfare, health and education; and thirdly, the organization of leisure and protection of the environment. These occupations will have to be greatly expanded, not merely continued on their present scale. In the area of welfare, for example, Schaff envisages an entire range of social needs being identified and catered for.

An obvious difficulty with such solutions is that they tend to be rather idealistic and utopian. They assume that an aggressive capitalist system gives rise to the problems of automation (in the sense that it is competitiveness and the drive for profit which make automation an irreversible process) but they assume away capitalism when it comes to posing solutions. Thus Schaff argues that in order to avoid mass unemployment, 'society will have to take over the implementation of the needs of its members' (p.346). However, public intervention at this level is difficult to imagine in a competitive market economy. It would imply a capacity to plan centrally which far exceeds anything we possess at present – not to mention the problem of planning for social needs rather than for private profit. Such alternatives, in the last analysis, therefore seem little more comforting or convincing than the view that solutions will arise spontaneously.

One thing that the present high levels of unemployment have amply demonstrated is that we remain a society geared very firmly to employment. People identify in a fundamental way with work, just as their social economic well-being depends upon access to a wage. This is the nature of the industrial society we live in; and whatever changes are eventually deemed necessary, to bring us closer to the kind of 'post-industrial' or 'leisure' society that writers like Schaff envisage as possible, they will have to start out from these existing realities.

FURTHER READING

Braun, E. and S. MacDonald (1978) *Revolution in Miniature*. Cambridge: Cambridge University Press.

Burgess, C. (1985) 'Skill implications of new technology', *Employment Gazette*, October. (London: Department of Employment).

Child, J. (1984) *Organization* (2nd ed.) Chapter 9: 'New technology and organization'. London: Harper and Row.

Cockburn, C. (1983) *Brothers: Male Dominance and Technological Change*. London: Pluto Press.

Cockburn, C. (1986) *Machinery of Dominance: Women, Men and Technological Know-how*. London: Pluto Press.

Forester, T. (ed.) (1985) *The Information Technology Revolution*. Oxford: Blackwell.

Francis, A. (1986) *New Technology at Work*. London: Oxford University Press.

Friedrichs, G. and A. Schaff (eds.) (1982) *Microelectronics and Society: For Better For Worse*. Oxford: Pergamon Press.

Marstrand, P. (ed.) (1984) *New Technology and the Future of Work and Skills*. London: Frances Pinter.

Wilkinson, B. (1983) *The Shopfloor Politics of New Technology*. London: Heinemann.

Williams, V. (1984) 'Employment implications of new technology', *Employment Gazette*, April. (London: Department of Employment).

ORGANIZATIONS

If the issues dealt with in Section Three were mostly concerned with aspects of the division of labour, there is another major dimension along which the structuring of work takes place and that is the division of power and authority. This 'vertical' dimension embodies the hierarchy of control which forms the basic structure of the modern large-scale organization. A closely related aspect of this has already been discussed in Chapter 9, namely the systematic methods of work organization (like Taylorism) which brought about the rationalization of labour. We considered these as part of the labour process and the employment relationship but they could equally have been included here, for they hinge on the central theme of the control that managerial groups exercise over subordinate groups of workers.

Historically these methods belong to that important period in the last quarter of the last century – from about the mid-1870s to 1900 – which saw the emergence of what today we would recognize as the modern industrial economy. In this period industry in America and Europe was transformed. The new work methods emerged against a background of new technologies, like chemicals and steel, together with the new manufacturing and mass production industries. During the 1880s the commercial office and government bureaucracy first appeared. And all these enterprises were being managed on a much larger scale than had hitherto been either necessary or possible. Altogether, an industrial and commercial landscape was taking shape which was quite different from the small-scale capitalism of only twenty or thirty years earlier.

Seen from another perspective, what was happening was the rise of the modern organization. Presthus has summarized this process in America as follows:

> Beginning about 1875, social, economic and political trends in the United States prepared the way for the 'organization society', characterized by large-scale bureaucratic institutions in virtually every social area. The master trends included the separation of ownership from management; increasing size and concentration in business; the decline of competition as the financial resources required for entry in

almost every sector became prohibitive; and the emergence of an employee society. (1979, p.84)

The importance of these changes is easily appreciated. Many of us will spend all or some part of our working lives in large organizations, and we will be their clients and come into other forms of contact on countless other occasions. This should not be exaggerated, because as much as half of total employment is still provided by small firms. Nevertheless, the organizational setting has had a profound effect on the nature of work.

In this final part of the book, we will look first, in Chapter 14, at the sociological study of organizations. This is a subject that in recent years has attracted an enormous amount of attention, and has been radically transformed in its approach. The classical writings have been reappraised and re-interpreted, and a whole new body of theory and research has been developed. Much of this, as we will see, has centred on the model of organizations as control structures.

This will be followed, in Chapter 15, by an account of the managerial approach to organizations – usually referred to as organizational analysis, or simply as organization theory. In contrast with the sociology of organizations, the emphasis here is on the improvement of performance, and on a model of organizations as systems for goal attainment. However, as we will see, organizational analysis is by no means 'managerialist' in the crude sense of being unaware of issues of conflict and control – even if these are not treated in quite the same way or given as much prominence as in sociological accounts.

Finally, Chapter 16 examines another area of great recent interest which, in a sense, makes common ground between the sociological and managerial approaches. This is the study of power in organizations. Here, the radical concept of power is applied to the relations within groups of managers, and the model of the organization as an arena of bargaining and influence is explored.

14

Structure and Control in Organizations

One of the major developments behind the rise of large-scale organizations has been the so-called division between ownership and control. In small-scale enterprises it is common for legal ownership and management to overlap and be vested in the same person or group. But increasingly, with modern large-scale organizations, day-to-day control is exercised by managers who are themselves salaried employees, whilst share ownership has become so diffuse that it would be impossible for all the shareholders actually to run a company. In reality, the issue is rather more complex, and the separation between ownership and control is by no means so clear-cut. Ownership of many of the largest corporations throughout the world can be traced to groups that exercise corporate control, not uncommonly families (for a recent account, see Hill, 1981, pp.71–6). However, the point we wish to raise here is that the growth of organizations has led to the rise of a separate and distinct managerial structure.

In this context, Offe (1976) has distinguished what he calls 'task continuous' and 'task discontinuous' forms of organization. The former would include the small owner-managed firm, the craft workshop and the partnership, which are run cooperatively by those who actually perform the work. Planning is simply an outgrowth of the work process itself, and any authority is based on the possession of skills. In contrast to this, task discontinuous organizations are far more typical of modern employment. They have a discrete authority structure, unrelated to those who do the work.

Such changes reflect the growth of *bureaucratic* forms of organizing work. In the early stages of industrialization the need to plan and administer work presented few problems, but once the size and complexity of plants had increased, administration came to be seen as something distinctive. Nowadays in all areas of economic life – in industry, government and both the public and private services – there are complex and highly developed administrative structures.

These structures, moreover, are set up as means of pursuing explicit corporate objectives – goals which are not necessarily shared by all of the members. Central processes in organizations therefore involve the *control* of activities. The mechanisms of controlling the behaviour of people in organizations are reflected in the structuring of the rewards and deprivations of work, with increasing pay, discretion and power as one ascends to senior levels, and decreasing amounts in the lower ranks. This encompasses the concern with alienation, discussed in Chapter 9, where the central issue involved workers being denied control over their working lives and the products of their labour. Certainly many of the problems of repetitive dehumanized work, so characteristic of the modern factory or office, have been attributed to the power structure and to systematic control in organizations. However, the sociology of organizations has developed a rather broader view than this. The control of organizational personnel is not seen as being confined to the labour process, nor does it stop short at the factory or office floor. It also applies in varying degrees to the more privileged layers of an organization's employees.

BUREAUCRACY

The term 'organization' can be thought of in two ways: firstly in terms of concrete, real-life organizations (factories, offices, etc.), and secondly in terms of the principle of structuring work on a hierarchical basis. Bearing this in mind, we can see that real-life organizations will embrace other principles of 'organizing' work than the purely hierarchical one – there will be a range of occupations, a social division of labour (based on gender, race, age, etc.) and perhaps trade unions. Now the significance of the bureaucracy in this context – in addition, that is, to the fact that bureaucracies are important in themselves for managing modern business – is that in this form of organization the two meanings of the term merge. We can study a real-life organization which approximates very closely to the pure principle of hierarchy.

Indeed, the defining feature of the bureaucracy is that it is solely concerned with the task of administration; it is a purely 'task discontinuous' type of organization. In contrast to other major forms of work, like manual and professional, no concrete task is performed in the bureaucracy. Instead, it carries out the task of maintaining a system of records upon which the direction and control of the work of others is based. Typical employees are clerical officers and secretaries. Indeed, the classic example of bureaucracy is the civil service, although other large white-collar organizations like banks, building societies and insurance companies also have strong bureaucratic elements.

Modern sociological thought on this subject is traced to Max Weber, whose study of bureaucracy has had an enormous influence both on the theory of organizations and on how we understand the impact of organizations on society at large (Weber, 1970, pp.196–244; 1964, pp.330–3). Weber wrote during the years spanning the turn of the century, towards the end of the period when the modern German nation became consolidated. Unlike the pattern of industrialization in Britain, the German industrial economy developed along highly centralized lines, and one aspect of this was the growth of a huge state apparatus. It was the experience of seeing this central state machine develop and spread that persuaded Weber of the varied implications of the bureaucratic form of organization.

The bureaucratic model

In Weber's (1970) account of bureaucracy the following basic elements were included: (1) a *staff* consisting of a body of employees whose full-time work was to administer the activities of the particular institution. The employee's post carries with it authority over specific areas, but it is a cardinal principle that the incumbent should not overstep the bounds of his or her authority. Such behaviour (for example, the use of formal authority to gain wider influence) might result in various forms of corruption; (2) a *division of labour* which assigns specific tasks to sub-units and individuals. The division of labour in bureaucracies is highly developed: departmental boundaries and individual jobs are closely specified and duties and responsibilities carefully set out; (3) the *hierarchy*, or division of power, involves the ranking of offices to provide clear lines of command. In bureaucracies the hierarchy also is typically very complex, its many levels providing a highly differentiated structure of authority; (4) *competence* refers to the basis upon which office is held. Factors like luck, favouritism or personal connections should play no part in the position that officials attain, advancement should be decided by expertise and ability alone. Thus organizations have to pay close attention to the process of selection, whereby these qualities can be identified in personnel; and (5) *objectivity* suggests that all dealings within the bureaucracy and with clients should be conducted on the basis of equal treatment according to a procedural routine. The objective conduct of business, free from any personal feelings, is the basis of the reliability of formal administration.

From the point of view of technical efficiency, Weber believed that the above characteristics gave far-reaching advantages, making the bureaucratic form of organization absolutely necessary in a modern economy:

> The decisive reason for the advance of bureaucratic organization has always been its purely technical superiority over any other form of organization. The fully developed bureaucratic mechanism compares with other organizations exactly as does the machine with the non-mechanical modes of production. . . . Today it is primarily the capitalist market economy which demands that the official business of the administration be discharged precisely, unambiguously, continuously and with as much speed as possible. Normally, the very large capitalist enterprises are themselves unequalled models of strict bureaucratic organization. (1964, pp.214–15)

Two things are apparent from this account. Firstly, any large-scale organization will in some measure have a bureaucratic structure. All have a lateral division of tasks and a vertical division of authority, and embrace principles of objectivity and competence. Yet some of these factors may vary quite considerably across different organizations. Some, for instance, may have a relatively relaxed division of labour, with work being accomplished in diffuse groups and with little attention paid to exact responsibilities. In the bureaucratic model, however, these factors are present in an exaggerated form. The civil service, for example, has an extremely complex hierarchy, in which close attention is given to differentials covering a whole range of fringe benefits, privileges and status symbols.

Secondly, it is obvious that the above factors present too faultless a picture. No real-life bureaucracy meets all of these requirements all of the time. Nor was it Weber's intention to describe actual patterns of behaviour. The model that he set out was what he termed an *ideal type*. The word 'ideal' here does not have the evaluative meaning it has in common usage; it refers instead to the pure idea that lay behind the reality. What Weber described was the consistent and logical form of bureaucracy, rather than its day-to-day operations.

Nevertheless, in reality organizations do approximate quite closely to Weber's model. People are mostly appointed on the basis of merit, tasks on the whole are clearly allocated, and clients are dealt with impartially. In other ways, the model also represents the *standard* that we expect from organizations. There is normally an outcry if official corruption is uncovered, and we would usually be affronted when dealing with bureaucracies to be treated according to the personal whim of the official. However, although values of objectivity and competence help to guarantee integrity in public life, and we tend to take them for granted, they are at bottom arbitrary and relative like all social institutions. In the historical past organizations were based on quite different rules, where, for example, it was quite normal for an office-holder to confer privilege on his relatives or favourites.

Organizational authority and rationality

In common with most sociologists, Weber was centrally concerned with the problem of social order. Why should people accept the roles allocated to them by some external power, and why do they obey the directives issued on its behalf? There can be many possible reasons. People may comply simply because they are coerced, or because they perceive some advantages in obeying, they may obey out of sheer habit, or even because they feel affection for the person issuing orders, and so on. However, if the motives people have for accepting rules reflect only factors like expediency or coercion, Weber reasoned, social order would hardly be stable in the long term. At some basic level there must be a feeling of solidarity with rules. This all-important voluntary element is embodied in a special type of social control, namely *authority*.

The crucial feature of all forms of authority as a basis of social control is that the power of senior officials should be accepted by those under control. The latter should believe that it is right and proper for people in senior positions to issue directives and equally justifiable that their orders be complied with. In short, authority should be regarded as a *legitimate* form of social control.

> . . . custom and personal advantage, purely affectual or ideal motives, do not, even taken together, form a sufficiently reliable basis for a system of imperative coordination. In addition, there is normally a further element, the belief in legitimacy. . . . No system of authority voluntarily limits itself to the appeal to material or affectual or ideal motives as a basis for guaranteeing its continuance. In addition, such a system attempts to establish and to cultivate the belief in its legitimacy. (Weber, 1964, p.325)

Weber distinguished three types of authority: (1) *charismatic authority* which is based on the personal qualities, heroic or mystical, of leaders; (2) *traditional authority* based on established customs and the right to rule of dominant groups sanctified by such customary beliefs; and (3) *rational authority* based on the legal occupancy of senior positions by those who exercise authority.

Mouzelis (1975, p.16), in his thorough account of the Weberian approach to bureaucracy, makes the important point that each of these types of authority gives rise to a different kind of organization. Movements based on charismatic leaders tend to be associated with a temporary and loose type of administrative structure. Traditional authority, vested in the inherited status of a king or lord, gives rise to a more permanent apparatus where officials owe their position to some privilege or contract granted by the superior. Finally, rational authority forms the basis of the modern work organization, and in particular the bureaucracy. Here the basis of order seems obvious: people conform with the directives of those in senior positions because they are paid to do so and because they may be dismissed if they refuse. A rational calculation on the part of the employee is inherent in this kind of contractual arrangement. But in addition to this Weber was convinced that bureaucracy was of fundamental importance in industrial society because of its distinctively rational structure.

We discussed this briefly in Chapter 9, and pointed out that rationality reflects the application of a formal structure of administration as the means of managing complex tasks. Bureaucracy thus permits the calculation and predictability of future outcomes, together with accountability and close control of activities. Bureaucratic authority has advantages over other types since rational action is in evidence throughout the organization, as well as in the organization's relations to its markets and clients. When people perceive that office-holders are competent, that decisions are taken formally, resources are accounted for, and so forth, this upholds the belief in legitimacy. Such beliefs are further supported by the fact that office-holders themselves are subject to the same impersonal rules. The appeal of rationality therefore remains independent of the personal qualities of leaders and so outlasts individuals, and is not based on the forces of tradition and habit which may come to be questioned. For these reasons, rational bureaucratic authority should prove to be by far the most stable form of authority.

Finally, all three authority types are themselves ideal types. Thus in real organizations authority will be a mixture of types, and there will always be traces of motives other than the purely rational. Senior management, for instance, are always very careful about projecting the right image, for they know full well that their personal charisma is important if they wish to command authority. Similarly, all forms of authority depend in part upon force of habit, indeed some organizations can be very traditional and hidebound in this respect. As Weber himself put it, all systems of authority rest on a *belief*, held by subordinates, and by virtue of which those exercising authority are accepted willingly. The belief is invariably complex and composed of several elements, including habit and personal charisma (Weber, 1964, p.382). Nevertheless, in a bureaucratic organization one type should predominate, namely the appeal that rational procedures have for the majority of members of the organization.

SOCIAL ACTION IN ORGANIZATIONS

Bureaucratic dysfunctions

A more obvious meaning attached to the idea of bureaucracy, however, presents a major problem with Weber's account, and that is that it has always seemed at odds with common-sense notions. 'Bureaucracy' in everyday terms usually means the exact opposite of the highly rational and efficient system that Weber seemed to refer to. The popular view of bureaucracy conjures up an image of unnecessary paperwork, time-consuming procedures, strict adherence to rules, and an unresponsiveness to clients. In short, administrative procedures often seem to be designed to get in the way of achieving goals, rather than rationally facilitating them. This critical, common-sense view has formed the basis of a lengthy 'debate with Weber' in which a great deal of modern writing and research has been cast. Later writers, particularly in the United States, stress the major 'dysfunctional' features that bureaucracies have. The post-Weberian analysis of bureaucracy, following Merton (1940) and Selznick (1943), has focused on the rigid and impersonal character of bureaucracy, contrasting this with the perfect form of administration that Weber appeared to be describing (Table 14.1).

It helps to separate out two different themes in this critique. Firstly there is the suggestion that bureaucracy is actually an *inefficient* form of organization. The question of efficiency is chiefly a managerial concern (one that we deal with in much more detail in the next chapter), but for the moment we can note that the emphasis here is on the inability of bureaucratic organizations to achieve their goals in a flexible way, or to respond to changes in their market environment.

Table 14.1 *Weber and his critics.*

The 'ideal type' model of bureaucracy	High degree of internal efficiency Rational: effective administrative means to corporate ends
The 'efficiency' critique of Weber's model	Bureaucracy as 'red tape': irrational Goal displacement: the displacement of corporate ends by administrative means Inflexible: unresponsive to environmental changes and demands
The 'social' critique of Weber's model	Erosion of individual democratic freedoms Depersonalization: the 'bureaucratic personality'

This common-sense view of bureaucracy as 'red tape' mounts an explicit challenge to the Weberian notion of bureaucracy as a highly rational means to an end. This criticism centres on the idea of *goal displacement*. What this refers to is the forms of incapacity that emerge in elaborate bureaucratic structures when officials become preoccupied with the administrative process itself. This can happen as a result of an extreme division of labour that allows the bureaucrat to see only a small part of the operation, and also because people's reputations and careers become bound up with established procedures. In any case, if the smooth running of the bureaucracy becomes the real goal of officials, the stated goals for which the bureaucracy was originally set up tend to slip into the background. This sort of shift, from ends to means, can be a familiar experience of dealing with centralized bureaucracies, where the quality of service appears to have been sacrificed to the goal of easy administration.

Secondly there is the criticism that bureaucracy has major *social* dysfunctions. Included here is Merton's (1940) original idea of the 'bureaucratic personality' as a narrow, one-dimensional kind of individual. This basic problem, that large-scale bureaucratic systems produce 'organization men' who are the harbingers of a new kind of bland, conformist middle class, has been a strong theme in American sociology (e.g. Mills, 1951). In a broader sense this reflects the *depersonalization* of social and economic life. Objectivity was mentioned as a key criterion of rational administration, but objectivity has a negative side. The price that has to be paid is that the quality of human relations, both within the bureaucracy and between the bureaucracy and its clients, becomes transformed into anonymous and calculative exchanges.

These socially dysfunctional features have major implications for the erosion of individual freedom. The state bureaucracy is in theory the servant of society, responsible for major forms of welfare provision, like health, education, social security and protection of the environment. Yet the belief that in some quite straightforward way the state distributes the services to which we are entitled can prove to be rather naive. 'The state' as a principle of government may stipulate this, but in reality the relationship of the state to society is mediated by the bureaucratic machine. At times the individual has little chance of redress against officialdom, and for all practical purposes has to accept the treatment he or she is meted out. Cases of 'bureaucratic abuse' give sufficient grounds for believing that the different departments of the modern state are remarkably autonomous, and that they can and often do appropriate wider powers from their official position (Weinstein, 1979). A great many officials of the state – the police, social security officers, welfare officials, immigration officials – in reality have wide-ranging forms of discretion over the way laws are interpreted, and consequently have very real power over the members of the public with whom they come into contact.

It now tends to be recognized, however, that these criticisms of the nature of bureaucracy were misjudged as criticisms of Weber. In the first place, it was indeed true that Weber regarded bureaucracies as a highly efficient form of administration. Without efficiency the whole basis of authority in large organizations would have been undermined. And this is certainly at odds with the goal-displacing picture of inflexible, bureaucractic organizations that critics have drawn. Yet, after all, how accurate is their viewpoint? Much of it relies upon appealing to common-sense views, or to anecdotal evidence. By comparison the emphasis on rationality, and the honest fulfilment of contractual obligations, is at least as well founded. If we take a broader comparative viewpoint, compared with organizations in some Third World countries or in socialist countries, where political factors intervene in commercial life far more prominently, the bureaucracies we are familiar with often do seem to be models of efficiency and fair dealing. These positive features therefore form the first impression we receive of bureaucracy, as Weber intended they should.

Secondly, fears about the impact of bureaucracy on society were actually consistent with the viewpoint that Weber held. As we saw in Chapter 9, he was chiefly concerned with the much broader issue of *rationalization* as the key historical trend in the development of industrial society. This meant a world dominated by the calculative logic of rational decision-making and the remorseless spread of bureaucratic rationality. It embraced fears of the erosion of individual freedom – and indeed the very efficiency of bureaucracy was what made it a potent threat. Of course, the fear of an overbearing state is as old as the idea of democracy itself, and certainly did not originate with Weber. Yet the idea that bureaucracy poses previously unforeseen problems is no less important today, while the threats that Weber identified when state bureaucracies and business corporations first appeared are perhaps more urgent now.

Therefore, considered as criticisms of Weber these points are somewhat irrelevant. The problems of bureaucratic inefficiency and the erosion of democratic freedoms were not radical new ideas, even in Weber's time, so he did not develop his 'ideal' model of bureaucracy in a state of ignorance or naivity. As Mouzelis (1975, p.43) has pointed out, the ideal type concept was not meant to describe a 'typical' or even an 'ideal' form of bureaucracy; it was a logical extension of the underlying principle of rationality. Nonetheless, although it has followed from a rather narrow interpretation of Weber, the detailed study of the 'dysfunctional' side of organizational life has added much to our understanding of how real bureaucracies and other large organizations work, and we can discuss this in more detail now.

The dynamics of bureaucracy

If we are to do justice to the full complexity of social action within organizations, it is necessary to see that much more is involved than just conformity to external rules. Formal authority is not merely accepted in some straightforward way by subordinates; those under authority do not necessarily obey automatically. Subordinates may resent the imposition of control and resist in whatever ways are available to them. Also, people in authority usually devote considerable efforts to persuasion aimed at shoring up the image of themselves as legitimate office-holders (much the same as the tactics of 'impression management' that are used by group members, as discussed in Chapter 5). Authority is thus a *dynamic* relationship, and legitimacy can come under threat at any time or ultimately be withdrawn by organization members. In other words, the conflict between bureaucratic control and individual resistance is a major source of instability, and the distinction has to be drawn between official expectations and real activities.

The discrepancy between formal rules and actual behaviour reflects one of the most persistent themes of sociology, that of the individual 'making out' in an established, sometimes coercive social structure, and the tactics developed to cope with externally imposed controls. In his classic study, *Work and Authority in Industry*, Bendix saw in the growth of bureaucratic work structures the increasing estrangement of employees from their work. When they seek to modify external control, in one way or another they overreach the strict limits of their office, and this resistance further prompts the penetration of formal authority.

> The strict separation between office and incumbent, between the position and the employee, is an ideal condition which is rarely achieved, in practice, especially with regard to salaried employees and skilled workers. Incumbents endow their work performance with personal qualities that range from dispensable idiosyncrasies to untransferable and often indispensable skills, so that some measure of identification of the employee with his position is unavoidable. . . . Managers endeavour to minimise or eliminate this 'silent bargaining' (and thereby to maximise the predictable performance of employees) by the strategic use of penalties, incentives and ideological appeals. (1956, pp.246–7)

271

These distinctions have often been referred to in terms of the difference between *formal* and *informal* organization. Informal structure is not so readily identifiable as the formal, since it is not officially recognized, yet it is no less important for behaviour. Informal structure includes all of the subtle customs and attitudes, the expectations and unwritten rules that stamp an organization with a specific character. These may involve general patterns of activity – the degree of formality of behaviour, the deference to those in authority that is expected, and the autonomy that people are normally allowed in their work. They also include the 'real' distribution of power, i.e. the possibility of particular departments or managers being highly influential while officially they have no more authority than others at their level. What is referred to as 'learning the ropes' by people newly recruited to an organization usually means gaining a working knowledge of this informal structure.

The ways in which informal actions serve to undermine rational authority have long been a favourite topic of sociological research (resistance to the formal constraints of Taylorist methods of work study on the part of work groups is one of the best known examples, as we saw in Chapter 10). However, the interplay between formal and informal spheres is in fact highly complex. In many cases, informal action serves to *support* formal rules – indeed it is often suggested that organizations would cease to operate without this kind of informal cooperation. Employees very often will take responsibility on themselves to see that tasks are completed, rather than merely following procedures, and this may involve short-cutting the formal rules. Furthermore, in even more subtle ways, formal institutions can exploit employees' willingness to take informal action for the benefit of management objectives. These include the formal acceptance, whether grudging or not, of informal practices which have become desirable or indispensable.

Thus patterns of action in organizations are influenced by many different and sometimes conflicting social rules. Informal codes of practice can bind behaviour just as tightly as formal rules, while the occupational values of groups like craftsmen and professionals, as well as trade unions, are no less important. In short, official rules and the formal structure compete with the informal rules of groups enjoying varying degrees of recognition from the organization's hierarchy.

In one way or another the classical empirical studies in the neo-Weberian tradition, such as Blau's *Dynamics of Bureaucracy* (1955), Gouldner's *Patterns of Industrial Bureaucracy* (1954) and Crozier's *The Bureaucratic Phenomenon* (1964), have all emphasized this tension between formal rules and social action. Impersonal rules and social responses are both equally important parts of the total organization.

Thus Gouldner distinguished between the varying content of rules, types of enforcement, and the motives which sustained acceptance, as well as the conditions under which the legitimacy of social order might be suspended. Bureaucratic patterns in which conformity had to be strongly enforced were distinguished from the genuine acceptance of authority because interests were widely represented, and these in turn were distinguished from conformity with the form rather than the essence of rules: 'punishment-centred', 'representative' and 'mock' bureaucracies. Similarly, in his study of government recruitment agencies, Blau stressed that competition between employees acted as an important mechanism of control. He too focused on the interplay between formal and informal, seeing in the 'daily operations and interpersonal relationships' the main dynamic of organizational change, namely the continual modification of formal procedures by social practice. Finally, in the rigidly bureaucratic factory that Crozier studied, major problems in an otherwise routine production task were created by machine breakdowns; and this gave the maintenance workers who dealt with breakdowns a degree of informal influence, which was reflected in their superior pay and general treatment by management. In this sense, Crozier indicated how an organizational authority structure could in effect become distorted as a result of special powers possessed by particular groups.

While such studies have stressed the *interplay* between formal rules and social action, in the end this is really a matter for interpretation. Others, who are more radically or perhaps pessimistically inclined, have seen things differently. Instead of viewing formal and informal spheres as competing rationalities, they have stressed the extent of formal control. Individuals who come under these controls will invariably put up resistance, but 'making out' in an oppressive bureaucratic environment frequently has a defensive character.

An example of the near-complete negation of individual freedom is offered in Goffman's famous study of mental institutions, *Asylums* (1968). Goffman emphasized that rules, ostensibly for the benefit of inmates, were in fact used coercively in order to make 'care' a relatively easy task for the hospital staff. He showed, for example, how treatment (particularly the issuing of drugs) could be used as punishment rather than cure, and how doctors often withheld treatment until patients had accepted the psychiatric diagnosis of their condition. Furthermore, patients' apparently bizarre behaviour could often be interpreted as attempts to gain a few basic rights (such as a degree of privacy) denied them in the artificial conditions of the asylum. The psychiatric profession usually regarded this as further evidence of the patient's illness. In other words, on the basis of his findings Goffman was arguing that the true purpose of bureaucratic rules lies in the way the majority of organizational members can be controlled for the benefit of the minority in power.

In mental institutions the power of staff over inmates was greatly amplified because these were what Goffman referred to as 'total institutions', where inmates live entirely within the system (another common example of which would be prisons). Total institutions served as an extreme case of the control that powerful groups exercise over others in organizations. Nevertheless, the issue of control more generally lies at the heart of the hierarchical structuring of work.

CONTROL IN ORGANIZATIONS

The notion of control that prevails in much of the literature on organizations reflects essentially managerial interests. This approach (which we will take up in the next chapter) focuses on the kinds of structure which best allow managers to regulate their subordinates' activities, with improved performance as the end in view. However, a much broader notion of organizational control has recently emerged and now constitutes a major new perspective. Here the whole structure of organizations is viewed as a mechanism for controlling employees' behaviour – and indeed their beliefs and motivations as well. With the emphasis squarely on the constraint and manipulation of members' activity, this represents a radical view of organizations and one which challenges more conventional views of the organization as a system for the attainment of corporate goals. (For accounts of this perspective, see Salaman, 1979, 1981; Clegg and Dunkerley, 1980, Chapter 13; Burrell and Morgan, 1979, Chapter 11; and Storey, 1983, Chapter 7.)

The origins of this more radical approach can partly be found in Marx's critique of capitalism. Focusing on the conflict between labour and capital, Marx viewed administrative control as an active force in the exploitation of labour. As we saw in Chapter 9, the Marxist view of the labour process is that the natural control of work of the craftsman is taken over by capitalist control, and replaced by an elaborate system of supervision. Thus the cooperation of workers in large enterprises is in no way spontaneous or willing, but rather an enforced integration of effort (Marx, 1974, pp.313–14).

Marxist writers have held to the idea of organizations as a control *over* productive labour. Baldamus, for example, has defined this as follows:

> . . . the organisation of industry, with all its complexities and diversities, ultimately revolves on a single process: the administrative process through which the employees' effort is controlled by the employer. This means that the entire system of industrial production will be viewed as a system of administrative controls which regulate quantity, quality and distribution of human effort. (1961, p.1)

Thus the hierarchy of supervision and management, production planning, work-pacing technology, indeed the whole edifice of organizational authority, is seen as representing an artificial structure which alienates the control of work from workers themselves.

Normative control and management

However, the concept of organizational control applied *within* the administrative structure has a further important feature. We usually think of managers and other administrative employees as being *in* control rather than *under* control. Yet organizations are highly complex structures, with extended hierarchies of rewards, status and power, as well as differences of occupation and function. With this go varying degrees of *commitment*. Very senior corporate managers receive such rewards of money, prestige and other benefits that protect them from insecurity that they normally identify very closely with organizational goals. However, in the middle and lower ranks commitment is more in doubt. For employees who make up the bulk of administration – the junior managers, supervisors, technical specialists – the rewards fall far short of those going to top management, albeit that a wide differential still separates them from the shopfloor. Employees in these positions, therefore, constitute part of the organization's problem of control.

Of course, some of the constraints on workers apply within the administrative structure as well. Managers and professionals may be dismissed if they fail to meet performance standards, and their jobs are subject to many other regulations. But while there is a degree of overlap, the constraints that apply to managers differ in important respects from those on workers. Because workers' effort tends to be controlled by direct and coercive means (like intensive supervision, systems of fines, and incentives for output), there is relatively little concern with engaging their loyalty. By contrast, the control exerted over managers is concerned far more centrally with their loyalty and commitment. In their case, rewards are not merely an exchange for effort, as they are with workers, but involve a crucial moral element, so that conformity arises from managers' own internal motivation. The essential *normative* element in organizational control is reflected here, namely the attempt to secure the self-involvement of managerial groups.

This brings us back to the Weberian account of bureaucracy. Weber, as we saw, stressed that control in bureaucratic organizations, although to some extent enforced, is also in a crucial sense accepted. People cooperate in systems of formal authority essentially because of the conviction that a particular form of rationality is operating. This in turn rests on the belief that organizations are governed by formal *rules*. The proper discharge of the duties of office, advancement based on merit, objective notions of competence, and so on, all constitute the basis of organizational legitimacy.

The idea of bureaucratic control as 'self-control' has informed much of the recent sociology of organizations. For example, Fox (1971, 1974) has described the organizational hierarchy in terms of two variables: the *discretion* that attaches to managerial jobs in the senior levels, which in turn reflects the fact that managers enjoy varying degrees of *trust*, and are held accountable only over the longer term. One of the pioneers of the radical approach to organizational control, Graeme Salaman, has put it this way:

> . . . forms of control vary in their effects. Some are highly alienative; others actually encourage normative commitment. The reason for variation in the sorts of organisational control employed for various groups is not only that the sort of work is more or less amenable to this or that form of control. It is also because it would generally be regarded as inapplicable and dangerous to expose senior organisational members in the crucial, decision-making jobs to alienative forms of control, because of the importance of their normative involvement. (1979, p.129)

Definite features of administrative structures serve to engage managers' commitment. At a fundamental level, because organizations are social systems, a distinctive *culture* develops within them, and like all cultures enforces a degree of conformity. The values and beliefs which make up organizational culture take the form of rules of behaviour, which define informal under-standings about how members are expected to act. Secondly, the *division of labour* within management also helps to sustain the central authority. This differs crucially from the division of labour on the shopfloor. As Child (1984, pp.26–7) has pointed out, workers' jobs tend to be fragmented by Taylorist work practices, giving routine and deskilled operations. But in managerial, technical and professional work, the division of labour is manifest in terms of the *specialization* of tasks. And whereas fragmentation is aimed at removing any discretion or freedom in workers' jobs, with specialization a good deal of discretion is retained. Thus managerial work becomes 'narrow in scope but founded on considerable depth of knowledge'.

As a result, while the division of labour tends to isolate workers, within management the effect is to create departments and units which are inter-dependent. Within these networks of relationships managers put pressure on one another for greater effort since they depend upon one another in their jobs. However, the important difference is that here organizational control appears to originate within the management group and does not seem so coercive – although of course it ultimately derives from external controls, like budgets and output targets. Thus it is common to hear managers complain about such pressure but not to resent it, because 'other people have their jobs to do'.

Professionals in organizations

With growing technological sophistication and the rise of many science-based industries, people with professional training and skills now form an increas-ingly important part of organizational workforces. Groups like engineers, technicians and accountants have become much more numerous and central in industrial and commercial organizations. Although such experts can be included simply as part of management, their role in organizations is in certain ways quite distinctive.

As we saw in Chapter 11, sociologists have come to regard the professions as a kind of occupational control strategy – a means by which groups seek to upgrade the rewards they obtain from employment by gaining recognition as professions and claiming professional status. Occupational groups organize themselves into professions, it is argued, essentially as a way of gaining control over their own market situation and working conditions (Johnson, 1972; Child and Fulk, 1982). What this means, however, is the *organizational* structures of control may be incompatible with the *occupational* controls upon which the profession bases itself. Thus within organizations the priorities of cost-cutting and tidy administration might be at odds with a professional orientation to 'best practice' in the performance of work. These problems are often made much worse because experts and specialists often have relatively little influence within management, despite the importance of their skills. In short, the organizational work setting may deny professionals the autonomy they expect and may be experienced as constraining.

Gouldner's (1957) noted distinction between 'cosmopolitans' and 'locals', for example, contrasted professional attachment to wider occupational ideals with the narrower commitment to an organizational career. Similarly, in Burns and Stalker's (1961) classic study of the Scottish electronics industry, the occupational identity of industrial scientists was seen to conflict with many features of their employment context. The scientists became isolated within firms, and found difficulty in fitting into the status conventions. In particular, their identification with technological change perpetually caused them to clash with management oriented to more stable operations.

However, it is important not to overgeneralize the conflict between professional loyalties and organizational employment. It is by no means always true that professionals experience organizations as hostile environments. Indeed, one line of argument has suggested the exact opposite, that professional training and work orientation actually resolve many problems of organizational control. As Salaman (1979, p.139) has argued, organizations are willing to confer superior rewards and privileges upon employed professionals in return for their 'responsible' approach to work, while for professionals applying their technical expertise to the problems the organization sets them means that any conflicts are reduced to minor matters.

The wide variety of organizational settings that professionals work in has been seen as the key to explaining the differences between occupations that are more or less successful in gaining professional status. Johnson (1972) has referred to three types of occupational control. Firstly, in organizations where professionals predominate (e.g. private practice, universities, research establishments) they usually achieve high levels of status. This 'collegiate' type of occupational control is typical of the senior professions. Secondly, occupations defined by 'corporate patronage' are found within large private corporations, where the employer defines the service he needs, and so shapes the development of the profession over time. Such professions (like accounting, engineering and computing) still enjoy considerable status, although they tend to be 'tied' to a particular employer. Thirdly, 'state mediation' refers to the creation by government bureaucracy of occupations that are only marginally professional. The ethics of such groups (e.g. teachers and social workers) reflect the rules of the employing agency rather than true occupational values, while control of the service provided resides with the state – all of which detract from professionalism.

It seems clear, however, that the nature of the organizational employer does not account for all of the variation in professional status. What does seem to be universally true is that *bureaucratic* work settings impede professional autonomy. Rigid division of labour, insistence on formal authority and a preoccupation with the detail of administration conflict sharply with a professional work ethic (Scott, 1966; Hall, 1968). But it is not obvious that such bureaucratic work settings are found only in the state sector, as Johnson seemed to suggest. Many large private corporations are run along strictly bureaucratic lines, whilst in the public sector there are organizations – hospitals within the National Health Service and universities are two examples that spring to mind – which operate very favourably for the professionals within them.

Within different sectors (private practice, private corporate, public) there may be as much variety in the status enjoyed by professionals as exists between sectors. Particularly in the private corporate sector, where many modern professions and technical occupations are found, studies have revealed that the levels of occupational control that professions enjoy can vary across a wide range. For example Kraft (1979) has argued that the occupation of computer programmer has become 'industrialized'. In the early years of commercial computing, when programming was an uncertain business, computer staff enjoyed high status. But increasingly the work has become rationalized and higher-level tasks hived off to systems analysts. In contrast to this, Watson (1977) gives an account of personnel officers as a profession of improving status. The tasks of labour management that they perform (often taken over at the expense of first-line supervisors) are crucial for profitability, and have brought to the personnel function levels of rewards comparable with other corporate professions, like accounting and engineering.

A different approach is taken by Armstrong (1985). Rather than try to predict the success of professions from the functions that they perform in organizations, he stresses *inter-professional competition* as being decisive for the relative standing of occupations. Accounting in particular, he points out, has been remarkably successful in achieving access to senior levels within organizations; and the profession has seen the 'language' of finance adopted as the chief strategy of organizational control in very many firms. Yet other professions that might have been equally successful, most notably engineering, have failed to gain anything like the prominence of accountants in top management. Only dynamic factors can explain these differences: the historic success of particular occupations in mounting collective campaigns to upgrade their status.

Organizational selection

The above forms of control are to an extent simply part of human interaction in organizations, or in the case of experts are reliant on occupational factors. But there is another means of control, namely organizational selection, which represents a strategy much more consciously and explicitly applied. Selection is the process whereby people are initially recruited into an organization, and then continue (as long as their promotion continues) to progress to the inner circles of organizational power. Although there are important technical functions served in chosing people who are competent to perform particular jobs, selection also has a crucial *political* function. The whole of the power structure of organizations rests to a very large extent on the hierarchy as a 'selective mechanism'. For it is vital in ensuring control over personnel that appropriate people are chosen to enter positions of authority. 'Appropriate' here refers to people who will not merely conform, but will actively pursue the goals of the organization, however defined. Thus considerable resources are normally devoted to the allocation of posts; and the procedures of selective recruitment and promotion become increasingly elaborate and formalized the further up the hierarchy one goes, comprising interviews and tests as well as criteria such as track record and past experience.

We might also add that selection automatically implies *rejection*. Thus selection is often portrayed as a 'gatekeeping' function, stressing that unsuccessful candidates are kept out, as well as the successful ones being let in. In this context, Blau and Schoenherr (1971) have emphasized that senior management usually have little need to resort to direct, coercive control because they are able to rely on gatekeeping. Selection ensures that potentially critical groups, which may challenge the settled practice, are simply not allowed entry; they remain as outsiders – or they do at least to the extent that selection is effective.

Given the secrecy and confidentiality which surrounds organizational selection, research on the subject is, not surprisingly, rather thin on the ground. However, Salaman and Thompson (1974) have contributed important empirical findings describing the interview procedures used in selecting candidates for officer training in the British army and for selecting management trainees in the Ford Motor Company (see also Salaman, 1979, pp.187–95). In the army case study, for example, a precisely defined military culture was used as the yardstick for selection. Although the language army selectors used to describe the characteristics they were looking for was apparently rather vague, the selectors themselves knew exactly what they meant. For instance, the capacity in a candidate to remain composed and to present a confident front, even when he had made an obviously incompetent decision, was highly rated, being defined as 'coolness' and 'natural leadership'. The usefulness of such an ability to an organization such as the army, where discipline is of the utmost importance, is readily apparent.

Organizational careers From the employee's point of view, the selection process is experienced in terms of his or her progress, or lack of progress, through the hierarchy – that is, in terms of career. Many sociologists have stressed the potency of career as a form of social control (Wilensky, 1968; Sofer, 1970; Presthus, 1979). The prospect of promotion offers huge potential rewards of material gains, prestige and power. Possibly the greatest appeal is that it resolves the contradiction between extrinsic and intrinsic rewards that appears to be the natural lot of manual workers. If manual workers want higher wages, they usually have to forego some other reward; they have to work overtime and so lose leisure, or perhaps take on dangerous work, or unpleasant work, or unsociable hours. With a career, however, increasingly interesting and responsible work is automatically matched by increasing financial rewards.

Career acts as both carrot and stick. If the rewards of promotion motivate management, so too does the fear of failure. Organizations typically are strewn with people who failed to get on, and their fate can be a cruel one in terms of the great psychological pressures that bear upon the unsuccessful. Certainly their presence acts as a constant reminder to the ambitious of the price of being passed over in the promotion race.

Promotion structures therefore engender a particularly intense kind of conformity. Becoming adept at manipulating the organization's belief systems and culture is essential for those with ambition. Learning to interact with colleagues and gaining recognition as an important participant in organizational life are the ingredients of success. The consequences of all this for social control are clear. Such a huge personal investment is involved that a career normally brings about increasing attachment to the organization and its ways of seeing and doing. As Salaman (1979, pp.140–1) put it, 'When the self is so enmeshed within the organisation, the distinction between personal priorities and organisational goals becomes relatively meaningless, and self-control becomes little different from organisational regulation.'

FURTHER READING

Burrell, G. and G. Morgan (1979) *Sociological Paradigms and Organisational Analysis*. London: Heinemann.

Clegg, S. and D. Dunkerley (1977) *Critical Issues in Organizations*. London: Routledge and Kegan Paul.

Clegg, S. and D. Dunkerley (1980) *Organization, Class and Control*. London: Routledge and Kegan Paul.

Eldridge, J.E.T. and A.D. Crombie (1974) *A Sociology of Organisations*. London: Allen and Unwin.

Etzioni, A. (1961) *A Comparative Analysis of Complex Organizations*. New York: Free Press.

McKinlay, J.B. (ed.) (1975) *Processing People: Cases in Organizational Behaviour*. London: Holt, Rinehart and Winston.

Morgan, G. (1986) *Images of Organization*. London: Sage.

Mouzelis, N. (1975) *Organization and Bureaucracy*. London: Routledge and Kegan Paul.

Reed, M. (1986) *Redirections in Organisational Analysis*. London: Tavistock.

Salaman, G. (1979) *Work Organisations: Resistance and Control*. London: Longman.

Salaman, G. (1981) *Class and the Corporation*. London: Fontana.

Salaman, G. and K. Thompson (eds.) (1980) *Control and Ideology in Organizations*. Milton Keynes: Open University Press.

15

Structure and Performance in Organizations

INTRODUCTION

Although there are different perspectives on organizations, and a proliferation of research and writing on the subject, it is possible to single out two predominant schools of thought. One is concerned with the sociology of organizations, and focuses on what Mouzelis has called 'the organizational problems of society's power structure' (1975, p.79). This corresponds broadly with the approach of the previous chapter, and owes much to the Weberian analysis of bureaucracy. The second is a managerial tradition deriving from F.W. Taylor's theory of scientific management and his studies of work administration. The concerns here are with the internal efficiency of organizations: the design of structure and the motivation of groups and individuals to perform in line with stated goals. To a large extent these two approaches have been mutually exclusive, not to say antagonistic. Writers interested in the 'problem' of organization tend not to regard organizational efficiency as an issue of first importance, and writers preoccupied with efficiency usually disregard awkward questions about the social and political impact of organizations. (Though there are notable exceptions in those who have tackled the problem of integrating the two approaches, e.g. Mouzelis, 1975; Perrow, 1980; and Albrow, 1980.)

However, we will now turn our attention to the managerial approach. Although in some ways it seems hardly necessary to have to justify this, the concerns of management merit our interest for a number of reasons. Modern large-scale organizations produce the goods and services of our material life, and the problems of providing these benefits efficiently affect all of society. Furthermore, since management has the power to direct activities in organizations, a knowledge of managerial priorities and objectives is necessary for a wider understanding of organizational behaviour. Organizations have many different objectives and engage in a variety of activities, so there is a problem in defining an initial perspective on organization theory and what we expect the theory to cover.

Organizations as systems A similarity with living organisms suggests itself, and while there are dangers in taking this analogy too far, it has proved a useful model and one which keeps cropping up in organizational analysis. The parts of an organization – departments, divisions – must integrate their efforts, just as the parts of any living organism are inter-dependent. Moreover, organizations may be viewed as existing in a competitive environment, as do plants and animals, and they have to adapt to environmental conditions or perhaps find their existence threatened.

Organizations have system boundaries in the sense that they may occupy a definite geographical area, although this isn't always the case. Government departments and multinational companies, for example, are dispersed over wide areas. Nonetheless, great care is taken in organizations to ensure that the membership is identified and kept under review. The writers who have developed the systems approach, however, have been at pains to emphasize that organizations should not be viewed merely as closed systems; to do this is to adopt a very static picture of how they operate (Elliott, 1980). Organizations have suppliers and clients; and there are wider social and economic forces that affect them, such as the labour market, the community, government legislation, and of course other organizations. Thus, organizations are open systems, and transactions across the organizational boundary take place continuously, so much so that it can be difficult in practice to define exactly where an organization stops and its environment begins.

Structure and performance It follows from the systems approach that organizations have a structure – an established set of relationships, with the emphasis on ordered and regularly occurring activities. Because tasks in organizations are almost always inter-dependent, it is essential that personnel act in a calculable and predictable manner. Hence performance and structure are inextricably linked. And, of course, the desire to improve performance is the underlying reason for studying the management process in organizations. This aim does not refer to the effectiveness of actual decisions taken in given circumstances (which is the central problem of business policy), but rather to the attempt to identify those structures of behaviour which contribute to the achievement of organizational goals.

Reference here is mainly to the *formal* structure of organizations – that is, the official hierarchy of positions, the division of labour and specified operating procedures. This is not to ignore the informal side of organizational activity. We focused on this in the previous chapter, and indeed as we shall see organizational analysis has increasingly taken serious notice of factors which lie outside the structure of formal authority. However, as Child (1984) has pointed out, only the formal structure is subject to control and planning by management, thus it remains the fundamental concern of organization theory. In practical terms, the design of an effective structure must reflect the objectives of the particular organization and the context in which it operates. Good management also means anticipating the changed circumstances which make structural development and adaptation necessary.

Goals and the problem of reification The formal nature of organization structure reflects the fact of goals having been identified and the criteria of achievement specified. Indeed, organizations are set up and designed explicitly as means of achieving certain goals. While some goals refer to broad aims, such as efficiency or the pursuit of profit, these afford little insight into the operations of a specific enterprise, and so more detailed goals are normally of interest.

For example, the management of a retail chain specializing in inexpensive furniture might well decide that the goal of quality is not its first priority. They may be content to put up with a certain proportion of customer complaints for a given volume of business. On the other hand, a high-class interior designer would be far more likely to regard quality as a goal that could not be compromised, and might regard a single dissatisfied customer as a threat to future business. Thus, while both firms have the same overall goal of selling furniture for profit, the more detailed breakdown of goals tells us much more about the different ways in which the two businesses will be run.

An important problem relating to the use of goal analysis is that of *reification*. This refers to the tendency of attributing human motives to social institutions, in this case of thinking about organizations as if *they* were pursuing the goals in question. Of course, only the personnel of organizations can pursue goals. Still, it is all too easy to refer to organizations as the active party – to speak of organizations controlling their personnel, adapting to their environments, and so on. The danger in viewing the organization as a purposeful entity is that one ends up with a highly abstract and artificial analysis. The people making decisions and the motives behind their actions tend to be overlooked. There is also the danger of unwittingly shielding the actions and motives of senior management from criticism by implying that it was 'the organization' that was responsible for particular decisions. Thus when analysing organizational goals, one must be clear that one is referring to the objectives officially sanctioned in the organization, and not to the goals that organizations pursue.

ORGANIZATIONAL ANALYSIS

Having discussed these introductory points, we can proceed to examine some of the ways in which the structure of organizations contributes to the achievement of the goals set by management.

There are several distinct but related aspects of organization structure. At its most basic level, formal structure refers to the physical shape of the organization – the distribution of jobs and lines of command – often set out in an organization chart, if the firm in question has one. At a more analytic level we can distinguish two main components of the management structure:

(1) the division of task or function – the division between groups, departments, specialisms and organizational divisions;
(2) the division of power and authority – the division between superordinate and subordinate which forms the organizational hierarchy.

This gives the familiar picture of organizations as pyramidal structures of laterally connected departments and hierarchical levels. Thus, for example, Salaman (1979, p.61) has defined structure as 'the way in which work is organised and control exercised', a definition in which we can see the twofold emphasis on relationships of communication and authority.

As well as these basic relationships, formal structure is identified with the major areas of managerial responsibility. John Child (1984, Chapter 1) has set out in some detail the requirements for the formulation and successful implementation of managerial plans. They include an established procedure for decision-making, with arrangements for the collection of information, the notification of decisions to groups and individuals, and a schedule for meetings. Another important managerial task is the control and coordination of activities. Here, operational procedures have to be set down in advance in order to specify areas of accountability and standards of performance; there must be a monitoring system to feed back information on performance to the right authority centres, and arrangements to correct operational activity in the light of any shortcomings. Thus the success and viability of an enterprise depend upon creating the most effective structure of administration, given the circumstances in which the organization is operating – one which distributes the necessary tasks, delegates required authority and controls the outcomes of actions.

The classical school

The established theory generally regarded as the starting point of organizational analysis is, as we have said, Taylor's scientific management. This was an approach which gave a decidedly formalistic slant to early theory. Taylor had developed a 'science' of the control of manual work that employers had applied to great advantage; and the first writers on organizations, the so-called classical school, set themselves the task of developing along similar lines a formal theory of administration. Many of them were or had been managers themselves, and they emphasized such practical aspects of administration as the importance of strict specialization in management, and the exercise of strong leadership with clear lines of authority. Henri Fayol, a French engineer, is regarded as the founder of the classical school, and other prominent writers included Gulick and Urwick, Mary Parker Follet, and Mooney and Reiley. (For discussion of the classical school, see March and Simon, 1958, Chapter 2; Pugh *et al.*, 1971; Mouzelis, 1975, Chapter 4; and Clegg and Dunkerley, 1980, pp.99–106.)

By modern standards their work was probably not very impressive. Their emphasis on the correct 'principles of management' had a slightly archaic flavour, like the search for some magic formula. Concepts were not clearly specified, nor were their claims based on any empirical research. Perhaps their major shortcoming was a failure to take human factors into account (in this they were the true heirs of Taylor) so that an appropriately designed structure was supposed to eliminate all further problems of control and integration. This is something that certainly cannot be assumed, indeed the central concern of modern organization theory has been precisely those behavioural factors ignored by the classical writers. Nonetheless, the classical school did tackle some of the basic problems of organization design. It cleared a space for organization analysis to develop, and their concerns with formal structure and the functions of management remain valid today.

The contingency approach

After the initial impact of the classical school, interest in organizations shifted to psychological and group aspects (dealt with under the human relations school in Chapter 6) and very little concern with structure was shown until as late as the 1950s. Then a new line of thought emerged which took a fresh look at structure and at the original focus on the principles of efficient administration. This was the so-called contingency theory. As with many important insights, the idea behind the theory was quite simple, namely that organization structure should be regarded as a contingent variable. In other words, the search of the classical theorists for universal principles of administration was held to be misguided; managers face circumstances which vary and change, and they must choose whatever structural arrangements are most appropriate in the prevailing context. The proper role of organization theory, therefore, is not to seek any 'one best way' to manage, but to provide insight and guidance for managers to help them formulate responses in the complex situations of organizational decision-making.

The general model implicit in contingency theory assumes that, for an organization to be effective, there must be an appropriate 'fit' between structure and context. Such a model can be set out as follows.

$$\text{CONTEXTUAL} \atop \text{FACTORS} \longrightarrow \text{ORGANIZATION} \atop \text{STRUCTURE} \longrightarrow \text{PERFORMANCE}$$

Thus structure is essentially seen as an *intervening variable*, which modifies the effect of contingent factors upon performance, given the context in which the organization operates. Structure is also essentially *adaptive* since it may need to be changed if the context is dynamic and makes demands that alter over time. (For discussion of contingency theory, see Burrell and Morgan, 1979, pp.164–81; and Child, 1984, pp.217–25.)

Contextual factors embrace all of the given elements which serve to constrain managerial decision-making, so the context may vary over time and from firm to firm in an almost endless variety of ways. However, it has proved possible to isolate some of the most important contextual variables. These include chiefly the type of *technology* an organization uses and the kind of *environment* in which it operates.

Technology As well as the hardware used in production, the term technology is used to refer to production methods and work organization. Thus technology has become a sort of shorthand term for the general task structure of an organization. A mass-production technology, for example, involves large numbers of semi-skilled operatives, and hence the task of labour management and supervision becomes critical. Conversely, science-based technologies generate tasks involving professional and technical skills, and employees with these sorts of ability tend to be self-regulating in their work. Craft technologies are similar in this respect. Thus different production technologies give rise to different systems of tasks, which in turn affect structure.

The best-known research on the technology–structure relationship is Joan Woodward's (1965) study of manufacturing firms in south-east Essex. Woodward obtained measures (some of them admittedly rather simple and crude) of three organizational variables: firstly, the commercial success of firms; secondly, their production technology (which she classified in three types: technologies that produce single units or small batches, mass-production, and process-production technologies); and thirdly, certain dimensions of structure (e.g. the number of levels in the hierarchy, the labour intensity, and the first line spans of control). These, we can see, cover the three variables in the contingency model above.

Woodward arrived at two major findings. (1) There was a link between structure and technology in that firms in the same technical category (say, all of the unit production firms) tended to have similar organization structures. (2) She then discovered that all three variables – technology, structure and performance – were related. She found that successful firms in each technical category had structural characteristics near the average for the category as a whole, while the firms with below average success fell in the extremes of the range of structural variables.

This seemed to imply that a given technology 'demands' a particular structure, and firms that obey this 'technological imperative' reap the rewards in terms of organizational efficiency and business success. Moreover, the relationship was clearly a contingent rather than an unvarying one. Thus, for example, in successful mass-production firms tasks tended to be clearly defined and the structure bureaucratic. By contrast, in continuous-process firms the technology was often advanced and science-based; firms employed a high proportion of professional and technical staff who required more flexible working arrangements, hence a bureaucratic structure was too rigid and tended to be associated with commercial failure.

Environment The environment with which an organization engages (like its technology) is chiefly defined by the decision to enter a particular product market. But once that initial choice has been made the environmental pressures it creates – pressures from competitors, from technical change, etc. – become part of the given context of decision-making. The general effect of environment on an organization is determined by the level of *uncertainty* it generates, i.e. whether the

287

environment is stable or the source of rapid and unpredictable change. The more uncertain and complex an organization's environment, the more internally differentiated that organization will tend to become because it will need to develop new functions to cope with environmental problems.

As an example of this link between environment and structure, we can consider the uncertainty created by raw material inputs to an organization. If inputs could always be precisely relied upon, the organization would need no separate purchasing and stock control functions. But this is rarely the case. In practice, organizations have to secure their supplies, monitor quality and suitability, and create buffer stocks to enable flows to be regulated. In this way a need is created for specialized functions to manage the interface with the environment.

Burns and Stalker's study *The Management of Innovation* (1961) was an early and very influential piece of research which focused on the organization–environment relationship. These researchers studied the Scottish electronics industry, which underwent rapid expansion in the post-war period under the impact of advances like television and the transistor. With rapid technical change and fierce competition, the firms upon which Burns and Stalker based their research existed in an extremely turbulent, uncertain environment. The researchers sought an explanation of survival and success in such an environment, and they found it in a particular kind of organization structure.

They distinguished two structural types, which they termed 'mechanistic' and 'organic' (1961, pp.119–25). The mechanistic structure was highly bureaucratic, with a strict division of authority and preoccupation with matters of internal efficiency. By contrast, organic structures were flexible and informal, with a good deal of sharing of responsibility, and lower-ranked staff had considerable influence delegated to them. Of crucial importance was the fact that the organic structure retained a strong sense of direction and commitment which embraced all the personnel.

> The distinctive feature of the organic system is the pervasiveness of the working organization as an institution. In concrete terms, this makes itself felt in a preparedness to combine with others in serving the general aims of the concern. . . . The individual's job ceases to be self-contained; the only way in which 'his' job can be done is by his participating continually with others in the solution of problems which are real to the firm. (p.125)

The organic structure was thus able to adapt to uncertain environments. Indeed, the research showed that firms that survived and prospered in the electronics industry at that time were the ones with organic structures. The firms which floundered (as many did) tended to be the ones with mechanistic structures, their problems arising from their inability to respond to new and unforeseen circumstances.

Once again, however, this was a contingent relationship. Burns and Stalker wished to avoid any suggestion that organic structures are always superior – indeed they can be very expensive in terms of the managerial time taken up in integrating activities. In an environment where there is little need for adaptability the mechanistic structure comes into its own.

Criticisms of contingency theory and managerial choice

More recently, organizational analysis has moved away from the consensus of opinion which made contingency theory the main school of thought in the 1960s and early 1970s, and we should now consider some of the criticisms that have been levelled at it.

Firstly, contingency theory suggested an unrealistic and oversimplified model of managerial activity. For although the theory stressed that there is no *one* best way to manage, it did assume that there was *a* best way given a limited number of contextual conditions. The reality, critics have pointed out, is far more complex than this. Managers are required to formulate policy and strategy in far more varied circumstances than ever contingency theory acknowledged, and in fact there is little convincing evidence that structural designs can be made to 'fit' the context of operations. Secondly, the simple *causal* link between structure and performance has also been challenged. Contingency theory proposed that an appropriate structure gives rise to high performance, but all the empirical research showed (or indeed ever could show) was a *correlation* between structure and performance. The direction of causation was assumed. Critics have therefore suggested that in some cases causality may run the other way. In other words, a more realistic and dynamic argument may be that it is the initial performance of organizations which determines the kinds of structure they are able to adopt (Child, 1984, pp.225–30).

A good illustration of this was provided by a company in which one of the authors of this book conducted some research. This was a highly successful manufacturer of surgical equipment, which had adopted a fully integrated management structure. Whilst it was possible that the structure had led to their success, it seemed equally likely that the reverse had happened, that once the company had achieved a dominant market position it then had the resources to develop its matrix structure. This involved a considerable managerial overhead (there was a network of inter-departmental teams permanently established to deal with many specific projects and problems of long-range planning), and it seemed rather unlikely that any company that had been performing badly would have been able to sustain this level of expenditure as a precondition of success.

A third criticism is that contingency theory plays down the importance of *power*, both the power of strategically placed managers and the power of the organization itself. In this context, Child (1972) has referred to the 'strategic choice' exercised by managers as the 'critical variable in organization theory'. Corporate groups with effective power in organizations have a great deal of discretion; their decisions are not predetermined by context and structure, nor are they without the power to enforce choices which suit their purposes irrespective of constraints placed upon them. Wood (1979) has similarly argued that management policy and the development of the organization's human resources are critical factors, and that firms have the capacity to organize themselves from within, rather than being forced to adapt to technical and market contexts. It would be naive not to recognize that organizations often exercise considerable control over their environments. Large-scale organizations dispose of enormous advertising revenues to stimulate markets, they can exert influence via political lobbying, and much modern technology comes under their control. Indeed, organizations with monopolistic powers over markets and potential competitors are readily able to sustain a poor level of performance, or an inappropriate structure, if they wish to do so for whatever reasons.

However, while the force of these criticisms has to be accepted, certain points in defence of contingency theory can be put forward. The model linking context, structure and performance perhaps inevitably involved simplification, but researchers like Woodward and Burns were well aware of this, and in their detailed accounts made a good deal of perceptive comment on the complexity of these relationships. For example, Woodward has frequently been criticized for an order of 'technological determinism' in her work, for suggesting that technology determines organization structure and that human choice plays no significant role. Such criticism is to an extent valid, since she did argue that technology seemed to have an effect on structure and performance of which managers were unaware. However, Woodward also stressed that technology acts only as a *constraint* on behaviour, and that within certain limits conscious choices are exercised.

Thus the contingency theorists' notion of decision-making as an activity partially constrained by structure, but displaying choice and variability, does not seem unreasonable. As Wood has suggested, it may be the popularizers of contingency theory who, with 'their limited reading of the work in which they purport to be rooted', are responsible for any oversimplification rather than the writers who conducted the classic studies (1979, p.353). Certainly these writers' empirical research took our understanding of organization and management a stage further, and their contributions remain extremely important.

MANAGERIAL PROBLEMS AND RESPONSES

Clearly, however, the criticisms that have been made of contingency theory have changed our notions of how managers go about their work. In reality decision-making involves multiple and often conflicting goals, and hence implies the search for workable compromises rather than permanent solutions.

For instance, the choice between rationalized versus flexible structures, which Burns and Stalker investigated, presents itself at many different levels in the organization. Thus the advantages of tight control of costs and labour in a rigidly designed system may be decisive in certain circumstances, but it may be necessary to switch to a more flexible, albeit less efficient system, which can absorb the uncertainties of production and supply, if circumstances change.

Moreover, even these choices rarely present themselves as simple alternatives. Managers may have to combine different elements of each approach, and they may need to make constant adjustments if the operational or market context changes. Therefore, rather than try to specify appropriate structural designs or the functional areas of responsibility, modern theory seeks to define the basic problems that managers face, and how in successful firms they go about resolving them. Invariably such central problems present themselves as actual dilemmas which entail the perpetual juggling of different demands.

Control and integration

Child (1984) has drawn attention to two fundamental managerial tasks, which reflect the basic structures of authority and the division of labour: these are the twin problems of *control* and *integration*.

(1) Control refers to the problem of regulating the activities of subordinates. We have spoken about the control of organizational work at length in previous chapters, but the control mechanisms typically used by management include standardized operating procedures, job specifications, the monitoring of performance, and assigning specific responsibilities. The problem involved here is part of the wider issue of choosing between bureaucratic structures and more flexible relationships. The essential point is that mechanisms for keeping tight control can be self-defeating. The experience of being closely supervised may demoralize people, it may make them surrender initiative and lose interest in their jobs. On top of problems of motivation, centralized control may cause related problems of inflexibility. Organizations remain responsive to change in part because of power being delegated to those with operational roles. Specialists keeping abreast of innovations in their field, middle managers aware of the state of markets and able to act on their knowledge – these strengths keep an organization adaptive. Too rigid a control structure tends to withdraw decision-making capacity from those close to the boundary with the environment.

Strategies of control aim·to resolve this dilemma by attempting to satisfy the conditions both of the centralization of control and its decentralization. They do this essentially by centralizing and decentralizing different kinds of power: major policy decisions are centralized, while operational responsibility is delegated. Thus, the typical structure of multinational and other large divisionalized companies will embrace a corporate headquarters with authority over things like product development, forward planning and major new investment, while the divisions and individual plants remain profit centres and hence responsible for operational efficiency.

This overall strategy is sustained by corporate management keeping a tight hold of the purse strings. The capital budget will be controlled from the corporate centre, and since important policy decisions always involve capital expenditure, this will effectively keep policy centralized. The plants and divisions are free to run their operations efficiently, but only within an established budget outside which their powers are strictly limited. Thus, within certain limits, this arrangement achieves the best of both worlds: central control over policy and organizational development, and an operational management able to take on-the-spot decisions.

(2) Turning to integration, within any large organization there are enormous problems ensuring that information reaches people in time and in sufficient detail to enable them to coordinate their activities. However, to develop a structure so that people *can* integrate their efforts is one thing, but whether they *will* integrate even with an efficient structure may be quite another matter. In other words, on top of the purely technical problems of the dissemination of information there are often behavioural difficulties of achieving integration. Moreover, separating the two aspects is really to oversimplify, for managers' willingness to cooperate has to be assumed in any formal system of communication.

A major cause of conflict in organizations, and lack of integration, involves the communications problems that arise out of the division of labour. Differences in outlook, occupational values and style of behaviour can become entrenched in organizations; and they can cause serious problems of co-operation. This diversity within management is encompassed by a general concept: *differentiation*. The term was defined in a well-known early empirical study by Lawrence and Lorsch as 'the difference in cognitive and emotional orientation among managers in different functional departments' (1967, p.11). These researchers found evidence of a general model linking differentiation and integration. They suggested that, other things being equal, there would be an inverse relationship between the two variables: the higher the differentiation, the lower the integration (or the higher the conflict), and vice versa.

Differentiation covers many aspects of behaviour. One very common source of conflict, which we discussed in the previous chapter, involves the difference between managers having a professional approach to their work and those with a bureaucratic orientation. Another important relationship, which is related to conflicting professional and bureaucratic orientations, is that between line and staff management. Line managers, within the central chain of command, and managers of staff or service departments typically experience problems with which they have to come to terms if the relationship between them is not to break down. Services which are centralized for economy and control become a scarce resource. Thus service managers find themselves under constant pressure for quicker and more comprehensive service, while line managers are often forced to compete for services in order to meet their own targets.

Lawrence and Lorsch themselves focused on major types of inter-group relations in organizations which give rise to recurring problems of integration. They looked at the relationships between production, sales, and research and development departments, and revealed typical patterns of conflict. For example, production managers favoured stable output and low product variation, as these helped them to meet production targets and stay within budget, while managers in sales desired the exact opposite. Rapid delivery and a high degree of variation helped salespeople to meet customer requirements. Similar problems arose between production and R&D: development engineers became preoccupied with the technical problems of product design and were oriented towards long-range planning; production managers, on the other hand, wanted engineers to be available to solve immediate practical problems. Differences along these and other dimensions caused managers to fail to communicate properly and to be unable to understand one another's problems.

The resolution of conflict

The distinction we have made between control and integration, although quite helpful in understanding managerial activity, can be rather artificial. In practice managers do not always simply issue orders and then leave subordinates to take care of lateral integration (although subordinates are usually more responsible for this). Managerial actions have a more *systematic* character, which include both order-giving and the necessary coordination. Nonetheless, if such systems are to be viable, the conflicts that can arise when orders are issued, or when attempts are made to integrate activities, must somehow be dealt with.

The obvious answer to the problem of excessive levels of conflict – given the above model showing that differentiation leads to conflict – would seem to lie in only having homogeneous bodies of managers. However, the solution is unfortunately not that simple. Organizations often require a wide range of specialist skills, as well as needing to allocate tasks to well-defined sub-units, both of which lead to high levels of differentiation. A contradiction therefore arises: for high performance, high levels of differentiation are required, but these lead to conflict which in turn has a deleterious effect on performance. What this means in practice is that conflict can never be wholly eliminated, and hence the resolution of conflict remains a central problem of management.

One of the most common management practices aimed at resolving conflict is the *mediation* of relationships of potentially high conflict. Here intermediate departments or channels of communcation intervene between the two groups concerned, in effect preventing them from coming into direct contact. For example, the relationships between production departments in mass assembly plants contain a major source of conflict in the problems that departments create for one another. Such departments are highly inter-dependent, since the product passes between them, and if the work of one department is not to specification it means that another department will be unable to do its work. In such cases, when problems of integration arise, production management in one department first approach some intermediate department (quality control or production engineering often fulfil this role) who then investigate the problem with production management in the department concerned. Thus potential confrontation may be avoided.

In fact there are many variants of structure and managerial practice designed to resolve the conflict that would otherwise be generated in organizations. In their research, Lawrence and Lorsch found that the most successful organizations had managed to achieve high levels of integration together with high levels of differentiation (i.e. at variance with the general rule) by means of effective mechanisms for continually resolving conflict as it arose. They report several such mechanisms, including special integrating groups, but also appropriate forms of motivation, influence and inter-personal style among integrating managers, which enabled them to understand and accommodate the points of view of other groups (1967, p.80). Similarly, Child (1984, pp.127–32) set out a number of different methods of integration. These ranged from simply making an individual manager responsible for liaison with another department, to highly elaborate matrix structures comprised of intersecting project teams. The point stressed in both these accounts is that particular organizations have levels of 'required integration' matching the context in which they operate. And the more powerful integrating mechanisms (and hence more costly in terms of managerial overheads) are appropriate only where an organization faces an extremely demanding task (highly uncertain environment, complex technical problems, competitive markets), otherwise the less sophisticated alternative methods are preferred.

FURTHER READING

Child, J. (1984) *Organization* (2nd ed.). London: Harper and Row.

Donaldson, L. (1985) *In Defence of Organization Theory*. Cambridge: Cambridge University Press.

March, J.G. and H.A. Simon (1958) *Organizations*. New York: Wiley.

O'Shaughnessy, J. (1976) *Patterns of Business Organization*. London: Allen and Unwin.

Perrow, C. (1970) *Organizational Analysis*. London: Tavistock.

Perrow, C. (1979) *Complex Organizations: A Critical Essay*. Glenview, Ill.: Scott, Foresman.

Pugh, D. (ed.) (1984) *Organization Theory* (2nd ed.). Harmondsworth: Penguin.

Rose, M. (1975) *Industrial Behaviour: Theoretical Developments since Taylor*. London: Allen Lane.

Sofer, C. (1972) *Organizations in Theory and Practice*. London: Heinemann.

16

Conflict and Power in Organizations

INTRODUCTION

> Organizations are neither the rational, harmonious entities celebrated in managerial theory, nor the arenas of apocalyptic class conflict projected by Marxists. Rather, it may be argued, a more suitable notion lies somewhere between these two – a concept of organizations as politically negotiated orders. Adopting this view, we can observe organizational actors in their daily transactions, perpetually bargaining, repeatedly forming and reforming coalitions, and constantly availing themselves of influence tactics . . . politics in organizations involve the tactical use of power to retain or obtain control of real or symbolic resources. In describing the processes of organizations as political acts, we are not making a moral judgement; we are simply making an observation about a process. (Bacharach and Lawler, 1980, pp.1–2)

From the discussion of organizations in the previous two chapters, the above picture that Bacharach and Lawler present of these two major schools of organization theory – the contrasting schools of managerial theory and Marxism – may seem rather oversimplified. For their part, as we saw in Chapter 15, managerialists were never quite so naive as the quotation suggests. Even the early theorists had a practitioner's eye for the problems of workers' resistance; and certainly more recent theory has been able to incorporate issues of behavioural conflict within management. Marxists, as we saw in Chapter 14, have lately been developing theories of conflict and control within organizational groups. But Marxist theory obviously doesn't imagine that 'apocalyptic class conflict' occurs within management.

However, the approach taken by Bacharach and Lawler is at least helpful in setting the scene, for the subject of power in organizations is one which can present problems – not so much in terms of understanding the actual arguments, but in appreciating what point there is in discussing managerial activity in these terms. Managerial work is typically thought of in terms of decisions made on the basis of training and experience. And within organizations 'politics' is often regarded with great distaste – as the main barrier to getting on with the job. Thus, an approach which seems to see organizational activity as nothing other than politics – which takes this activity from the margins and places it at the focus of attention – might seem perverse and hard to accept. It seems helpful therefore to look at power as a concept which retains the best of both the managerialist and Marxist approaches. It is useful to see power as a radical idea, but applied in the context of the managerial concern for decision-making.

The managerial approach quite deliberately restricts itself to the formally sanctioned aspects of behaviour in organizations, since its aim is the effective control of organizational tasks. While this approach does take account of some aspects of conflict and power, the extent to which it can do this will always be limited. Thus, in spite of undoubted progress and refinements in organization theory since the days of the classical writers, some of the processes underlying real organizational activity are bound to be overlooked, or at least explained inadequately.

The behavioural limits on rationality To begin with, any focus on organizations as structures for achieving goals runs the risk of becoming too prescriptive. Too great an emphasis on goal achievement, and an obsession with efficiency and effectiveness, can mean that we are not explaining how organizations really operate. Decision-making has often been thought of as a purely rational process, emerging out of the application of expertise. But in reality managers do not act jointly to resolve problems in a purely un-problematic way – decision-making is also a *human* process constrained by the limits on people's abilities.

Writers on organization and management have for some time been aware of the deficiencies of human rationality. For instance, March and Simon (1958, pp.137–71) used the term 'bounded rationality' to point out that decision-making is only rational up to a certain point. Managerial action is rarely optimal in the sense of the best solution being sought and found. In practice, a *satisfactory* solution, one that will cope with the problem in hand, is the most common outcome. The reason, quite simply, is that decision-making and problem-solving between managers involves the expenditure of a good deal of time and effort.

A good example of this is provided by budgeting behaviour. If budgets were in reality what they are supposed to be in theory, that is optimal systems of cost control, then a firm's or department's budget would be overhauled on a regular basis. In fact this rarely happens. Certain operations may be re-costed in detail, but for the remainder an incremental rather than optimal approach is taken. In other words, savings are made by reducing existing costs by some pre-determined amount, often set rather arbitrarily. In this sense, decision-making is frequently described as a *search process*. Defining alternative courses of action, and testing their relative efficiency, happens only to a limited extent because once a satisfactory solution has been found the search tends to stop.

Conflict and power As well as the simple fact of human abilities being limited, any preoccupation with formal management tasks, like planning and control, also risks neglecting factors outside the structure of formal authority. The behavioural limits on decision-making corrected this bias to some extent. But the processes of conflict and power in organizations are far more important in shaping managerial activity. We saw in the previous chapter that formal organization structures invariably contain the means for resolving conflict. However, to represent conflict merely as something that has to be resolved is to fail to explain it in its own right.

In this sense, organizations may be thought of as comprising a dual reality. On one level there is a set of relationships which represent the organization as an *operating system* – these would include the actions of managers in problem-solving, as well as the view of organizations as systems for rational goal-attainment. But there is also a parallel system based on the internal *struggle for power*. Much informal managerial activity – the deals and favours that inevitably are a part of real life in organizations – would be included here, as would the pursuit of self-interest and the defence of departmental interests against other conflicting groups. In this vein, Burns (1969) has referred to organizations as 'plural social systems'.

> Business enterprises are cooperative instrumental systems assembled out of the usable attributes of people. They are also places in which people compete for advancement. Thus, members of a business concern are at one and the same time cooperators in a common enterprise and rivals for the material and tangible rewards of successful competition with each other. The hierarchical order of rank and power, realized in the organization chart, which prevails in all organizations is both a control system and a career ladder.

The fact that the political side of organizations has been largely ignored until quite recently, plus the suggestion that power in organizations can actually be the decisive factor in decision-making, has meant that organizational politics is increasingly regarded as a key explanation of managerial behaviour.

THE CONCEPT OF POWER

The concept of power has always proved difficult to define, even though a common-sense grasp of the term seems easy enough. This is partly because the activity being described is itself dynamic and complex. For example, suppose someone has been influenced to follow a course of action against their original inclination. Has power been exercised over them? The answer might be yes, if their compliance was obtained with the use of threats, but no, if the advantages of a particular course of action of which they were unaware had simply been pointed out to them. However, if they were persuaded by force of argument, then it might be quite difficult to determine whether or not power had been used. It would depend upon exactly how aggressively the case was put:

whether threats were implied or whether the case was merely stated enthusiastically.

The complex nature of these types of behaviour is reflected in the number of terms similar to power, such as authority, control and influence, which are often used interchangeably in normal conversation. In social science analysis, however, one would want to know how precisely they differ from the notion of power. Do the different terms refer to types of power, or are they quite separate forms of behaviour?

Various definitions of power have been offered in answer to these questions. In an early attempt the political scientist Robert Dahl (1957) argued that a common-sense definition along the following lines was a useful starting point: 'A has power over B to the extent that he can get B to do something that B would otherwise not do.' This raised the essential issue of *resistance* on the part of B, because his wishes are being overridden, and hence of *conflict* between A and B. Certainly for Dahl, and many others, the acid test of a power relationship was the existence of this conflict of interests between persons or groups.

The framework for the sociology of power, originally set out by Weber, put forward a definition which also stressed the resistance of those under power. But for Weber power represented the *potential* to act in certain ways. Weber was interested in the way power could most often be effective when used as a threat rather than actually being exercised. Thus he spoke of the probability or chance of groups or individuals prevailing over others: 'We understand by "power" the chance of a man or a number of men to realize their own will in a communal action even against the resistance of others who are participating in the action' (Weber, 1970, p.180). We can also see that Weber's definition stressed power as a *collective* phenomenon. This use of the term is certainly appropriate within organizations, where groups of one kind or another – teams, departments, divisions – typically exercise power as the product of collective and social relationships. Even where power appears to be exercised by an individual, often its true basis lies in some group or other collectivity. The power of managers, for example, represents a mandate from the legal owners of the firm and is exercised on their behalf.

In addition, in order to arrive at the root causes of power we need to take account of behaviour that, in a sense, doesn't take place. According to Bachrach and Baratz (1962), this 'other face of power' reflects the ability of powerful groups to prevent various options or choices from even being considered. The original view expressed by Dahl – that power is reflected in the actions of the powerful – only looked at actual decisions and the groups which prevailed over them, so that even those who are overruled will still take part in the decision-making process. But what of the groups which are never admitted to the decision arena in the first place? Bachrach and Baratz argued that real power in this sense is exercised by suppressing their preferences. Thus, power in the form of 'non-decision-making' does not necessarily involve resistance or overt conflict at all. Indeed, the fact that those under power are never permitted to resist, or to engage in conflict, is a measure of the degree of power exercised over them.

Steven Lukes (1974) has taken the argument even further, saying that we need a fully radical view of power. This would include power that is exercised by preventing people from forming conscious preferences or choices. Such a type of power might apply, for example, to the way in which the social horizons of many working class people are narrowed and constrained by education and upbringing. They perceive that certain ambitions and aspirations are simply 'not for them' – which means that they may never challenge the economic position of the middle and upper classes. This formed the basis of Lukes's 'three-dimensional view of power'. The first dimension was the most obvious one, of power observable in the clash of interests between decision-makers (as stressed by Dahl). The second referred to the interests of certain groups being excluded from a particular bargaining arena (as emphasized by Bachrach and Baratz). The third, or radical, dimension referred to certain groups under power never being able to consciously formulate their real interests.

Organizational power

These different approaches and definitions should help in understanding the terms related to power, and in particular in focusing on the specific forms of power that are of interest in organizations. If we consider the amount of resistance offered by those under power, and also the strength of the sanctions brought to bear by those in power, then the different types of power can be seen to fall within a continuum. This represents the extent of conflict between the interests of the 'in-power' group and the 'under-power' group (Figure 16.1).

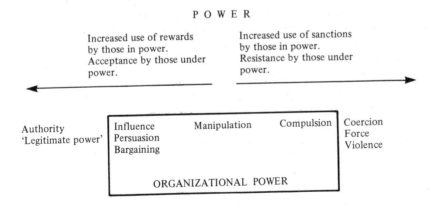

Figure 16.1 *Types of power.*

As the figure shows, power covers a very broad range of behaviours, from almost pure agreement to the resort to violence. The topic of this chapter, organizational power, clearly applies to a much narrower band of activities. Forms of violent coercion would need to be left out when speaking of power in organizations – or at least power in the kinds of commercial and public sector organization we are most familiar with.

In addition, the concept of authority overlaps with that of power, and the two terms can be quite ambiguously related. As we saw in Chapter 14, Weber regarded authority, in the sense of power accepted as legitimate by the under-group, as being of vital importance for maintaining social order; and within organizations authority remains the basis of formal control. Yet if authority is *purely* consensual it is doubtful whether we would speak of power being exercised. However, authority is nearly always backed up by sanctions, so the resort to power remains a choice for the group in authority. Thus the other dimensions of power, discussed by Bachrach and Baratz and by Lukes, can be placed in the same category as authority – even though these authors make the point that the agreement of the under-group is hardly freely given.

In practice the confusion between power and authority need not detain us, because authority and these other 'hidden' dimensions of power are not of central importance here. For organizational power refers essentially to lateral relations within management. This means focusing upon a range of activities of which bargaining and influence remain central (Abell, 1975).

THE ORGANIZATION AS A POLITICAL SYSTEM

The concern with power in organizations includes, first and foremost, an emphasis on *process* rather than structure. Although hierarchical position is one important power resource, it is not accepted that real power necessarily mirrors the formal hierarchy. Furthermore, managerial decision-making is seen as a *political* activity. People never suspend the pursuit of individual interests, nor cease to identify with the sectional loyalties which support them. So there are practical reasons for studying these political processes, since anyone who is to prosper, or even survive, in organizations must be able to bargain effectively for a share of resources. In short, they need to be equipped to play the game of organizational politics.

Thus, while power can be seen in terms of power *over* subordinates (which was the perspective we followed in the previous chapter), the emphasis here will be on the *use* of power and the range of tactics that people employ. This does not always mean the pursuit of career and self-interest. There is also a vitally important sense in which this power struggle and the broader attainment of organizational goals actually overlap and mutually support each other. It reflects management's responsibility for organizational development, and for designing an organization structure which is competent to meet a changing environment. Given the tendency of all institutions to resist change and settle into a routine, decision-makers in the real world often have their hands full merely getting organizations started towards change. Yet organizations must be made to adapt if they are to survive and prosper. It is only by deploying power that managers can intervene in the change process and guide their organizations along desired paths. First, though, we need to know something of the power resources that different groups are able to draw upon and about the organizational arena in which power is exercised.

Power resources

The social psychologists French and Raven, in a now-classic study (1959), developed a scheme of five categories of power, which reflected the different bases or resources that power holders rely upon. They identified reward, coercive, legitimate, referent and expert power.

Reward power depends upon the ability of the power wielder to confer valued material rewards, such as promotions or increases in pay or responsibility. *Coercive power* is the reverse side of this coin, in the sense that those who have the power to reward usually also have the power to punish. Thus coercive power might refer to the ability to demote or to withhold other rewards. In both cases, it is the desire for valued rewards or the fear of having them withheld that ensure the obedience of those under power. *Legitimate power* is identical with authority, and depends upon the belief of individuals in the right of senior people to hold their positions, and their consequent willingness to accept the power holder. *Referent power* is based on the 'charisma' of the power holder. Here the person under power desires to identify with these personal qualities, and gains satisfaction from being an accepted follower. Lastly, *expert power* rests on the skills or expertise of the person holding power. Unlike the others, this type of power is usually highly specific and limited to the particular area in which the expert is trained and qualified.

There are, however, certain defects in the French and Raven scheme. Their reward and coercive forms of power are not in fact power resources in themselves – they merely describe the actions of people who have other power resources. So, for example, senior managers with formal positions in the organizational hierarchy (legitimate power) can confer or withhold pro-motions. In addition, their legitimate and referent forms of power are taken directly from Weber's typology of authority, although without the addition of his third type, namely traditional authority (see Chapter 14). Still, French and Raven's approach does serve to emphasize the fact that within organizations people can call upon a range of different bases of power and influence.

Although hierarchical rank – legitimate power – is obviously a crucial power resource, when we consider power as a political process the focus of interest shifts to the resources that people can mobilize irrespective of their official positions. Here expertise, or French and Raven's expert power, represents an important power resource. Professionals, technical experts and tradespeople, who are employed in organizations for their specific skills, derive power from the fact that the organization depends upon that skilled work being performed. The 'expert power' of the professional or the tradesman very frequently comes into conflict with formal authority. In the long run this is a struggle for control in which experts are unlikely to prevail. The organization is still the employer and retains the ultimate power to hire and fire. Experts are also self-defeating in certain respects – it is often part of the expert's job to streamline and automate operations, and thereby to eliminate the need for his or her own skill. However, while there is innovation and growth in an organization expert power is enhanced, and in these kinds of circumstances experts can be highly influential, albeit in an informal way.

An attempt to explain power in more universal terms involves the twin concepts of *uncertainty* and *dependency* – ideas which have been developed most fully by Hickson *et al.* (1971) in their 'strategic contingencies' theory of power. Uncertainty for an organization stems from its system of operations (the technology and work organization) and from the environment. Reducing the uncertainty of operations is vital for management, and hence groups of employees who 'cope with uncertainty' thereby gain influence and power. The more strategic the form of uncertainty for a particular organization, the more powerful will the group which controls it become. Therefore organizations become heavily dependent on the groups which cope with central areas of uncertainty. For example, Crozier (1964) has shown how skilled workers were able to exploit a source of residual uncertainty in an otherwise routine production system. Machine breakdowns were the only major contingency that disrupted operations. The organization was thus dependent on the maintenance crews which dealt with breakdowns, which enabled these workers to enhance their status and rewards.

Another important study using this approach is Pettigrew's *The Politics of Organizational Decision-Making* (1973). This was based on an expanding computer system in a retailing organization, and examined the impact of this huge new resource on organizational politics. The first computer was installed in the 1950s, when commercial data-processing was a very uncertain business. Skills of a high order were involved, and the company itself was anxious to get the system working due to a rapid expansion in their volume of business. All these factors made the organization heavily dependent on the group of programmers in charge of the installation, and this was reflected in the programmers' total control of computer operations – a clear example of expert power. However, the programmers simply didn't fit into the organization. It was traditional and bureaucratic, while the programmers were university graduates who behaved and dressed casually, and who worked outside normal hours setting up the installation. They came to regard the firm's employees as dull and authoritarian, while the employees regarded the programmers as arrogant and immature. The very powerful antipathy between the two groups put paid to the programmers ever becoming an integral part of the organization; and senior management in particular greatly resented having to rely upon the programmers' skills. Pettigrew charts the struggle that ensued as management tried to undermine the programmers' control of technical information – by, for example, breaking up the programming function and hiving-off parts of it to other staff. For their part, the programmers sought to protect their power base by mystifying their skills and withholding information. In this way this professional group challenged formal authority essentially by seeking to retain the dependence of the organization upon their expertise.

The bargaining process

Having examined the bases of power in organizations, we can now turn to look at the organizational setting in which the political process takes place. It is important to bear in mind here, as we stressed earlier, that management is not the harmonious group it is often made out to be. Persistent conflict exists within management which is manifest in a variety of ways: in the manipulation of information, in hostility and lack of trust in inter-group relations, and in unwillingness to cooperate with colleagues. While it is possible for conflict to escalate to the point where it becomes highly destructive of organizational effort, where groups isolate themselves and become suspicious and hostile, even in the normal process of reaching joint decisions conflict and cooperation occur together. Therefore if joint decisions are to be arrived at, and conflict continually resolved, a negotiation or bargaining model of organizational interaction is implied.

Several recent studies have explored the notion of organizational decision-making as a process of negotiation (Abell, 1975; Bacharach and Lawler, 1980; Pfeffer, 1981). They stress that decisions are not simply 'made' or 'taken' but rather they *emerge* from interaction. Rules and relationships within organizations are outcomes of negotiation, constantly created and recreated, they are never merely part of an established structure. Conflict plays a central role in this, because it is conflicts of interest which cause people to use their power resources to bargain for outcomes favourable to themselves.

Yet conflict does not merely occur at random. It can also be a direct result of the formal structure of organizations. As we saw above, specialization and departmentalization within management create sub-units with discrete tasks and goals, and they also develop their own distinctive commitments and outlooks. While this differentiation is necessary for organizational performance, nevertheless the goal conflict it gives rise to creates the motives behind conflict.

The early writers of the classical school thought that goals were normally integrated. Under their model, the overall goal of the organization, being itself highly complex, is supposedly broken down into various sub-goals and allocated to specific units via the division of labour. The organization structure formally unites these sub-goals and hence the overall goal is achieved. We can see that this model must to an extent be true, otherwise little would ever get done in organizations. The goal of one department has to be formulated in accordance with the needs of other departments with which it interacts. But equally clearly the view of organizations as structures for the rational pursuit of goals is much too simplistic. Goals may in fact be poorly defined and provide an inadequate guide to behaviour; the real goals that actors pursue may be subtly different (or indeed very different) from stated goals; personal goals (the pursuit of promotion, power, income, security) may clash with official goals; and goals may change over time, or the original goals may be displaced by other real goals.

Thus, in practice, in the interaction between various groups of managers, goals are *made* to integrate as actors bargain about what constitutes acceptable performance.

DECISION-MAKING AS A POLITICAL PROCESS

Power itself is a dynamic concept. But if we only look at the *power resources* that actors possess, to some extent we receive a static picture of the negotiation process, as if actors merely command influence in some fixed proportion of their expert power or position power. In reality organizational politics is more dynamic even than this, and new sources of power can be generated actually in the process of negotiation itself. French and Raven were aware of this. They noted that there was also a 'subjective' side to power – people may not actually possess certain power resources, but as long as they can persuade others that they do they can still gain the substance of power. Implied here is a *tactical* conception of decision-making, in which power seekers can amplify (or reduce if they choose the wrong tactics) the power resources at their disposal.

For example, probably the most basic power tactic is the *control of information*. Information flows to high-ranking organizational members as part of the normal process of decision-making, and the possession of important information naturally reinforces their formal power. But lower-ranking members can also mobilize this particular resource to their advantage. They can exploit the fact that they are directly involved with the work process to gain control of strategic information. Withholding information, releasing information at the moment likely to cause maximum embarrassment to your opponent, and even distorting information are all very common tactics in the power game.

The range of tactics that people adopt in pursuit of their individual and sectional interests has become the subject of a highly refined theory of power in organizations, which has been reviewed in detail by Bacharach and Lawler

(1980). We have no space to go fully into their survey here, although we will indicate some of its main points.

Coalitions and interest groups

One common power tactic involves the formation of *sponsor–protégé relationships*. These are informal alliances between a senior and junior manager in which the protégé may assist the more senior person in some specialist area: he may perform various detailed work (e.g. write reports, speeches) and he may provide the senior manager with intelligence reports. In return the sponsor will guide the career of the protégé. Sponsors often have clusters of protégés; and when the sponsor moves up or out, to a better job, he may move his whole team with him. In this way corporate management is frequently made up of interlocking cliques of senior people and their followers.

But by far the most important power tactic is *coalition-formation* (indeed, sponsor–protégé relationships are a special kind of coalition). Coalition-formation represents the essence of political action, since it holds out the possibility of groups actually creating power for themselves. When interest groups face powerful opposition, a viable course of action is for them to join forces with other similar groups. A coalition, then, is *an informal relationship between two or more interest groups for the purpose of increasing their joint power in relation to some other group or groups.*

The obvious reason why groups should form coalitions is the gains they expect to make. But this doesn't take us very far. The more important question concerns the conditions under which groups might expect to gain little or much from forming a coalition. At least three factors can be distinguished here.

(1) The most important objective condition is usually the *relative power* of the interest groups involved, for this decides whether a winning coalition can be formed. Thus, if two weaker groups have sufficient power together to override a third group with which they are in conflict, then other things being equal it is likely they will form the coalition. On the other hand, if their joint power is still insufficient to prevail against the third group, they may well decide that the coalition is not worth forming.

(2) Managerial *differentiation* also plays a part. Interest groups in which the members are very different from each other, and have conflicting priorities, are usually only capable of forming unstable coalitions. So even if an issue does arise over which such groups might usefully pool resources, they may find day-to-day cooperation so difficult that they have to pursue their interests separately.

(3) In certain ways the *issue at stake* can itself become a condition of formation. Firstly, if it is a specific issue, resolved once and for all at a given time, then the most unlikely groups may be tempted into a temporary coalition because they know there will be no lasting commitment. Secondly, a highly important issue – one in which the potential gains are large, or where the very

survival of the groups is at stake – may also force into a coalition groups that would otherwise never contemplate joint action.

The circumstances in which groups might expect to gain more from going it alone are readily identified as the reverse of those that produce coalitions. Thus if an interest group is especially powerful it will not need to engage in a coalition. Similarly, if it is highly differentiated from other organizational groups its members may decide that they share no interest with other groups. In such circumstances the costs of coalition-formation – the most obvious one being that any spoils have to be shared – are liable to outweigh the benefits. Moreover, benefits can be transformed into costs: interacting with colleagues, which is a rewarding experience among people of like mind, can itself become a burden if they share little in common.

Perhaps the most widespread example of organizational staff likely to rely upon interest group tactics is *professionals*. Employed professionals (engineers, technical specialists, etc.) very often have a degree of expert power, perhaps conferred by control of strategic technology. They are likely to be differentiated from other organizational members in terms of occupational values, and their technical qualifications may also make them mobile and independent of the organization to a certain extent. Thus they are quite likely to pursue their interests via their profession rather than the organization. The interest group tactic represents true political behaviour only where it is actively chosen, or where it is used as an occupational strategy. However, in organizational terms it may often amount to opting out of the political game. The programmers in Pettigrew's (1973) case study, discussed above, seemed to present a good example of this kind of orientation. They clearly did see the organization in terms of the technical problems it provided rather than as secure employment. In the long term they seemed to be storing up trouble for themselves by choosing to defend an isolated position and not seeking wider organizational influence. On the other hand, of course, one might regard a defensive tactic as the only sensible course given their extreme social distance from other groups in the organization. In any case, the programmers managed to preserve some of their status, and their skills gave them the option of seeking other employment.

Human rationality in decision-making

While these structural factors influence coalition-formation, they are not the whole story. In practice, losing coalitions form quite frequently. For, as we have stressed, decision-making is a human and political process, and factors other than the purely rational calculation of costs and benefits enter into it.

To begin with, coalition-formation is an *indeterminate* process, one in which there is always uncertainty as to the outcome. This is so for several reasons. People's information is never perfect nor their judgments completely objective. Thus when we speak of the gains and losses involved in a coalition, the unspoken qualifier is that these are always people's *expectations* of gains and losses. In addition, important elements in the political process are non-comparable. One can never say exactly how much power a potential ally or adversary has, and thus one can never be entirely sure in advance whether the combination of these powers would produce a winning coalition.

More important, though, is the *tactical* nature of the organizational power game. Leadership, the deployment of resources and the formation of intelligent alliances are all going to be decisive. These are open-ended factors, which involve initiative and which take shape only as part of the political process. It follows that it is possible only with hindsight to say that so-and-so would inevitably win, or could never have won. At the time of conflict, each participant had the opportunity of winning, otherwise of course no certain loser would ever enter the political arena. Indeed, the essence of political action lies in the ability to convert an apparently weak position into a winning one via the intelligent use of tactics.

Another reason why losing coalitions may be formed stems from the subtle and dynamic nature of political processes. Gains other than purely material ones may be had from coalition membership. Being part of such power cliques, playing the game of organizational politics, is far more rewarding than being left on the sidelines. Moreover, material gains may eventually be forthcoming, since a losing coalition today may be the basis of a winning coalition in the future. Thus, people often judge this kind of group experience as being useful as well as enjoyable. They are right to do so, because coalitions are an integral part of organizational life, and to be an active participant in these crucial processes is to be pursuing one's own career in the long term.

CONCLUSION

The study of negotiation and power, then, has some very positive things to recommend it: the stress on 'real' organizational activity is refreshing when compared with the overly formal and prescriptive approach of the managerial theorists, while the ability to manipulate power is vital for organizational as well as managerial development. The mere fact that this side of the management role has been played down until quite recently encourages an interest in power – any new approach which promises to take our understanding forward is naturally welcome. However, in concluding we should perhaps take a step back and cast a more critical eye over some of these claims.

In their quotation at the beginning of this chapter, Bacharach and Lawler argued that the power and politics emphasis is no moral judgment but purely an observation. But this claim is almost bound to be misleading. The view of managers as 'perpetually bargaining' and 'repeatedly forming coalitions' does contain a value judgment. The Machiavellian image casts managers in a dramatic and rather exciting role. Similarly, the claim to be describing how organizations 'really are', which is frequently tagged on to theories of power and politics, is also evaluative. The strong appeal to common sense asks us to accept the truth of the theories even before the evidence is brought out.

Taking a wider view to include other schools of thought, or aspects of organizational activity other than power, we can see that the discussions in previous chapters are still obviously important for organizational behaviour. For example, Dalton's excellent study *Men who Manage* (1959) reminds us that power play by managers may influence the 'dynamics, development, re-organization and evolution of the organization' – but the fact remains that formal codes of practice prevail, whether or not they are partially undermined by informal activity.

> . . . however irregularly the informal operates to make changes, to check the extremes of official – or other informal – action; or however purely evasive or organizationally superfluous the informal may be, the formal restrains it in at least three ways. First, the formal largely orders the direction the informal takes. Second, it consequently shapes the character of defences created by the informal. And third, whether the formal is brightly or dimly existent in the blur of contradictions, it requires overt conformity to its precepts. (p.237)

So we now have three possible positions as regards these different approaches to organizations. Firstly, there is the viewpoint expressed in this chapter, by exponents of the power approach, that power and negotiation are the 'name of the game' in organizations, and remain the *decisive* factor in decision-making (e.g. Pettigrew, 1973; Bacharach and Lawler, 1980). Secondly, the opposing view, put forward for example by Dalton, while not ignorant of the importance of the pursuit of self-interest, ultimately takes the *managerialist* line – seeing organizations in the last analysis as rational goal-attainers, there to do the jobs they were established for. And thirdly, the viewpoint expressed by Burns (1969) above argues simply for an *interplay* between these two spheres, and suggests that there is both cooperation and conflict present in the 'plural social system' of organizations.

In setting out these different approaches to power, it seems fairly clear that the search for a resolution between them would probably be a false hope. For these are not competing theories, giving either 'true' or 'false' explanations of events. Rather, they are *perspectives* – ways of seeing organizational activity, and ways of emphasizing some aspect of it. Ultimately the need for so many different approaches reflects the inability to describe the 'reality' of organizations. But, short of that, organizational behaviour clearly is highly complex and variable. To seek to encapsulate it within a single theory may be asking rather a lot, particularly when different observers will have their own preferred perspective, and the uses to which the theory is being put will vary across a wide spectrum.

FURTHER READING

Abell, P. (1975) *Organizations as Bargaining and Influence Systems*. London: Heinemann.

Bacharach, S.B. and E.J. Lawler (1980) *Power and Politics in Organizations*. London: Jossey-Bass.

Kakabadse, A.P. (1983) *Politics of Management*. Aldershot: Gower.

Lee, R. and P. Lawrence (1986) *Organizational Behaviour: Politics at Work*. London: Hutchinson.

Lukes, S. (1974) *Power: A Radical View*. London: Macmillan.

Lukes, S. (ed.) (1986) *Power*. Oxford: Blackwell.

Pettigrew, A. (1973) *The Politics of Organizational Decision-Making*. London: Tavistock.

Pfeffer, J. (1981) *Power in Organizations*. Marshfield, Mass.: Pitman.

References

Abell, P. (ed.) (1975) *Organizations as Bargaining and Influence Systems*. London: Heinemann.

Abercrombie, N. and J. Urry (1983) *Capital, Labour and the Middle Classes*. London: Allen and Unwin.

Adams, J.S. (1965) 'Inequity in social exchange', in L. Berkowitz (ed.) *Advances in Experimental Social Psychology* Vol. 2. New York: Academic Press.

Adams, J.S. and P.R. Jacobsen (1964) 'Effects of wage inequities on work quality', *J. of Abnormal and Social Psychology*, 69, 19–25.

Adams-Webber, J. (1981) 'Empirical developments in personal construct theory', in H. Bonarius, R. Holland and S. Rosenberg (eds.) *Personal Construct Psychology*. London: Macmillan.

Alan Smith, K. (1981) 'The coming of age of the social sciences', in *Report of Working Party of the Undergraduate Courses Board, Committee for Business and Management Studies*. Council for National Academic Awards: London.

Albrow, M. (1980) 'The dialectic of science and values in the study of organizations', in G. Salaman and K. Thompson (eds.) op. cit.

Alderfer, C.P. (1972) *Existence, Relatedness and Growth*. New York: Free Press.

Allen, V.L. (1975) *Social Analysis*. London: Longman.

Allen, V. and D.A. Wilder (1979) 'Group categorization and attribution of belief similarity', *Small Group Behaviour*, 110, 73–80.

Argyle, M. (1983) *The Psychology of Interpersonal Behaviour*. (4th ed.) Harmondsworth: Penguin.

Argyle, M. and M. Cook (1976) *Gaze and Mutual Gaze*. Cambridge: Cambridge University Press.

Argyle, M., A. Furnham and J.A. Graham (1981) *Social Situations*. Cambridge: Cambridge University Press.

Armstrong, P. (1985) 'Changing management control strategies: the role of competition between accountancy and other organisational professions', *Accounting, Organizations and Society*, 10, 124–48.

Arsenault, A. and S. Dolan (1983) 'The role of personality, occupation and organization in understanding the relationship between job stress, performance and absenteeism', *J. of Occupational Psychology*, 56, 227–40.

Attwood, M. and F. Hatton (1983) ' "Getting on". Gender differences in career development: a case study in the hairdressing industry', in E. Gamarnikow, D.

Morgan, J. Purvis and D. Taylorson (eds.) *Gender, Class and Work*. London: Heinemann.

Bacharach, S.B. and E.J. Lawler (1980) *Power and Politics in Organizations*. London: Jossey-Bass.

Bachrach, P. and M.S. Baratz (1962) 'The two faces of power', *American Political Science Rev.*, 56, 947–52.

Bainbridge, L. (1978) 'The process controller' in W.T. Singleton (ed.) *The Analysis of Practical Skills*. Lancaster: MTP Press.

Baldamus, W. (1961) *Efficiency and Effort*. London: Tavistock.

Bales, R.F. and P.E. Slater (1955) 'Role differentiation in small decision-making groups', in T. Parsons *et al.* (eds.) *Family, Socialization and Interaction Processes*. New York: Free Press.

Bamforth, K. (1965) 'T-group methods within a company', in G. Whitaker (ed.) *ATM Occasional Papers*. Oxford: Blackwell.

Banks, M.H., P.R. Jackson, E.M. Stafford and P.B. Warr (1982) *The Job Components Inventory Mark 2*. Sheffield: Manpower Services Commission Training Studies.

Barker, C. (1983) 'The psychotherapist', in W.T. Singleton (ed.) *Social Skills*. Lancaster: MTP Press.

Barker, J. and H. Downing (1980) 'Word processing and the transformation of the patriarchial relations of control in the office', *Capital and Class*, 10, 64–99.

Barrett, P. and P. Kline (1980) 'Personality factors in the EPQ', *Personality and Individual Differences*, 1, 317–23.

Barron, I. and R. Curnow (1979) *The Future with Microelectronics*. Milton Keynes: Open University Press.

Bass, B.M. (1981) *Stogdill's Handbook of Leadership*. New York: Free Press.

Bass, B.M., P.C. Burger, R. Doktor and G.V. Barrett (1979) *Assessment of Managers: An International Comparison*. New York: Free Press.

Bass, B.M. and E.R. Valenzi (1974) 'Contingent aspects of effective management styles', in J.G. Hunt and L.L. Larson (eds.) *Contingency Approaches to Leadership*. Carbondale: Southern Illinois University Press.

Bass, B.M., E.R. Valenzi, D.C. Furnow and R.J. Solomon (1975) 'Management styles associated with organizational task, personal and interpersonal contingencies', *J. of Applied Psychology*, 60, 720–29.

Bell, D. (1948) ' "Screening" leaders in a democracy', *Commentary*, 5, 368–75.

Bell, D. (1980) 'The social framework of the information society', in T. Forester (ed.) op. cit.

Bendix, R. (1956) *Work and Authority in Industry*. New York: Wiley.

Benson, I. and D. Lloyd (1983) *New Technology and Industrial Change*. London: Kogan Page.

Beynon, H. (1984) *Working for Ford*. (2nd ed.) Harmondsworth: Penguin.

Billings, A.G. and R.M. Moos (1981) 'The role of coping responses in attenuating the impact of stressful life events', *J. of Behavioural Medicine*, 4, 139–57.

Blackburn, R.M. and M. Mann (1979) *The Working Class in the Labour Market*. London: Macmillan.

Blackler, F.H.M. and C.A. Brown (1980) 'Job redesign and social change: case studies at Volvo', in K.D. Duncan, M.M. Gruneberg and D. Wallis (eds.) op. cit.

Blau, P.M. (1955) *The Dynamics of Bureaucracy*. Chicago: University of Chicago Press.

311

Blau, P.M. and R.A. Schoenherr (1971) *The Structure of Organizations*. New York: Basic Books.

Blauner, R. (1964) *Alienation and Freedom*. Chicago: University of Chicago Press.

Boot, R.L., A.G. Cowling and M.J.K. Stanworth (1977) *Behavioural Science for Managers*. London: Edward Arnold.

Braun, E. and S. MacDonald (1978) *Revolution in Miniature*. Cambridge: Cambridge University Press.

Braverman, H. (1974) *Labor and Monopoly Capital: The Degradation of Work in the Twentieth Century*. New York: Monthly Review Press.

Bray, D.W., R.J. Campbell and D.C. Grant (1974) *Formative Years in Business: A Long-Term AT&T Study of Managerial Lives*. New York: Wiley.

Brenner, M. (1982) 'Actors' powers', in M. von Cranach and R. Harré (eds.) *The Analysis of Action*. Cambridge: Cambridge University Press.

Brett, J.M. (1980) 'The effect of job transfer in employees and their families', in C.L. Cooper and R. Payne (eds.) op. cit.

Brighton Labour Process Group (1977) 'The capitalist labour process', *Capital and Class*, 1, 3–26

British Psychological Society (1981) 'Principles governing the employment of psychological tests', *Bull. of the British Psychological Society*, 34, 317–18.

Brown, D. and M.J. Harrison (1980) 'The demand for relevance and the role of sociology in business studies degrees', *J. of Further and Higher Education*, 4, 54–61.

Brown, G.W. and T. Harris (1978) *Social Origins of Depression: A Study of Psychiatric Disorder in Women*. London: Tavistock.

Buchanan, D.A. and D. Boddy (1983) *Organizations in the Computer Age*. Aldershot: Gower.

Burns, T. (1969) 'On the plurality of social systems', in T. Burns (ed.) *Industrial Man*. Harmondsworth: Penguin.

Burns, T. and G.M. Stalker (1961) *The Management of Innovation*. London: Tavistock.

Burnstein, E. (1983) 'Persuasion as argument processing', in I.M. Brandstatter, J.H. Davis and G. Stocker-Kreichgauer (eds.) *Group Decision Processes*. London: Academic Press.

Burrell, G. and G. Morgan (1979) *Sociological Paradigms and Organisational Analysis*. London: Heinemann.

Cameron, R. and D. Meichenbaum (1982) 'The nature of effective coping and the treatment of stress related problems: a cognitive–behavioural perspective', in L. Goldberger and S. Breznitz (eds.) *Handbook of Stress: Theoretical and Clinical Aspects*. London: Macmillan.

Caplan, R.D., S. Cobb, J.R.P. French, R. van Harrison and S.R. Pinneau (1975) *Job Demands and Worker Health*, pp.75–160. U.S. Department of Health, Education and Welfare/NIOSH.

Carchedi, G. (1977) *On the Economic Identification of Social Classes*. London: Routledge Direct Editions.

Carey, A. (1967) 'The Hawthorne studies: a radical criticism', *American Sociological Rev.*, 32, 403–16.

Carrell, M.R. and J.E. Dittrich (1978) 'Equity theory: the recent literature, methodological considerations and new directions', *Academy of Management Rev.*, 3, 202–10.

Carruthers, M. (1980) 'Hazardous occupations and the heart', in C.L. Cooper and R. Payne (eds.) op. cit.

Cartwright, D. and A. Zander (1968) (eds.) *Group Dynamics: Research and Theory*. (3rd ed.) New York: Harper and Row.

Carver, C.S. and D.C. Glass (1978) 'Coronary-prone behaviour patterns and interpersonal aggression', *J. of Personality and Social Psychology*, 36, 361–6.

Cathcart, E.P. (1928) *The Human Factor in Industry*. Oxford: Oxford University Press.

Cattell, R.B. (1967) *The Scientific Analysis of Personality*. Harmondsworth: Penguin.

Chesney, M.A. and R. Rosenman (1980) 'Type A behaviour in the work setting', in C.L. Cooper and R. Payne (eds.) op. cit.

Child, J. (1972) 'Organizational structure, environment and performance: the role of strategic choice', *Sociology*, 6, 1–22.

Child, J. (1978) 'The myth at Lordstown', *Management Today*, October.

Child, J. (1984) *Organization*. (2nd ed.) London: Harper and Row.

Child, J. and J. Fulk (1982) 'Maintenance of occupational control: the case of professions', *Work and Occupations*, 9, 155–92.

Child, J., R. Loveridge, J. Harvey and A. Spencer (1984) 'Microelectronics and the quality of employment in services', in P. Marstrand (ed.) *New Technology and the Future of Work and Skills*. London: Frances Pinter.

Chinoy, E. (1955) *Automobile Workers and the American Dream*. New York: Doubleday.

Claridge, G.S. (1970) *Drugs and Human Behaviour*. London: Allen Lane.

Clarke, D.D. (1983) *Language and Action: A Structural Model of Behaviour*. Oxford: Pergamon Press.

Clegg, C. and M.J. Fitter (1978) 'Management information systems: the Achilles Heel of job redesign', *Personnel Rev.*, 7, 5–11.

Clegg, S. and D. Dunkerley (1980) *Organization, Class and Control*. London: Routledge and Kegan Paul.

Cliffe, T. (1970) *The Employers' Offensive*, London: Pluto Press.

Cooley, M. (1981) 'The Taylorisation of intellectual work', in L. Levidow and B. Young (eds.) op. cit.

Cooper, C. L. (1975) 'How psychologically dangerous are T-groups and encounter groups?', *Human Relations*, 28, 249–60.

Cooper, C.L. and R. Payne (eds.) (1980) *Current Concerns in Occupational Stress*. Chichester: Wiley.

Cox, T. (1980) 'Repetitive work', in C.L. Cooper and R. Payne (eds.) ibid.

Craig, C., E. Garnsey and J. Rubery (1983) 'Women's pay in informal payment systems', *Employment Gazette*, April. (London: Department of Employment.)

Crompton, R. and G. Jones (1984) *White Collar Proletariat: Deskilling and Gender in Clerical Work*. London: Macmillan.

Crompton, R. and S. Reid (1982) 'The deskilling of clerical work', in S. Wood (ed.) op. cit.

Crossman, E.R.F.W. and J.E. Cooke (1962) 'Manual control of slow response systems', in E. Edwards and F.P. Lees (eds.) *The Human Operator in Process Control*. London: Taylor and Francis.

Crowder, N.A. (1960) 'Automatic tutoring by instrinsic programming', in A.A. Lunsdaine and R. Glaser (eds.) *Teaching Machines and Programmed Learning*. Washington: N.E.A.

Crozier, M. (1964) *The Bureaucratic Phenomenon*. London: Tavistock.

Cutler, A. (1978) 'The romance of labour', *Economy and Society*, 7, 74–95.

Dahl, R.A. (1957) 'The concept of power', *Behavioral Science*, 2, 201–5.

Dahrendorf, R. (1959) *Class and Class Conflict in Industrial Society*. London: Routledge and Kegan Paul.

Daley, M.R. (1979) 'Burnout: smouldering problems in protective services', *Social Work*, 24, 375–9.

Dalton, M. (1959) *Men who Manage*. New York: Wiley.

Deem, R. (1981) 'The teaching of industrial sociology in higher education: an exploratory analysis', *The Sociological Rev.*, 29, 237–51.

de Waele, J.P. and R. Harré (1976) *Personality*. Oxford: Blackwell.

Dobb, M. (1963) *Studies in the Development of Capitalism*. London: Routledge and Kegan Paul.

Doeringer, P.B. and M.J. Piore (1971) *Internal Labor Markets and Manpower Analysis*. Lexington, Mass.: D.C. Heath.

Downs, S. and P. Perry (1982) 'How do I learn?', *J. of European Industrial Training*, 6, 27–32.

Downs, S. and P. Perry (1984) *Developing Skilled Learners: Learning to Learn in the Youth Training Scheme*. Sheffield: Manpower Services Commission, R&D Publication No. 22.

Downs, S. and P. Perry (1986) 'Can trainers learn to take a back seat?' *Personnel Management*, March.

Duncan, K.D., M.M. Gruneberg and D. Wallis (eds.) (1980) *Changes in Working Life*. Chichester: Wiley.

Drazen, M., J.S. Nevid, N. Pace and R.M. O'Brien (1982) 'Worksite-based behavioural treatment of mild hypertension', *J. of Occupational Medicine*, 24, 511–14.

Duck, S.W. (1973) *Personal Relationships and Personal Constructs: A Study of Friendship Formation*. Chichester: Wiley.

Duranti, A. and E. Ochs (1979) 'Left-dislocation in Italian conversation', in T. Givon (ed.) *Syntax and Semantics* Vol. 12: *Discourse and Syntax*. New York: Academic Press.

Durbeck, D.C., F. Heinzelmann, J. Schacter, W.I. Haskell, G.H. Payne, R.T. Moxley, M. Nemeroff, D.D. Limoncelli, L.B. Arnoldi and S.M. Fox (1972) 'The National Aeronautics and Space Administration: U.S. Public Health Service Health Evaluation and Enhancement Programme', *American J. of Cardiology*, 30, 784–90.

Edwardes, M. (1984) *Back from the Brink*. London: Pan Books.

Edwards, P.K. (1979) ' "The awful truth about strikes in our factories": a case study in the production of news', *Industrial Relations J.*, 10, 7–11.

Edwards, R., M. Reich and D.M. Gordon (eds.) (1975) *Labor Market Segmentation*. Lexington, Mass.: D.C. Heath.

Eldridge, J.E.T. (1968) *Industrial Disputes*. London: Routledge and Kegan Paul.

Eldridge, J.E.T. (1971) *Sociology and Industrial Life*. London: Nelson.

Elger, A. (1979) 'Valorisation and deskilling: a critique of Braverman', *Capital and Class*, 7, 58–99. Reprinted in S. Wood (ed.) (1982) op. cit.

Elliott, D. (1980) 'The organization as a system', in G. Salaman and K. Thompson (eds.) op. cit.

Elliott, P. (1972) *The Sociology of Professions*. London: Macmillan.

Entwistle, N.J. and J.D. Wilson (1977) *Degrees of Excellence: The Academic Achievement Game*. London: Hodder and Stoughton.

Esland, G. (1980) 'Professions and professionalism', in G. Esland and G. Salaman (eds.) *The Politics of Work and Occupations*. Milton Keynes: Open University Press.

European Trade Union Institute (ETUI) (1980) 'The Impact of Microelectronics on Employment in Western Europe in the 1980s. Brussels: ETUI.

Evans, M.G. (1970) 'The effects of supervisory behavior on the path–goal relationship', Organizational Behavior and Human Performance, 5, 277–98.

Evans, M.G. (1973) 'The moderating effect of internal versus external control on the relationship between various aspects of job satisfaction', Studies in Personnel Psychology, 5, 37–46.

Evans, M.G., M.M. Kiggundu and R.J. House (1979) 'A partial test and extension of the job characteristics model of motivation', Organizational Behavior and Human Performance, 24, 354–81.

Evison, R. and R. Horobin (1983) How to Change Yourself and Your World. Sheffield: Co-counselling Phoenix.

Eysenck, H.J. (1953) Uses and Abuses of Psychology. Harmondsworth: Penguin.

Eysenck, H.J. (1985) Decline and Fall of the Freudian Empire. Harmondsworth: Viking.

Eysenck, H.J. and S.B.G. Eysenck (1976) Psychoticism as a Dimension of Personality. London: Hodder and Stoughton.

Exley, M. (1977) 'A job satisfaction study in H.M. Customs and Excise: a participative approach to research management and a contingency approach to research design', Personnel Rev., 6, 12–20.

Fazio, R.H., L.M. Cooper, K. Dayson and M. Johnson (1981) 'Control and the coronary-prone behaviour pattern: responses to multiple situational demands', Personality and Social Psychology Bull., 7, 97–102.

Ferguson, D.A. (1973) 'Comparative study of occupational stress', Ergonomics, 16, 649–64.

Ferster, C.B. and B.F. Skinner (1957) Schedules of Reinforcement. New York: Appleton.

Fiedler, F.E. (1967) A Theory of Leadership Effectiveness. New York: MacGraw-Hill.

Fiedler, F.E. (1970) 'Leadership experience and leader performance – another hypothesis shot to hell', Organizational Behavior and Human Performance, 5, 1–14.

Fiedler, F.E. (1982) 'Are leaders an intelligent form of life? A long neglected question of leadership theory', Abstracts, 20th International Congress of Applied Psychology, 113.

Fiedler, F.E., P.M. Bons and L. Hastings (1975) 'The utilization of leadership resources', in W.T. Singleton and P. Spurgeon (eds.) Measurement of Human Resources. London: Taylor and Francis.

Fiedler, F.E. and M.E. Chemars (1984) Improving Leadership Effectiveness: The Leader Match Concept. Chichester: Wiley.

Fiedler, F.E. and A.F. Leister (1977a) 'Intelligence and group performance: a multiple screen model', Organizational Behavior and Human Performance, 20, 1–11.

Fiedler, F.E. and A.F. Leister (1977b) 'Leader intelligence and task performance: a test of a multiple screen model', Organizational Behavior and Human Performance, 20, 11–14.

Fiedler, F.E. and L. Mahar (1979) 'The effectiveness of contingency model training: validation of leader match', Personnel Psychology, 32, 45–62.

Field, R.H.G. (1979) 'A critique of the Vroom–Yetton contingency model of leadership behaviour', Academic Management Rev., 4, 249–57.

Fleishman, E.A. and E.F. Harris (1962) 'Patterns of leadership behavior related to employee grievances and turnover', Personnel Psychology, 15, 43–56.

Fleishman, E.A., E.F. Harris and H.E. Burtt (1955) *Leadership and Supervision in Industry*. Columbus: Ohio State University, Bureau of Educational Research.

Fodor, E.M. and T. Smith (1982) 'The power motive as an influence on group decision making' , *J. of Personality and Social Psychology*, 42, 178–85.

Fogarty, M., I. Allen and P. Walters (1981) *Women in Top Jobs 1968–1979*. London: Heinemann.

Forester, T. (ed.) (1980) *The Microelectronics Revolution*. Oxford: Blackwell.

Forester, T. (ed.) (1985) *The Information Technology Revolution*. Oxford: Blackwell.

Fox, A. (1971) *A Sociology of Work in Industry*. London: Collier-Macmillan.

Fox, A. (1974) *Beyond Contract*. London: Faber and Faber.

Fox, A. (1977) 'The myths of pluralism and a radical alternative', in T. Clarke and L. Clements (eds.) *Trade Unions Under Capitalism*. London: Fontana.

French, J.R.P. and B. Raven (1959) 'The bases of social power', in D. Cartwright (ed.) *Studies in Social Power*. Ann Arbor, Mich.: Institute for Social Research.

Frese, M. (1982) 'Occupational socialization and psychological development: an underemphasized research perspective in industrial psychology', *J. of Occupational Psychology*, 55, 209–24.

Freshwater, D.L. (1982) *Basic Skills Analysis*. Sheffield: Manpower Services Commission.

Friedman, A. (1977) 'Responsible autonomy versus direct control over the labour process', *Capital and Class*, 1, 43–57.

Friedman, M. and R.H. Rosenman (1974) *Type A Behaviour and Your Heart*. New York: Knopf.

Friedrichs, G. and A. Schaff (eds.) (1982) *Microelectronics and Society: For Better For Worse*. Oxford: Pergamon Press.

Gallie, D. (1978) *In Search of the New Working Class*. London: Cambridge University Press.

Ganster, D.C., B.T. Mayers, W.E. Sime and G.D. Tharp (1982) 'Managing occupational stress: a field experiment'. *J. of Applied Psychology*, 67, 533–42.

Ghiselli, E.E. (1963) 'Intelligence and managerial success', *Psychological Reports*, 12, 898.

Gibson, J.J. (1968) *The Senses Considered as Perceptual Systems*. Boston: Houghton Mifflin.

Glass, D.C. (1977) *Behavior Patterns, Stress and Coronary Disease*. Hillsdale, N.J.: Lawrence Erlbaum.

Goethals, G.R. and J.M. Darley (1977) 'Social comparison theory: an attributional approach', in J.M. Suls and R.L. Miller (eds.) *Social Comparison Perspectives*. Washington, D.C.: Hemisphere.

Goffman, E. (1968) *Asylums*. Harmondsworth: Penguin.

Goffman, E. (1971) *The Presentation of Self in Everyday Life*. Harmondsworth: Penguin.

Goldthorpe, J.H., D. Lockwood, F. Bechofer and J. Platt (1968) *The Affluent Worker: Industrial Attitudes and Behaviour*. Cambridge: Cambridge University Press.

Goode, W.J. (1957) 'Community within a community: the professions', *American Sociological Rev.*, 22, 194–200.

Goodfellow, M.M. (1983) 'The schoolteacher', in W.T. Singleton (ed.) *Social Skills*. Lancaster: MTP Press.

Goodrich, C.L. (1975) *The Frontier of Control*. London: Pluto Press.

Gospel, H. (1983) 'The development of management organization in industrial relations: a historical perspective', in K. Thurley and S. Wood (eds.) *Industrial Relations and Management Strategy*. Cambridge: Cambridge University Press.

Gouldner, A.W. (1954) *Patterns of Industrial Bureaucracy*. Glencoe, Ill.: Free Press.

Gouldner, A.W. (1955) *Wildcat Strike*. London: Routledge and Kegan Paul.

Gouldner, A.W. (1957) 'Cosmopolitans and locals', *Administrative Science Quarterly*, 2, 281–306.

Gowler, D. and K. Legge (1982) 'The integration of disciplinary perspectives in problem-oriented organizational research', in N. Nicholson and T.D. Wall (eds.) *The Theory and Practice of Organizational Psychology*. London: Academic Press.

Greene, C.N. (1975) 'The reciprocal nature of influence between leader and subordinate', *J. of Applied Psychology*, 60, 187–93.

Greene, C.N. (1979) 'Questions of causation in the path goal theory of leadership', *Academic Management J.*, 22, 22–41.

Grice, H.P. (1975) 'Logic and conversation', in P. Cole and J.L. Morgan (eds.) *Syntax and Semantics* Volume 3: *Speech Acts*. London and New York: Academic Press.

Guest, D., R. Williams and P. Dewe (1980) 'Workers' perceptions of changes affecting the quality of working life', in K.D. Duncan, M.M. Gruneberg and D. Wallis (eds.) op. cit.

Guilford, J.P. (1967) *The Nature of Human Intelligence*. New York: McGraw-Hill.

Guilford, J.P. (1982) 'Cognitive psychology's ambiguities: some suggested remedies', *Psychological Rev.*, 89, 48–59.

Gyllenhammar, P.G. (1977) 'How Volvo adapts work to people', *Harvard Business Rev.*, 55, 102–13.

Hackman, J.R. (1980) 'Changing views of motivation in work groups', in K.D. Duncan, M.M. Gruneberg and D. Wallis (eds.) op. cit.

Hackman, J.R. and G.R. Oldham (1975) 'Development of the job diagnostic survey', *J. of Applied Psychology*, 60, 159–70.

Hackman, J.R. and G.R. Oldham (1976) 'Motivation through the design of work: test of a theory', *Organizational Behavior and Human Performance*, 16, 250–79.

Hakim, C. (1980) 'Census reports as documentary evidence: the Census Commentaries 1801–1951', *The Sociological Rev.*, 28, 551–80.

Hall, J. (1971) 'Decisions decisions', *Psychology Today*, June.

Hall, R.H. (1968) 'Professionalisation and bureaucratisation', *American Sociological Rev.*, 33, 92–104.

Halpin, A.W. and B.J. Winer (1957) 'A factoral study of the leader behavior descriptions', in R.M. Stogdill and A.E. Coons (eds.) *Leader Behavior: Its Description and Measurement*. Columbus: Ohio State University, Bureau of Business Research.

Halsey, A.H., A.F. Heath and J.M. Ridge (1980) *Origins and Destinations: Family, Class and Education in Modern Britain*. Oxford: Clarendon Press.

Harré, R. (1979) *Social Being: A Theory for Social Psychology*. Oxford: Blackwell.

Harrell, T.W. and M.S. Harrell (1945) 'Army classification test scores for civilian occupations', *Educational and Psychological Measurement*, 5, 229–39.

Harrison, R.V. (1976) 'Job stress as person–environment misfit'. Paper presented to annual meeting of the American Psychological Association, Washington D.C.

Heinzelmann, F. (1975) 'Psycho-social implications of physical activity', in *Employee Physical Fitness in Canada*. Ottawa: National Health and Welfare, Information Canada.

Hemphill, J.K. (1950) 'Leader behavior description'. Columbus: Ohio State University, Personnel Research Board (mimeo).

Herzberg, F., B. Mausner and B.B. Snydeman (1959) *The Motivation to Work*. New York: Wiley.

Hickson, D.J., C.R. Hinings, C.A. Lee, R.E. Schneck and J.M. Pennings (1971) 'A strategic contingencies theory of intraorganizational power', *Administrative Science Quarterly*, 16, 216–29.

Hill, G.W. (1982) 'Group versus individual performance: are N+1 heads better than one?', *Psychological Bull.*, 91, 517–39.

Hill, S. (1976) 'The new industrial relations?' *British J. of Industrial Relations*, 14, 214–19.

Hill, S. (1981) *Competition and Control at Work*. London: Heinemann.

Hofstede, G. (1978) 'Value systems in forty countries'. Proceedings of the 4th International Congress of the International Association for Cross-Cultural Psychology.

Hollander, E.P. (1958) 'Conformity, status and idiosyncrasy credit', *Psychological Rev.*, 65, 117–27.

Hollander, E.P. (1961) 'Emergent leadership and social influence', in L. Petrullo and B.M. Bass (eds.) *Leadership and Interpersonal Behavior*. New York: Holt, Rinehart and Winston.

Hollander, E.P. (1978) *Leadership Dynamics: A Practical Guide to Effective Relationships*. New York: Free Press.

Holroyd, K.A. and R.S. Lazarus (1983) 'Stress, coping and somatic adaptation', in L. Goldberger and S. Breznitz (eds.) *Handbook of Stress: Theoretical and Clinical Aspects*. London: Macmillan.

Horner, M. (1972) 'Toward an understanding of achievement-related conflicts in women', *J. of Social Issues*, 15, 157–75.

House, R.J. (1971) 'A path goal theory of leader effectiveness', *Administrative Science Quarterly*, 16, 321–38.

Hughes, E. (1975) 'Professions', in G. Esland, G. Salaman and M. Speakman (eds.) *People and Work*. Edinburgh: Holmes-McDougall and Open University Press.

Huws, U. (1982) *Your Job in the Eighties: A Woman's Guide to New Technology*. London: Pluto Press.

Hyman, R. (1983) 'White-collar workers and theories of class', in R. Hyman and R. Price (eds.) *The New Working Class? White-Collar Workers and their Organizations*. London: Macmillan.

Hyman, R. (1984) *Strikes*. (3rd ed.) London: Fontana.

Hyman, R. and T. Elger (1981) 'Job controls, the employers' offensive and alternative strategies', *Capital and Class*, 15, 115–49.

Ide, T.R. (1982) 'The technology', in G. Friedrichs and A. Schaff (eds.) op. cit.

Ivancevich, J.M. (1978) 'The performance to satisfaction relationship: a causal analysis of stimulating and non-stimulating jobs', *Organizational Behavior and Human Performance*, 22, 350–65.

Jamous, H. and B. Peloille (1970) 'Professions or self-perpetuating systems?', in J.A. Jackson (ed.) *Professions and Professionalization*. London: Cambridge University Press.

Janis, I.L. (1972) *Victims of Groupthink*. Boston: Houghton Mifflin.

Janis, I.L. (1982) 'Decisionmaking under stress', in L. Goldberger and S. Breznitz (eds.) *Handbook of Stress: Theoretical and Clinical Aspects*. London: Macmillan.

Jemmot, J.B., J. Borysenko, M. Borysenko, D.C. McClelland, R. Chapman, D. Meyer and H. Benson (1983) 'Academic stress, power motivation and decrease in secretion rate of salivary secretory immuno globulin A', *The Lancet*, 8339, 1400–2.

Johnson, T. (1972) *Professions and Power*. London: Macmillan.

Jones, E.E. amd H.B. Gerard (1967) *Foundations of Social Psychology*. New York: Wiley.

Kasl, S.V. (1980) 'The impact of retirement', in C.L. Cooper and R. Payne (eds.) op. cit.

Katz, R. and G. Farris (1976) 'Does performance affect LPC?' Boston: Massachusetts Institute of Technology (mimeo).

Kelly, G.A. (1955) *The Psychology of Personal Constructs*. New York: Norton.

Kelly, J.E. (1982) *Scientific Management, Job Redesign and Work Performance*. London: Academic Press.

Kelly, J.E. and C.W. Clegg (1982) *Autonomy and Control at the Workplace*. London: Croom Helm.

Kemp, N.J., C.W. Clegg and T.D. Wall (1980) 'Job redesign: content, process and outcomes', *Employee Relations*, 2, 5–14.

Kemp, N.J., T.D. Wall, C.W. Clegg and J.L. Cordery (1983) 'Autonomous work groups in a greenfield site: a comparative study', *J. of Occupational Psychology*, 56, 271–88.

Kimmons, G. and J.H. Greenhaus (1976) 'Relationship between locus of control and reactions of employees to work characteristics', *Psychological Reports*, 39, 815–20.

King, A. (1982) 'A new Industrial Revolution or just another technology', in G. Friedrichs and A. Schaff (eds.) op. cit.

Klein, L. (1979) 'Some problems of theory and method', in R.G. Sell and P. Shipley (eds.) *Satisfaction in Work Design*. London: Taylor and Francis.

Klein, L. (1981) 'Trebor factory, Colchester, Essex: appraisal', *Architects' Journal*, June.

Kline, P. (1980) 'Burt's false results and modern psychometrics: a comparison', *Supp. to the Bull. of the British Psychological Society*, 33, 20–3.

Kline, P. (1983) *Personality: Measurement and Theory*. London: Hutchinson.

Kline, P. (1986) *A Handbook of Test Construction*. London: Methuen.

Korda, M. (1976) *Power in the Office*. London: Weidenfeld and Nicolson.

Kraft, P. (1979) 'The industrialization of computer programming: from programming to "software production" ', in A. Zimbalist (ed.) op. cit.

Lamm, H. and D.G. Myers (1978) 'Group-induced polarization of attitudes and behavior', in L. Berkowitz (ed.) *Advances in Experimental Social Psychology* Vol. 2. New York: Academic Press.

Landy, F. (1982) 'Models of man: assumptions of theorists', in N. Nicholson and T.D. Wall (eds.) *The Theory and Practice of Organizational Psychology*. London: Academic Press.

Lane, T. and K. Roberts (1971) *Strike at Pilkingtons*. London: Fontana.

Latham, G.P. and J.J. Blades (1975) 'The practical significance of Locke's theory of goal setting', *J. of Applied Psychology*, 60, 122–4.

Lawrence, P.R. and J. Lorsch (1967) *Organization and Environment*. Cambridge, Mass.: Harvard University Press.

Lazarus, R.S., J.B. Cohen, S. Folkman, A. Kanner and C. Schaefer (1980)

'Psychological stress and adaptation: some unresolved issues', in H. Selye (ed.) *Selye's Guide to Stress Research* Vol. 1. New York: Van Nostrand.

Lee, D. and H. Newby (1983) *The Problem of Sociology*. London: Hutchinson.

Levidow, L. and B. Young (eds.) (1981) *Science, Technology and the Labour Process* Vol. 1. London: CSE Books.

Levidow, L. and B. Young (eds.) (1985) *Science, Technology and the Labour Process* Vol. 2. London: Free Association Books.

Lewis, S. and C.L. Cooper (1983) 'The stress of combining occupational and parental roles: a review of the literature', *Bull. of the British Psychological Society*, 36, 337–40.

Likert, R. (1961) *New Patterns of Management*. New York: McGraw-Hill.

Likert, R. (1977a) 'Management styles: the human component', *Management Rev.*, 66, 23–8, 43–5.

Likert, R. (1977b) 'Past and future perspectives on System 4', Proceedings of the Academy of Management.

Lindblom, C. (1959) 'The science of muddling through', *Public Administration Rev.*, 19, 79–88.

Littler, C.R. (1978) 'Understanding Taylorism', *British J. of Sociology*, 29, 185–202.

Littler, C.R. (1982) 'Deskilling and changing structures of control', in S. Wood (ed.) op. cit.

Littler, C.R. and G. Salaman (1982) 'Bravermania and beyond: recent theories of the labour process', *Sociology*, 16, 251–69.

Locke, E.A. (1968) 'Toward a theory of task motivation and incentives', *Organizational Behavior and Human Performance*, 3, 157–89.

Locke, E.A. (1976) 'The nature and causes of job satisfaction', in M.D. Dunnette (ed.) *Handbook of Industrial and Organizational Psychology*. Chicago: Rand McNally.

Lockwood, D. (1958) *The Blackcoated Worker*. London: Allen and Unwin.

Loveridge, R.J. (1983) 'The professional negotiator: roles, resources and the run of the cards', in W.T. Singleton (ed.) *Social Skills*. Lancaster: MTP Press.

Lukes, S. (1974) *Power: A Radical View*. London: Macmillan.

Lupton, T. (1963) *On the Shop Floor*. Oxford: Pergamon Press.

Lupton, T. and I. Tanner (1980) 'Work design in Europe', in R.D. Duncan, M.M. Gruneberg and D. Wallis (eds.) op. cit.

Luthans, F. and R. Kreitner (1975) *Organizational Behavior Modification*. Glenview, Ill.: Scott, Foresman.

Luthans, F., R. Paul and D. Baker (1981) 'An experimental analysis of the impact of a contingent reinforcement intervention on salesperson's performance behaviors', *J. of Applied Psychology*, 66, 314–23.

Maher, J.P. (1976) 'Situational determinants of leadership behaviour in task oriented small groups', *Dissertation Abstr. International*, 37, 693–4.

March, J.G. and H.A. Simon (1958) *Organizations*. New York: Wiley.

Marglin, S.A. (1974) 'What do bosses do? The origins and functions of hierarchy in capitalist production', *Rev. of Radical Political Economics*, 6, 33–60. Reprinted in A. Gorz (ed.) *The Division of Labour*. Hassocks, Sussex: Harvester Press, 1976.

Marsh, P. (1982) 'Rules in the organization of action', in M. von Cranach and R. Harré (eds.) *The Analysis of Action*. Cambridge: Cambridge University Press.

Martin, J. and C. Roberts (1983) *Women and Employment: A Lifetime Perspective*. London: HMSO Books.

Martin, R. (1981) *New Technology and Industrial Relations in Fleet Street*. Oxford: Oxford University Press.

Martin, R. and J. Wallace (1986) *Working Women in Recession: Employment, Redundancy and Unemployment*. Oxford: Oxford University Press.

Martindale, D. (1977) 'Sweaty palms in the control tower', *Psychology Today*, October.

Marx, K. (1973) *Grundrisse*. Harmondsworth: Penguin.

Marx, K. (1974) *Capital* Vol. 1. London: Lawrence and Wishart.

Marx, K. (1975) *Early Writings*. Translated by R. Livingstone and G. Benton. Harmondsworth: Penguin.

Maslow, A.H. (1954) *Motivation and Personality*. New York: Harper.

Matsui, T., M. Kagawa, J. Nagamatsu and Y. Ohtsuku (1977) 'Validity of expectancy theory as a within-person behavioural choice model for sales activity', *J. of Applied Psychology*, 62, 764–7.

Mayo, E. (1943) 'Forward', in F.J. Roethlisberger and W.J. Dickson, op. cit.

McCall, G.I. and I.L. Simmons (1966) *Identities and Interaction*. New York: Free Press.

McClelland, D. (1961) *The Achieving Society*. Princeton: Van Nostrand.

McClelland, D. and R.E. Boyatzis (1982) 'Leadership motive pattern and long-term success in management', *J. of Applied Psychology*, 67, 737–43.

McClelland, D. and D.H. Burnham (1976) 'Power is the great motivator', *Harvard Business Rev.*, 54, 100–10.

McGregor, D. (1960) *The Human Side of Enterprise*. New York: McGraw-Hill.

McHenry, R. (1981) 'The selection interview', in M. Argyle (ed.) op. cit.

McKenna, E. (1983) *Undergraduate Business Education: A Reappraisal*. Discussion paper, London Chamber of Commerce and Industry.

Merton, R.K. (1940) 'Bureaucratic structure and personality', *Social Forces*, 18, 560–8.

Mettlin, C. (1976) 'Occupational careers and the prevention of coronary-prone behaviour', *Social Science and Medicine*, 10, 367–72.

Michaels, C.E. and P.E. Spector (1982) 'Causes of employee turnover: a test of the Mobley, Griffeth, Hand and Meglino model', *J. of Applied Psychology*, 67, 53–9.

Michener, H.A. and E.J. Lawler (1975) 'Endorsement of formal leaders: an integrative model', *J. of Personality and Social Psychology*, 31, 216–23.

Mikes, P.S. and C.L. Hulin (1968) 'Use of importance as a weighting component of job satisfaction', *J. of Applied Psychology*, 52, 394–8.

Miles, R.M. (1980) 'Organization boundary roles', in C.L. Cooper and R. Payne (eds.) op. cit.

Miller, E.J. (1975) 'Sociotechnical systems in weaving 1953–70: a follow-up study', *Human Relations*, 28, 349–86.

Miller, G.A. (1956) 'The magical number seven, plus or minus two: some limits on our capacity for processing information', *Psychological Rev.*, 63, 81–97.

Miller, N. and M.B. Brewer (1984) 'The social psychology of desegregation: an introduction', in N. Miller and M.B. Brewer (eds.) *Groups in Contact*. London: Academic Press.

Mills, C.W. (1951) *White Collar*. New York: Oxford University Press.

Miner, J.B. (1980) *Theories of Organizational Behavior*. Hinsdale, Ill.: Dryden Press.

Mitchell, T.R., C.M. Smyser and S.E. Weed (1975) 'Locus of control: supervision and work satisfaction', *Academy of Management J.*, 18, 623–31.

Mobley, W.H. (1977) 'Intermediate linkages in the relationship between job satisfaction and employee turnover', *J. of Applied Psychology*, 62, 237–40.

Mobley, W.H., S.O. Horner and A.T. Hollingsworth (1978) 'The evaluation of precursors of hospital employee turnover', *J. of Applied Psychology*, 63, 408–14.

Moorhouse, P. (1981) 'Production management', in W.T. Singleton (ed.) *Management Skills*. Lancaster: MTP Press.

Moorhouse, P. (1983) 'The industrial sales team', in W.T. Singleton (ed.) *Social Skills*. Lancaster: MTP Press.

Moos, R.H. and A.G. Billings (1982) 'Conceptualizing and measuring coping resources and processes', in L. Goldberger and S. Breznitz (eds.) *Handbook of Stress: Theoretical and Clinical Aspects*. London: Macmillan.

Moscovi, S. and G. Paicheler (1978) 'Social comparisons and social recognition: two complementary processes of identification', in H. Tajfel (ed.) *Differentiation between Social Groups: Studies in the Social Psychology of Intergroup Relations'*, European Monographs in Social Psychology, 14. London: Academic Press.

Mouzelis, N. (1975) *Organization and Bureaucracy*. London: Routledge and Kegan Paul.

Muchinsky, P.M. (1977) 'A comparison of within- and across-subjects analyses of the expectancy-valence model for predicting effort', *Academy of Management J.*, 20, 154–8.

Mumford, E. (1976) 'A strategy for the redesign of work', *Personnel Rev.*, 5, 33–9.

Murphy, L.R. (1984) 'Occupational stress management: a review and appraisal', *J. of Occupational Psychology*, 57, 1–15.

Myers, C.S. (1924) *Industrial Psychology in Great Britain*. London: Cape.

Nash, A.N., J.P. Muczyk and F.L. Vettori (1971) 'The relative practical effectiveness of programmed instruction', *Personnel Psychology*, 24, 397–418.

Neimeyer, G.J. and J.E. Hudson (1985) 'Couple's constructs: personal systems in marital satisfaction', in D. Bannister (ed.) *Issues and Approaches in Personal Construct Theory*. London: Academic Press.

Nemeroff, W.F. and J. Cosentino (1979) 'Utilizing feedback and goal setting to increase performance appraisal interviewer skills of managers', *Academy of Management J.*, 22, 566–76.

Newman, J.D. and T. Boehr (1979) 'Personal and organizational strategies for handling job stress: a review of research and opinion', *Personnel Psychology*, 32, 1–43.

Nichols, T. and H. Beynon (1977) *Living with Capitalism*. London: Routledge and Kegan Paul.

Nord, W. (1969) 'Beyond the teaching machine: the neglected area of operant conditioning in the theory and practice of management', *Organizational Behavior and Human Performance*, 4, 375–401.

Ochs, E. (1983) 'Planned and unplanned discourse', in E. Ochs and B.B. Schieffelin (eds.) *Acquiring Conversational Competence*. London: Routledge and Kegan Paul.

Ochs, E. and B.B. Schieffelin (1983) 'Topic as a discourse notion: a study of topic in the conversations of children and adults', in E. Ochs and B.B. Schieffelin (eds.) ibid.

Offe, C. (1976) *Industry and Inequality*. London: Edward Arnold.

Orpen, C. (1978) 'Work and non-work satisfaction: a causal-correlational analysis', *J. of Applied Psychology*, 63, 530–2.

Park, B. and M. Rothbart (1982) 'Perception of out-group homogeneity and levels of social categorization: memory for the subordinate attributes of in-group and out-group members', *Journal of Personality and Social Psychology*, 42, 1051–68.

Parry, N. and J. Parry (1976) *The Rise of the Medical Profession*. London: Croom Helm.

Perrow, C. (1980) 'Zoo story or life in the organizational sandpit', in G. Salaman and K. Thompson (eds.) op. cit.

Pettigrew, A. (1973) *The Politics of Organizational Decision-Making*. London: Tavistock.

Pfeffer, J. (1981) *Power in Organizations*. Marshfield, Mass.: Pitman.

Philo, G., P. Beharrell and J. Hewitt (1977) 'One-dimensional views: television and the control of information', in P. Beharrell and G. Philo (eds.) *Trade Unions and the Media*. London: Macmillan.

Pollert, A. (1981) *Girls, Wives, Factory Lives*. London: Macmillan.

Poppleton, S.E. (1981) 'The social skills of selling', in M. Argyle (ed.) *Social Skills and Work*. London: Methuen.

Porter, L.W. (1962) 'Job attitudes in management: I. Perceived deficiencies in need fulfillment as a function of job level', *J. of Applied Psychology*, 46, 375–84.

Porter, L.W. and E.E. Lawler (1968) *Managerial Attitudes and Performance*. Homewood, Ill.: Dorsey Press.

Potter, R.M.C. (1983) 'The statesman', in W.T. Singleton (ed.) *Social Skills*. Lancaster: MTP Press.

Presthus, R. (1979) *The Organizational Society*. London: Macmillan.

Price, K.H. and H. Garland (1981) 'Compliance with a leader's suggestions as a function of perceived leader/member competence and potential reciprocity', *J. of Applied Psychology*, 66, 329–36.

Pritchard, R.D. and M.S. Sanders (1973) 'The influence of valence, instrumentality, and expectancy on effort and performance', *J. of Applied Psychology*, 57, 55–60.

Pugh, D.S., D.J. Hickson and C.R. Hinings (1971) *Writers on Organizations*. Harmondsworth: Penguin.

Randall, G.A. (1981) 'Management education and training', in W.T. Singleton (ed.) *Management Skills*. Lancaster: MTP Press.

Rhodes, P.S. (1983) 'The prediction of success in business studies students', *Business Education*, 4, 31–5.

Richbell, S. (1976) 'Participation and perceptions of control', *Personnel Rev.*, 5, 13–9.

Rice, A.K. (1958) *Productivity and Social Organization*. London: Tavistock.

Rice, B. (1982) 'The Hawthorne defect: persistence of a flawed theory', *Psychology Today*, February.

Roberts, C. and S. Wood (1982) 'Collective bargaining and job redesign', in J.E. Kelly and C.W. Clegg (eds.) op. cit.

Robey, D. (1977) 'Computers and management structure', *Human Relations*, 30, 963–76.

Rodger, A. (1952) *The Seven Point Plan*. Windsor: NIIP/NFER-Nelson.

Roethlisberger, F.J. and W.J. Dickson (1943) *Management and the Worker*. Cambridge, Mass.: Harvard University Press.

Rose, M. (1975) *Industrial Behaviour: Theoretical Developments since Taylor*. London: Allen Lane.

Rose, R.M., C.D. Jenkins and M.W. Hurst (1978) 'Air traffic controller health change study: a prospective investigation of physical, psychological and work related changes'. Galveston: University of Texas (mimeo).

Rosen, B. and T.H. Jerdee (1977) 'Influence of subordinate characteristics on trust and use of participative decision strategies in a management simulation', *J. of Applied Psychology*, 62, 628–31.

Rosenman, R.H., R.J. Brand, D. Jenkins, M. Friedman, R. Straus and M. Wurm (1975) 'Coronary heart disease in the western collaborative group study', *J. of the American Medical Association*, 233, 872–7.

Rotter, J.B. (1966) *Generalized Expectancies for Internal versus External Control of Reinforcement*. Psychological Monographs: 80.

Routh, G. (1980) *Occupation and Pay in Great Britain 1906–79*. London: Macmillan.

Roy, D. (1952) 'Quota restrictions and goldbricking in a machine shop', *American J. of Sociology*, 57, 427–42.

Roy, D. (1954) 'Efficiency and the "fix": informal inter-group relations in a piecework machine shop', *American J. of Sociology*, 60, 255–66.

Rubery, J. (1980) 'Structured labour markets, worker organization and low pay', in A. Amsden (ed.) *The Economics of Women and Work*. Harmondsworth: Penguin.

Sacks, H., E. Schegloff and G. Jefferson (1974) 'A simplest systematics for the organization of turn-taking for conversation', *Language*, 50, 696–735.

Salaman, G. (1979) *Work Organisations: Resistance and Control*. London: Longman.

Salaman, G. (1981) *Class and the Corporation*. London: Fontana.

Salaman, G. and K. Thompson (1974) Media Booklets 1 and 2. *People and Organisations* DT352. Milton Keynes: Open University Press.

Salaman, G. and K. Thompson (eds.) (1980) *Control and Ideology in Organizations*. Milton Keynes: Open University Press.

Schaff, A. (1982) 'Occupation versus work', in G. Friedrichs and A. Schaff (eds.) op. cit.

Schaffer, R.H. (1953) *Job Satisfaction as Related to Need Satisfaction in Work*. Psychological Monographs: 67.

Schieffelin, B.B. (1983) 'Talking like birds: sound play in a cultural perspective', in E. Ochs and B.B. Schieffelin (eds.) *Acquiring Conversational Competence*. London: Routledge and Kegan Paul.

Schneider, J. and E.A. Locke (1971) 'A critique of Herzberg's incident classification system and a suggested revision', *Organizational Behavior and Human Performance*, 6, 441–57.

Schriesheim, C.A. and D. Hosking (1978) 'Review essay of F.E. Fiedler, M.M. Chemers, and L. Mahar: "Improving Leadership Effectiveness: The Leader Match Concept' ", *Administrative Science Quarterly*, 23, 496–505.

Schriesheim, C.A., R.J. House and S. Kerr (1976) 'Leader initiating structure: a reconciliation of discrepant research results and some empirical tests', *Organizational Behavior and Human Performance*, 15, 297–321.

Schriesheim, C.A. and C.J. Murphy (1976) 'Relationships between leader behavior and subordinate satisfaction and performance: a test of some situational moderators', *J. of Applied Psychology*, 61, 634–41.

Schriesheim, C.A. and A.S. de Nisi (1981) 'Task dimensions as moderators of the effects of instrumental leadership: a two-sample replicated test of Path–Goal leadership theory', *J. of Applied Psychology*, 66, 589–97.

Scott, R. (1966) 'Professionals in bureaucracies: areas of conflict', in H.M. Vollmer and D.M. Mills (eds.) *Professionalization*. Englewood Cliffs, New Jersey: Prentice-Hall.

Sear, Baroness (1985) 'There is much to be done', *Training and Development*, January.

Seligman, M.E.P. (1975) *Helplessness: On Depression, Development and Death.* San Francisco: Freeman.

Selye, H. (1936) 'A syndrome produced by diverse nocuous ages', *Nature*, 138, 32.

Selye, H. (1975) 'Stress', in *Employee Physical Fitness in Canada.* Ottawa: National Health and Welfare, Information Canada.

Selye, H. (1983) 'History and present status of the stress concept', in L. Goldberger and S. Breznitz (eds.) *Handbook of Stress: Theoretical and Clinical Aspects.* London: Macmillan.

Selznick, P. (1943) 'An approach to a theory of bureaucracy', *American Sociological Rev.*, 8, 47–54.

Sherif, M. and C.W. Sherif (1982) 'Production of intergroup conflict and its resolution: robbers' cave experiment', in J.W. Reich (ed.) *Experimenting in Society: Issues and Examples in Applied Social Psychology.* Glenview, Ill.: Scott, Foresman.

Sherif, M., O.J. Harvey, B. White, W.R. Hood and C.W. Sherif (1961) *Intergroup Conflict and Cooperation: The Robbers' Cave Experiment.* Norman: University of Oklahoma Press.

Simpson, D.H. (1981) *Commercialization of the Regional Press.* Aldershot: Gower.

Singleton, W.T. (1978) 'Final discussion', in W.T. Singleton (ed.) *The Analysis of Practical Skills.* Lancaster: MTP Press.

Singleton, W.T. (1983) 'Final discussion', in W.T. Singleton (ed.) *Social Skills.* Lancaster: MTP Press.

Skinner, B.F. (1954) 'The science of learning and the art of teaching', *Harvard Educational Rev.*, 24, 86–97.

Skinner, B.F. (1971) *Beyond Freedom and Dignity.* Harmondsworth: Penguin.

Slocum, J.W. and H.P. Sims (1980) 'A typology for integrating technology, organization and job redesign', *Human Relations*, 33, 193–212.

Smith, A. (1982) *The Wealth of Nations.* Harmondsworth: Penguin.

Smith, F.J. (1977) 'Work attitudes as predictors of attendance on a specific day', *J. of Applied Psychology*, 62, 16–19.

Sofer, C. (1970) *Men in Mid-Career.* Cambridge: Cambridge University Press.

Sorge, A., M. Hartmann, M. Warner and I. Nicholas (1982) 'Technology, organization and manpower: applications of CNC manufacturing in Great Britain and West Germany', in N. Bjorn-Anderson, M. Earl, O. Holst and E. Mumford (eds.) *Information Society: For Richer For Poorer.* Amsterdam: North Holland.

Sorrentino, R.M. and R.G. Boutillier (1975) 'The effect of quantity and quality of verbal interaction on ratings of leadership ability', *J. of Experimental and Social Psychology*, 11, 403–11.

Spearman, C. (1904) 'General intelligence objectively determined and measured', *American J. of Psychology*, 14, 201–93.

Spearman, C. (1927) *The Abilities of Man.* New York: Macmillan.

Steers, R.M. and S.R. Rhodes (1978) 'Major influences on employee attendance: a process model', *J. of Applied Psychology*, 63, 391–407.

Stephenson, G.M. (1981) 'Inter-group bargaining and negotiation', in J.C. Turner and H. Giles (eds.) *Intergroup Behaviour.* Oxford: Blackwell.

Sternberg, R.J. (1985) *Beyond IQ: A Triarchic Theory of Human Intelligence.* Cambridge: Cambridge University Press.

Sterns, L., R.A. Alexander, G.V. Barett and F.M. Dambrot (1983) 'The relationship of extraversion and neuroticism with job preferences and job satisfaction for clerical employees', *J, of Occupational Psychology*, 56, 145–53.

Stewart, A., K. Prandy and R.M. Blackburn (1980) *Social Stratification and Occupations*. London: Macmillan.

Stogdill, R.M. (1948) 'Personal factors associated with leadership: a survey of the literature', *J. of Psychology*, 25, 35–71.

Stogdill, R.M. (1974) *Handbook of Leadership: A Survey of Theory and Research*. New York: Free Press.

Stonier, T. (1983) *The Wealth of Information*. London: Methuen.

Storey, J. (1983) *Managerial Prerogative and the Question of Control*. London: Routledge and Kegan Paul.

Strube, M.J. and J.E. Garcia (1981) 'A meta-analytic investigation of Fiedler's contingency model of leadership effectiveness', *Psychological Bull.*, 90, 307–21.

Tajfel, H. (1978) 'Social categorization, social identity and social comparison', in H. Tajfel (ed.) *Differentiation between Social Groups*. London: Academic Press.

Tajfel, H. (1981) 'Social stereotypes and social groups', in J.C. Turner and H. Giles (eds.) *Intergroup Behaviour*. Oxford: Blackwell.

Taylor, L. and P. Walton (1971) 'Industrial sabotage: motives and meanings', in S. Cohen (ed.) *Images of Deviance*. Harmondsworth: Penguin.

Taylor, R. (1980) *The Fifth Estate*. London: Pan Books.

Taylor, S.M. and J.A. Sniezek (1984) 'The college recruitment interview: topical content and applicant reactions', *J. of Occupational Psychology*, 57, 157–68.

Thompson, P. (1983) *The Nature of Work*. London: Macmillan.

Thompson, P. (1986) 'Crawling from the wreckage: the labour process and the politics of production', paper presented to Aston/UMIST 4th Labour Process Conference.

Thompson, V. (1961) *Modern Organization*. New York: Knopf.

Thurstone, L.L. (1938) *Primary Mental Abilities*. Chicago: University of Chicago Press.

Trist, E.L. and K.W. Bamforth (1951) 'Some social and psychological consequences of the longwall method of coal-getting', *Human Relations*, 1, 3–38.

Turner, H.A. (1969) *Is Britain really Strike-Prone?* Cambridge: Cambridge University Press.

Turner, J.C. (1982) 'Towards a cognitive redefinition of the social group', in H. Tajfel (ed.) *Social Identity and Intergroup Relations*. Cambridge: Cambridge University Press.

Turner, J.C. and H. Giles (eds.) (1981) *Intergroup Behaviour*. Oxford: Blackwell.

Vernon, P.E. (1971) *The Structure of Human Abilities*. London: Methuen.

Vroom, V.H. (1964) *Work and Motivation*. New York: Wiley.

Vroom, V.H. (1976) 'Leadership', in M.D. Dunnette (ed.) *Handbook of Industrial and Organizational Psychology*. Chicago: Rand McNally.

Vroom, V.H. and A.G. Jago (1978) 'On the validity of the Vroom–Yetton model', *J. of Applied Psychology*, 63, 151–62.

Vroom, V.H. and P.W. Yetton (1973) *Leadership and Decision-Making*. Pittsburgh: University of Pittsburgh Press.

Wagner, U. and P. Schönbach (1984) 'Links between educational status and prejudice: ethnic attitudes in West Germany', in N. Miller and M.B. Brewer (eds.) *Groups in Contact*. London: Academic Press.

Wahba, M.A. and C.B. Bridwell (1976) 'Maslow reconsidered: a review of research on the need hierarchy theory', *Organizational Behavior and Human Performance*, 15, 212–40.

Wainright, H. (1984) 'Women and the division of labour', in P. Abrams and R. Brown (eds.) *UK Society*. London: Weidenfeld and Nicolson.

Wall, T. (1980) 'Group work redesign in context: a two-phase model', in K.D. Duncan, M.M. Gruneberg and D. Wallis (eds.) op. cit.

Wall, T. (1982) 'Perspectives on job redesign', in J.E. Kelly and C.W. Clegg (eds.) op. cit.

Wall, T. and J.L. Cordery (1982) *Work Design and Supervisory Practice*. Social and Applied Psychology Unit, Memo 470. University of Sheffield.

Wallis, D. and D. Cope (1980) 'Pay-off conditions for organizational change in the hospital service', in K.D. Duncan, M.M. Gruneberg and D. Wallis (eds.) op. cit.

Wanous, J.P. (1974) 'A causal-correlational analysis of the job satisfaction and performance relationship', *J. of Applied Psychology*, 59, 139–44.

Wanous, J.P. and A. Zwany (1977) 'A cross-sectional test of need hierarchy theory', *Organizational Behavior and Human Performance*, 18, 78–97.

Watson, O.M. (1970) *Proxemic Behaviour: A Cross-Cultural Study*. The Hague: Mouton.

Watson, T.J. (1977) *The Personnel Managers*. London: Routledge and Kegan Paul.

Weaver, C.N. (1980) 'Job satisfaction in the United States in the 1970s', *J. of Applied Psychology*, 65, 364–7.

Weber, M. (1964) *The Theory of Social and Economic Organization*. New York: Free Press.

Weber, M. (1970) From Max Weber: *Essays in Sociology*. Translated by H.H. Gerth and C.W. Mills. London: Routledge and Kegan Paul.

Wedderburn, D. (1978) 'Swedish experiments in work organisation', in D. Gregory (ed.) *Work Organisation*. London: SSRC.

Wedderburn, D. and R. Crompton (1972) *Workers' Attitudes and Technology*. Cambridge: Cambridge University Press.

Weinstein, D. (1979) *Bureaucratic Opposition: Challenging Abuses at the Workplace*. New York: Pergamon Press.

Welford, A.T. (1973) 'Stress and performance', *Ergonomics*, 16, 567–80.

West, J. (1982) 'New technology and women's office work', in J. West (ed.) *Work, Women and the Labour Market*. London: Routledge and Kegan Paul.

Wilensky, H.L. (1968) 'Careers, life-styles and social integration', in B. Glaser (ed.) *Organizational Careers*. Chicago: Aldine.

Wilkinson, B. (1983) *The Shopfloor Politics of New Technology*. London: Heinemann.

Williams, V. (1984) 'Employment implications of new technology', *Employment Gazette*, April. (London: Department of Employment).

Winter, D.G. (1978) *Navy Leadership and Management Competencies: Convergence among Tests, Interviews and Performance Ratings*. Boston: McBer.

Wood, S. (1979) 'A reappraisal of the contingency approach to organization', *J. of Management Studies*, 16, 334–54.

Wood, S. (ed.) (1982) *The Degradation of Work?* London: Hutchinson.

Woodward, J. (1965) *Industrial Organization: Theory and Practice*. London: Oxford University Press.

Yates, D. (1986) 'Is dual labour market theory dead?', paper presented to Aston/UMIST 4th Labour Process Conference.

Zimbalist, A. (1979) *Case Studies on the Labor Process*. London: Monthly Review Press.
Zimbardo, P.G., C. Harey, W.C. Banks and D. Jaffe (1973) 'The mind is a formidable jailer: a Pirandellian prison', *New York Times Magazine*, 8 April, 38–60.

Author Index

Subject Index

academic attainment, 55, 68
action, social, 11–12, 202–3, 257, 268–73
action research, 163
affordances, 30
alienation, 173, 174–5, 186–7, 264, 274
anal stage, 60
appearance, 109
appraisal, of situations, 39
authority, types of, 266–8, 299–300, 301
autonomic nervous system, 55
autonomous work groups, 163–4, 166
avoidance learning, 23

bargaining, organizational, 303–4
basic skills analysis, 34
behaviour modification, 26, 27
benevolent autocrat, 141
body posture, 109; movement, 109
boundary-spanning roles, 40, 41
bounded rationality, 296
bureaucracy, 174, 263, 264–8
bureaucratic abuse, 270; control, 194, 275, 277–8; dysfunctions, 268–71
burnout, 41

career, 278–80 (*see also* women's careers)
caution shift, 124
central nervous system, 54
circumspection, 111
classical school, the, 285–6, 303–4
clerical work, 219, 224, 234, 235, 243, 253–5, 264
closed situations, 105
coalition formation, 305
commonality, 110
conditionability, 54
conditioned stimulus, 20; response, 20
conflict, industrial, 202–11; organizational, 296–7, 303–4; social, 12; sociological model of, 204–6; resolution of, 293–4; workplace, 198–202

conformity, in groups, 9–10
constancies, in perception, 30–1
contact hypothesis, 127
contagion, in groups, 137
content theories of motivation, 78–83
contingency theory, 286–90
continuous process technology, 142–3, 186–9, 248
control, frontier of, 199; and the labour process; 179, 196, 198; managerial, 169–200; managerial systems of, 291–2; in organizations, 274–80, 263–4 (*see also* bureaucratic control); organizational versus occupational, 276–8
coping strategies, 46–8
coronary heart disease, and stress, 44–6
cross resistance effect, 47
culture, organizational, 276; workgroup, 199–202

decision-making in organizations, 304–7
defence mechanisms, 59
defined situations, 105
denial, 60
depersonaii ition, 126, 269
deskilling, 182, 191–5, 222, 225–7
deviate, 119
differentiation, in management, 292, 305; in work groups, 166–7
discrimination learning, 20
displacement, 60
division of labour, 171, 180–2, Chapter 11 *passim*, 261, 265, 276
dual labour markets, 215–6

effort bargain, 85
ego, 58
enfolders, 136
enlargers, 136
environment, organizational, 287–90

334